The Unrepe

The Unrepentant Renaissance

FROM PETRARCH
TO SHAKESPEARE
TO MILTON

Richard Strier

The University of Chicago Press   CHICAGO & LONDON

RICHARD STRIER is the Frank L. Sulzberger Distinguished Service Professor in the Department of English and in the College at the University of Chicago. He has coedited several interdisciplinary essay collections and is the author of many articles and two books, *Resistant Structures: Particularity, Radicalism, and Renaissance Texts* and *Love Known: Theology and Experience in George Herbert's Poetry*, the latter published by the University of Chicago Press.

The University of Chicago Press, Chicago 60637
The University of Chicago Press, Ltd., London
© 2011 by The University of Chicago
All rights reserved. Published 2011.
Printed in the United States of America

20 19 18 17 16 15 14 13 12 11   1 2 3 4 5

ISBN-13: 978-0-226-77751-1 (cloth)
ISBN-10: 0-226-77751-0 (cloth)

Library of Congress Cataloging-in-Publication Data
Strier, Richard.
   The unrepentant Renaissance : from Petrarch to Shakespeare to Milton / Richard Strier.
      p.   cm.
   Includes bibliographical references and index.
   ISBN-13: 978-0-226-77751-1 (hardcover : alk. paper)
   ISBN-10: 0-226-77751-0 (hardcover : alk. paper)   1. European literature—Renaissance,
1450–1600—History and criticism. 2. English literature—Early modern, 1500–1700—
History and criticism. 3. Petrarca, Francesco, 1304–1374—Criticism and interpretation.
4. Shakespeare, William, 1564–1616—Criticism and interpretation.   I. Title.
   PN721.S835 2011
   809'.89409024—dc22   2010050570

♾ This paper meets the requirements of ANSI/NISO Z39.48-1992 (Permanence of Paper).

To my students, over the years, in
"Renaissance Intellectual Texts" at the University of Chicago

CONTENTS

ACKNOWLEDGMENTS

It was with the help of the students in my graduate seminar, "Renaissance Intellectual Texts," given periodically at the University of Chicago since the late 1970s, that I developed the courage to wander beyond the bounds of English literature into the wider world of Renaissance texts and ideas. My experience with these students—some of whom are now famous professors (you know who you are!)—allowed me to feel at home enough in texts by Petrarch, Erasmus, Loyola, Descartes, and other Continental figures to write about them in detail. I could not have embarked on this project without the experience and support of our shared endeavor. This is truly a significant debt, and one that I am delighted to be able to acknowledge in the dedication of this book.

But of course that is not the end of my debts. There is a small group of friends and colleagues whose voices and points of view I have internalized so deeply that I feel I am in dialogue with them even if I am not (as I often am) literally so. This group has long included Stephen Greenblatt, Frank Whigham, and Michael Murrin. Kathy Eden has recently entered the circle. My Renaissance colleagues in the English department have long been a source of inspiration and instruction: David Bevington, Joshua Scodel, Michael Murrin (again), and my newest and extremely shrewd and generous colleague, Bradin Cormack. Janel Mueller cotaught the original version of the course that led to this book. William Veeder sat through and responded sagely to accounts of various chapters and readings through many a sacred Wednesday lunch over the years.

Other friends and colleagues responded helpfully to particular chapters. For comments on what became the first chapter, I am grateful to James Turner, and to audiences at Vanderbilt (especially Deak Nabers), CCNY, Hope College (especially John Cox), and Emory University (especially Rick Rambuss), to the members of the Chicago-area faculty Renaissance Seminar, and to the graduate workshop on the history of political and social thought at the University of Chicago. A request from Michael Schoenfeldt provided the happy occasion for me to work on Petrarch and Shakespeare. For comments (not always agreeing, but always helpful) on this material, especially with regard to Petrarch's *Rime*, I am grateful to my colleagues in Italian literature, Justin Steinberg and Armando Maggi, to the members of the Western Mediterranean workshop at the university, and to Gordon Braden, Michael Murrin, David Quint, Leonard Barkan, William West, and Robert von Hallberg. For further comments, I am grateful to Frank Whigham and Lars Engle. The third and central chapter of this book began as a paper for a terrific conference on Renaissance ethics organized by the late Marshall Grossman at the University of Maryland. The argument benefited from comments (at various times) by Stephen Greenblatt, Glenn Most, Loy D. Martin, and Robert David Cohen, as well as from discussion at the Renaissance workshop at the University of Chicago (where Steven Pincus, Joshua Scodel, and Jeffrey Collins were especially helpful), at the Shakespeare Association of America (SAA), and at the Heyman Center for the Humanities at Columbia University, where comments from Akeel Bilgrami, Kathy Eden, and Ed Mendelson were bracing. The appendix on seduction was for an SAA seminar on that fine topic. John Kerrigan commented and disagreed helpfully on the appendix on *Macbeth*.

The chapter on *The Comedy of Errors* began in another excellent SAA seminar. I am greatly indebted to that group, especially to the papers and comments of Matthew Steggle and Kent Cartwright. I received helpful responses to later versions from David Bevington and Ted Leinwand, and also at the Waterloo conference on Elizabethan religion and theater, at the University of Chicago Society of Fellows draft group, at the Vanderbilt group on early modern cultural studies, at the Columbia University Shakespeare Seminar (especially from my respondent, Rich McCoy), at the CUNY Graduate Center, and at the Pittsburgh Consortium for Medieval and Renaissance Studies (where I particularly profited from remarks by Jonathan Arac).

I accumulated many debts in working on the chapter on Montaigne and Descartes. My experience has been that Montaigne scholars are an especially generous group. I am deeply indebted to my colleague Philippe Desan (not least for lending me books from his amazing library), and to my friend and fellow wine fanatic George Hoffmann, who corresponded with me about this material over a number of years. Kevin Hart and Charles Larmore also gave me the benefit of their views on Montaigne, and Charles directed me to highly relevant work of his that I might not otherwise have discovered. Kathy Eden read the chapter with her eagle eye and superb knowledge of Renaissance rhetoric and philology. The chapter began as a keynote address for a Renaissance prose conference at Purdue organized by Charles Ross and Angelica Duran, and I am grateful to the lively audience there, at Carnegie Mellon, and at the early modern workshop at the University of Chicago. Lisa Ruddick and Dr. Jeffrey Stern, two friends who are not Montaigne or Descartes scholars but who are deeply interested in questions of selfhood and identity, also read the chapter closely; they both made extraordinarily helpful comments (I wish I knew enough about Kohutian self-psychology to follow up on Jeffrey's).

The chapter on Milton began in the East Coast Milton Seminar. I am grateful to Regina Schwartz for that invitation and for leading an exceptionally probing discussion spearheaded by Michael Lieb. For written comments and lively conversation about the revised version of that piece (and much else), I am grateful to Victoria Kahn. The appendix on *The Reason of Church-Government* began in a session on discipline at the Renaissance Society of America organized by Kenneth Graham, who is working on that topic, and who made valuable comments at and after that session and shared some of his own relevant work with me. The paper was also helpfully and penetratingly discussed at a meeting of the Northwestern University British Studies group.

Finally, I want to thank Alan G. Thomas, my editor at the University of Chicago Press, for his belief in this project and for finding me excellent readers for both the partial and the whole manuscript. The first reader of the whole was wonderfully appreciative and described the aims and structure of the book better, I think, than I could have myself. The second reader was extremely useful to me by virtue of loving only "90 percent" of the manuscript. This reader had shrewd comments throughout, but I especially profited from the comments on the baneful 10 percent. This included the appendix on devout humanism, which indeed needed to be rescued from its earlier alliance with the Pascal of *The Provincial Letters*, and the introduction, which has been overhauled from its original state. In these revisions I benefited from the generosity of many friends who offered commentary: Bradin Cormack (most detailed of all!), William West, Edward Muir, Joshua Scodel, and again, Lisa Ruddick, and Robert von Hallberg. Though I may be "unrepentant," I hope not to be ungrateful.

As always, I have benefited from the steady intelligence, good judgment, and unflagging support of my wife, Camille Bennett.

*

Some material in this book appeared previously and in different form in the following publications and is used by permission of the publishers: a version of chapter 1 appeared in *Reading the Early Modern Passions: Essays in the Cultural History of Emotion*, ed. Gail Kern Paster, Katherine Rowe, and Mary Floyd-Wilson (Philadelphia: University of Pennsylvania Press, 2004), copyright © 2004 by University of Pennsylvania Press; part of chapter 2 appeared in *Blackwell's Companion to Shakespeare's Sonnets*, ed. Michael Schoenfeldt (Oxford: Blackwell, 2007); a version of chapter 3 appeared in *Reading Renaissance Ethics*, ed. Marshall Grossman (New York: Routledge, 2007); part of chapter 4 appeared in *Shakespeare and Religious Change*, ed. Kenneth J. E. Graham and Philip D. Collington (Basingstoke, Hampshire: Palgrave Macmillan, 2009), reproduced with permission of Palgrave Macmillan; some material in the appendix to chapter 4 appeared in *Resistant Structures: Particularity, Radicalism, and Renaissance Texts* (Berkeley: University of California Press, 1995), copyright © 1995 by the Regents of the University of California; a version of chapter 5 appeared in *Prose Studies* 29 (Fall 2007); a version of chapter 6 appeared in *Religion and Culture in the English Renaissance*, ed. Claire McEachern and Debora Shuger (Cambridge: Cambridge University Press, 1997).

Back to Burckhardt
(Plus the Reformations)

VALUES AND COUNTERVALUES

Reason, patience, and moderation of anger; a proper understanding of the inferiority of the physical to the spiritual; ordinary decency and morality; a rejection of materialism and worldliness; an assertion of the need for humility—these are certainly recognized and widely voiced values in the early modern or "Renaissance" period. Such values are part of the inherited and continuous Christian tradition, and some were reinforced by key aspects of the classical revival, especially by certain aspects of Stoicism and Platonism. Who could possibly have seriously opposed them? This book is dedicated to discussing some of the movements and texts of the period that, in fact, did so. *The Unrepentant Renaissance* tries to make apparent, through careful readings of particular texts—mostly but not only literary ones—that it was possible in the period to praise the opposites of the worthy qualities listed in my opening sentence. The chapters that follow treat, in order, texts that oppose (or at least do not accept as unquestioned values) reason, patience, and moderation of anger; a proper understanding of the inferiority of the physical to the spiritual; ordinary decency and morality; a rejection of materialism and worldliness; an assertion of the need for humility. That is why these texts are all, as my title suggests, "unrepentant."

The works treated span the period in Europe from the early fourteenth to the late seventeenth centuries; they include texts in Latin, but many more in some of the major vernaculars: Italian, Spanish, French, and English. My argument, therefore, is that opposition to the most commonly voiced values and virtues of the period was not only possible but also continuous and important throughout Europe and throughout the period. I do not wish to contest the predominance of the widely voiced (one might say "official") values and virtues, but I do mean to suggest that alternatives to them were fully and perhaps surprisingly available. What I hope will emerge from all this is a sense of the period as more bumptious, full-throated, and perhaps perverse than that which has prevailed in a good deal of recent literary scholarship, especially with regard to England.[1]

It might be said, therefore, that this book represents something like a "return to Burckhardt."[2] There is a sense in which this is true, and I am happy to proclaim it. But where Burckhardt's great book basically ends its story at the beginning of the sixteenth century and treats only Italy, this study includes the Reformation as well as, let's call it, the Renaissance, and continues its story well into the period when the two movements are interacting.[3] I argue that the Reformation and the Counter- or Catholic Reformation, as well as the Renaissance, contributed to the opposition to certain elements of the Christian-Stoic-Platonic synthesis that produced the "official" and, one might wrongly think, unquestioned values of the period. From the perspective of European history as a whole, the Renaissance and the Reformations can all be seen as contributing to the creation of a culture that was no longer, as Burckhardt said of the previous period, "essentially clerical" (1:211).

As my mention of the Reformations is intended to suggest, this does not mean that the new culture was therefore fundamentally secular. It does, however, mean that from the early fourteenth to the seventeenth century, the status of the ordinary layperson (to adopt a contested term) was elevated and shifted

1. It should be said that the problem I am addressing in the scholarship does not, by and large, exist with regard to a figure like Machiavelli. But I do note that Mark Hulliung, in *Citizen Machiavelli* (Princeton: Princeton University Press, 1983), felt that he had to attempt to rescue Machiavelli from overly respectable readings.

2. The reference is to Jacob Burckhardt, *The Civilization of the Renaissance in Italy*, intro. Benjamin Nelson and Charles Trinkaus, trans. S. G. C. Middlemore, 2 vols. (New York: Harper and Row, 1958). *Die Cultur der Renaissance in Italien: Ein Versuch* appeared in 1860.

3. I prefer to refer to "the Renaissance" rather than the "early modern" period since the former term captures the period's own ideology about itself, and the latter term seems horribly Whiggish. On the Renaissance's sense of itself as such, and the importance of this, see Herbert Weisinger, "The Self-Awareness of the Renaissance as a Criterion of the Renaissance," *Papers of the Michigan Academy of Science, Arts and Literature* 29 (1944): 561–67, and Erwin Panofsky, " 'Renaissance'—Self-Definition or Self-Deception?," in *Renaissance and Renascences in Western Art* (1960; New York: Harper and Row, 1969), 1–41 (see also chap. 2, "Renaissance and Renascences"). On "Renaissance" versus "early modern," see inter alia, the "Forum" in *American Historical Review* 103 (1998): 51–124.

from the periphery to the center of European culture. As we will see, all three movements—Renaissance, Reformation, and Counter-Reformation—either celebrated or acknowledged this development. Burckhardt's emphasis on Renaissance individualism is justly famous, but his recognition of the importance of civic life to the phenomenon he is describing has not been widely seen. This recognition is why he begins his book with a series of chapters on the Italian "states," meaning city-states "whether," as he says, "republics or despotisms."[4] He insisted that "the fact that nobles and burghers dwelt together within the walls of the cities" was a fact of "vital importance," and even more so was the fact of their relatively fluid interaction (2:353).[5] To make this interaction possible was, for Burckhardt, the fundamental role of Renaissance values and of the revival of the classics (not exactly the same for him).[6]

So, with the larger chronological, geographical, and religious scope in mind, let me now specify the ways in which this book indeed represents a return to

4. The first ten chapters of *Civilization of the Renaissance* are on the Italian states. The quotation is from 1:143, where Burckhardt attributes the "chief reason" of the phenomena he is describing to "the character of these states, whether republics or despotisms." This sentence suggests that while Hans Baron was certainly right to suggest the importance of republican ideology to the Italian Renaissance, Burckhardt, despite his focus on the great princes, was not entirely unaware of this. For Baron, see *The Crisis of the Early Italian Renaissance: Civic Humanism and Republican Liberty in an Age of Classicism and Tyranny*, rev. ed. (Princeton: Princeton University Press, 1966). For current thinking about the "Baron thesis," see *Renaissance Civic Humanism: Reappraisals and Reflections*, ed. James Hankins (Cambridge: Cambridge University Press, 2004). For Baron on Burckhardt, see "The Limits of the Notion of 'Renaissance Individualism': Burckhardt after a Century," in *In Search of Florentine Civic Humanism: Essays on the Transition from Medieval to Modern Thought* (Princeton: Princeton University Press, 1988), 2:155–81.

5. See also, for instance, *Civilization of the Renaissance*, 1:143, 180 and 2:401. This emphasis seriously throws into question David Norbrook's insistence on Burckhardt's elitism and (supposed) interest in "legitimating inequalities" (see "Life and Death of Renaissance Man," *Raritan* 8 [Spring 1989]: 99). This emphasis also provides me with a way to respond to a worry raised by Edward Muir as to whether Burckhardt's analysis of fourteenth- and fifteenth-century Italy can be applied to sixteenth- and seventeenth-century England. Patrick Collinson's emphasis on the amount of local civic participation (and ideology) in England in the period, amounting to seeing the English polity as a "monarchical republic," helps make the connection to Burckhardt plausible. Collinson's essay, "The Monarchical Republic of Queen Elizabeth I," appeared in *Bulletin of the John Rylands Library* 69 (1987): 394–24; it is reprinted in his *Elizabethan Essays* (London: Hambledon, 1994), 31–58. For responses to and further developments of Collinson's thesis, see *The Monarchical Republic of Early Modern England: Essays in Response to Patrick Collinson*, ed. John F. McDiarmid (Farnham, Surrey: Ashgate, 2007).

6. For the complexity of Burckhardt's view of the revival of the classics, see *Civilization of the Renaissance*, 1:175 (and the whole chapter which begins there).

Burckhardt. Aside from believing that there was a major shift in European culture (or "civilization") beginning in Italy in the late thirteenth century, I accept the view that there were many persons in the period who "knew little of false [or any] modesty" (1:144) and were committed to being recognized as—dare I say it?—"individuals." Obviously there have always been individuals, but there has not always been individualism—an ideology that placed a value on distinctiveness and personality. Burckhardt notes *unico* and *singolare* becoming, in the relevant period, terms of praise (1:143n).[7] And he accepts the moral neutrality of this. In commenting on Cellini's autobiography, Burckhardt remarks, "It does not spoil the impression when the reader often detects him bragging or lying; the stamp of a mighty, energetic, and thoroughly developed nature remains" (2:330). Burckhardt recognizes that one form of individuality was a deliberate amorality or immorality; he points to "Werner von Urslingen, whose silver hauberk bore the inscription, 'The enemy of God, of pity, and of mercy'" (2:441). Burckhardt may not quite share the delight of his colleague and admirer, Nietzsche, in such figures—Nietzsche asserts that "in the days of the Renaissance, the criminal was a flourishing species of humanity"—but Burckhardt does see such figures as tapping into something central in the period, and he does not see them merely as "appalling" (2:441).[8] He spends very little time condemning them; he sees their existence as a historical necessity; and he notes, very coolly, that "we shall be more reserved in our judgment of them when we remember that the worst part of their guilt—in the estimate of those who record it—lay in their defiance of spiritual threats and penalties, and that to this fact is due that air of horror with which they are represented as surrounded" (2:441).

7. On the Hegelian background to this, see William Kerrigan and Gordon Braden, *The Idea of the Renaissance* (Baltimore: Johns Hopkins University Press, 1989), 11. I am happy to say that Kerrigan and Braden share my sense of the continuing relevance of Burckhardt.

8. Friedrich Nietzsche, *The Will to Power* (sec. 740), quoted and translated in Wallace K. Ferguson, *The Renaissance in Historical Thought: Five Centuries of Interpretation* (Boston: Houghton Mifflin, 1948), 207–8. For Burckhardt on individuality and wickedness, and on Nietzsche, see Richard Sigurdson, *Jacob Burckhardt's Social and Political Thought* (Toronto: University of Toronto Press, 2004), 213. William N. West, in "Jacob Burckhardt's Untimely Observations," *Modern Language Quarterly* 68 (2007): 27–50, cites Nietzsche calling Burckhardt "my great, my greatest teacher" (41–42). This seems to me quite important, and I would posit a more substantive connection between the two thinkers than that of the "full irony" with which West sees them both occupying their positions (50), though I would deny the political affinity that Norbrook asserts (see note 5 above). Sigurdson's chapter on Burckhardt and Nietzsche seems to me an excellent account of their intellectual affinities and political differences.

I also agree with Burckhardt in seeing the period as one in which it was possible to regard enjoyment of the things of this world as something not clearly
negative and even, at times, as praiseworthy. In his chapter "The Outward
Refinement of Life," Burckhardt speaks of "the well-paved streets of the Italian cities" and notes that "we read in the novelists of soft, elastic beds, of costly
carpets and bedroom furniture . . . of the abundance and beauty of the linen"
(2:370). But again, what is important is not so much the fact of these things
as the ideology concerning them. In his book on the family, Alberti asserts
(through his spokesperson, Lionardo) that "intellect, judgment, memory, appetite, anger, reason, and discretion" are among other "divine forces [*divine
forze e virtú*], by which man outdoes all other animals in strength, in speed,
and in ferocity [*velocità e ferocità*]," and that these are "capacities given to us
to be amply used."[9] It is very much worth noting, I would argue, that appetite
(though *l'apetito dell'animo*), anger, and ferocity appear on this list along with
the more familiar virtues and capacities. Alberti's basic view is that "[m]an
is by nature suited and able to make good use of the world, and he is born to
be happy" (136/161). Leonardo Bruni sees the city of Florence as admirable
not only in its public spaces and buildings but in the homes of its private citizens.[10] Personal pride and civic pride, public and private, went together. Bruni
praises the Florentines (in another fascinating list) for being "eager for glory,
brilliant in giving advice, industrious, generous, magnificent, pleasant, affable,
and, above all civilized" (*glorie avide, pollentes consilio, industrii, liberales,
magnifici, jocundi, affabiles, maximeque urbani*).[11] One of Burckhardt's main
examples of a Renaissance figure who lived and articulated the ideal of the full
life—in this particular case, without crime—is the "philosopher of practical
life," Luigi Cornaro. Burckhardt quotes passages of total self-satisfaction from
Cornaro. His friends "are wise, learned, and distinguished people of good positions"; his city house "is beautiful" and comfortable, as are his villas in the
hills and on the plain (from which he has drained the marshes); and his life,

9. Leon Battista Alberti, *The Family in Renaissance Florence*, trans. Renée Neu Watkins
(Columbia: University of South Carolina Press, 1969), 133; *I Libri della Famigilia*, ed. Ruggiero
Romano and Alberto Tenenti (Turin: Einaudi, 1980), 158. In subsequent citations of this work,
I give first the page numbers of the translation and then of the Italian edition.

10. Leonardo Bruni, *Panegyric to the City of Florence*, in *The Earthly Republic: Italian Humanists on Government and Society*, ed. Benjamin G. Kohl and Ronald G. Witt (Philadelphia:
University of Pennsylvania Press, 1978), 140.

11. Ibid., 174 (translation slightly altered). For the Latin, see the edition in Hans Baron, *From
Petrarch to Leonardo Bruni: Studies in Humanistic and Political Literature* (Chicago: University of Chicago Press, 1968), 263.

up to and through advanced old age, is filled with pleasure and thoroughly worldly enjoyment (2:332–33).

WHENCE THE GLOOM?

The picture of the Renaissance and Reformations that I have sketched is deeply at odds with the picture that has characterized a great deal of literary study of the period, certainly with regard to England, for the past few decades, and indeed for decades before that. One doesn't hear much, in this scholarship and criticism, of man being "born to be happy" in this world. Being "civilized" is equated with being repressed rather than being "jocund," "affable," or "liberal."[12] One might think that this is because, in England, the Renaissance and the Reformation are temporally and culturally coincident, but I have already suggested that the two great movements need not and should not be seen, in large cultural effect, as in opposition (though certainly they were in opposition in some important respects).[13] There are signs that the dour picture may be changing—one critic has risked "being a messenger of good news"—but I believe (though I would be jocund to be wrong about this) that the dark view still largely predominates.[14]

But where does the dour picture come from, the picture of the period as conservative (dedicated to law and order, reason and moderation, and so forth)

12. Here the influence, along with Foucault (see note 18 below), is Norbert Elias, *The Civilizing Process*, trans. Edmund Jephcott, 2 vols. (1939; New York: Pantheon Books, 1978).

13. Nietzsche saw the Renaissance and the Reformation as "born of related impulses." See section 93 of *The Will to Power*, trans. Walter Kaufmann and R. J. Hollingdale (New York: Random House, 1967), 57.

14. Leonard Barkan, *Transuming Passion: Ganymede and the Erotics of Humanism* (Stanford: Stanford University Press, 1991), 3. Barkan's work points to two (often conjoined) fields in which the view of the period tends to be less dour than it is in the work of the New Historicists: in the work of scholars of English literature who are deeply involved with Renaissance art history, and (sometimes) in the field of gay and queer studies. Stephen Orgel's *Impersonations: The Performance of Gender in Shakespeare's England* (Cambridge: Cambridge University Press, 1996) generally treats English culture in the period as less anxious about sexual and gender issues than it is usually taken to be, especially given the period's own condemnations of the dread practice of "sodomy" and our period's insistence on the power and pervasiveness of patriarchy. Jonathan Goldberg's *The Seeds of Things: Theorizing Sexuality and Materiality in Renaissance Representations* (New York: Fordham University Press, 2009) asserts the presence in English Renaissance (not, I note, "early modern") literature of non-normative (Lucretian) ontology and of non-normative conceptions of sexuality—pleasure oriented and nonprocreative.

and dominated by various kinds of anxieties and repressions? I would see it as coming from both "Old" and New Historicism, and from the surprising resurgence of Old Historicism in what might be called "the new humoralism." The conservatism of works like Tillyard's *The Elizabethan World Picture* (1943) and *Shakespeare's History Plays* (1946) or Lily Bess Campbell's *Shakespeare's Tragic Heroes: Slaves of Passion* (1952) hardly needs, at this point, to be demonstrated. These works are simply not in play—in their own names at least—at this point. Much more important, and still relevant as an influence and model, is the picture of the period put forth by the scholars and critics whose work constitutes the New Historicism.[15]

Preeminent among these, of course, is Stephen Greenblatt, whose most important book explicitly announces itself as a retreat from Burckhardt's picture of the period. The title *Renaissance Self-Fashioning* has caused a good deal of confusion—with Greenblatt often taken to be expounding the position that he is critiquing—but there is no doubt that he meant to ironize the notion that self- (or any other) "fashioning" is something that an agent can do.[16] Burckhardt took the project of treating selves, states, and all activities "as works of art" to be the hallmark of the period.[17] Greenblatt claims, and I see no reason not to believe him, to have begun his project from a Burckhardtian point of view. He had intended to study "the role of human autonomy in the construction of identity" in sixteenth- and early seventeenth-century England. He found, however, that in all the texts and documents he examined carefully, the human subject "began to seem remarkably unfree" (*RSF*, 256). The Foucault of *Discipline and Punish*, in tandem with Clifford Geertz, displaced the Burckhardtian framework.[18] A culture is seen, borrowing from Geertz, as

15. In this paragraph and elsewhere, I take "New Historicism" to be contrasted with Old Historicism, not with New Criticism. On this ambiguity, see Richard Strier, *Resistant Structures: Particularity, Radicalism, and Renaissance Texts* (Berkeley: University of California Press, 1995), 67–68.

16. *Renaissance Self-Fashioning from More to Shakespeare* (Chicago: University of Chicago Press, 1980; reissued with a new preface, 2005). Hereafter cited parenthetically in the text as *RSF*.

17. The opening section of Burckhardt's *Civilization of the Renaissance* is entitled "The State as a Work of Art"; it includes a subsection on "war as a work of art." For courtly and public social life as "a matter of art," see 2:377; for domestic life as "a matter of deliberate contrivance," 2:397.

18. Michel Foucault, *Discipline and Punish: The Birth of the Prison*, trans. Alan Sheridan (New York: Random House, 1979).

"a set of control mechanisms"; self-fashioning became "in effect the Renaissance version of these mechanisms" (*RSF*, 3).[19] It became something done to the self rather than something the self does; the self is the object rather than the agent of such "fashioning."

My aim in this section of the introduction is to propose a way of reading the texts of the period that allows for the genuine existence and affirmation of the things that Burckhardt saw in the period, and even of those that Nietzsche did. I will contrast this way of reading, which shows such things to be present without being undermined or ironized, with ways of reading that either insist on such ironies or deny the historical existence of such features. I will consider Renaissance and Reformation texts. In relation to New Historicism, the Renaissance work that I will examine is one of the most "apparently" (as Greenblatt would say) radical of humanist texts, Thomas More's *Utopia* (1516); Reformation values will be considered with regard to William Tyndale (1494–1536) and to Shakespeare's *Othello* (1603–4). For the "new humoralism," I will consider the readings in Michael Schoenfeldt's *Bodies and Selves in Early Modern England*.[20] The issue here is not so much the interpretation of particular texts—though that is the acid test—as it is of contrasting ways of reading. As my title suggests, this book argues that expressions of self-assertion, perversity, and worldly contentment can be truly "unrepentant" in the period, and that the texts expressing such attitudes need not be fissured, anxious, or self-contradictory.

Greenblatt does not describe himself as a deconstructive reader or as a reader "against the grain"; his approach to every figure and text in the period is, rather, "resolutely dialectical": "If we say that there is a new stress on the executive power of the will, we must say that there is the most sustained and relentless assault upon the will; if we say that there is a new social mobility,

19. The phrase is taken from Clifford Geertz, *The Interpretation of Cultures* (New York: Basic Books), 44. It might be said that in Greenblatt's account, Geertz's views are darkened in much the same way that the figures and texts of the Renaissance are. Geertz's conception of cultural "control mechanisms" is intended to explain the development of individuals, through choices, not to deny their self-fashioning ability. Geertz is trying to defend the study of particular cultures and individuals against generalized norms. He sees cultural constraints, as opposed to biological ones, as leaving the objects of them "much less precisely regulated." Becoming human, says Geertz, "is becoming individual, and we become individual under the guidance of cultural patterns" (52). "Guidance" is a much less determining notion than "control mechanisms" originally suggested, and than Greenblatt's use of the phrase suggests.

20. Michael C. Schoenfeldt, *Bodies and Selves in Early Modern England* (Cambridge: Cambridge University Press, 1999).

we must say that there is a new assertion of power by both family and state to determine all movement within the society; if we say that there is a heightened awareness of the existence of alternative modes of social, theological, and psychological organization, we must say that that is a new dedication to the imposition of control upon those modes and ultimately to the destruction of alternatives" (*RSF*, 1–2). In each of these formulations, the clauses that represent what "we say" (or are likely or tempted to say) represent versions of what might fairly be called the Burckhardtian view of the period; the clauses that sternly represent what we "must" say represent the corrective view (or opposing forces). This does represent a more complex picture of the period than Burckhardt's, and may indeed highlight post-fifteenth-century developments (centralized monarchies, the Council of Trent, etc.). But what is notable about Greenblatt's presentation of this "dialectic" is that in each case he is committed to demonstrating the triumph of the right-hand (negative, coercive) clauses in each of the pairings over the left-hand (affirmative) ones. The picture is less of a dialectic than an undermining. His effort is not simply to show that these forces coexist in the period, but to show that they coexist in such a way that the Burckhardtian positive features can never be seen as existing, within a text or an individual, in a non-undermined way.

So let me proceed now to my first test case in what might be called affirmative rather than undermining reading: More's *Utopia*. For Greenblatt, More's aim in book 2 of *Utopia*—the detailed account of the imagined society—is to construct a society in which "modern individuality," in fact all individuality and inwardness, becomes impossible (*RSF*, 37). In abolishing private property, the Utopians are eliminating private selves—indeed, they are eliminating selves: Utopia is "a society designed to reduce the scope of the inner life" (*RSF*, 53). The first thing that should be said is that this is a very odd way to understand the goal of Utopian communism. More (or his imaginary narrator, Hythlodaeus) goes out of his way to stress the elimination of material scarcity and of the pervasive and devastating moral, psychological, and sociological effects of such scarcity.[21] But Greenblatt is constantly in the position of arguing against the text. He acknowledges that the Utopian workday of no more

---

21. See Thomas More, *Utopia*, ed. Edward Surtz, S.J. (New Haven: Yale University Press, 1964), 77, 147, et passim. This is the paperback edition. For the Latin, I have used *The Complete Works of St. Thomas More* (New Haven: Yale University Press, 1965), vol. 4, *Utopia*, ed. Edward Surtz, S.J., and J. H. Hexter. Page numbers to the Latin refer to this text. The English translation is the same in the paperback and in the *Complete Works*. In citing the translation, I give the page number in the paperback followed by the page number in the *Complete Works* volume.

("often" less [75, 135]) than six hours—an astonishing idea in the early modern period—could be seen as "far from discouraging individuation . . . but rather designed to permit its greatest flourishing" (40). But he quickly goes on to discount this possibility. He notes that some Utopians end up working a longer day. What he does not mention is that those who do this *choose* to do so ("if anyone should prefer to devote himself to his trade" [70]; *si quis arte suae malit insumere* [128]). And these people too, like all the Utopians, enjoy the sumptuous communal meals with music, fancy desserts, and so forth. Greenblatt emphasizes the limitations on Utopian choice in leisure activities, but the text states that the Utopians spend their (universally distributed) leisure time according to individual choice (*suo cuiusque arbitri* [126]). The main entertainments offered to them are indeed public lectures, but the text emphasizes, again, that there are many different sorts of lectures precisely to accommodate differences in taste and "natural inclination" in different persons (*prout cuiusque fert natura* [128]). Throughout this passage on leisure, the variety of preferences and natural inclinations among individuals is highlighted (note the repetition of *cuius*).[22]

In the society imagined, freedom of choice, on the basis of individual preference or capacity, is accommodated not only with regard to leisure activities (which include games, conversation, and music as well as lectures), but also with regard to occupations (69/127); travel (82/147); possession of fools (113/193); farming (where everyone is required to do some, but those who by nature enjoy it [*natura delectat* (114)] can stay longer [62/115]); health care (home or hospital [78/141]); the end of life (suicide *in extremis* is an option [108/187]); marriage (110/188); and religious beliefs and practices (133/221, 142/233). From this point of view, what is striking about the imagined society is how deeply—within its multifarious rules and structures—individual choice and respect for individual "natures" is built into it.[23]

22. For a brilliant discussion of the way in which the word *cui* works in *Utopia* as contrasted with the way in which it works in Cicero (particularly, in *De Officiis*), see Bradin Cormack, *A Power to Do Justice: Jurisdiction, English Literature, and the Rise of Common Law, 1509–1625* (Chicago: University of Chicago Press, 2007), 107–9.

23. Humanist pedagogy might be seen as having this same mixture of set structures and respect for individual difference. See, for instance, Erasmus, *De Pueris Instituendis*, in William Harrison Woodward, *Desiderius Erasmus Concerning the Aim and Method of Education* (New York: Teachers College, Columbia University, 1964), 195–96; Erasme, *Declamatio de Pueris Statim a Liberaliter Instituendis*, ed. and trans. Jean-Claude Margolin (Geneva: Droz, 1966), 409, 411 (in French). For an overview, see Rebecca Bushnell, *A Culture of Teaching: Early Modern Humanism in Theory and Practice* (Ithaca: Cornell University Press, 1996), chap. 3.

But where the Greenblattian (New Historicist) approach is even more misleading—and characteristically so—in darkening the text is with regard to the
"theoretical celebration of pleasure" in Utopia (*RSF*, 52). Along with communism, the commitment to pleasure is a central feature of the society presented.
Like Alberti, the Utopians believe that the soul is "born for happiness" (*Utopia*, 92/161–63). This might be seen as a distinctly "Renaissance" orientation
from a Burckhardtian perspective. It cannot be allowed to stand. Greenblatt
discounts it by pointing out that the Utopians believe in a hierarchy of pleasures. He states correctly that they place sexual intercourse in the same
category as defecation and scratching an itch, and he quotes the narrator's rhetorical question about a life devoted to such pleasures: "Who does not see that
such a life is not only disgusting but wretched?" (*RSF*, 43; *Utopia*, 101/177). But
what Greenblatt does not and perhaps cannot note, and what I would stress,
is that a few lines later this passage takes a turn. The narrator adds, "yet they
enjoy even these pleasures and gratefully acknowledge the kindness of mother
nature who, with alluring sweetness [*blandissima suavitate* (176)] coaxes her
offspring to that which of necessity they must constantly do" (101/177). And,
as to sex in Utopia, Greenblatt does not mention the most striking custom: the
"strictly observed" practice (*illi serio ac severe observant* [188]) of having both
partners of a potential marriage inspect the other naked to make sure that each
of them finds the potential spouse physically appealing (110/189). So obviously
the fact that certain pleasures are "lower" than others does not mean that these
"lower" pleasures are unimportant or to be disregarded or renounced.[24] The
clergy who do choose to renounce such pleasures—they are not required to—
are considered quite irrational, though very holy (*Utopia*, 138/227).[25]

24. Greenblatt revisits the topic of Utopian pleasure in a recent essay by that title in *Cultural Reformations: Medieval and Renaissance in Literary History*, ed. Brian Cummings and
James Simpson (Oxford: Oxford University Press, 2010), 305–320. He here acknowledges the
place of pleasure in Utopia somewhat more fully—"The Utopians certainly do not condemn
the pleasure of the flesh—on the contrary, they recognize and enjoy the satisfaction that comes
with eating or excreting or scratching an itch" (312). Even this, however, is rather muted, and
the pleasures of sex are notably missing from this list (as is, still, any reference to the premarital
nude inspections).

25. Comparing the ascetic to the non-ascetic clergy, Hythlodaeus says that *Hos* [the latter]
Utopiani prudentiores, at illos [the former] *sanctiores reputant*, and he goes on to note that if the
ascetics purported to be relying on reason they would be laughed to scorn (*si rationibus nitteren-
tur irriderent* [226]). My friend Richard G. Stern objected to an earlier formulation in which I
had said that More/Hythlodaeus presented the ascetic priests as "very holy, but quite insane."

To say that the Utopians only "profess to value pleasure" is therefore a major misrepresentation (*RSF*, 44).[26] And there is another such, of the same darkening kind. Along with communism and hedonism, the most salient feature of Utopia is its commitment to religious toleration: "[T]hey count this principle among their most ancient institutions, that no one should suffer for his religion" (*Utopia*, 133/219). This commitment too must be undermined; it suggests a too strongly "Renaissance" perspective.[27] Greenblatt points to the existence of excommunication in Utopia. He rightly notes that it is highly dreaded and, moreover, "reinforced by the threat of physical punishment" (*RSF*, 56). If excommunicated persons do not demonstrate repentance, they are "seized and punished by the senate for their impiety" (*Utopia*, 140/229). This concern for repentance hardly betokens an indifference to the inner life, but that is passed over here. Greenblatt has found his "dialectic": "It is here, in this crushing of impiety, that all the coercive powers of Utopian society" come together; moreover, "the form of their union, in this commonwealth celebrated for its tolerance, is the precise form of the operation of the Holy Inquisition: excommunication, public shaming, the attempt to waken guilt, the grim transfer of the unrepentant sinner from the religious to the secular arm" (*RSF*, 56).

It is true that the text does not exactly say this, but it comes pretty close (and Surtz accepts "saner" as a translation of *prudentiores*).

26. Richard Halpern's more Marxist-inflected account of *Utopia* (and Utopia) is similarly committed to showing the Utopian commitment to pleasure not to be what it seems; he claims that it is "mostly defined negatively" and that it is actually a "rejection" of bodily pleasures. See *The Poetics of Primitive Accumulation: English Renaissance Culture and the Genealogy of Capital* (Ithaca: Cornell University Press, 1991), 172. Halpern's chapter is odd in that it begins with a brilliant critique of the reading of Utopia as a "totalitarian" state, and of the "conservative tradition of *Utopia* criticism" that has exaggerated the unpleasantness of the society described, but he then goes on to state, quite accurately, that he too intends to "explore the 'unpleasantness' of Utopia" (140–41). He insists that Utopia secretly values what it pretends to despise (gold—see 146 and 168), and that the economy described is actually one of potential scarcity rather than realized abundance (168–69). Halpern states more explicitly than Greenblatt does that any proper reading of book 2 "has as its prerequisite the disruption of Utopia's discursive self-sufficiency" (151).

27. See Burckhardt's chapter "Religion and the Spirit of the Renaissance" (2:473–83), and the very end of his study (2:513–16); Roland H. Bainton, "Man, God, and the Church in the Age of the Renaissance," in *The Renaissance: Six Essays* (1953; New York: Harper and Row, 1962), 77–96; and George Huntston Williams, "Erasmus and the Reformers on Non-Christian Religions and *Salus Extra Ecclesiam*," in *Action and Conviction in Early Modern Europe*, ed. Theodore K. Rabb and Jerrold E. Seigel (Princeton: Princeton University Press, 1969), 319–70.

"darkeary" is undetermined.

Here Greenblatt would seem to have found a deep—and dark—contradiction. Toleration has apparently turned into its opposite.

However, as Greenblatt acknowledges in a footnote—it would have spoiled the point to put it in the text—what "impiety" means in the passage about the impious being "seized and punished by the senate" is immoral behavior (*RSF*, 266n70). The "impious" person in Utopia is not being punished for his beliefs. Even the atheist, in Utopia, is not physically punished. This is a huge matter.[28] The atheist does suffer some constraints—inability to hold office and inability to argue his position "in the presence of the common people"—but the authorities "do not punish him in any way" (*nullo afficiunt supplicio*). Moreover, they do not "compel him by threats to change his views," and they do not wish him to profess beliefs that he does not hold. They understand that belief cannot be compelled—a central tolerationist premise (*persuasum habeant, nulli hoc in manu esse, ut quicquid libet, sentiat* [222])—so instead, they discuss the matter with him in private (135/223).[29] This is truly a "utopian" treatment of heresy. But it might be objected—although Greenblatt does not seize on this—that Utopia does have a state religion. This seems to be a point where the cleft foot indeed sticks out. But here too, the text is quite consistent. The state religion puts forth only the most generalized conceptions of the divinity, "so as not to detract from any of the private devotions" (142–43/233). Utopus, the founder of the society, considered the possibility that God "desired a varied and manifold worship" (133/221), and the priests of the state religion continue to respect this possibility. We are a long way from the Inquisition. I would suggest that book 2 of *Utopia*, the most sustained attempt in the period, serious or not, to imagine "alternative modes" of social, religious, and psychological organization should be fully acknowledged and appreciated.[30]

28. Edward Surtz, like Greenblatt, also downplays this important point. See Surtz's note in the paperback edition (*Utopia*, 135).

29. For an overview of the development of the idea of religious toleration from the sixteenth to the early eighteenth century in Europe, see Perez Zagorin, *How the Idea of Religious Toleration Came to the West* (Princeton: Princeton University Press, 2003). For More's contribution, see Sanford Kessler, "Religious Freedom in Thomas More's *Utopia*," *Review of Politics* 64 (2002): 207–29.

30. In the essay "Utopian Pleasure" (see note 24 above), Greenblatt does try to give More credit for the "Utopian" aspects of Utopia: "In the long run, the most interesting story is not his [More's] conservative recuperation of Catholic doctrines" (319). But Greenblatt's account of Utopian society here is even more insistent on its (supposed) lack of true religious toleration. He takes the way persons who deny the immortality of the soul and the afterlife are treated to be central to the society, since he sees these beliefs as more fundamental to the society than

Let me turn now to actual rather than Utopian religion. An inability or unwillingness to acknowledge the positive dimension of the Reformation is a trait shared by Greenblatt and almost all the New Historicists as well as by a number of revisionist historians and literary critics following them.[31] C. S. Lewis, in a memorable passage in the *Oxford History of English Literature*, describes what he calls "the beautiful, cheerful integration of Tyndale's world."[32] Greenblatt must also oppose this—he substitutes "nervous alliance" for "cheerful integration"—though he concedes that "it is quite true that Tyndale utterly denies the medieval distinction between religion and secular life" (*RSF*, 112). The important point is that what is being dismissed or only faintly acknowledged here, in a concessive clause, is a giant revolution in sensibility and worldview—one that will feature largely in *The Unrepentant Renaissance*: a conception of life in the world as compatible with, and even constituting, the highest form of spiritual life. To deny "utterly" the medieval distinction between religion and secular life is to make (or participate in) this revolution, and precisely to allow for the cheerful integration of which Lewis writes.

The Reformation gets lost in Greenblatt's treatment of *Othello*. Again, sexuality is a key issue. Greenblatt assumes that the rigorist view is normative for Christianity. He quotes St. Jerome's endorsement of the Stoic view that to love

communism (317). He acknowledges that the text "does not disclose what happens to those freethinkers who are not cured of their 'madness,'" but he hypothesizes a particular punishment for them (enslavement). The basis for this is that these persons "would presumably" be treated the way that adulterers are (315). Again, the passage in which it is explicitly stated that the authorities "do not punish him [the denier of providence, etc.] in any way" (*nullo afficiunt supplicio*) is suppressed. The connection to adulterers is never made (or suggested) in the text, and the reference to the harsh treatment of that class of persons is treated as part of the picture of Utopian society as self-underminingly repressive, while the fact that the society makes explicit provisions for divorce (and remarriage) on the basis of both ill-treatment and characterological incompatibility (*Utopia*, 111; 189/191) is never mentioned.

31. For New Historicism and the Reformation, see Strier, *Resistant Structures*, chap. 4. The central figure among the historians is Eamon Duffy, especially in *The Stripping of the Altars: Traditional Religion in England, 1400–1580* (New Haven: Yale University Press, 1992). For literary critics sharing Duffy's perspective, see inter alia, James Simpson, *Burning to Read: English Fundamentalism and Its Reformation Opponents* (Cambridge: Belknap Press of Harvard University Press, 2007), and Regina M. Schwartz, *Sacramental Poetics at the Dawn of Secularism: When God Left the World* (Stanford: Stanford University Press, 2008). For a critique of the "Reformation as loss" view, see Richard Strier, "Martin Luther and the Real Presence in Nature," *Journal of Medieval and Early Modern Studies* 37 (Spring 2007): 271–303.

32. The quotation is from C. S. Lewis, *English Literature in the Sixteenth Century, Excluding Drama* (Oxford: Clarendon, 1954), 190.

one's spouse too ardently is adultery, and cites Calvin, along with various late medieval and sixteenth-century confessors, as also endorsing it (*RSF*, 248-49). In fact, Calvin's endorsement of this view is muted,[33] but the important point is that Greenblatt never gives the Protestant revaluation of celibacy and marriage its full weight. He does acknowledge—again in a concessive clause—that "there is, to be sure, in all shades of Protestantism an attack on the Catholic doctrine of celibacy and a celebration of married love" (*RSF*, 248). But once again this acknowledgment, as the construction suggests, is perfunctory. Passages about lust and jealousy are quoted (*RSF*, 249) from Roland M. Frye's "The Teachings of Classical Puritanism on Conjugal Love," but the main thrust of Frye's essay is ignored. Frye's primary aim is to demonstrate, with many examples, "classical Puritanism to have inculcated a view of sexual life in marriage as [quoting Milton] the 'Crown of all our bliss.'" Frye shows Thomas Gataker, in a sermon on marriage published in 1620, arguing that to represent Christianity as a damper placed on the joys of living is a tactic of the demonic. Frye sees Gataker as "typical here," and quotes William Gouge, in his very popular *Of Domesticall Duties* (1634), stating that although married couples should certainly behave properly in public, "an husband's affection to his wife cannot be too great."[34]

This perspective allows us truly to historicize what is happening in *Othello*. Consider the exchange, in the scene following the great central one of Othello's temptation and fall, between Othello and Desdemona concerning Desdemona's hand.[35] Here we can see an appreciation of sexuality alternating with an ascetic, specifically Catholic negative view of exactly the same phenomenon. When Desdemona, at Othello's request, gives Othello her hand, he notes that

33. Calvin calls the view "severe, though not undeserved" in *Institutes of the Christian Religion*, ed. John T. McNeill, trans. Ford Lewis Battles, (Philadelphia: Westminster, 1960), 2.8.44. Greenblatt, interestingly, does not quote the view from Calvin directly but from Lawrence Stone, who ignores the qualification in Calvin's statement (the reference is to Stone, *The Family, Sex, and Marriage in England, 1500–1800* [New York: Harper and Row, 1977], 499). My colleague David Bevington has reminded me that Stone is one of the purveyors of the dour view of the period.

34. I have cited Frye's "The Teachings of Classical Puritanism on Conjugal Love" as it appears in *On Milton's Poetry: A Selection of Modern Studies*, ed. Arnold Stein (Greenwich, Conn.: Fawcett, 1970), 98, 104, 106; hereafter cited in the text. The article originally appeared in *Studies in the Renaissance* 2 (1955): 148–59.

35. For *Othello* as "Shakespeare's *Paradise Lost*," see Richard Strier, "Excuses, Bepissing, and Non-being: Shakespearean Puzzles about Agency," in *Shakespeare and Moral Agency*, ed. Michael D. Bristol (London: Continuum, 2010), 65.

it "is moist."[36] She answers, quite candidly and wonderfully, that it should be so: "It yet hath felt no age, nor known no sorrow" (3.4.37). She is happy and healthy, and happy to be both of these. Othello responds:

> This argues fruitfulness and liberal heart:
> Hot, hot, and moist. This hand of yours requires
> A sequester from liberty, fasting and prayer,
> Much castigation, exercise devout,
> For here's a young and sweating devil, here,
> That commonly rebels. 'Tis a good hand,
> A frank one.
>
> (3.4.38–44)

While "fasting and prayer" may be confessionally neutral, "castigation" and "exercise devout" are not. The alternation here is not, in England, part of a culturally necessary dialectic. Instead of seeing Othello as expressing, with the help of Iago, a "quite orthodox" anxiety about adultery with one's spouse (*RSF*, 250), one can see the play as showing, to a largely Protestant audience, the way in which what would have been perceived as a specifically Catholic view of sexuality within marriage can serve as a deeply dangerous and destabilizing psychic force. Iago can be seen as demonic in exactly Gataker's terms. Whether or not it is true that, were it not for Iago's interventions, Othello would have "prove[d] to Desdemona / A most dear husband" (2.1.288–89), it is certainly true that the view of sexuality that Iago prompts in Othello would have been seen as medieval and, in the sixteenth-century present, Catholic.[37] "Classical" Puritans and many other Protestants did not share that view. In a Protestant context, the moist hand need not be castigated; within marriage, it could be allowed its "liberty."

While it is fair to say that no single book as influential as *Renaissance Self-Fashioning* has appeared in the field of English Renaissance studies since 1980, one of the striking developments in the field, as I have already noted,

---

36. I quote from *Othello*, ed. E. A. J. Honigmann (Surrey: Thomas Nelson, 1997), 3.4.36; references appear hereafter in the text.

37. I am not definitively taking a stand on the highly contentious and uncertain matter of Shakespeare's own religious commitment (if any), but I do think that the plays quite consistently present asceticism and sexual disgust as pathological.

has been the emergence of what I have described as "the new humoralism." The scholar-critics involved in this "movement" have taken Galenic psycho-physiology (humor theory) as the key to the period's distinctive thought about and representation of persons (though how this period's use of the theory is different from that of earlier periods is left unclear). Their focus might be said to be on selves in the period as physiocultural rather than sociocultural formations (though obviously these frameworks interact).[38] Preeminent in this group are Gail Kern Paster and Michael C. Schoenfeldt.[39] I have taken the latter's work as my example because Schoenfeldt can be seen as more interested in the ethical dimensions of the theory and Paster as more interested in what she thinks of as its "phenomenological" dimension.[40] From my point of view, the important feature of this work is that it, too, presents the period in dark and dour terms. Schoenfeldt clearly wishes to present his conception of self-discipline in the period, particularly with regard to food, under the banner of Foucauldian liberation rather than Foucauldian social control—so a difference is here proclaimed from New Historicism (12)—but the emphasis of the book keeps slipping from liberation to anxiety.[41]

Schoenfeldt's basic view is that "the early modern regime," meaning its psychological "regime" or system, "seems to entail a fear of emotion," so that the great positive value becomes self-control, "the capacity to control rather than

38. For general discussion of this kind of work, see Mary Floyd-Wilson, Matthew Greenfield, Gail Kern Paster, Tanya Pollard, Katherine Rowe, and Julian Yates, "Shakespeare and Embodiment: An E-Conversation," *Literature Compass* 2 (2005): 1–13; and Richard Strier and Carla Mazzio, "Two Responses to 'Shakespeare and Embodiment: An E-Conversation,'" *Literature Compass* 3 (2005): 15–31.

39. For Paster, see *The Body Embarrassed: Drama and the Disciplines of Shame in Early Modern England* (Ithaca: Cornell University Press, 1993), and especially, *Humoring the Body: Emotions and the Shakespearean Stage* (Chicago: University of Chicago Press, 2004). For Schoenfeldt, see *Bodies and Selves*. For a collection that extends the humoral approach in an environmentalist direction, see *Environment and Embodiment in Early Modern England*, ed. Mary Floyd-Wilson and Garrett A. Sullivan, Jr. (Basingstoke, Hampshire: Palgrave Macmillan, 2007).

40. For their own comments on the difference between their approaches, see Paster, *Humoring the Body*, 21, and Schoenfeldt, *Bodies and Selves*, 15 (cited hereafter in the text). For doubts about the appropriateness of presenting a physiological theory as a "phenomenology," see my response to the "E-Conversation" cited in note 38 above.

41. The work of Foucault to which Schoenfeldt primarily appeals is *The Use of Pleasure*, vol. 2 of *The History of Sexuality*, trans. Robert Hurley (New York: Random House, 1985), esp. part 1, chap. 4.

to vent emotion" (15–16).[42] This leads him to place a modified version of Stoicism at the center of the period's values, and to claim that "when Stoics are criticized in the early modern period, it is more typically for their pride than for their suppression of emotion" (17). This is an assertion that he elsewhere contradicts, but that his framework—fear of emotion as normative—leads him to make.[43] The trouble with this perspective is not simply that it presents what may be the most widely voiced value system of the period as too thoroughly dominant, or that it treats a framework (a version of Galenic medicine) that is filled with contradictions, crudities, and crippling ambiguities as a subtle and coherent system (Burckhardt, interestingly, had no use for it).[44] The major problem is that even more than Greenblatt's "dialectical" approach, Schoenfeldt's "humoral" approach produces readings that are extraordinarily and consistently conservative, readings that entirely support the rule of order, reason, and restraint.[45] This, together with the systematizing ("world picture")

42. Compare Paster: since "humoral subjectivity" is characterized by "a high degree of emotional lability," this explains "the call for emotional regulation by self and by external social disciplines"; see also her presentation of Othello's "dread of embodied emotion" as normal in "the early modern cultural imaginary" (*Humoring the Body*, 19, 72).

43. For places where Schoenfeldt contradicts this claim (or seems to), see *Bodies and Selves*, 85–86, 112, 164. For a sustained argument against this claim, see chapter 1 below. Paster begins *Humoring the Body* with a passage stating that Christ's passions "never proceeded beyond their due measure," and she uses this as an example of anti-Stoicism (1). It is so insofar as a certain kind of Aristotelian position is so, but, as we will see in chapter 1 below, robust Renaissance anti-Stoicism defended vehement and, indeed, indecorous passions.

44. Here is Burckhardt on humors theory: "It sounds almost ludicrous when an otherwise competent observer considers Clement VII to be of a melancholy temperament, but defers his judgment to that of the physicians, who declare the Pope of a sanguine-choleric nature; or when we read that the same Gaston de Foix, the victor of Ravenna, whom Giorgione painted and Bambaja carved, and whom all the historians describe, had the saturnine temperament. No doubt those who use these expressions mean something by them; but the terms in which they tell us their meaning are strangely out of date in the Italy of the sixteenth century" (2:303–4). On the incoherence of the early modern physiological "system," see not only the conclusion of Anne Ferry quoted by Schoenfeldt (20), who somehow sees this incoherence as positive (recoding it as flexibility), but, more important, the recent study of Robert Burton, a figure regularly cited by the humoralists as an exponent of the system, which shows Burton to be doing essentially a send-up or deconstruction of it. See Angus Gowland, *The Worlds of Renaissance Melancholy: Robert Burton in Context* (Cambridge: Cambridge University Press, 2006), chap. 2, "Dissecting Medical Learning."

45. Paster is much more wary of conservative values, seeing them in class and gendered terms, but one can see the framework pushing her in the same direction as Schoenfeldt. For

impulse, is what most deeply links the new humoralists to the Old Historicists.
As in Campbell's *Shakespeare's Tragic Heroes: Slaves of Passion*, passion, in
both Schoenfeldt and Paster, is almost always presented as "seething" or something of the sort. Guyon's utter destruction of the Bower of Bliss in book 2
of *The Faerie Queene* (2.11.83) is presented by Schoenfeldt as an instance of
rather than a departure from temperance (70). Guyon's intensity is justified by
the picture of the emotions that Spenser, and virtually everyone in the period,
is seen as holding: "The temperance Spenser portrays throughout the book
is . . . a dynamic, even frantic maintenance of order in the face of perpetual
insurrection" (73). The figure of weakness of the will (Acrasia) who presides
over the Bower of Bliss generates "overheated love" that "melts the stone"
from which, according to Schoenfeldt, a Renaissance or early modern self is
composed (71).

This mention of the (supposed) positive stoniness of the Renaissance self
leads directly into Schoenfeldt's chapter on Shakespeare's sonnets. The intention of the sonnets as a whole is to demonstrate the importance of "the rational
self-control of moderation" (90) in the face of the mental and physical pathol-
ogy of erotic desire (see, e.g., 75, 83). That Shakespeare—like Petrarch before
him—might have seen something paradoxically positive in erotic obsession
cannot be allowed by Schoenfeldt (this positive viewpoint in both Shakespeare
and Petrarch is the burden of my second chapter below). The centerpiece of
Schoenfeldt's chapter on the sonnets is, courageously and consistently enough,
a defense of the position apparently asserted in sonnet 94, "They that have
power to hurt, and will do none," a poem that praises those who are "as stone, /
Unmoved, cold." Schoenfeldt associates "power to hurt" with aristocratic possession of weapons (92), but the context seems pretty clearly to be one of erotic
and emotional "power to hurt," a much more complex matter. Schoenfeldt
wants to take the praise of the stony people at face value, and he is deeply ir-
ritated by Edward Hubler's assertion that it is "preposterous" to do so (84, 90,
93).[46] But Hubler's reading of the sonnet as "ironic" is based on its relation
to the other sonnets in Shakespeare's volume, and William Empson's similar

instance, with regard to *The Taming of the Shrew*, Paster warns us, quite unhappily, that it is
anachronistic to take Katherine's compliance at the end of the play as merely "strategic," since
"in the reciprocities of humoralism [between the physical and the psychical], external compliance means internal alteration" (134).

46. See Edward Hubler, *The Sense of Shakespeare's Sonnets* (Princeton: Princeton University
Press, 1952), 103.

reading draws on many Shakespearean texts outside the sonnets.[47] Schoenfeldt mocks the idea that Shakespeare may have thought that there was "some
ethical joy implicit in the virtue of giving" (93), but this is exactly what Hubler
and Empson are able to show, and it is a position that was highly available in
the period, in both secular and theological contexts. It is what Luther called
the "freedom of a Christian."[48] A more generous, less purely defensive picture
of selfhood was unquestionably possible in the period—even, or especially, for
Shakespeare.

With regard to George Herbert, Schoenfeldt has a great deal of trouble
with Herbert's defenses of strong, even indecorous emotion (111–13).[49] Where
Schoenfeldt is convincing is in the view that Herbert's attitude toward earthly
and bodily pleasures is almost always negative.[50] Humoralism may not be as
important in the poetry as Schoenfeldt asserts, but it may actually be justified
to speak of "the immense anxiety that for Herbert suffused situations of con-
sumption" (129)—in his life as well as in his poetry.[51] The important question,
however, is whether there are larger implications in Herbert's anxieties and

47. William Empson, *Some Versions of Pastoral* (1935; Norfolk, Conn.: New Directions,
1960), chap. 3. Empson notes that sonnet 94 would not strike one as incoherent or ironic "if it
was Shakespeare's only surviving work" (86).

48. See *The Freedom of a Christian*, in *Martin Luther: Selections from His Writings*, ed. John
Dillenberger (Garden City, N.Y.: Doubleday, 1961), 67, 70, 73–76. For Seneca's *De Beneficiis* as
the primary secular (classical) source for Shakespeare's commitment to "the virtue of giving,"
see John M. Wallace, "*Timon of Athens* and the Three Graces: Shakespeare's Senecan Study,"
Modern Philology 83 (1986): 349–63.

49. For a discussion of this theme in Herbert's poetry, see 53–58 below.

50. I have argued for this view myself. See Richard Strier, "George Herbert and the World,"
Journal of Medieval and Renaissance Studies 11 (1981): 211–36.

51. With regard to humoralism, I am not sure that I see "Confession," for instance, as "particularly organic" (105), since its picture of the self seems to be primarily artifactual. Moreover,
the poem seems truly to be treating the self, not the body—a distinction that is either nugatory or
crucial depending on one's understanding of the status of humoralism. The critique of Burckhardt's conception of the Renaissance "self" that John Jeffrey Martin purports to offer in *Myths
of Renaissance Individualism* (Basingstoke, Hampshire: Palgrave Macmillan, 2004) seems to
me simply to identify aspects of the conception of self that Burckhardt presents, including the
"porous" aspect so beloved especially of Paster (see Burkhardt, *Civilization of the Renaissance*,
2:484–509). I am not sure that a reading of "The Collar" is deepened or made more accurate
by seeing it, as Schoenfeldt does, as about an imbalance in "humoral fluids" (110–11) or that it is
coherent to see the spiritual transgression imagined in the poem as caused by "the excess of humoral choler" (130). The confusion of reasons and causes is an endemic feature of the humoral
framework, as is the implied physiological determinism.

fastidiousness. Can his wariness toward the physical—and the worldly and the social—be extended (as Schoenfeldt implies) to early modern persons, especially Protestants, in general?[52] I would argue that the negativity of Herbert's attitudes was personal to him and contradicts the attitudes that normally flow from a strong commitment to Reformation theology.[53] Again, sexuality is a test. Herbert insisted, "Virginity is a higher state than matrimony."[54] But the whole realm of bodily and social life is at issue. Luther proclaimed the holiness of the peasant working in the field; Tyndale saw urination as a potentially holy act (a prime example of "cheerful integration").[55] When, once in his poetry, Herbert did present low service as potentially "divine," even there he could not help but see it as "drudgerie" ("The Elixir," lines 17–18). Even his attitude toward temperance is pinched.[56] Herbert translated Luigi Cornaro's treatise on temperance, and Schoenfeldt's correct placement of this in the context of Herbert's general wariness contrasts sharply with Burckhardt's use of Cornaro (as we have seen) as a model of happy and flourishing worldliness.

Finally, let me say a few words about Milton and anxiety. *Paradise Lost* is Schoenfeldt's final case. Milton may, in his life and habits, have been just as fastidious as George Herbert; Schoenfeldt suggests this, and there is a fair amount

---

52. Herbert's lack of civic humanism is the focus of Malcolm Mackenzie Ross's *Poetry and Dogma: The Transfiguration of Eucharistic Symbols in Seventeenth-Century English Poetry* (New Brunswick: Rutgers University Press, 1954), chap. 6. This view is only partly modified by Christina Malcolmson's *George Herbert and the Protestant Ethic* (Stanford: Stanford University Press, 1999).

53. For the strength of Herbert's commitment to the central doctrine of Reformation theology—justification by faith—see, inter alia, Richard Strier, *Love Known: Theology and Experience in George Herbert's Poetry* (Chicago: University of Chicago Press, 1983), and Gene Edward Veith, Jr., *Reformation Spirituality: The Religion of George Herbert* (London: Associated University Presses, 1985).

54. *The Country Parson (A Priest to the Temple)*, in *The Works of George Herbert*, ed. F. E. Hutchinson (Oxford: Clarendon, 1945), 236. See also the canceled stanzas to "The Church-porch," in which Herbert had asserted that "A Virgin-bed" has "a speciall Crowne" (though he did add "If it concurr with vertue"), and in which Herbert was worried that his position might "seem Monkish" (6). The revised stanza purports to see virginity and faithful marriage as equal options, and purports to "gladly welcome" legitimate sexuality, but remains highly monitory and anxious.

55. See Luther's *The Babylonian Captivity of the Church*, translated as *The Pagan Servitude* in *Selections from His Writings*, 311; and Tyndale's *The Parable of the Wicked Mammon*, in *Doctrinal Treatises . . . by William Tyndale*, ed. Rev. Henry Walker (Cambridge: Parker Society, 1848), 100.

56. See Strier, "George Herbert and the World," 215–21.

of evidence for it. But *Paradise Lost* is not a fastidious poem.[57] Schoenfeldt very much likes and agrees with W. B. C. Watkins that "Milton from beginning to end is preoccupied with eating" (135). But the quotation from Watkins in Schoenfeldt that begins in this way ends with the sentence: "Neither the denizens of Paradise nor of Heaven miss a meal, invariably described with unabashed enjoyment."[58] "Unabashed enjoyment" is notably missing from Schoenfeldt's account of any activity. Even in his treatment of angelic feasting, which he notes is surprisingly lavish, Schoenfeldt speaks of a fantasy of "disciplined surfeit" (137) where Milton stresses divine plenitude and angelic lack of anxiety ("secure / Of surfeit" [5.638–39]).[59] Schoenfeldt does not comment on the verb that Milton uses to describe the dining of the prelapsarian Adam and Eve, a verb used with complete unselfconsciousness—"To thir Supper Fruits *they fell*" (4.331). And where Milton stresses the elegance and unsparingness of the meal that Eve prepares for Raphael, Adam, and herself, Schoenfeldt stresses temperance (138), a word that does not appear in the passage—true, Eve "tempers dulcet creams" (5.34), but that is a different matter. Schoenfeldt wants Adam and Eve to "stuff themselves" at the Fall (149), but Eve alone "engorged without restraint"; of the forbidden fruit, Adam eats "his fill" (9.791, 1005). The framework of dietary temperance and intemperance only partially works and does not seem to be Milton's focus.[60] But the major question, again, is where does Schoenfeldt show us the "liberating aspects of the exercise of self-

57. See Joshua Scodel, *Excess and the Mean in Early Modern English Literature* (Princeton: Princeton University Press, 2002), chap. 9. Scodel's view of temperance is much more capacious and nonrepressive than that of Schoenfeldt. Scodel points to positive conceptions of excess as well as of moderation in the period, and he stresses the presence of pleasure in Milton's Eden, albeit through "pleasurable restraint."

58. The quotation from Watkins is from *An Anatomy of Milton's Verse* (Baton Rouge: Louisiana State University Press, 1955), 117.

59. Throughout, citations of Milton's poetry are from John Milton, *Complete Poems and Major Prose*, ed. Merritt Y. Hughes (New York: Odyssey, 1957).

60. Schoenfeldt's idea that the Fall is a matter of "conduct before food" (131) is hyperbolic, to say the least. The forbidden fruit is never, even at the moment of Eve's Fall, a matter primarily of food. That it is dinner time—"the hour of Noon drew on" (9.739)—is only a very small part of Eve's decision to taste the fruit. Her soliloquy before the fatal plucking and eating (9.745–79) is focused primarily on the apparent fact of the fruit's effect on the serpent. And to say that prelapsarian dietary experience is (in Milton's words elsewhere) "a perpetuall childhood of prescription" is completely misleading, since, before the Fall, Adam and Eve have only "This one, this easy charge" (4.421)—a line that is quoted by Schoenfeldt, but not taken seriously, since he asserts that "their diet is clearly prescribed" (133). There are no "dietary laws" before the Fall. Such laws concern categories of foods (from animals with cloven hoofs, and so forth).

discipline" in the poem (168)?[61] Where is "unabashed enjoyment," if "every meal"—and every other physical action—is "a moral test" (132)? Milton would not have insisted on happy angelic eating and, emphatically, on happy unfallen sex if the point were merely that now we are to disdain these things, or only to experience them with due anxiety. Milton was against refraining when God sends a cheerful hour, and he warned his countrymen not to worry that Christianity might seem "too luscious" in its marital and sexual doctrines.[62]

UNREPENTANT PARTS

The Unrepentant Renaissance is divided into three parts. The first, entitled "In Defense of Passion and the Body," consists of three chapters. Chapter 1, "Against the Rule of Reason," takes up the issue of attitudes toward passion in the period, especially toward the "negative," unruly passions of anger and impatience. It shows that both the humanist and the Reformation traditions included eloquent defenses of passion—even (and perhaps especially) of the negative passions. The chapter treats anti-Stoical expository texts by Petrarch, Salutati, Erasmus, Luther, and others, and literary texts by Shakespeare and George Herbert. It shows that *The Comedy of Errors*, a much-underestimated play, includes a sustained defense of impatience, and it then goes on to take up the question of anger and impatience in *King Lear*. The chapter shows that while *Lear* is certainly aware of the costs of anger, the play also defends anger as appropriate in a number of situations, and even as having a special "privilege." The privileged status of complaint, and raw aggressive emotion, is then shown to be thematized and asserted in the poetry of George Herbert.

Chapter 2, "Against Judgment," considers erotic passion. It treats Petrarch's *Canzoniere* and Shakespeare's sonnets and (as I have already suggested) establishes a continuity rather than a discontinuity between them. This involves a major revaluation of what Petrarch was doing in his volume. The chapter argues that Petrarch's is an antitranscendental sequence, that he places a high value on the body, and that he sees erotic obsession as something to live with,

---

No categories are forbidden before the Fall, only the one particular tree among "all the Trees / In paradise that bear delicious fruit / So various" (4.422–24).

61. Goldberg, *The Seeds of Things*, notes of Schoenfeldt that "the labor that entrances him is the labor of denial" (90–91).

62. On not refraining, see the first sonnet to Cyriack Skinner (*Complete Poems*, 169); on Milton's fear of Christian doctrine being perceived to be "too luscious," see *The Doctrine and Discipline of Divorce* (ibid., 705b).

and even to accept, rather than as something only to be despised and rejected. Extreme lucidity about his complex, painful, and soul-endangering psychological and spiritual situation is seen as leading Petrarch neither to the ability nor even to the unalloyed desire to change it. When Petrarch is seen in this way, the continuities with Shakespeare emerge: the rejection of moral judgment, the world of conscious and more or less happy self-delusion, the mode of lucidly impotent self-diagnosis.

"Against Morality," the third chapter in the book and the final one in its first section, moves from exploring morally ambivalent self-defense of dubious behavior to examining outright defenses of criminal or otherwise bad behavior. Chapter 3 argues that Shakespeare was fully capable of occupying what we would describe as a Nietzschean point of view (here I invite, but I hope deflect, the charge of anachronism). The chapter begins with a section entitled "The Happy Criminal" and treats *Richard III* (recall Burckhardt on Werner von Urslingen). The next section of the chapter tries to explain (following Dr. Johnson and others) what it is that makes Falstaff, despite his obvious moral flaws, attractive. This section goes on to see the rejection of Falstaff—on unimpeachable grounds of morality and decorum—as something that haunted Shakespeare for the rest of his career, and as something that he increasingly repudiated.

"Against Morality" is followed by two appendices: The first, "Shakespearean Seduction," analyzes in detail how Richard III succeeds in seducing Lady Anne Neville as she is accompanying to burial the corpse of her husband, whom, she knows, Richard has killed. The second, "Morality and the Happy Infant," treats *Macbeth*. Appendix 2 is necessary because I myself would have raised the issue of *Macbeth* as an objection to "Against Morality," since *Macbeth* is a play that seems (and largely is) utterly conventional in its moral and political values. My analysis shows that Shakespeare had to do some special and very particular work to get this play to be so.

Part 2 of the book, "In Defense of Worldliness," consists primarily of a long chapter on (again) *The Comedy of Errors*. This fourth chapter, "Sanctifying the Bourgeoisie," treats the play as Shakespeare's most extended presentation and celebration of urban, specifically commercial and bourgeois life (again apparently risking anachronism, though here relying on some economic history). The Protestant conception of companionate marriage and inner-worldly sanctity is shown to triumph over a specifically Catholic conception of sanctity apart from the world.

The appendix to this chapter, "Sanctifying the Aristocracy," shows that it was not just Protestantism in the period that adjusted to the growing power, wealth, literacy, and cultural importance of Christians not in orders. One of the founding texts of the Catholic Reformation, Ignatius Loyola's *Spiritual Exercises* (published 1548, but completed earlier) is shown to be a work of very modified asceticism, a work dedicated to helping anyone who gets the benefit of it to live a Christian life in the world—in whatever status. I identify two problems, however, in the Catholic attempt at "sanctified worldliness": its focus on aristocratic life and its attempt to retain a penitential focus. The discussion then shows that François de Sales's *Introduction to the Devout Life* (1609) deals brilliantly with these tensions but also continues to manifest them, as do, with less subtlety, some non-Puritan English Protestant texts by the young George Herbert and the older John Donne.

The third and final section of the book is devoted to the defense of pride in the period (I take sex to have been treated, at least in a basic way, in this introduction and in chapter 4). The final section consists of two chapters, "Self-Revelation and Self-Satisfaction in Montaigne and Descartes" (chapter 6) and "Milton on Humility" (chapter 7). These chapters address the question of why each of these authors felt impelled and justified, in Milton's words, "to venture and divulge unusual things" of themselves, to do so not only in writing but in print, and to do so unrepentantly. Chapter 6 analyzes Montaigne's essay "On Repentance" (1592) and then Descartes's *Discourse on the Method* (1637). It shows the first of these texts—amazingly—to eschew humility, and the second to adopt it only intermittently, clearly disingenuously, and for reasons that have nothing at all to do with the normal reasons for such assertion.

The final chapter argues that Milton too had little use for humility. The chapter shows his ethical framework to be fully classical, fully Aristotelian. Milton consistently espouses the distinctively Aristotelian virtue of "great-souledness" (*megalopsychia*, or "proper pride"), a virtue that is extremely difficult to incorporate in a Christian framework. Key passages in the prose (including *On Christian Doctrine*) are examined, but the important argument touches the major poetry. "Proper pride"—also espoused by Montaigne and Descartes—is shown to be crucial to *Paradise Lost*; and both *Samson Agonistes* and *Paradise Regained* are read as versions of the heroic tradition. The book ends with an appendix that takes up the influential claim that in one of Milton's major tracts against the bishops (*The Reason of Church-Government*), he appeals to authority rather than to reason. The question mark in the title—"Lordly Command?"—is meant to suggest that such a speech-act is neither the mode of Milton's pamphlet nor the way in which Milton envisioned God communicating to man. Human dignity, in both Milton's audience and God's, had to be respected. Lordly commands, for Milton, were never acceptable—even from God.

We return to unashamedness, and so we return to Burckhardt. For him, lack of repentance was a primary feature of the Renaissance "individual."[63] The historical and fictional characters studied in this book, whether religious or secular, whether Protestant, Catholic, or humanist (or some combination), felt no need or were unwilling to repent of some of their strongest, most unruly passions, of their enjoyment (however defined) of life in the world, and of what Burckhardt called their "personal force."[64] Even poor Petrarch did not want to be cured. George Herbert was willing to disturb God. Ignatius and François de Sales assure the rich that they can be spiritual. The one character studied who does not (in some sense) enjoy being unrepentant, Shakespeare's Macbeth, had to be imagined entirely outside of a Renaissance framework. The rest, historical or fictional, are all, in varying ways, unrepentant.

---

63. See *Civilization of the Renaissance*, 2:473, 514; also 1:144.
64. Ibid., 1:147 (with Dante as the exemplar).

1

In Defense of Passion and the Body

Against the Rule of Reason: Praise of Passion from Petrarch to Luther to Shakespeare to Herbert

RENAISSANCE

In Petrarch's little book on the state of learning in his time (*On his own Ignorance, and that of Many Others*), he explains his preference for Cicero over Aristotle. Aristotle, Petrarch concedes, defines and distinguishes the virtues and vices with great insight. Yet, Petrarch reports, "when I learn all this, I know a little bit more than I knew before, but mind and will remain the same as they were, and I myself remain the same."[1] He then goes on to make a key distinction, one that Plato, for instance, would not make, and one that explains the centrality of rhetoric:

> It is one thing to know, another to love; one thing to understand, another to will. [Aristotle] teaches what virtue is, I do not deny that; but his lesson lacks the words that sting and set afire and urge toward love of virtue and hatred of vice or, at any rate, does not have enough of such power.

Here the ethical life is conceived primarily in affective terms, and knowledge is seen as insufficient to produce affect—"What is the use of knowing what virtue is if it is not loved when it is known?" It is not the concepts alone but rather the words in which the ethical concepts are expressed "that sting and set afire and urge." The most important authors, therefore, from an ethical point of view, are those, says Petrarch, like Cicero, who "stamp and drive deep into the heart

---

1. Francesco Petrarca, *On his own Ignorance, and that of Many Others*, trans. Hans Nachod, in *The Renaissance Philosophy of Man*, ed. Ernst Cassirer, Paul Oskar Kristeller, and John Herman Randall, Jr. (Chicago: University of Chicago Press, 1948), 103.

the sharpest and most ardent stings of speech" (*acutissimos atque ardentissimos orationis aculeos precordiis admovent infliguntque*).[2] The violence of this imagery is intentional. Effort and violence are required to penetrate what is clearly seen as the object of ethical teaching: the heart.[3]

This stress on the centrality of affect is crucial not only to the humanist defense of rhetoric, but also (and this is a closely related theme) to the defense of the active life, of life within rather than outside of the ordinary political and social world. Coluccio Salutati's letter to Peregrino Zambeccari (1398) appears to concede the greater sublimity, delight, and self-sufficiency of the contemplative life, but Salutati (chancellor of the Florentine republic from 1375 to 1406) insists that though the active life is "inferior," it is nonetheless "many times to be preferred."[4] Part of the work of the letter is to blur the distinction between the kinds of life. Salutati suggests that not bodily placement but state of mind is determinative. In a certain state of mind, "the city will be to you a kind of hermitage," and paradoxically, one can be distracted and tempted in solitude (108). But Salutati's major thesis is that detachment from the world is not, in fact, a good thing, especially with regard to one's feelings. The most surprising (and passionate) section of the letter is a scathing attack on detachment.

The focus of the issue is the appropriateness of grief. Imagining (as is inevitable in the context) the would-be contemplative as a male householder, Salutati begins at the personal level, asking, "Will he be a contemplative so completely devoted to God that disaster befalling a dear one or the death of relations will not affect him?" (112). What is being imagined here, though not named as such, is the state of Stoic *apathia*. What ordinary folk take to be occasions for grief (or for anger) are the normal tests for the achievement of this state. In the *Tusculan Disputations*, the ideal Stoic is presented as receiving the news of the death of his child with the words, "I was already aware that I

---

2. Ibid., 104. I have used the Latin text in Francesco Petrarca, *De Ignorantia* (*De sui ipsius et multorum ignorantia*), ed. and trans. Enrico Fenzi (Milan: Mursia, 1999), 268 (in Italian).

3. On images of rhetoric as a form of violence in the period, see Wayne A. Rebhorn, *The Emperor of Men's Minds: Literature and the Renaissance Discourse of Rhetoric* (Ithaca: Cornell University Press, 1995), esp. chap. 3. Debora K. Shuger, *Sacred Rhetoric: The Christian Grand Style in the Renaissance* (Princeton: Princeton University Press, 1988), 125, denies that these images are primarily to be read in terms of aggression.

4. Coluccio Salutati, "Letter to Peregrino Zambeccari," trans. Ronald G. Witt, in *The Earthly Republic: Italian Humanists on Government and Society*, ed. Benjamin G. Kohl and Ronald G. Witt (Philadelphia: University of Pennsylvania Press, 1978), 111; the letter in this translation is hereafter cited by page in the text.

had begotten a mortal."[5] Salutati's critique is not that this response is impossible, but that it is undesirable. He adds to the list of disasters that should move a person a case that transcends the personal, a case that represents the ultimate disaster for a civic humanist and republican patriot: "the destruction of his homeland." None, Salutati implies, should not be moved—to grief, and perhaps to anger—at this.

Salutati is, in fact, skeptical about the possibility of such a person. His deeper point, however, is that such a being would not be a person:

> If there were such a person [unmoved by such things], and he related to other people like this, he would show himself not a man but a tree trunk, a useless piece of wood, a hard rock and obdurate stone. (112)

Human beings, for Salutati, are defined by their affections, and these affections are seen as fundamental to social life: "If there were such a person . . . *and he related to other people like this*." Sociality and affectivity are seen as defining the human, and as inextricably linked. The Stoic sage—autonomous, unmoved, always detached—is seen as "useless" at best, and destructive at worst. Aristotle saw the person who had no need for a polis as "either a beast or a god."[6] Salutati eliminates the second possibility.

The final point Salutati makes about such a creature is perhaps the most interesting and historically significant of all. Zambeccari, in planning to give up the cares and commitments of ordinary life and detach himself from disquieting passions, clearly sees himself as following a religious, and especially a Christian path (see his letter to Salutati quoted in Salutati's response [101]). Salutati's answer to this is his trump card. Not only would the detachment from cares and passions that Zambeccari imagines be a betrayal of the fundamental nature of his humanity, it would also not be Christian. Were Zambeccari to succeed in becoming a contemplative unmoved by any human situations, Salutati asserts that Peregrino would not thereby "imitate the mediator of God and man, who represents the highest perfection." For Salutati, *imitatio Christi* means precisely to be passionate and moved:

> For Christ wept over Lazarus, and cried abundantly over Jerusalem, in these things, as in others, leaving us an example to follow.

5. The statement is attributed to Anaxagoras in Cicero, *Tusculan Disputations*, trans. J. E. King, Loeb Classical Library (Cambridge: Harvard University Press, 1945), 3.24.

6. *The Politics of Aristotle*, trans. Ernest Barker (1946; New York, 1958), 1.2.14 (6).

Through this appeal to the figure depicted in the Gospels, Salutati sharply distinguishes the Christian from the Stoic tradition—indeed, from the entire tradition of the classical sage.[7] In a remarkable essay, "The Paradox of Socrates," Gregory Vlastos, one of the great recent scholars of Greek moral philosophy, considers the limits of Socratic ethics. Vlastos points first to the conception of knowledge as both necessary and sufficient for moral goodness. He thinks it, on empirical grounds, not necessary for morality and, more important, not sufficient for it. Knowledge can remain inert. Here Vlastos agrees with Petrarch, who insisted that "it is better to will the good than to know the truth."[8] But Vlastos's critique of Socrates goes further. After discussing the limits of the "virtue as knowledge" view, Vlastos moves to a more personal and more unusual critique. "I will put all my cards on the table," he says, "and say that beyond [Socrates's philosophical limitations] lay a failure of love."[9] Vlastos argues that the trouble with Socrates is not that he didn't care about the souls of his fellows—he obviously did—but that he didn't care enough. He was, ultimately, too detached:

> The care is limited and conditional. If men's souls are to be saved, they must be saved his way. And when he sees they cannot, he watches them go down the road to perdition with regret but without anguish.

To cap his point, Vlastos moves to Salutati's: "Jesus wept for Jerusalem."

In many ways, the text in which the humanist critique of Stoicism culminates is Erasmus's *Praise of Folly* (1511–16).[10] Vives's treatise on the soul (1538) is probably the most sustained philosophical treatment of this view, and was immensely influential, but the *Encomium Moriae* is the literary masterpiece of

---

7. See Pierre Hadot, *Exercices spirituels et philosophie antique* (1981; 3rd ed. rev., Paris: Institut d'Etudes Augustiniennes, 1993), and "Forms of Life and Forms of Discourse in Ancient Philosophy," trans. Arnold Davidson and Paula Wissing, *Critical Inquiry* 16 (1990): 483–505.

8. Petrarch, *On his own Ignorance*, 105.

9. Gregory Vlastos, "The Paradox of Socrates," introduction to *The Philosophy of Socrates*, ed. Gregory Vlastos (Garden City, N.Y.: Doubleday, 1971), 16; subsequent quotations from Vlastos are also to this page.

10. For the composition and revision of the text, see Desiderius Erasmus, *The Praise of Folly*, trans. Clarence H. Miller (New Haven: Yale University Press, 1979), xxxiii–iv. This translation indicates the layers of composition. Page references throughout are to this translation and hereafter appear in the text.

this humanist tradition.[11] Obviously, it is a tricky work and has several rhetorical modes. In a great deal of the text, the praise of folly is ironic, and sometimes the critique of contemporary practices (especially with regard to war and religion) does not even maintain the fiction of praise. As Folly says, sometimes she seems "to be composing a satire rather than delivering an encomium" (115).[12] In the richest and most interesting parts of the text, however, the praise of folly is either semi- or fully serious, and it is in these moments that the text is most anti-Stoical. In arguing for her special relation to happiness and pleasure, Folly is perfectly willing to accept the central premise of Stoic ethics—"according to the Stoic definition, wisdom consists in nothing but being led by reason and, conversely, folly is defined as being swept along at the whim of emotion" (28).[13] Folly is pleased with this definition, since it seems to cede her so much of human life (that guided by emotion). Erasmus cannot be seriously praising "being swept along," but the sense that human life would be very limited were it restricted to the nonaffective may not be entirely tongue in cheek ("in order to keep human life from being dreary and gloomy, what proportion did Jupiter establish between reason and emotion?").[14] The texture of the argument gets more complex when Folly moves from the defense of pastimes to more major features of social life. She notes that those who scorn pastimes insist that friendship "takes precedence over everything else" (31). She then presents the Stoic sage as incapable of lasting friendship through an incapacity to overlook faults:

> [I]f it should happen that some of these severe wisemen should become friendly with each other, their friendship is hardly stable or long-lasting, because they are so sour and sharp-sighted that they detect their friends' faults with an eagle eye. (32)

11. For the importance of Vives in this regard, see Maureen Flynn, "Taming Anger's Daughters: New Treatment for Emotional Problems in Renaissance Spain," *Renaissance Quarterly* 51 (1998): 864–86, esp. 877–80; and see Carlos G. Noreña, *Juan Luis Vives and the Emotions* (Carbondale: Southern Illinois University Press, 1989).

12. See Sister Geraldine Thompson, *Under Pretext of Praise: The Satiric Mode in Erasmus' Fiction* (Toronto: University of Toronto Press, 1973), chap. 2.

13. Miller's footnotes document the accuracy of Folly's account.

14. Walter Kaiser's treatment of the text in *Praisers of Folly: Erasmus, Rabelais, Shakespeare* (Cambridge: Harvard University Press, 1963) is perhaps overly inclined to de-ironize the praise, but is a useful guide to a positive view of many of Folly's positions.

Again, Folly's praise of "being well-deceived," as Jonathan Swift would later put it, is not fully serious, but it is also not fully ironized (as it is in Swift).[15] As Erasmus presents the phenomenon, even through Dame Folly, this state is uncomfortably akin to a highly recognizable conception of charity, which, for instance, "suffereth long" and "covereth all sins."[16]

The opposition between Stoic wisdom and social life is continued, in a mostly unserious vein, a few pages later—"Bring a wiseman to a party: he will disrupt it either by his gloomy silence or his tedious cavils" (39). But the moral status of adapting to circumstances (44) is as vexed here as it is in the companion text to *Folly*, More's *Utopia*, where the theatrically inflected and sociable philosophy of "accommodation" (*philosophia civilior, quae suam novit scenam, eique sese accommodans*) is both praised—by the character named More—and subject to devastating critique by the Platonist and eulogizer of Utopia, Raphael Hythlodaeus: "[Y]ou will be made a screen for the wickedness and folly of others."[17] Folly, in Erasmus's text, says that "true prudence," as opposed to the rigidity of the sage, "recognizes human limitations and does not strive to leap beyond them." Such "prudence" is willing to overlook faults tolerantly or, and here the irony reemerges, "to share them in a friendly spirit"—exactly, in a different register, Hythlodaeus's critique. This, of course, is folly, as Folly happily concedes—as long as her philosophical opponents "will reciprocate by admitting that this is exactly what it means to perform the play of life" (44). That was "More's" point.

It is at this moment of complex irony and non-irony that the issue of emotion resurfaces. "First of all," says Folly, beginning her oration yet again, "everyone admits that emotions all belong to Folly" (45). This is why, she explains (again with complete accuracy), "the Stoics eliminate from their wiseman all emotional perturbations as if they were diseases."[18] Folly, however, in an uncharacteristically sober moment, straightforwardly endorses the alternative Aristotelian position—"But actually the emotions not only function as guides

15. See Swift's *A Tale of a Tub*, sec. 9, "A Digression Concerning the Original, the Use and Improvement of Madness in a Commonwealth," in *"Gulliver's Travels" and Other Writings by Jonathan Swift*, ed. Ricardo Quintana (New York: Random House, 1958), 342.

16. See 1 Cor. 13:4 and Prov. 10:12 (Authorized Version).

17. *The Praise of Folly* is dedicated to More and its title puns (in Greek) on his name (*Encomium Moriae*). For both the Latin and English quotations from More, see *Utopia*, ed. Surtz and Hexter, 98 (Latin), 103 (English). (See intro., n. 21.)

18. On the importance of this metaphor of emotions as diseases, see Martha C. Nussbaum, *The Therapy of Desire: Theory and Practice in Hellenistic Ethics* (Princeton: Princeton University Press, 1994), esp. chaps. 1–4 and 13.

to those who are hastening to the haven of wisdom, but also, in the whole range of virtuous action, they operate like spurs or goads, as it were, encouraging the performance of good deeds." This returns us to Petrarch's "ardent stings," the idea that emotions can be potential "spurs" to virtue. In something closer to her own voice, Folly states that she knows that "that dyed-in-the-wool Stoic, Seneca, strenuously denies this, removing all emotion whatever from his wise-man." Folly's critique joins Salutati's here. Seneca is Folly's representative (or super) Stoic, and she claims that in denying emotion to his wise man, Seneca "is left with something that cannot even be called human; he fabricates some new sort of divinity that never existed and never will . . . he sets up a marble statue of a man, utterly unfeeling and quite impervious to all human emotion." Returning to the issue of normal social life, Folly then asks:

> Who would not flee in horror from such a man, as he would from a monster or a ghost—a man who is completely deaf to all human sentiment . . . no more moved by love or pity than a chunk of flint . . . who never misses anything, never makes a mistake, who sees through everything . . . never forgives anything, who is uniquely self-satisfied, who thinks he alone is rich, he alone is healthy, regal, free. (45)

This is a brilliant characterization of Stoic autonomy, capturing the Stoic practice of paradoxically redefining the normal terms of social life ("he alone is rich," etc.).[19] It is also a devastating critique, and it is hard to see that there is much significant undercutting of Folly here.

The peroration of the *Encomium* is the moment of the text in which the praise of Folly is unquestionably sincere. Echoes of the Pauline praise of folly over and against the wisdom of the world are sounded (127–29), but the most lyrical and exultant section of the text is the final movement, which begins (again), "First of all, Christians essentially agree with Platonists" (133).[20] Unlike Salutati, Erasmus is not here defending normal emotional reactions; the affection that he defends is not normal grief but, as the reference to Plato would suggest, a specialized version of love. Plato is praised for asserting that "the madness of lovers is the height of happiness" (136). Unlike Salutati, Erasmus

19. On Stoic redefinition, see, inter alia, Malcolm Schofield, *The Stoic Idea of the City* (New York: Cambridge University Press, 1991).

20. For a sustained analysis of the peroration and its sources (though with some attempt to recuperate it for orthodoxy), see M. A. Screech, *Erasmus: Ecstasy and "The Praise of Folly"* (London: Duckworth, 1980).

does not connect the turn to the Bible with the critique of Stoicism, but it is clear that his vision of Christianity has affect at its center. In the polarity between Stoicism and Augustinianism in Renaissance thought, Erasmus clearly stands (with Folly) squarely in the "Augustinian" camp.[21]

REFORMATION

The critique of Stoicism is an important strand in the humanist tradition, especially in the civic humanist tradition, but the pull of Stoicism, of dualism, and even of asceticism, remained strong among the humanists as well.[22] Even the Epicurean Utopians, who primarily value the mental pleasures but also, as we have seen, accept bodily pleasure gratefully, think of the celibate and ascetic among their priests as less sensible but holier (*sanctiores*) than the non-ascetic priests.[23] It is only in the Reformation tradition that the attack on Stoicism and asceticism is freed from ambivalence.[24] It is to the reformers and especially to Luther that we must turn for the most full-throated defenses of passion and of imperfection in the period. Folly's horror at the Stoic wise man is given a theological underpinning by Luther. The Reformation can be seen as an antihumanist movement—its attack on the dignity of man comes to mind—but in its sociological implications, the Reformation joined with the most robust forms of civic and Erasmian humanism in providing a positive account of ordinary human behavior and psychology in the world.[25]

21. For this polarity, see William J. Bouwsma, "The Two Faces of Humanism: Stoicism and Augustinianism in Renaissance Thought," in *A Usable Past: Essays in European Cultural History* (1975; Berkeley: University of California Press, 1990), 19–73. The importance of Augustine for the Renaissance defense of affectivity is one of the major theses of Shuger, *Sacred Rhetoric* (see note 3 above).

22. See Charles Trinkaus, *Adversity's Noblemen: The Italian Humanists on Happiness* (New York: Columbia Studies in the Social Sciences, 1940); George W. McClure, *Sorrow and Consolation in Italian Humanism* (Princeton: Princeton University Press, 1991); and see Petrarch, *The Life of Solitude*, trans. Jacob Zeitlin (Urbana: University of Illinois Press, 1924). On the pull of dualism, see Trinkaus, *In our Image and Likeness: Humanity and Divinity in Italian Humanist Thought* (Chicago: University of Chicago Press, 1970).

23. See More, *Utopia*, 226 (Latin), 227 (English), for the two kinds of priests. On the Utopian gratitude even for pleasures recognized as lower, see the introduction, 11, above.

24. For a similar view, see Bouwsma, "Renaissance and Reformation: An Essay on Their Affinities and Connections," in *A Usable Past*, 225–46.

25. For more on Reformation (and Counter-Reformation) accommodation with ordinary social life, see chapter 4 below; for antihumanism in Reformation theology (but not ecclesiology), see chapter 6 below.

One of the great paradoxes of Reformation theology is that the doctrine of sin is what yields the humane and comforting consequences of this theological framework. Luther rejected the conception of sin as primarily having to do with or emanating from the body. He insisted (probably correctly) that "flesh" and "spirit" in the Pauline epistles were not used in the Platonic sense—were not equivalent, in other words, to body and soul. Luther asserted that flesh, according to St. Paul, "means everything that is born of the flesh, i.e. the entire self, body and soul, including our reason."[26] Fleshliness or carnality, from this point of view, is fundamentally the condition of egotism or self-regard—the condition of being, as Luther wonderfully put it, *incurvatus in se* (curved, or turned, into oneself).[27] Being "spiritual," from this point of view, would be a matter of being turned away from self-regard. Beware, warned Luther, "of all teachers who use these terms differently, no matter whom they may be, whether Jerome, Augustine, Ambrose, Origen, or their like, or even," he somewhat mysteriously adds—perhaps with Erasmus in mind—"persons even more eminent than they."[28]

Luther's reinterpretation of the central terms of Christian and philosophical anthropology had, as he well knew, profound and far-reaching implications. The theology of grace is necessitated by it, as is the entire Reformation rethinking of sanctity. The doctrine of grace flows from the reinterpretation of "flesh" and "spirit" because it seems truly impossible to imagine the self willing itself out of self-regard. All sorts of other things are possible. To do great works of charity (for instance) in order to lay up treasures in heaven seemed, to Luther, an elaborate and dangerous form of self-regard, of working "in order to attain

26. Luther, "Preface to Romans," in *Selections from His Writings*, 25. Hereafter works by Luther cited either by title and page number alone or parenthetically in the text following a quotation refer to this collection edited by Dillenberger (see intro., n. 48). On Paul's view, see, inter alia, John A. T. Robinson, *The Body: A Study in Pauline Theology* (Chicago: Regnery, 1952), esp. chap. 1.

27. The Pauline (biblical) conception of man is that he is "curved in upon himself to such an extent that he bends not only physical but also spiritual goods toward himself, seeking himself in all things." See Martin Luther, *Lectures on Romans*, ed. and trans. Wilhelm Pauck, Library of Christian Classics (Philadelphia: Westminster, 1961), 218–19. For the Latin, see the edition of Luther's *Römerbriefvorlesung* by Johannes Ficker, vol. 56 of *Luthers Werke* ([1883–]; Weimar: Böhlau, 1938), 356; hereafter, this edition of Luther's works, the Weimar edition (or *Weimar Ausgabe*), is cited as *WA* and identified by volume number. On how Luther's use of *curvatus* differs from Augustine's apparently similar usage, see Anders Nygren, *Agape and Eros*, trans. Philip S. Watson (1953; New York: Harper and Row, 1969), 713.

28. "Preface to Romans," 25.

some benefit, whether temporal or eternal."[29] Only a force from outside the self could change so fundamental and "natural" an orientation, the orientation to what Luther called "works-religion": "Nature of itself cannot drive it out or even recognize it, but rather regards it as a mark of the most holy will."[30] Grace, in the form of faith, can do this through convincing the person that he or she is already in possession of the ultimate good (salvation) that his or her works were striving to obtain. The psychological impact of this conviction is what Luther meant by the "freedom" of a Christian, and it should by now be clear why he thought that only grace could provide this freedom. Already having grace—beyond what one could ever have earned—takes away the need for self-regard and allows works to be done "out of pure liberty and freedom," seeking "neither benefit nor salvation," since the graced person "already abounds in all things."[31] Tyndale echoes Luther when he explains that the regenerate "are in eternal life already, and feel already in our hearts the sweetness thereof."[32]

When this conception of the impossibility and non-necessity of merit is put together with the conception of sin as not primarily concerned with the body, the whole rationale for asceticism and renunciation of the world disappears. Salutati's suggestion that holiness is a state of mind rather than a particular set of activities comes to fruition here. Luther sees the ascetic life as full of super-stitions; but most of all, as he explains in his *Commentary on Galatians* (1531), he finds it an inducement to pride, since

> those which lurk in caves and dens, which make their bodies lean with fasting, which wear hair [shirts], and do other like things, [do so] with this persua-sion and trust, that they shall have a singular reward in heaven above all other Christians. (161)[33]

The word "saint," as Luther understood it, is improperly restricted to "hermits and monks which did certain great and strange works" (160). Among those to whom the word "saint" used to be wrongly restricted, Luther much prefers

---

29. *The Freedom of a Christian*, 79.

30. Ibid., 72.

31. Ibid., 70.

32. Tyndale, *Parable of the Wicked Mammon*, 65 (see intro., n. 55).

33. A complete translation based on earlier English versions was edited by Philip S. Watson (London, 1953). There is also an edition published by Baker Books (Grand Rapids, Mich., 1979).

those like Augustine and Ambrose, "which lived not so strait and severe a life," but rather

> were conversant among men, and did eat common meats, drank wine, and used cleanly and comely apparel, so that in a manner there was no difference between them and other honest men as touching the common custom, and the use of things necessary to this life. (161)[34]

According to Luther, the conception of sainthood or holiness as asceticism not only encouraged pride in its practitioners but also, and this is perhaps even more important, encouraged a false and psychologically dangerous moral and spiritual perfectionism in serious Christians. This theme always produced autobiography in Luther, and these autobiographical excurses were always meant to reassure his readers. In the *Commentary on Galatians*, Luther's greatest treatment of the Pauline conception of flesh and spirit (translated into English by "certain godly learned men" early in the 1570s), Luther noted: "When I was a monk, I thought I was utterly cast away, if at any time I felt the concupiscence of the flesh" (148).[35] And by "concupiscence of the flesh," he does not mean primarily sexuality; he acknowledges sexual desire as one of its meanings, but one that "the schoolmen" (those "inept asses") mistakenly and disastrously took to be definitive (*Illi inepti asini nullam sciverunt tentationem quam libidinem*).[36] In the autobiographical passage quoted above, he immediately explains what he means by *concupiscentia*—"that is to say, if at any time, I felt any evil motion, fleshly lust, wrath, hatred, or envy against any brother." Luther had diligently employed all the prescribed and recommended penitential and

34. Those familiar with Kierkegaard will recognize here the "knight of faith," as opposed to the tragic hero or "knight of infinite resignation." Persons of faith are likely, from a perspective looking for the extraordinary, "to disappoint, for externally they have a striking resemblance to bourgeois philistinism"; what they succeed in doing is "absolutely to express the sublime in the pedestrian"; they exist in the ordinary world in such a way that their difference from ordinary worldly existence "constantly expresses itself as the most beautiful and secure harmony with it." See Søren Kierkegaard, *Fear and Trembling*, ed. and trans. Howard V. Hong and Edna H. Hong (Princeton: Princeton University Press, 1983), 38, 41, 50.

35. For the preface "To the Reader" of the Elizabethan translation, see either the Watson or the Baker Books edition cited in note 33 above.

36. For the Latin, see *WA, Tischreden* 4, no. 5097 (cited below as *TR* followed by the entry number). The correction of this mistaken understanding is one of the major themes of the 1531 Galatians commentary. Along with the passages quoted in the text, see, inter alia, in Watson's edition, 143–44, 212–13, 402, and 408.

devotional practices, but was "continually vexed" with one sort of "evil motion" or another. This led him to misery. He knew he would never be perfect, and he despaired. Only when he came to recognize the true depth of human sinfulness, and the need for grace to come "from without," was he freed from this torment of conscience.[37] The grace that comes from without transforms the recipient's relation to God and to "works"—it allows the graced person to experience God as loving and giving rather than as judging and demanding—but it does not change the believer from being partly a creature of "the flesh." The saving transformation is attitudinal, not ontological. The "righteousness" that is required for salvation is *imputed to* the believer; it is not literally and actually imparted to him or achieved by him.[38] As Luther puts it in the 1531 Galatians commentary, this means that, when faced with the persistence of sinful impulses, Luther could tell himself:

> Martin, thou shalt not utterly be without sin, for thou hast yet flesh; thou shalt therefore feel the battle thereof, according to that saying of Paul: "The flesh resisteth the spirit." Despair not therefore. (149)

"Despair not therefore"—that was the essential message from Luther to himself and to his readers. Perfection is impossible. Luther insisted (against the prevailing exegesis) that when Saint Paul spoke of the law of sin in his members and the battle with the flesh, Paul was not "speaking in the person of the ungodly" (146). Paul is speaking there as one of the regenerate—"at once righteous and a sinner" (*simul justus et peccator*).[39] The regenerate are not free from sin and, correlated with this, are not free from passion—"the holiest that live have not yet a full and continual joy in God, but have their sundry passions" (127). As an example of this, Luther points to the depiction in the scriptures of the lives and emotional experiences of the prophets and apostles. The saints are depicted as falling into sin: "David fell horribly . . . Peter also fell most grievously," and yet they are models of holiness (157). To say that the saints are not "without all feeling of temptations or sins" is to say, Luther

---

37. Luther tells this story, his conversion story, again and again (see, for instance, *TR*, nos. 335 and 5285). The most famous version, narrated in relation to the phrase *justitia Dei* is in the 1545 preface to Luther's Latin writings (in *Selections from His Writings*, 11).

38. This is the difference, Luther explained, between the philosophical and the religious understanding of "righteousness." See *Commentary on Galatians*, 100–101, 131–32; preface to Latin writings, 11–12.

39. *Commentary on Galatians*, 130; for the Latin, see *WA* 40:368.

insists, that they are not "very stocks and stones" (158). This is part of what makes their examples religiously and humanly valuable. "Assuredly Mary felt great grief and sorrow of heart when she missed her son"; David in the Psalms "complaineth that he is almost swallowed up with excessive sorrow of the greatness of his temptations and sins." Luther has only reprehension for what he calls (in the Elizabethan translation) the "imagination" that "the monks and schoolmen had of their saints, as though they had been very senseless blocks, and without all affections" (158). And he makes the key intellectual-historical connection, explaining that "the saints of the Papists are like to the Stoics, who imagined such wise men as in the world as were never yet to be found." Luther saw such figures just as Folly did—as "monsters" (159, 162).

This valuation of the acceptability, indeed necessity, of passions—even negative ones like fear, anger, and impatience—in the life of the godly was not a position unique to Luther. Just as Luther loved the psalms (and the Book of Job) for their uncensored emotionality and sincerity, Calvin felt the same way.[40] Calvin alludes to his own conversion experience in the preface to his commentary on the Psalms, and he noted that readers of his commentary would observe that "in unfolding the internal affections both of David and of others, I discourse upon them as matters of which I have familiar experience."[41] Luther thought that the line from Psalm 22 that Jesus quoted from the Cross—"My God, my God, why hast thou forsaken me?" (Matt. 27:46)—represented "the greatest words in all the Scripture" (*TR*, no. 5493). Calvin was particularly keen to explain the godliness of this verse. He argues that a crucial feature of this question and others like it in the Bible, in Job, and in the Psalms is that, while such questions are certainly complaints and even rebukes, they are complaints addressed to God—and therefore acts of faith. "What point would there be in crying out to him," Calvin asks, "if they hoped for no solace from him?"[42] Luther thought that only "speculative" (as opposed to experiential) theologians condemned impatience (*TR*, no. 228). Calvin discusses Christian patience at length, and is more invested in this notion than Luther is, but Calvin nonetheless insists that "patiently to bear the cross is not to be utterly

---

40. For Luther's comment that "whoever wrote the Book of Job" was "a real theologian," see *TR*, no. 475.

41. John Calvin, "The Author's Preface" to *The Commentary on the Book of Psalms*, trans. Rev. James Anderson (Edinburgh: Calvin Translation Society, 1845), 1:xlviii; for Calvin's reference to his "sudden conversion" from being "obstinately devoted to the superstitions of Popery," see 1:xl.

42. Calvin, *Institutes*, 3.2.21 (see intro., n. 33); cited hereafter in the text. See also *Commentary on the Book of Psalms*, 1:182, 357.

stupefied" (*Institutes*, 3.8.9). Like Luther, he notes that "among the Christians there are also new Stoics, who count it depraved not only to groan and weep but also to be sad and care ridden." Calvin's response to this is as strong as Luther's: "We have," he said, "nothing to do with this iron philosophy." He makes the same point that Salutati did about what "imitating Christ" means. This "iron philosophy," Calvin writes,

> our Lord and Master has condemned not only by His word, but also by His example. For He groaned and wept both over his own and others misfortunes. And he taught his disciples in the same way.

And of course Jesus did this, Calvin notes, "to recall godly minds from despair" (*Institutes*, 3.8.10).

HOWL: THE REJECTION OF PATIENCE

It should now be clear that both the humanist and the Reformation traditions provided powerful defenses of the validity and even the desirability of ordinary human emotions and passions. Texts from both traditions expressing such a view were, as we have seen, widely available. The rest of this chapter is devoted to ways that the Renaissance and Reformation defenses of passion entered into English vernacular literature, both sacred and profane, in the sixteenth and seventeenth centuries, drawing on examples from two plays of Shakespeare and from the religious lyric.[43]

I will begin with *The Comedy of Errors*, a play that is overtly aware of both humanist and Reformation traditions. Certainly performed (and perhaps composed) for the Christmas Revels of a learned audience (at Gray's Inn, 1594), it flaunts its classical knowledge: in its title, its obvious use of classical sources and allusions, and its dramaturgy.[44] It flaunts its biblical and theological aware-

---

43. Christopher Tilmouth's *Passion's Triumph over Reason: A History of the Moral Imagination from Spenser to Rochester* (Oxford: Oxford University Press, 2007) recognizes both humanist and Reformation anti-Stoicism, but as its title suggests, sees a chronological shift from rationalist to antirationalist ethical thinking ("moral imagination") in England from the turn of the seventeenth century forward. As this chapter shows, my view is that the two strands coexist from the beginning of the European Renaissance onward, and I am not as certain as Tilmouth is that rationalist ethics ceases to be the dominant ethical framework in the course of the seventeenth century in England.

44. On the Gray's Inn performance, see the introduction to *The Comedy of Errors*, ed. R. A. Foakes (London: Methuen, 1962), xxiii, and the extract from *Gesta Grayorum* given in appendix 2

ness in its use of the Ephesian setting—associated by Saint Paul with exorcists and "curious arts" (Acts 19:13–19)—and in its spectacular comic allusion to the "whole armor of God" passage in Paul's epistle to the inhabitants of that city (Eph. 6:11–17; *Errors*, 3.2.143–45). The play begins on a moment of Stoic resignation—"[P]roceed, Solinus, to procure my fall, /And by the doom of death end woes and all"—but its most striking thematic, thoroughly enacted in its dramaturgy, is its low estimate of human intellectual capacity.[45] Every assertion of such capacity in the play is ironized. Speaking of the relative lack of hair of humans compared to beasts, Dromio of Syracuse asserts that what "Time" (the cosmos) "hath scanted men in hair, he hath given them in wit," but Antipholus of Syracuse replies by noting that "there's many a man hath more hair than wit" (2.1.79–82). When Dromio of Ephesus confidently asserts, "I know what I know" (3.1.11), we know that he is mistaken. As Bertrand Evans observes, *The Comedy of Errors* is unique in the Shakespearean corpus "in the universal depth of the participants' ignorance." In other plays, Evans notes, Shakespeare allows characters ignorant of a situation occasional glimpses of the truth, even though dimly and obliquely, but in this play, he is unrelenting. As Evans says, though truth "beats at them [the characters] incessantly, it beats in vain."[46]

The most reflective character in the play, Antipholus of Syracuse, has exceedingly little faith in the powers of the mind. He believes in "dark-working sorcerers that change the mind" (1.2.99); he is unsure whether sleeping and waking can be distinguished (2.2.181–83); he speaks of his "earthy gross conceit / Smother'd in errors, feeble, shallow, weak" (3.2.34–35); and he thinks that only a benign transcendental force can keep him—and all of us?—from wandering "in illusions": "Some blessed power deliver us from hence" (4.3.41–42). But while the play is extremely skeptical about human intellectual capacity, it has no doubt about the human capacity for feeling—in both senses of the term, physical and emotional. This awareness leads to a series of remarkable jokes, all of which simultaneously demean human intellectual capacity and assert the capacity for feeling. It is highly significant, moreover, that these jokes are always made by social inferiors who are being or have been assaulted.

---

of this edition (115–17). Unless otherwise specified, all quotations from the play are from this edition (sometimes with slightly altered punctuation).

45. For the question of whether this emphasis has a confessional significance in the sixteenth century, see chapter 4, note 79, below, and the references there given.

46. Bertrand Evans, *Shakespeare's Comedies* (Oxford: Clarendon, 1960), 4–5.

In the first error, Dromio of Ephesus encounters an uncomprehending and increasingly angry Antipholus of Syracuse. When Adriana, the wife of Antipholus of Ephesus, asks this Dromio about her husband—"Didst thou speak with him? knowst thou his mind?"— the poor servant replies, "Ay, ay, he told his mind upon my ear" (2.1.47–48). Communication fails on one level of sense (semantic) but succeeds on another (somatic). Adriana picks up the conceit—"Spoke he so doubtfully, thou couldst not feel his meaning?"—and Dromio responds thus: "Nay, he struck so plainly I could too well feel his blows; and withal so doubtfully, I could scarce understand them" (2.1.47–54). The pain, if nothing else, is clear. This is not an isolated moment. A similar set of jokes occurs in the scene that immediately follows. We get another case of "telling" a meaning upon a body when the Syracusan Antipholus confuses his own Dromio with the one that he has just encountered—and beaten. He tells this Dromio to behave himself, "Or I will beat this method in your sconce." Dromio replies:

> Sconce call you it? so you would leave battering,
> I had rather have it a head; and you use these
> blows long, I must get a sconce for my head, and
> insconce it too, or else I shall seek my wit in my
> shoulders; but I pray, sir, why am I beaten?
>
> (2.2.34–39)

Dromio will have to relocate his "wit," since his head is being treated as a mere physical object, but his question truly arises from a sensible being—in both meanings, rational and sensate. And his question resonates: "[S]ir, why am I beaten?" Yet another form of the joke occurs in the opening scene of the next act, when, in claiming (wrongly) to know what he knows, Dromio of Ephesus gives another example of "sensible" inscribing:

> If the skin were parchment and the blows you gave were ink,
> Your own handwriting would tell you what I think.
>
> (3.1.13–14)

What he "thinks" is what he has felt. It is not truth that beats incessantly at the servants; it is their masters.[47]

47. In an important essay, Maurice Hunt has called attention to the social realities that lay behind this theme and recurrent "stage-business" in the play. See "Slavery, English Servitude,

This emphasis on the reality of suffering, apart from comprehension, leads to a major motif in the play: the critique of patience.[48] In another set of puns equating social with bodily phenomena, Dromio of Ephesus responds to Antipholus of Syracuse's question about Antipholus's "thousand marks" (money) with a reference to bearing "some marks" of his master's beatings upon, of course, his "pate." And here Dromio adds, in a pregnant phrase, "If I should pay your worship those again, / Perchance you will not bear it patiently" (1.2.81–86). This issue arises most powerfully in the play in the context of another relationship of subordination, that of wife to husband.[49] As Robert A. Kaster notes, in the context of ancient Rome, "in social relations *patientia* is almost always implicated in establishing hierarchy and expressing differentials of power."[50] When we first meet Adriana, the wife of Antipholus of Ephesus, she is annoyed that her husband has not come home for dinner, the midday meal. Her sister, Luciana, tells her to "be patient." Adriana, however, refuses to be "bridled," saying, "There's none but asses will be bridled so" (2.1.14).[51] She agrees with Kaster's analysis that "*patientia* could be said to define the essence of slavery."[52] At this point, Luciana brings out the big gun of

---

and *The Comedy of Errors*," *English Literary Renaissance* 27 (1997): 31–56. The last third of this essay blunts its force because, as Hunt himself acknowledges (45), "it introduces the notion of figurative rather than literal enslavement (and risks confusing the two ideas)."

48. James L. Sanderson deserves credit for first noticing the prominence and "substance" of the theme in the play. See "Patience in *The Comedy of Errors*," *Texas Studies in Literature and Language* 16 (1975): 603–18. Sanderson's treatment, however, sees the play as supporting rather than criticizing the Stoic ideal, and critiquing "the folly of impatience" (609).

49. For an extended discussion of the treatment of marriage in *Errors*, see chapter 4 below.

50. See Robert A. Kaster, "The Taxonomy of Patience, or When is '*Patientia*' Not a Virtue," *Classical Philology* 97 (2002): 138.

51. Some in Shakespeare's audience might have thought that overly verbal women should be "bridled so," and treated like animals, but it is not at all clear that Shakespeare thought this, or that he saw Adriana in this way. Female "shrews" or "scolds" were sometimes put in bridles, or "branks," which included metal rods that extended into the woman's mouth, and were sometimes led around in public in this way. There are illustrations of such bridles in Joan Hartwig, "Horses and Women in 'The Taming of the Shrew,'" *Huntington Library Quarterly* 45 (1982): 285–94 (illus., 289–91); in Valerie Wayne, "Refashioning the Shrew," *Shakespeare Quarterly* 17 (1984): 159–87 (illus., 160); and in the "Texts and Contexts" edition of *Taming of the Shrew*, ed. Frances E. Dolan (New York: Bedford Books, 1996), 291. Whatever one thinks of Petruchio's "taming" of Kate, his methods are certainly a departure from the much more brutal ones of the shrew-taming tradition. See Wayne, "Refashioning," 170, and "A Merry Jest of a Shrewd and Curst Wife Lapped in Morel's Skin for Her Good Behavior," in Dolan's edition of *Shrew*, 257–88.

52. Kaster, "The Taxonomy of Patience," 138.

conservative Elizabethan ideology: the Chain of Being. The Chain requires female subordination, which should be especially true in creatures "[i]ndued with intellectual sense and souls" (2.1.22). This speech is problematic in a number of ways.[53] We have already noted the status of "intellectual sense" in the play, and the speech equivocates (as its uncertain grammar indicates) between *homo* and *vir* in its claims about "man": "The beasts, the fishes . . . Are their *males* subjects . . . *Man*, more divine" (2.1.18–20).[54] Adriana, however, takes a different tack. She first presents subordination as demeaning—"This servitude makes you to keep unwed" (2.1.26)—but then returns to the issue of patience, of not being moved to anger or complaint. In posing the case of a wife who has been betrayed by a husband, Adriana denies the idea that her unmarried sister has any right to speak:

> Patience unmov'd! no marvel though she pause;
> They can be meek that have no other cause.

Adriana's next lines are a remarkably powerful defense of this critique of counsels to patience. The essential point is that it is easy to call for a certain kind of behavior to be changed, and in doing so to ignore the feeling that underlies, and justifies, the behavior:

> A wretched soul, bruis'd with adversity,
> We bid it quiet when we hear it cry;

53. Foakes's notes on this passage assume that Luciana's view is unquestionably correct, and that Shakespeare accepted it. Peter Holbrook's developmental scheme forces him to see *Errors* as "more committed to traditional notions of social hierarchy than later plays," while at the same time acknowledging that *Errors* contains "contradictory ideological impulses" ("Class X: Shakespeare, Class and the Comedies," in *A Companion to Shakespeare's Works*, ed. Richard Dutton and Jean E. Howard, vol. 3, *The Comedies* [Oxford: Blackwell, 2003], 74–55). Thomas Hennings, one of the few scholars who does not see Luciana as the play's spokesperson on the theme of marriage, notes that "because Luciana speaks to the Elizabethan commonplace of wifely obedience, scholars have held her moral voice in high esteem" ("The Anglican Doctrine of Affectionate Marriage in *The Comedy of Errors*," *Modern Language Quarterly* 47 (1986): 91–107, esp. 95).

54. For the uncertain grammar, see "Man . . . the master . . . Indued with . . . souls . . . are masters." The eighteenth-century editor Edward Capell apparently noticed the problem, and changed "Man" to "Men" and "master" to "masters." Foakes includes the emendation in his collation, but does not comment on the problem.

> But were we burden'd with like weight of pain,
> As much, or more, we should ourselves complain.
>
> (3.1.34–37)

Dromio of Ephesus, we recall, made a similar point about patient "bearing," and the play as whole can be seen as endorsing Adriana's position. In only one case is patience clearly presented as appropriate. When Antipholus of Ephesus is barred from his house, Balthasar urges, "Have patience, sir" (3.1.85). The reasons that Balthasar provides are not cosmological but social and prudential, and Antipholus agrees to "depart in quiet" (3.1.107). This seems to be a case of common sense all around, but it brackets the issue of Antipholus's pain. The problem returns, however, in its normative form, in another scene in which Adriana refuses Luciana's urging that she have patience. Hearing of the courtship of her sister by her apparent husband, Adriana says, "I cannot, nor I will not, hold me still" (4.2.16–17). And the matter surfaces again in a later scene where, yet once more, a servant is beaten. When Antipholus of Ephesus is given a rope by Dromio of Ephesus rather than the money for which he has sent the other Dromio, Antipholus of Ephesus begins beating his Dromio with the rope. The officer with Antipholus of Ephesus counsels, "Good sir, be patient" (4.4.18). Dromio then rightly points out that, in traditional teaching, " 'tis for me to be patient, I am in adversity," and the puns start recurring. Antipholus of Ephesus calls Dromio a "senseless" (meaning nonsense-speaking) villain, to which the servant replies: "I would I were senseless, sir, that I might not feel your blows" (4.4.22–24).

Adriana, however, remains key to the critique of patience in the play. After the Syracusan Antipholus avoids danger by running into a "priory," the Abbess appears onstage. She makes a long speech denouncing Adriana for her impatience, and then something remarkable happens. Luciana, who has been all along the voice of patience and meek obedience, speaks up when her sister is silent, urging her not to stand quietly by: "Why bear you these rebukes and answer not?" (5.1.89). And Adriana does answer. She refuses the Abbess's command, "Be patient" (5.1.102), and the play, through the development of the fifth act, supports this refusal.[55] But that is not the last word on the subject of patience. In the midst of the scene, a messenger who is a servant of Antipholus of Ephesus enters to announce that his purportedly mad master has broken loose and turned the tables on Dr. Pinch, the exorcist called in to deal with

---

55. This argument is developed in chapter 4 below.

his supposed demonic possession. The Ephesian Antipholus and his Dromio have

> bound the doctor,
> Whose beard they have sing'd off with brands of fire,
> And ever as it blaz'd, they threw on him
> Great pails of puddled mire to quench the hair
>
> .   .   .   .
>
> His man with scissors nicks him like a fool.
>
> (5.1.170–75)

And while all this is going on, the messenger recounts, "My master preaches patience to him" (174).

King Lear is, among other things, Shakespeare's most extended meditation on the problematics of patience.[56] I will not treat the play fully here, but I will offer an initial sketch of some of the ways it does (and does not) participate in the humanist and Reformation critique of being "unmoved." Clearly the play is aware of the cost of irrational anger. Lear can never undo the effects of his initial act of rage. This is part of what it means for the play to be a tragedy. Yet, as the play develops, and Lear becomes a character who is, arguably, "[m]ore sinned against than sinning" (3.2.60), the moral status of rage in the play undergoes a transformation.[57] The villains in the play tend to be the spokespersons for calm, for "reason," and for decorum.[58] Regan admonishes Lear, "I pray, sir, take patience" (2.4.113/127), and she speaks of herself and Goneril as "those that mingle reason with your passion" (2.4.204/223).

The culmination of this development in the play is Lear's great protest against common sense and prudence, in the speech beginning, "O reason not

56. My treatment of this topic will contrast rather sharply with that of John F. Danby in "*King Lear* and Christian Patience: A Culmination," *Poets on Fortune's Hill: Studies in Sidney, Shakespeare, Beaumont and Fletcher* (London: Faber, 1952), 108–127.

57. For my text of *Lear*, I have used René Weis's facing page Quarto and Folio edition, *King Lear: A Parallel Text Edition* (London and New York: Longman, 1993). In my citations, when both texts include the line or lines cited, I have given the act, scene, and line number in the Quarto text as it appears in Weis's edition followed by the line number in the Folio text from this edition (when act and scene are the same in both). I am aware, that, unlike the Folio, the Quarto text does not include act divisions, but since it does not include scene numbers either, the argument for indicating the latter but not the former in the Quarto text seems to me unpersuasive.

58. On the moralism of the wicked characters in *Lear*, see chapter 3 below.

the need" (2.4.234/253). This speech is a call for generosity, for the rejection of calculation in the face of "need." It echoes the Reformation critique of giving alms for "reasons"—in relation, that is, either to one's own salvation or to the "merit" of the object (Luther notes that "a joyful, willing, and free mind serves one's neighbor willingly, and takes no account of gratitude or ingratitude, of praise or blame, of gain or loss").[59] And the speech rejects discretion as well as calculation. It picks up a notion developed earlier in the act through the plainspoken figure that Kent becomes in disguise. "Caius" is startlingly badly behaved. He cannot contain his contempt for Oswald, and he insults everyone around (and over) him. When the Duke of Cornwall speaks for decorum and questions whether Kent as Caius has any proper "reverence" for authority and social position, Kent replies, "Yes sir, but anger hath a privilege" (2.2.63/66). Kent is clearly using "privilege" here in its legal sense of an exemption from a normal obligation. Lear is attempting to claim this privilege in his speech on need.[60] He rejects meekness, urging the gods to "fool me not so much" as to let him bear his situation "tamely."[61] He wants to be touched with "noble anger" (2.4.245–46/264–65)—the anger that is connected to honor and to heroic (or merely integral) identity.[62]

59. Luther, *The Freedom of a Christian*, 76; see also Tyndale, *Parable of the Wicked Mammon*, 98; and Calvin, *Institutes*, 3.7.6 ("we are not to consider" what "men merit of themselves").

60. Gordon Braden's *Renaissance Tragedy and the Senecan Tradition: Anger's Privilege* (New Haven: Yale University Press, 1985) uses Kent's defense of indecorum in anger as the subtitle for the book, and quotes the line on the second page of its introduction, but since Braden is interested in the general issue of self-presentation by characters in Renaissance drama, he does not keep the focus on anger. *Lear* ends up being barely mentioned (215–16).

61. The Quarto reading is "To bear it lamely." This is probably a misreading of "tamely." The Quarto version of this speech seems not to have been corrected against the manuscript, since it begins "O reason not the deed." For the 1608 Quarto in facsimile (with corrected Quarto readings also reproduced), see *The Parallel "King Lear," 1608–1623*, prepared by Michael Warren (Berkeley: University of California Press, 1989).

62. The connection between anger and honor is central to *The Iliad* and therefore, of course, to the entire heroic tradition; see Gregory Nagy, *The Best of the Achaeans: Concepts of the Hero in Archaic Greek Poetry* (Baltimore: Johns Hopkins University Press, 1979), esp. 73–74, 142–44; James M. Redfield, *Nature and Culture in "The Iliad"* (Chicago: University of Chicago Press, 1975), 103–6; and Leonard C. Muellner, *The Anger of Achilles: "Menis" in Greek Epic* (Ithaca: Cornell University Press, 1996), chaps. 4–5. Aristotle defines anger as a painful desire to punish [someone who has afflicted one with] undeserved belittlement; see Aristotle, *The "Art" of Rhetoric* 2.2 (1378a), trans. J. H. Freese, Loeb Classical Library (Cambridge: Harvard University Press, 1926), 172–73. The connection between anger and the possibility of a perceived

Yet even in this speech, the situation is complex. Just before he asks for "noble anger," Lear asks the heavens to "give me that patience," and insists, "patience I need." How can he follow the prayer for patience with a prayer for anger? The answer might seem to be that Lear imagines that "noble anger" might be compatible with or enabled by patience, that such anger is not a form of excess or madness. But the speech itself undercuts this fantasy. The prayer for "noble anger" turns into a vision of "revenges," and the vision of revenges turns into the rant of madness: "I will do such things, / What they are, yet I know not; but they shall be / The terrors of the earth"(2.4.250–52/269–71.)[63] The play accepts the Stoic equation of anger with madness. When Kent asks Lear, "where is the patience now / That you so oft have boasted to retain" (3.4.54–55/17–18), Kent is trying to keep Lear from going mad. Seneca saw the connection of anger to madness as the strongest argument for the sage not to indulge in anger, since "never will the wise man cease to be angry, if once he begins" because the world is so full of injustices and vices.[64] *Lear* can be seen as accepting the Stoic equation (anger leads the perceptive to madness), but rejecting the Stoic conclusion (anger is therefore to be avoided). The play may well present madness as the price that must be paid for a certain kind of wisdom rather than seeing the inevitability of madness as the reason why the wise man must renounce anger. Part of what makes the play a tragedy is its acceptance of the Stoic equation, its awareness that "noble anger" is indeed a fantasy, an unstable category.[65] Yet the play commits itself to anger nonetheless. Lear's

diminution of the self is a major theme of Philip Fisher's *The Vehement Passions* (Princeton: Princeton University Press, 2002), esp. chap. 10.

63. Interestingly in the context of Lear renouncing "women's weapons" and condemning "unnatural hags," the classical model for this rant is an outraged female. Kenneth Muir, in his edition of *King Lear* (1952; London: Methuen, 1972), notes that Joseph Ritson associated these lines with Golding's translation of Ovid's *Metamorphosis* 6.784–85—"The thing that I doe purpose on is great, what ere it is; / I know not what it may be yet"—where the speaker is Procne. Even closer to Lear's lines is Medea's vaunt, in the opening soliloquy of Seneca's *Medea*, that she will do "[s]avage, unheard-of, horrible things, evils fearful to heaven and earth alike" (lines 45–46). See Seneca, *Tragedies*, ed. and trans. John G. Fitch, Loeb Classical Library (Cambridge: Harvard University Press, 2002), 1:347. I owe this reference to my colleague Michael Murrin.

64. Seneca, *De Ira* 2.9, in *Moral Essays*, trans. John W. Basore, Loeb Classical Library (Cambridge: Harvard University Press 1928), 1:183.

65. On the instability of "noble anger" in the Greek (literary) context, see Ruth Padel, *Whom Gods Destroy: Elements of Greek and Tragic Madness* (Princeton: Princeton University Press, 1995); in the political and public context, see Danielle S. Allen, *The World of Prometheus: The Politics of Punishing in Democratic Athens* (Princeton: Princeton University Press, 2000).

apocalyptic rage, his dialogue with the elements, is borrowed from Senecan tragedy and is clearly on the verge of madness.[66] Yet the passion that animates Lear's rage at how he has been treated is also seen as enabling his newfound sympathy for all victims of injustice. Madness and "noble anger" do indeed go together in the play. The idea of the mighty and powerful willingly exposing themselves "to feel what wretches feel" is a mad idea, but it has an undeniable moral grandeur—just as Lear's own attempt at enacting this fantasy by stripping has the dimensions of both lunacy and magnificence.[67]

The obvious contrast to Lear's response to injustice is Gloucester's. Gloucester rises to moral heroism—"Though I die for't, as no less is threatened me, the King, my old master, must be relieved" (3.3.16–17)—and he suffers horribly as a consequence, yet he would rather lose his life than his patience toward the gods.[68] He chooses (he believes) suicide in order not to "fall / To quarrel with [the gods'] great opposeless wills" (4.4/5.38). He takes the posited objective reality of "opposeless" (not being alterable by opposition) to imply the subjective condition (and moral necessity) of not opposing.[69] He articulates a Stoic, perhaps especially Senecan, conception of suicide as moral freedom and political resistance, idealizing a time "When misery could beguile the tyrant's rage / And frustrate his proud will" (4.4/5.63–64).[70] Even after Edgar has contrived the apparent miracle for Gloucester and presented suicide as a demonic temptation and the gods as benign, Gloucester is still eager to die quietly. In fact, he can be said to make another suicide attempt. When Oswald appears, chortling with delighted opportunism, and rather

---

66. On apocalypticism in Senecan tragedy, see Braden, *Renaissance Tragedy and the Senecan Tradition*, 5–8, 55–56.

67. The Duke of Albany can be seen as rising to "noble rage" in his denunciation of Goneril, especially in the much longer Quarto version, but even this has an element of rant ("Humanity must perforce prey on itself / Like monsters of the deep" [Q 4.2.47–48]) and of madness (in Albany's fantasy of allowing himself, Hercules-like, to "dislocate and tear / [Goneril's] flesh and blood" [Q 4.2.61–64]).

68. I have given the Quarto reading of lines 16–17 of this scene. The Folio has "If I die for it."

69. Compare S. L. Goldberg, *An Essay on "King Lear"* (Cambridge: Cambridge University Press, 1974), 85.

70. There is disagreement in the scholarship as to whether Seneca's attitude toward suicide is normal within the Stoic tradition or whether it contains new elements or emphases. For the view that suicide has a special place in Seneca's thought, and that he lays unusual emphasis on a general right to suicide, see J. M. Rist, *Stoic Philosophy* (Cambridge: Cambridge University Press, 1969), 246–49. Rist's view is supported by Miriam Griffin, "Philosophy, Cato and Roman Suicide" *Greece and Rome* 33 (1986): 64–77 (part 1), 192–202 (part 2).

grandly and impersonally announces to Gloucester that "The sword is out /
That must destroy thee," Gloucester too understands this moment as a happy
opportunity: "Now let thy friendly hand," he urges, "Put strength enough to't"
(4.6.215–20/4.5.220–25). This renewed desire to die is probably to be seen as
produced by Gloucester's encounter with the mad Lear. Gloucester responds
to Lear's person and Lear's madness with admirable pity and affection, but
Gloucester does not respond to Lear's savage indignation. Gloucester never
directly responds to the picture of universal injustice and wickedness that
Seneca said would drive the wise man mad if he were once to allow himself
to be moved by it, the picture that does drive Lear mad (Seneca mentions the
judge "who will condemn the same deeds that he himself has committed" and
insists that there is no place in society not filled with "crime and vice").[71] When
Lear finally does bring himself to acknowledge Gloucester calmly, he knows
what Gloucester needs and wants to hear: "I know thee well enough; thy name
is Gloucester. / Thou must be patient" (4.6.165–66/170–71).[72]

Gloucester dies a lovely, quiet death, in which "two extremes of passion,
joy and grief" (that is, pity) simultaneously assert themselves and cancel themselves out, so that his heart "burst[s] smilingly" (5.3.192–93/190–91). He goes
gently. The play would seem to present this death as a sort of ideal—one connected, perhaps, to Edgar's conception of "ripeness." But Lear does not go
gently, and his death cannot be assimilated to any conception of "ripeness,"
whether Stoic or Christian.[73] The play refuses to wrap up when it should,

71. *De Ira* 2.7 (181), 2.9 (183).

72. Danby can only see this moment as ironic (*"King Lear* and Christian Patience," 122).

73. J. V. Cunningham is convinced that "Ripeness is all" must be read in Christian terms
(*Woe or Wonder: The Emotional Effect of Shakespearean Tragedy* [Chicago: University of Chicago Press, 1960], 7–13). I find William Elton's demonstration that the phrase is indistinguish-
able between Stoic and Christianized contexts convincing (see *"King Lear" and the Gods* [San
Marino: The Huntington Library, 1968], 101–7. In the Quarto, where Lear's final lines are to
say to himself, "Break heart, I prithee break" (5.3.303), the contrast between Lear's death and
Gloucester's, both focusing on the sufferer's "heart," is even sharper. Whereas Gloucester's
death is passive and (we are told) happy, Lear's death, in the Quarto version, is willed, yet not a
suicide. It remains more passionate and urgent than calmly resigned (or happily overburdened);
it remains anti-Stoical. The Folio gives the "Break heart" line to Kent (5.3.297). It is tempting to
think that Dylan Thomas's "Do not go gentle into that good night" is based on *Lear*, but, if so,
the poem is more optimistic about the cosmos than Shakespeare's play is: "[W]ise men at their
end know dark is right"; and the night is "good" (Dylan Thomas, *Collected Poems* [New York:
New Directions, 1957], 128).

presenting us with the corpse of Cordelia, murdered through a piece of bad timing: "Great thing of us forgot!" (5.3.230/211). Having earlier had his "great rage" cured—by a medical practitioner in the Quarto—Lear regains the great rage here.[74] Entering, as both of the early printed versions specify, with the corpse of Cordelia in his arms, Lear insists on the opposite of patience:

> Howl, howl, howl, howl! O you are men of stones.
> Had I your tongues and eyes, I would use them so
> That heaven's vault should crack.[75]
> (5.3.250–52/231–33)

We are back to the "privilege" of anger—cosmologized, so that it truly knows "no reverence." The "men of stones," here, are statues, of course, mere simulacra of persons, but they are also, as Folly and others would remind us, Stoic sages.

HOLY HOWLING

It may seem odd to approach the devotional poetry of George Herbert immediately after contemplating the supreme blasphemy of *Lear*, but Herbert, in his context, is as radical in his defense of unfettered emotion as Shakespeare is in his. Herbert is the great spokesman, in English poetry, for the Reformation defense of passion.[76] His lyrics are modeled on the Psalms, which he clearly sees, as Luther does, as expressions of the full range of emotions of the human heart in dialogue with God.[77] And Herbert sees Jesus's words on the cross in just the way Calvin does—as words spoken from the heart, in agony, in sincerity, and as part of a dialogue.[78] In "Longing," Herbert writes:

---

74. The "great rage" is "cured" in the Quarto (4.7.75–76); whereas it is "killed" in the Folio (4.6.72–73). The process is explicitly medical in the Quarto, where a doctor presides over it; in the Folio, the doctor is replaced by a gentleman.

75. The stage direction is identical in both the Quarto and the Folio: "Enter Lear with Cordelia in his arms." I have given the Quarto version of Lear's lines. The Folio has one fewer "howl," and elides "I would" to "I'd."

76. For a fuller development of this argument, see Strier, *Love Known*, chap. 7 (see intro., n. 53).

77. For Luther's view of the Psalms, see 41 above.

78. See Calvin, *Commentary on the Book of Psalms*, 1:182, 357; *Institutes*, 3.2.21.

My throat, my soul is hoarse;
My heart is wither'd like a ground
Which thou dost curse.
My thoughts turn round,
And make me giddie; Lord, I fall,
Yet call.[79]

It must be acknowledged that at times, like most other figures in the period, Herbert does feel the pull of Stoic equanimity—"the pliant minde, whose gentle measure / Complies and suits with all estates" ("Content," lines 13–14). And at times he also feels the pull of Stoic *apathia*. For example, in "Constancie," the "honest man" who must "treat / With sick folks, women, those whom passions sway / Allows for that, and keeps his constant way" (lines 26–28). Yet Herbert's most distinctive and important poetry is poetry of passion—poetry that, in the seventeenth century and beyond, was in fact extremely important to "sick folks, women, those whom passions sway."[80] Herbert knows that the priority he gives to unvarnished and unbridled emotion may seem odd, may seem to contradict the claims of both art and decorum. But he takes this priority to be God's.

In "Sion," one of a whole set of ironic architectural poems in *The Temple*, Herbert explains why God has given up wanting to be served as he was, on his own command, in Solomon's temple, with magnificent materials and elaborate art ("most things were of burnished gold," and the whole structure "embellished / With flowers and carvings, mysticall and rare").[81] It turns out,

79. "Longing," lines 7–12, in *The Works of George Herbert* (see intro., n. 54). All subsequent quotations of Herbert's poetry are also from this edition and are cited in the text.

80. On the importance of Herbert's poetry to women, as both readers and writers, in the seventeenth century, see Helen Wilcox, "Entering the Temple: Women, Reading, and Devotion in Seventeenth-century England," in *Religion, Literature, and Politics in Post-Reformation England, 1540–1688*, ed. Donna B. Hamilton and Richard Strier (Cambridge: Cambridge University Press, 1996), 187–207. Ann Collins, one of the poets discussed in Wilcox, may have been an invalid (a suggestion I owe to my former student, Sarah Skwire). For Herbert's extraordinary importance to a later female writer with health problems, see Simone Weil, *Waiting for God*, trans. Emma Craufurd (New York: Putnam, 1951), 68–69; and Jacques Cabaud, *Simone Weil: A Fellowship in Love* (New York: Channel, 1964), 168–69, 237.

81. On the architectural poems as a group, see Richard Strier, "George Herbert and Ironic Ekphrasis," *Classical Philology* 102 (January 2007), special issue, *Ekphrasis*, ed. Shadi Bartsch and Jas Elsner, 96–109.

as Herbert puts it with typically audacious and humorous understatement, that "all this glorie, all this pomp and state" does not "affect" God much (lines 7–8). What does "affect" him, apparently, is affect. In place of all the pomp and state, God has chosen to inhabit the intimate and peculiar world of human emotionality:

> There thou art struggling with a peevish heart,
> Which sometimes crosseth thee, thou sometimes it:
> The fight is hard on either part.
> Great God doth fight, he doth submit.
> (lines 13–16)

The final couplet of the stanza sums up the account of God's preferences:

> All Solomons sea of brasse and world of stone
> Is not so deare to thee as one good grone.[82]
> (lines 17–18)

Why God should condescend to do this, why he should wish to deal with something so apparently unattractive, so childish, petulant, and irritably demanding as "a peevish heart," why he should place such a value on "one good grone"—the poem, thus far, has recorded these odd preferences, but not explained them. The final stanza provides the "explanation":

> And truly brasse and stones are heavie things,
> Tombes for the dead, not temples fit for thee:
> But grones are quick, and full of wings,
> And all their motions upward be;
> And ever as they mount, like larks they sing;
> Their note is sad, yet musick for a King.
> (lines 19–24)

The final line alludes directly to the Psalms (with David as singer), but the "King" here is not David but God. Why the struggling heart is a better temple for God than a great building is explained by the contrast between "dead"

---

82. For the "sea of brasse" see—as Hutchinson points out in *The Works of George Herbert*, 515—1 Kings 7:23.

and living things (compare "O you are men of stones"). "Grones are quick"—
"quick" is the crucial word here, as it is in other Herbert poems (see the end of
"Love unknown," where God works to have the individual believer be "new,
tender, quick"). Groans are products of human emotional responsiveness; they
have "wings" because of their "motions upward," their expression of desire for
succor, relief, and love.[83] "Man groaning for grace" was the essential picture of
piety for Luther and Calvin.[84] The special kind of "King" that God is values
heartfeltness—sincerity—more than anything else.

Herbert knows that this is as strange a picture of divinity as it is of kingship. He knows that this conception of the "music" God enjoys is as far from
traditional pictures of heavenly decorum as the complaining speaker of a
poem like "Longing" is from some models of "saintly" behavior. "Gratefulnesse" is another exploration and celebration of the oddness of God's preferences. It imagines the impact of human neediness on a traditional picture of
heaven. God does not reason the need or worry about his great (or graced)
palace:

> Perpetuall knockings at thy doore.
> Tears sullying thy transparent rooms,
> Gift upon gift, much would have more,
>
> > And comes.
> >
> > (lines 13–16)

After explaining, once again, that God "didst allow us all our noise" and has
"made a sign and grone" his joys (lines 18–20), Herbert acknowledges the full
oddness of this, and provides a whimsical explanation. God is one of those
Renaissance aristocrats who likes folk music (recall Orsino's special preference for songs that are rural, old, and plain):

83. James Turner has wonderfully remarked to me that Herbert's image here "seems de-
liberately to flout the etymological connection between passion and passivity" (personal
communication).

84. See Jared Wicks, *Man Yearning for Grace: Luther's Early Spiritual Teaching* (Weis-
baden: F. Steiner, 1969); Heiko Oberman, "*Simul Gemitus et Raptus*: Luther and Mysticism," in
The Reformation in Medieval Perspective, ed. Steven E. Ozment (Chicago: Quadrangle Books,
1971); Thomas F. Torrance, *Calvin's Doctrine of Man* (London: Lutterworth, 1952). For a nice
passage on groaning in Calvin, see *Institutes*, 2.1.3.

> Not that thou hast not still above
> Much better tunes than grones can make;
> But that these countrey-aires thy love
> > Did take.[85]
>
> > (lines 21–24)

What all of this serves to do is to license Herbert to express his longing with full, unabashed, relentless, infantile intensity. He "howls":

> Wherefore I crie, and crie again;
> And in no quiet canst thou be,
> Till I a thankfull heart obtain
> > Of thee.
>
> > (lines 25–28)

Perhaps the clearest expression of the privileged status of emotion in Herbert is in the poem entitled "The Storm." The first stanza of this poem postulates a situation that would make one of Lear's storm fantasies come true. Lear asks that the gods make the storm affect the consciences of sinners and criminals: "Close pent-up guilts, / Rive your concealèd centres (3.2.57–58])." [86] Herbert asserts that "tempestuous times / Amaze poore mortals, and object their crimes" (lines 5–6). But here again what Herbert is interested in is not human moral and psychological vulnerability but the extraordinary power of this vulnerability to have the effect of successful rhetoric (as the Renaissance conceived it) on God—to "move / And much affect thee" (lines 4–5). The body of this poem gives the most powerful account in English of the "privileged" religious status of human psychological and moral need. Again Herbert praises importunate knocking (compare Luke 11:9):

> A throbbing conscience spurred by remorse
> > Hath a strange force:
> It quits the earth, and mounting more and more
> Dares to assault thee, and besiege thy doore.
>
> > (lines 9–12)

---

85. For Orsino's account of the kind of songs he likes, see *Twelfth Night*, ed. J. M. Lothian and T. W. Craik (London: Methuen, 1975), 2.4.43–48.

86. I quote the Quarto; the Folio substitutes "concealing continents" for "concealèd centres."

What "Sion" presents as "music," what "Gratefulnesse" first presents as "noise" but then presents as "countrey-aires," is here presented in its most raw, unaesthetic, and indecorous form—"There is stands knocking, to thy musick's wrong, / And drowns the song" (lines 13–14). And the status of this painfully sincere and visceral, this "throbbing" human longing, is truly privileged:

> Glorie and honour are set by, till it
> An answer get.
> (lines 15–16)

No one reasons this need—not even God.

CHAPTER 2

Against Judgment:
Petrarch and Shakespeare at Sonnets

Petrarch and Shakespeare figured in the previous chapter with regard to "praise of passion"—Petrarch as spokesperson, in Latin prose, for an anti-Stoic position that Shakespeare, and many others, later develop further. In this chapter, Petrarch functions as a great vernacular poet, the model for all Renaissance sonneteers, including, as we will see, Shakespeare. Shakespeare is almost always seen as an "anti-Petrarchan," but I will argue that, despite what seem to be sharp differences, once we see Petrarch's sonnets and the other poems in the *Canzoniere* correctly—as resisting rather than embracing dualism and disembodiment—then the deep continuity between his poems and Shakespeare's emerges.[1]

---

1. This thesis aligns me with the perspective of Gordon Braden's "Shakespeare's Petrarchism," in *Shakespeare's Sonnets: Critical Essays*, ed. James Schiffer (New York: Garland, 1999), 163–83, and against that of Joel Fineman's *Shakespeare's Perjured Eye: The Invention of Poetic Subjectivity in the Sonnets* (Berkeley: University of California Press, 1986), insofar as Fineman insists on the absolute distinctiveness of Shakespeare's sonnets, especially of the sonnets to the "dark lady," and sees Petrarch merely as a Neoplatonist. But Fineman regularly acknowledges the complexity of Petrarch's achievement, and the way in which Petrarch's sonnets do not actually stand in clear contrast with Shakespeare's. For such moments in *Shakespeare's Perjured Eye*, see 9, 56, 85, and especially 122: "Petrarch worries over much the same kind of issues that later become the thematic center of Shakespeare's sonnets." For an article that does present Shakespeare's sonnets as "innovative within the tradition of sonnet writing, largely because they are so anti-Platonic," see Douglas Trevor, "Shakespeare's Love Objects," in *A Companion to Shakespeare's Sonnets*, ed. Michael Schoenfeldt (Malden, Mass.: Blackwell, 2007), 227.

DOLCE ERROR

The funniest interchange in Petrarch's *Secretum* occurs at a very intense moment in the dialogue, a moment in which Franciscus and Augustinus are focusing on the stakes and value of Petrarch's love for Laura. Augustinus pulls out the big gun; Petrarch is guilty of idolatry: "She has distracted you from love of the Creator to love of one of the creatures."[2] Franciscus defends himself by asserting that "loving her has increased my love of God." Augustinus counters that loving God for having created Laura reverses "the right order of things" and places the physical over the spiritual. Franciscus insists that he has not "loved her body more than her soul." His proof of this is that his feelings have not changed as Laura has grown older: "The bloom of her youth has faded with the passage of time, but the beauty of her mind—which made me love her in the first place and [made me] afterwards continue to love—has increased." Augustinus responds with the coup de grace: "Are you serious? You mean that if that same mind had been in an ugly, gnarled body, you would have loved it just as much?" Here Franciscus immediately starts to backpedal.

In beginning with this passage, I mean to suggest that "Augustinus" was right about this last point—Laura's body did indeed matter to Petrarch—and I mean to suggest that Petrarch, and not only "Franciscus," knew this. But "Augustinus" has to be seen to be right only from a descriptive point of view—not necessarily from a moral one. I will argue that in the *Canzoniere*, Petrarch's most important lyric poems, the "scattered rhymes" (*Rime sparse*) that he so carefully collected and arranged, there is a sustained insistence on the importance and value of the bodily and the mortal. In the poems gathered in the *Rime*, as I will present them, Petrarch resists the ethical implications of the Platonism—or the Platonized Christianity—to which he is, metaphysically and religiously, committed. He accepts the soul-body dualism of Platonism, but he refuses to give the soul an absolute priority and to dismiss and devalue the body. He refuses, in other words, to adopt a transcendental perspective—though, as we shall see (and as the *Secretum*, among many other of his works, shows), he was fully aware of such a perspective.[3] John Freccero has praised Donne's love poetry for

2. Francis Petrarch, *My Secret Book*, trans. J. G. Nichols (London: Hesperus, 2002), 63; page references for the English in the text are to this edition.

3. For Neoplatonism in the *Secretum*, see ibid., 23–24; for how directly the Platonism of "Augustinus" in the *Secretum* contradicts the position of the historical Augustine, and on the fact that Petrarch certainly knew this, see Carol Everhart Quillen, *Rereading the Renaissance: Petrarch, Augustine, and the Language of Humanism* (Ann Arbor: University of Michigan Press,

"rescuing" human love from "angelic mysticism," for defending the distinctly human sphere of love from "the neo-Petrarchan and neoplatonic dehumanization of love."[4] I want to argue that, regardless of what "neo-Petrarchans" did, Petrarch does exactly what Freccero credits Donne with accomplishing.[5]

To return to the *Secretum*, we should note that Augustinus's attack on Franciscus goes even deeper than the latter's attitude toward the body. After Augustinus has successfully critiqued Franciscus's erotic obsession, Franciscus says, "I am ashamed, I suffer for it, and I repent it; but I cannot get beyond it" (*Pudet, piget et penitet, sed ultra non valeo*).[6] This brings up the issue with which the *Secretum* both begins and ends: the matter of the will. At the beginning of the dialogue, Augustinus claims that Franciscus has willed his "unhappy state" (not yet specified). As a good Platonist (in ethics as well

---

1998), chap. 5, esp. 191–95. Oscar Büdel brilliantly contrasts Petrarch's poetry with the Platonism of the *stilnovisti* in "Illusion Disabused: A Novel Mode in Petrarch's *Canzoniere*," in *Francis Petrarch, Six Centuries Later*, ed. Aldo Scaglione (Chapel Hill: University of North Carolina Press, 1975), 128–51, esp. 129–30. See also J. W. Lever: "Laura was indeed the living manifestation of heavenly virtue; but she remained part of the natural world, not to be spirited away in concept and symbol" (*The Elizabethan Love Sonnet* [London: Methuen, 1956], 3). As Joel Fineman points out—somewhat against the grain of his own argument (see note 1 above)—Giordano Bruno, a serious philosophical Platonist, saw Petrarch in the love poetry as insufficiently Platonic, as either a mad sensualist or (Bruno's preferred view) a sustained ironizer of such a figure (Giordano Bruno, *The Heroic Frenzies*, trans. Paul Eugene Memmo, Jr. [Chapel Hill: University of North Carolina Press, 1964], 64–65; quoted in Fineman, *Shakespeare's Perjured Eye*, 327n25).

4. John Freccero, "Donne's 'Valediction: Forbidding Mourning,'" *English Literary History* 30 (1963): 336. I do not mean, hereby, to endorse this as a view of Donne's love poetry as a whole, though Freccero is convincing, if perhaps overly systematic and Dantescan, on the particular poem that he analyzes. Donne's attitude toward the body varies wildly within the "Songs and Sonnets." My colleague Armando Maggi has remarked that "Freccero is right about 'the angelic mysticism' of neo-Petrarchan poetry, but only if seen as a generic concept, not in its concrete manifestations, because, for example Michelangelo, in his poems, is both very neoplatonic and very physical. And some of the women poets of the Italian Renaissance are much less 'angelic' than Freccero claims" (personal communication).

5. Freccero does not address this issue in his direct treatment of Petrarch because he insists that Petrarch's lyrics do not actually have a subject matter. See Freccero's "The Fig-Tree and the Laurel: Petrarch's Poetics," in *Literary Theory / Renaissance Texts* (Baltimore: Johns Hopkins University Press, 1986), 20–32, esp. 21. According to Freccero, Petrarch's is "a poetry whose real subject matter is its own act," and Freccero mocks those who think to find a representation of psychology (or anything else) in Petrarch's "autonomous universe of autoreflexive signs without reference to an anterior logos" (27).

6. English from *My Secret Book*, 80; Latin from Francesco Petrarca, *Prose*, ed. G. Martellotti et al. (Milan: Riccardi, 1955), 184.

as metaphysics), Augustinus holds that "anyone who has fully recognized his unhappiness wants to be happy; and anyone who wants this tries to achieve it." He also holds the optimistic view, important for this kind of ethics, that "anyone who tries to achieve [happiness] is able to achieve it" (6). Franciscus has difficulty believing that the whole issue of happiness is a matter of knowledge and the will, but the problem that emerges is whether the movement from recognition (or "full" recognition) of the condition of being unhappy leads as directly as Augustinus states that it does to the desire to be happy (this leaves aside the questions of whether the desire leads to action on its basis, and that action to its success). Franciscus appears to grasp very clearly everything that Augustinus says. Yet in their very last exchange, Franciscus asserts, "But I cannot restrain my desires" (*Sed desiderium frenare non valeo*), whereat Augustinus rightly notes, "We are getting back to the old bone of contention. You are saying your will is impotent [*voluntatem impotentiam vocas*]" (93).[7] Petrarch shows in the dialogue the failure of Socratic ethics.[8] In the lyrics, he goes further and at times seems to accept the perversion of his will, his inability to desire what he knows to be the highest good. The sustained presentation, in the first person, of simultaneous awareness of and resistance to moral evaluation—of the failure of clear-eyed moral analysis to determine the self-conscious agent's behavior, his affective commitment, and even his self-evaluation—can be seen as Petrarch's great contribution to European love poetry. This idea (or vision) of the self is not unprecedented, but Petrarch's sustained focus on it is, and might well constitute a revolution.[9]

7. Gordon Braden argues that this is a slight mistranslation, and that the Latin (*Prose*, 214) is even stronger here, and should be translated not as "you are saying your will is impotent," but as "what you are calling impotence is actually willfulness" (personal communication). This seems to me a useful, and clarifying, correction.

8. Needless to say, my reading of the *Secretum* differs from that of Thomas Roche, Jr., *Petrarch and the English Sonnet Sequences* (New York: AMS Press, 1989), 7, who says of the dialogue, "There can be no doubt who is right" (meaning "Augustinus"). My reading of the *Secretum* is in accord with that of Quillen (see note 3 above), and with Hans Baron, *Petrarch's "Secretum": Its Making and Its Meaning* (Cambridge, Mass.: Medieval Academy of America, 1985), esp. 221–22. My readings of the *Canzoniere* and of Shakespeare's sonnets are equally opposed to those of Roche.

9. For this perspective on Petrarch's achievement, and for a consideration of the precedents for it, from Vergil and the Roman elegists to the *stilnovisti* and Dante, see Jennifer Petrie, *Petrarch: The Augustan Poets, the Italian Tradition, and the "Canzoniere"* (Dublin: Irish Academic Press, 1983), chaps. 5–7. See also Marco Santagata, *Amate e amanti: Figure della lirica amorosa fra Dante e Petrarca* (Bologna: Il Mulino, 1999), 172: "Nella poesia di Petrarca i temi,

Anyone who thinks that Petrarch's sonnets are somehow simple and straightforward pieces should be disabused by opening the volume and reading its first poem (there is abundant evidence that Petrarch carefully arranged the order of the *Canzoniere*).[10] I can think of no other authorially arranged collection of lyrics—other perhaps than "The Church" section of George Herbert's *The Temple*—that begins with so complex a poem.[11] Moreover, I can think of no other collection of love lyrics that begins with what is essentially a palinode. Petrarch opens by addressing his readers—there is no pretense that these poems are not written to be widely read—and he does so in an oddly intimate way, as if his readers were already familiar with the poems: "You who hear" (*Voi ch'ascoltate*) rather than "You who will hear."[12] Moreover, the self that is writing to these readers (or hearers) has a complex relation to what it is that the readers "hear."[13] They hear "those sighs with which I nourished my heart during my first youthful error" (*quei sospiri ond'io nudriva 'l core / in sul mio primo giovenile errore*). One would think that the speaker would distance himself from such *errore*, but he states, with extraordinary care and precision, that he was then "in part another man from what I am now" (*quand'era in*

---

le immagini, il lessico del dolore e della sofferenza amorosi conoscono un incremento senza precedenti."

10. On Petrarch's careful and continuous arranging of the order of the *Rime*, see Ernest Hatch Wilkins, *The Making of the "Canzoniere" and Other Petrarchan Studies* (Rome: Edizioni di Storia e Letteratura, 1951); for the composition, dating, and placement of the first poem in the *Rime*, see 151–52, 190–93. On the richness of the opening sonnet, in itself and in relation to the volume as a whole, see Bruce Merry, "Il primo sonetto del Petrarca come modello di lettura," *Paragone* 25 (1974): 73–79.

11. "The Church" section of *The Temple* begins with "The Altar," on the complexities of which see, most recently, Strier, "George Herbert and Ironic Ekphrasis," 96–109, esp. 106–9, and the references there given (see chap. 1, n. 81). For the care with which George Herbert arranged his lyrics, one has only to compare the earlier version of the volume ("the Williams manuscript" version) and the final version. For a helpful chart, see *The Works of George Herbert*, liv–v (see intro., n. 54).

12. Wilkins notes that "the writing of No. 1 proves that Petrarch now [probably 1347] had in mind the idea of publication" (*The Making of the "Canzoniere,"* 15). Wilkins also points out (148) that what is now poem number 34, the sonnet "Apollo, s'ancor vive il ben desio," was the opening poem for the first version of the *Canzoniere*. Quotations from Petrarch's *Rime* are taken from *Petrarch's Lyric Poems: The "Rime Sparse" and Other Lyrics*, ed. and trans. Robert M. Durling (Cambridge: Harvard University Press, 1976). Throughout, translations are Durling's unless otherwise noted.

13. On the role of the reader in the *Canzoniere*, see William J. Kennedy, *Rhetorical Norms in Renaissance Literature* (New Haven: Yale University Press, 1978), 241.

parte altr'uom da quel ch'i' sono). The speaker is not wholly reformed; he is still *in parte* the person caught in the juvenile error. The reader is justifiably mystified. In what sense can one still participate in what one recognizes as a "juvenile error"? Augustine's (the real Augustine's) theory of imperfect conversion—Saint Paul's theory—would seem to be at work here.[14]

Instead, however, of continuing to elaborate on the complexity of the relation between his past and present selves, the speaker of poem 1 returns, in the second quatrain of the octave, to thinking about his readers. He hopes that they will be connoisseurs of poetry, appreciating the "varied style in which I weep" (line 5). Most of all, he hopes that they will see and share the experience behind the style, and offer the poet not only moral but emotional understanding—"I hope to find pity, not only pardon" (*spero trovar pietà, non che perdono*). The sestet shifts to the way the speaker is in fact different from his past self. He is now afflicted with deep shame, not merely embarrassment: "I was the talk of the town" (*come al popol tutto / fabula fui*), and he presents his *vario stile* as mere "raving" (*mio vaneggiar*) that has produced in him not only the feelings that have already been named and enacted—shame and repentance—but also a particular cognitive ability. He now has the ability to know something clearly, and what he has thus come to know constitutes the last line of the sonnet, "that whatever pleases in the world is a brief dream" (*che quanto piace al mondo è breve sogno*). The upshot of the whole process described and evoked in the poem is a grand metaphysical reflection, not an identifiably Christian moral. Obviously a "brief dream" is different from a solid and enduring reality, but it is also not necessarily something one would want to reject.

As we move through Petrarch's volume, the complexities enunciated in the opening sonnet persist. There continues to be a contrast between the speaker's present and his past, but this conflict persists in being different from the one we would expect. In poem 55 (not a sonnet), the speaker recounts that in his "no longer fresh" age, he is still basically the same person that he was earlier, still burning with love. Instead of improving, he fears that "my second error [*'l secondo error*] will be the worse" (line 6). Error, along with love and pain, seems to be a constant. Poem 59, "Perché quel che mi trasse ad amar" (Because that which drew me to love) begins to raise the issue of the will. The speaker

---

14. For the differences between "Augustinus" in the *Secretum* and the historical Augustine, see note 3 above. For the historical Augustine's theory of incomplete conversion, and on how this differed from the prevailing way of conceiving of conversion in his time, see Peter Brown's discussion of book 10 of *The Confessions*, in *Augustine of Hippo: A Biography* (Berkeley and Los Angeles: University of California Press, 1967), 177–81; for Augustine and Paul, see 150–52.

has to decide how to deal with the fact that he has apparently been barred from the sight of his beloved. This situation does not lead to any diminishment of the lover's passion, and this steadiness is seen not as a natural fact but as something like a decision or a commitment: the current deprivation "by no means dissuades me from my firm desire"—and the willfulness is even stronger in the Italian, where the words for volition are more prominent (*del mio firmo voler già non mi svoglia*). The power of the bodily presence of the lady is evoked, but the memory of that "splendor" is seen as equally strong. The poet laments the loss of the *dolce vista*, but insists that his commitment to continuing his feelings, despite their cost to him, is a matter of honor. By dying well, honor is gained (*ben morendo onor s'acquista*), and the poem ends with a clear assertion: "I do not wish Love to loose me from such a knot" (*non vo' che da tal nodo Amor mi scioglia*).[15]

As we shall see, this image of the knot (*nodo*) recurs throughout the poetry. The poet's bondage is always seen as having, at least potentially, a relation to his will that is not simply negative. Poem 61, "Benedetto sia 'l giorno e 'l messe et l'anno" (Blessed be the day and the month and the year), and poem 62, "Padre del Ciel" (Father of Heaven), both sonnets, are an odd pair. But they dramatize Petrarch's position. Each section of poem 61 begins with a formal blessing, some version of the opening "Benedetto sia." The poet accepts, sees as sacred, his entire situation—his pain, his poems, the fame they have garnered (lines 12–13), and his bondage: her eyes have "bound" him (*duo begli occhi che legato m'ànno* [line 4]). In the following sonnet, the poet (let's call him "Petrarch") addresses the Christian God and asks to turn to another life (*torni / ad altra vita*).[16] Petrarch notes that he has now been in bondage, "subject to a pitiless yoke" (*sommesso al dispietato giogo*), for eleven years, and asks that his "wandering" (though bound) thoughts be led to "a better place."[17] We learn what the better place is—Calvary—by learning that the day of the poem is Good Friday. The contrast with the asserted "blessedness" of the previous poem could not be sharper. Yet it is important to see that "Padre del Ciel" is entirely in the optative mode. There is no suggestion that the "turn" to another

15. Durling's translation weakens the force of the ending by reversing the penultimate and final lines of the original.

16. Durling's translation is somewhat misleading here, since he translates *ch'io torni* as "that I may *return*."

17. It should be noted that "subject to" does not quite capture the willing submission suggested by the original.

life that the speaker feels that he wants has actually occurred, or has even be-gun. His thoughts, in the present, still wander.

In poem 68, the "holy sight" of the city of Rome leads the poet to bewail his "evil" past, but—and Petrarch's poems are filled with significant adversa-tives—"with this thought another jousts" (*Ma con questo pensier un altro gios-tra*), namely, the thought that time is passing and the poet should return to see "our lady" (*la donna nostra*), that is, Laura. The poem ends with the speaker in a state of puzzlement as to the outcome of this conflict within himself—"Which will win I don't know" (*Qual vincerà non so*)—and with the acknowledgment that this conflict is hardly new to him. The next poem, the sonnet "Ben sapeva io" (I knew well), despite its ominous beginning, presents the poet as having experienced some sort of momentary and miraculous feeling (beyond what "natural counsel" can do) that has allowed him freedom from "the hands" of Amor. In the final tercet, however, a countermiracle occurs: "Love" asserts its power—"behold your ministers" (*ecco i tuoi ministri*)—and the speaker declares that the person is wicked who resists or hides himself from his des-tiny (*al suo destino / mal chi contrasta et mal chi si nasconde*).[18] "Destiny," a pagan concept, and one that does not allow for free will, shows (to return to the puzzlement of the previous sonnet) which side will win. The interesting question, however, is not whether heaven or destiny is the more important term for the speaker—though that is interesting—but how the speaker feels about this *destino*. He seems, in "Ben sapeva io," rather calmly resigned to it. The next poem, number 70, is a canzone in which the speaker puts himself in the whole tradition of Provençal and *stilnovisti* love poetry; he quotes (as he believes) Arnaut Daniel, Cavalcanti, Dante—and himself.[19] The speaker denies that his condition of erotic longing is externally caused: "[W]ho deceives me but myself. . . . Nay, if I run through the sky from sphere to sphere, no planet condemns me to weeping" (lines 31–34). The poem ends with Petrarch con-templating his inability to appreciate the inner, moral structure of the creation (poem 70, 44–45).[20] He further notes that if he ever returns to "the true splen-

18. Durling's translation, "one cannot fight against or hide from his destiny," changes the meaning of the line from acting badly if one resists to being unable to do so. Petrarch's line repeats *mal*.

19. For excellent overviews of these traditions, see, inter alia, Maurice Valency, *In Praise of Love: An Introduction to the Love Poetry of the Renaissance* (New York: Macmillan, 1958), and Mariann Sanders Regan, *Love Words: The Self and the Text in Medieval and Renaissance Poetry* (Ithaca: Cornell University Press, 1982).

20. These lines are quite difficult (conceptually, not linguistically); my paraphrase is an ap-proximation of their meaning.

dor" (*al vero splendor*), his eye will not be able to stay still, it is so weakened by its own fault (*l'occhio non po star fermo, / così l'à fatto infermo / pur la sua propria colpa*),[21] for which even the transforming power of the lady's beauty cannot be blamed (the final line of poem 70 refers the reader back to the great metamorphosis canzone, poem 23).

Again, poem 70 seems very calm about its *propria colpa*. In contrast, in poem 99, a sonnet, Petrarch's earnest exhortation to others who, like him, have experienced disappointed hopes, to devote themselves to "the highest good, which never fails," turns into comedy. A rather blunt hypothesized voice rebukes the poet in the final tercet for his inability "now more than ever" to follow his own advice. The sonnet on the sixteenth year of Petrarch's devotion (poem 118) may seem more genuinely conflicted, but it too seems to present the will's puzzlement as a kind of comedy. The play with terms for will and capacity is too willful: "I wish I wished more, and I do not wish more, and by not being able to do more, I do as much as I can" (*vorrei piu volere, et più no voglio, / et per più non poter fo quant'io posso*).[22] The final line, again, seems more resigned and accepting than anguished—"nor for a thousand turnings about have I yet moved." There may even be a hint of self-approval here. Poem 129, the canzone "Di pensier in pensier" (From thought to thought), confronts the fact that Petrarch enjoys his life of sighs and tears—"I would hardly wish to change this bitter, sweet life of mine" (lines 20–21)—and it celebrates, as Oscar Büdel argues, "the mode of conscious adoption of illusion."[23] The poet confesses in line 37 that he finds that his soul "approves its own deception" (*del suo proprio error l'alma s'appaga*).[24] The *propria colpa* of poem 70 has turned into *proprio error* in "Di pensier in pensier." Self-reproach has disappeared, though analytical awareness has not. The poet knows that he is in "error," and in lines 49–52 consciously prefers "sweet deception" (*dolce error*) to the bleakness of reality (*il vero*).

21. The tense structure of these lines, in which the future inability is expressed in the present tense (*non po*) intensifies the assertion of inability.

22. My translation is slightly altered from that of Durling, who, I think, improperly interrupts the series of "and's" by translating the second *et* in the passage quoted as "but"). Heather Dubrow quotes this sonnet and comments usefully on it in *Echoes of Desire: English Petrarchism and Its Counterdiscourses* (Ithaca: Cornell University Press, 1995), 18–19, but she does not seem to see any comedy or self-mockery in the poem.

23. Büdel, "Illusion Disabused," 139; see also Gordon Braden, *Petrarchan Love and the Continental Renaissance* (New Haven: Yale University Press, 1999), 18.

24. I have substituted "approves" for Durling's "is satisfied with."

"Di pensier in pensier" is not Petrarch's final word on the matter, but it is a major statement. In poem 132, the questioning sonnet "S'amor non è" (If it is not love), Petrarch seems truly and deeply puzzled by his enjoyment of his sufferings, by the role of his will in his sufferings, and by the question of "consent": "If I consent to [my suffering], it is very wrong of me to complain" (*s'io 'l consento, a gran torto mi doglio*). Yet in poem 141, a sonnet meditating on the self-destructive behavior of butterflies, the speaker notes, quite calmly, that his soul "consents to its own death" (*al suo morir l'alma consente*). In poem 207, the canzone "Ben mi credea passar mio tempo omai" (I strongly believed that I could now pass my time), Petrarch returns to the position of "Di pensier in pensier," though now in moral rather than in cognitive terms: "sweet poison" (*dolce veleno*) replaces "sweet error" (*dolce error*)—"still I do not repent that my heart is overwhelmed with sweet poison" (lines 83–84). He returns to the matter of "honor"—recall his words about dying well in poem 59—now affirming "I shall stand firm on the field" (lines 92–93). "Ben mi credea" ends with Petrarch happily proclaiming that evil, or at least misfortune, is his good: "There is no good in the world that is equal to my ill" (*ben non à mondo che 'l mio mal pareggi*).[25]

Like "Di pensier in pensier," the monumental canzone that begins the second section of the *Rime*—poem 264, "I' vo pensando" (I go thinking)—takes as its subject "thought."[26] Here one voice (one thought), like that of Augustinus in the *Secretum*, insists on the freedom and potency of Petrarch's will, as we read in lines 32–33: "As long as the body is alive, you have in your own keeping the rein of your thoughts" (*Mentre che 'l corpo è vivo / ài tu 'l freno in bailia de' penser tuoi*).[27] But the poem replaces a Platonic vision of the soul's (or intellect's) wings (lines 6–8) with an Aristotelian—or, perhaps better, Augustinian—

---

25. Durling's translation, "There is no good in the world that is equal to my ills," seems to me to soften the force and starkness of the line by importing the plural. David Quint (in a private communication) has expressed skepticism about my "Satanic" reading of this line, but I think that the allusion is appropriate.

26. On the way that the role of this canzone is marked in Petrarch's manuscript, see Wilkins, *The Making of the "Canzoniere,"* 190–93.

27. On the closeness of "I' vo pensando" to the *Secretum*, see Baron, *Petrarch's "Secretum,"* 47–57. Baron argues, along with Wilkins, in *The Making of the "Canzoniere,"* 153 (though not in later works), that the canzone and the original version of the *Secretum* were composed in the same year, namely 1347 (before Petrarch had heard of Laura's death, and in the same period in which he composed *De Otio Religiosum*). For Baron's dating of the composition of the *Secretum*, see 1–46. Wilkins (190–93), intriguingly suggests that poems 1 and 264, the opening poems for each section of the *Rime*, were composed at about the same time. Fineman sees the poetry as

insistence on habit (*costume* in line 105, *usanza* in line 125). The conception of habit involved here is Augustinian rather than Aristotelian because while habit is morally neutral in Aristotle's *Ethics*, in Augustine's *Confessions* habit (*consuetudo*) is almost always, as here, morally and spiritually negative.[28] In a typically remarkable and complex phrasing (lines 46–47), Petrarch presents himself as one who has spent many years "awaiting a day that, luckily for our salvation, will never come" (*aspettando un giorno / che per nostra salute unqua non vene*). What Joel Fineman says of Shakespeare's relation to the "dark lady" is exactly à propos here: the lady is "spur to a desire that knows better than itself."[29] The final line of "I' vo pensando" is "I see the better, and I lay hold on the worse" (*veggio 'l meglio et al peggior m'appiglio*).[30] This line is translated from Ovid's *Medea* in the *Metamorphoses*, but the context seems more resigned than tragic.[31] Pleasure remains "by habit" strong in Petrarch, even in the face of death (lines 125–26). Analytical clarity only intensifies the dilemma; it does not resolve it.[32] As Wilkins says, "I' vo pensando" is "not a poem of moral conversion" but rather "a poem of profound moral conflict."[33] In one of the last poems in the *Canzoniere* on the matter of choice, Petrarch decides, first, not to accuse himself for his erotic devotion, as he has done, but rather to excuse himself—or

much more "reticent" than the *Secretum*, and as somehow repressing or being unable to "speak" what the prose work is able to acknowledge (*Shakespeare's Perjured Eye*, 122).

28. Habit, of course, defines character for Aristotle (see *Nicomachean Ethics* 1103a17–26, in *Nicomachean Ethics*, trans. Martin Ostwald [1962; New Jersey, 1999]; hereafter *NE*). Aristotle normally thinks of habit in relation to the virtues (though, of course, each of the virtues has its opposite). In the *Confessions*, "habit" is consistently associated with sexual pleasure and need—see, for instance, *delectationes consuetudinis meae* and *consuetudo satiandae insatiabilis concupiscentiae* in 6.12, *pondus hoc consuetudo carnalis* in 7.17, and the imagined dialogue between *consuetudo violenta* and continence at the end of book 8 (*St. Augustine's "Confessions,"* trans. William Watts, Loeb Classical Library [Cambridge: Harvard University Press, 1912], 1:318, 384, 459).

29. Fineman, *Shakespeare's Perjured Eye*, 54.

30. Again, as in sonnet 118 (see note 22 above), Durling translates an *et* as "but."

31. For *video meliora proboque, / deteriora sequor*, see *Metamorphoses* 7.21–22 (Ovid, *Metamorphoses*, trans. Frank Justus Miller, Loeb Classical Library [Cambridge: Harvard University Press, 1977], 1:342). For the significance, in the Roman and in later contexts, of a male poet taking on the psychology of a woman afflicted with love-madness, see W. R. Johnson, *A Latin Lover in Ancient Rome: Readings in Propertius and His Genre* (Columbus: Ohio State University Press, 2009). Johnson suggests that whenever this occurs in poetry, "the myth of male erotic self-control" is put into question (147).

32. See Petrie, *Petrarch*, 157.

33. Wilkins, *The Making of the "Canzoniere,"* 191.

rather, to praise himself—"I used to accuse myself and now I excuse, rather I praise myself" (*I' mi soglio accusare, et or mi scuso, / anzi mi pregio*). The sestet of this sonnet (poem 296) explains that any soul would change its natural mode (*'l suo natural modo*) of loving its natural objects—something like life, liberty, and the pursuit of happiness (*d'allegrezza . . . di libertà, di vita*)—and choose, as the final line of the sonnet states, "to die content with such a wound, and to live in such a knot" (*di tal piaga / morir contento, et vivere in tal nodo*).

The "knot" is Petrarch's recurrent figure for bondage of the will. But it is also his image for what makes the human condition ontologically unique. In writing of "[t]hat subtle knot that makes us man," Donne is (whether consciously or not) echoing Petrarch.[34] In poem 214, "Anzi tre di creata era alma" (Three days ago, a soul was created), a sestina, Petrarch states that he will not be cured from the "wound" he received on first seeing Laura until "my flesh shall be free/from that knot for which it is more prized" (*la carne sciolta / fia di quel nodo ond'è 'l suo maggior preggio*). Throughout the *Rime*, Petrarch remains committed to the special, positive status of the "knot" that body and soul together form. He is constantly aware of Platonic dualism, and he constantly resists it.[35] Even in his most visionary moments—for example, poem 90, "Erano i capei d'oro a l'aura sparsi" (Her golden hair was loosed to the breeze), where the knots are literal—Petrarch is aware that though Laura's walk seems to him "not that of a mortal thing" (*Non era l'andar suo cosa mortale*), she is not, like Vergil's Venus (the model for the line), "a goddess who looks like a woman" but rather "a woman who looks like a goddess."[36] At the very end of the sonnet, Petrarch insists on this; he asserts that if Laura "were not such now" (*se non fosse or tale*), it would not matter. She is not a goddess

34. "The Exstasie," line 64. One would think from the title of Marianne Shapiro's *Dante and the Knot of Body and Soul* (New York: St. Martin's, 1998) that Dante uses the image in this way, but he, in fact, uses the image differently, as Shapiro's own analysis shows (15–16).

35. This assertion places me in opposition to Thomas M. Greene, in *The Light in Troy: Imitation and Discovery in Renaissance Poetry* (New Haven: Yale University Press, 1982), who seems to equate Christianity (rather than Platonism) with body-soul dualism (125, 129), and who sees in Petrarch the absence "of qualifications to pathos" (129). Greene is committed to a view of literary history that sees enacted in most Renaissance texts, and especially Petrarch's, "a disruption of classical equilibriums by a modern metaphysical fissure" (142). This view seems to me to darken Petrarch's poetry, and to understate the equilibrium that, as I will try to show, it often attains. At one point in his discussion, with regard to poem 188, the sonnet "Almo sol" (Life-giving sun), Greene does suggest a less schematic view (140).

36. Ibid., 112.

but something mortal (*cosa mortale*)—however powerful and lasting the impact of her youthful self on the poet.

The phrase *cosa mortale* recurs in poem 248, "Chi vuol veder" (Whoever wishes to see), a sonnet written, as David Kalstone puts it, in Petrarch's "majestic public manner."[37] Here Petrarch invites everyone interested in seeing the most sublime of sublunary sights—"all that Nature and Heaven can do among us"—to gaze upon Laura, but the whole poem is a carpe diem addressed to such would be admirers. It has the full classical sense of the vulnerability of the extraordinary—"to the extraordinary, life is short and old age is rare" (*inmodicis brevis est aetas et rara senectus*) says Martial.[38] Petrarch takes it as a fact that death "steals first the best" (lines 5–6), and he knows in a full sense that, as he puts it in line 8, "this beautiful mortal thing passes, and does not endure" (*cosa bella mortal passa et non dura*)—like the "brief dream" of the first poem in the *Rime*. Laura's mortality was built into the sequence from the beginning, and Petrarch's awareness of it is part of what makes him see Laura's qualities as to be especially prized. Poem 311, the magnificent sonnet about the nightingale—"Quel rosigniuol che s'i soave piagne" (The nightingale that so sweetly weeps)—comments directly on the fantasy that, as we have seen, "Erano i capei d'oro" both voiced and subtly resisted. In "Quel rosigniuol," written after Laura's death, Petrarch hears and appreciates the sweet mourning of the bird's song; it reminds him of his own hard lot (*dura sorte*), but he quickly takes personal responsibility for his grief, stating in lines 7–8 that "I have no one to complain of but myself, who did not believe Death reigns over goddesses" (*'n dee non credev'io regnasse Morte*). As the repeated references to luck or destiny (*sorte . . . ventura*) and the choice of *dee* suggest, the content here is, again, purely classical, so that the final recognition comes across as philosophical rather than specifically Christian—in poem 311, line 14, "nothing down here both pleases and endures" (*nulla qua giù diletta et dura*).[39]

37. David Kalstone, *Sidney's Poetry: Contexts and Interpretations* (Cambridge: Harvard University Press, 1965), 114.

38. *Epigrams* 6.29.8, translated (awkwardly) as "To unwonted worth comes life but short, and rarely old age," in Martial, *Epigrams*, trans. Walter C. A. Ker, Loeb Classical Library (Cambridge: Harvard University Press, 1968), 1:374–75. I am not claiming that Petrarch knew this poem but am using it, rather, as an illustration of a widespread classical topos. Petrarch certainly knew some of Martial's poetry, but how much is unclear. See Guido Martellotti, "Petrarca e Marziale," *Rivista di Cultura Classica e Medioevale* 2 (1960): 388–93.

39. Greene's darkening of Petrarch's poetry (see note 35 above) is quite clear in his treatment of this final line of "Quel rosigniuol." Greene says, "The closing line will deny that any earthly thing pleases" (123). But the line does not deny that. It denies that any earthly thing *that pleases*

Yet, in the face of this recognition, Petrarch does not turn to the transcendental. While he does see Laura's death in Platonic terms, as untying the "knot" that links soul to body, he almost never full-throatedly celebrates this untying, and he never denigrates the body. When, in the sonnet "O misera et orribil visione!" (poem 251), Petrarch is trying, as in "Chi vuol veder," to prepare himself for Laura's death, he speaks of the possibility that she has exited from "her lovely inn" (*uscita . . . del bell'albergo*). Whenever he speaks of Laura's inanimate body, Petrarch always, as here, softens the Platonic ontology with a positive adjective. Even when he uses the body-as-prison metaphor, for example in poem 306, the very Dantescan sonnet "Quel sol che mi monstrava il cammin destro" (That sun which showed me the right way [to go to heaven]), Petrarch presents Laura's body as both "her terrestrial prison" (*'l suo carcer terrestro*) and "my light" (*'l mio lume*). Petrarch uses the prison image most emphatically for Laura's body in poem 325, the canzone "Tacer non posso" (I cannot be silent), yet her body there is "the beautiful prison" (*la bella pregione*) in line 9 and "that beautiful earthly prison of hers" (*quel suo bel carcere terreno*) in line 101.[40] In a sonnet on what death has done in taking Laura (poem 283), Petrarch describes death as having loosed Laura's ardently virtuous soul from "the most charming and most beautiful knot" (line 4).[41] In poem 300, the passionate sonnet "Quanta invidia io ti porto, avara terre" (How I envy you, greedy earth), Petrarch envies everything that has contact with Laura after her death; in the octave, he envies the greedy earth that embraces her body, and heaven which, just as *cupidamente*, gathered to itself Laura's spirit, "freed from her beautiful members" (*de le belle membra sciolta*). Poem 301, another sonnet—"Valle che de' lamenti miei se' piena" (Valley, full of my laments)—builds on the appreciation of the preceding poem for "the beautiful members" from which Laura's spirit has been freed. Here Petrarch returns to the place of Laura's death, "whence she went naked to Heaven" (*ond'al Ciel*

---

also endures. So committed is Greene to denying the presence of pleasure in the line that he later misquotes it (125) by leaving the reference to pleasure out (*Nulla qua giù dura* rather than *nulla qua giù diletta et dura*).

40. Here I disagree with the comments on this image in Petrie, *Petrarch*, 55. I would argue, moreover, that even when Petrarch uses the image to refer to his own body, he generally uses it remarkably gently, as in poem 32, in which "this hard and heavy earthly burden" (*'l duro et greve / terreno encarco*) melts like snow (lines 6–7), and poem 349, in which "the earthly prison" quickly turns into a "heavy garment" (lines 9–11). Unsurprisingly, lines 6–8 of "I' vo pensando," discussed above, are an exception.

41. Durling's addition of "bodily" before "knot" here seems clarifying, but is actually misleading. The Italian does not include such a word.

nuda è gita [line 13]). But instead of celebrating and ending on this celestial nudity, the final line salutes what Laura left behind—"her beautiful vesture" (*lasciando in terra la sua bella spoglia* [line 14]).

For the most part, Petrarch does not present the "naked" soul as beautiful—poem 278, with its oddly erotic presentation of bodilessness, is an exception. In that canzone, "Che debb'io far" (What shall I do?), Laura's invisible form is in Paradise, set free—not from a loathsome sink, but rather, in a phrase that captures both physicality and temporality, "from the veil that here shadowed the flower of her years" (*di quel velo / che qui fece ombra al fior degli anni suoi*). Moreover, the truly consoling thought is the Pauline, anti-Platonic one that Laura "will be clothed with it [this veil, her body] another time" (*per rivestersen poi / un'altra volta*). In poem 302, "Levommi il mio penser" (My thought lifted me up)—the sonnet that follows "Valle che de' lamenti miei se' piena"—Petrarch imagines Laura in heaven. There she is presented as saying that although she experiences a well-being that cannot be held by the human intellect (*Mio ben non cape in intelleto umano*), she is nonetheless waiting for two things: for Petrarch himself (*te solo aspetto*), "and for that which you loved so much, and which remained down there, my lovely veil" (*quel che tanto amasti / et là giuso è rimaso, il mio bel velo*)—which apparently she also misses.

Petrarch's task as a poet is to celebrate, even after her death, Laura's earthly existence. Poem 282, a sonnet celebrating Laura's constant postmortem "returns" to Petrarch, makes it clear that what he values in these returns are the earthly signs by which he knows her—her walk, her voice, her face, even her clothing (line 14).[42] "Che debb'io far" (poem 268), in which we have already seen Petrarch's commitment to Laura's reincarnation, ends with the poet imagining Love telling him "not to extinguish" Laura's fame, "which sounds in many places still by your tongue." Unlike what Apollo tells the young Milton in "Lycidas," fame, for Petrarch, is an earthly matter, defended as such by Franciscus in the *Secretum* (87) and presented similarly in "I' vo pensando" (lines 66–67).[43] In a specifically autobiographical sonnet (poem 308), Petrarch

42. Ramie Targoff writes of this poem, which begins by speaking of how Laura often returns to console Petrarch with her eyes, "lest we imagine her posthumous form has been reduced to a set of eyes, he describes his encounter with her as if she were still embodied" ("Passion," in Cummings and Simpson, *Cultural Reformations*, 618 [see intro., n. 24]). Targoff, however, does not focus on the antitranscendental element in the *Rime* because her aim is to contrast Petrarch with Wyatt and the whole lyric tradition of the English Renaissance (632–34).

43. See Jacob Burckhardt, "The Modern Idea of Fame," in *The Civilization of the Renaissance*, 1:151–62 (see intro., n. 2), and the discussion in Kerrigan and Braden, *The Idea of the*

sees his (unachievable) poetic goal as quite literally incarnational—"nor with my style her beautiful face can I incarnate" (*né col mio stile il suo bel viso incarno* [line 8]). The best he can do is to shadow forth (*ombreggiare*) some of Laura's earthly virtues. Her divine part (*divina parte*) is entirely beyond him—"there fails my daring, my wit, and my art" (*ivi manca l'ardir, l'ingegno, et l'arte*). In another late sonnet, poem 345, Petrarch rebukes himself for missing Laura on earth; he tries to take consolation in her heavenly existence, knowing that "her being in Heaven ought to quiet my cruel state" (lines 5–6). But the only way in which he can find consolation and become calm is through seeing Laura there with his internal eye (*con l'occhio interno*) as "more beautiful than ever" (*piu bella che mai*).

One of the final poems in the sequence is a visionary canzone (poem 359) in which Petrarch imagines the beatified Laura sitting "on the left side of [his] bed" (a placement that is surely significant). Laura rebukes Petrarch for his inability—or rather, his unwillingness—to focus on her life in heaven: "Does it displease you so much that I have left this misery . . . ?" She urges him to use the wings of his soul, and to leave his poetry behind. But the poetry is here characterized in one of those oddly positive Platonic formulations—"these sweet deceptive chatterings of yours" (*queste dolci tue fallaci ciance*).[44] In imagining this colloquy, Petrarch sees himself as still admiring and bound by the "golden knot" (*l'aureo nodo*) of Laura's hair. She explains to him that she is a naked spirit (*Spirito ignudo sono*), and that what he has admired so much, and continues to admire, has been dust for years, yet "to help you from your troubles, it is given to me to seem such"—that is, to appear to him in her bodily form (lines 60–63a). Petrarch can only be comforted by a vision of Laura clothed in her body—which, as "she" points out, she will be again, and again, more beautiful than ever (*et ancor quella / sarò più che mai bella*) (lines 63–64).

The final poem of the sequence (poem 366), is a prayer to the Virgin to free Petrarch from his devotion to *mortal belezza* (line 85); yet in lines 121–22, he offers as his most promising feature his ability "to love with such a marvelous faith a bit of frail mortal earth" (*poca mortal terra caduca / amar con si mira-*

Renaissance, 19–34 (see intro., n. 7). For "Lycidas," lines 70–84, on fame as "no plant that grows on mortal soil," see Milton, *Complete Poems* (see intro., n. 59).

44. On the attitude toward poetry here, see Brenda Deen Schildgen, "Overcoming Augustinian Dichotomies in Defense of the Laurel in Canzoni 359 and 360 of the *Rime sparse*," *Modern Language Notes* 111 (1996): 149–63. Schildgen emphasizes the irresolvability of the dispute with "the Augustinian exemplar" in these closing poems of the sequence (162–63).

bile fede).[45] But what Petrarch really wanted—as the postmortem poems 315–17 (all sonnets) made clear, and as poem 12 (another sonnet) hoped for—was not to meet Laura in heaven, or even after the resurrection of their bodies, but to grow old with her on earth, with mortal bodies. He imagines them both with white hair, chatting amiably about his devotion to her, which would no longer make her afraid, his love having been freed from lust by the normal processes of nature. That is the vision of which he feels most cheated, and which neither heaven nor resurrection will be able to provide.[46]

"I AM THAT I AM"

With this picture of Petrarch's *Rime sparse* in mind, we can now approach Shakespeare's sonnets and see the continuities, as well as the differences, between these poems and Petrarch's. At times, the continuities are obvious. The sonnet numbered 106 in the Shakespeare collection,[47] "When in the chronicle of wasted time," is unproblematically Petrarchan; it celebrates the beauty of the beloved as appropriate to the powers of the poets and prophets of the past, powers that exceeded those of writers in the present (including the author)—though for Shakespeare the framework of the past writers is medieval rather than, in Petrarch's case, classical (see the *Rime*, poem 186, in which Homer and Vergil would have praised Laura, and poem 187, in which they are

45. I have departed from Durling's translation ("a bit of deciduous mortal dust"). On this final poem retaining "a residual justification" of Petrarch's love for Laura, see Kenelm Foster, "Beatrice or Medusa," in *Italian Studies Presented to E. R. Vincent*, ed. C. Brand, K. Foster, and U. Limentani (Cambridge: Heffer, 1962), 54.

46. I am greatly indebted to Lisa Barca, a Ph.D. student in Italian at the University of Chicago, who directed my attention to these three sonnets.

47. The role that Shakespeare played in the publication of the Quarto volume *Shake-speares Sonnets*, by Thomas Thorpe in 1609 is undetermined. The prevailing view has been that the sonnets were "pirated," but this has been challenged by Katherine Duncan-Jones in "Was the 1609 *Shake-speares Sonnets* Really Unauthorized?" *Review of English Studies*, n.s. 34 (1983): 151–71, and in her Arden edition of the sonnets (London: Thomas Nelson, 1997), 12–13, 31–41. Shakespeare's authorship of the sonnets that appear in the 1609 Quarto is widely accepted, the only ones in dispute being the two sonnets that appear last in the volume. The order of the sonnets in the 1609 Quarto may or may not be authorial, and so the arrangement of the volume has a very different status than that of Petrarch's volume. Unless otherwise noted, I have used, for my modernized text, the Duncan-Jones edition (though I have at times Americanized spellings); for the Quarto text, I have used the reproductions of the pages in *Shakespeare's Sonnets*, ed. Stephen Booth (New Haven: Yale University Press, 1978). These two editions of the sonnets are hereafter distinguished by the editors' names.

needed to do so). Even the "blasphemy" that Helen Vendler attributes to sonnet 106 "in secularizing Messianic prophecy" is matched or perhaps exceeded by Petrarch, who, in the fourth sonnet in the *Rime*, sees a direct parallel between the circumstances of Christ's birth and those of Laura's: "He, when he was born, did not bestow himself on Rome. . . . And now from a small village, He has given us a sun."[48]

Heather Dubrow has remarked that "anti-Petrarchism" is as difficult to define as "Petrarchism," and she shrewdly notes that the terms have a way of melding into each other.[49] It turns out that even some of the most obviously "anti-Petrarchan" poems in the volume of "Shake-speares sonnets" are, in some ways, deeply Petrarchan.[50] Sonnet 130, "My mistress' eyes are nothing like the sun," would seem to be a textbook case of "anti-Petrarchism." It refuses to apply to the person of the woman in question any of the standard descriptive hyperboles. The speaker presents himself as a determined and plain-speaking "realist"—as Cornwall says of Kent in *King Lear*, "he cannot flatter, he."[51] He knows what is what: "If snow be white, why then her breasts are dun." His tone seems to soften at the beginning of the second quatrain, where we get a moment of aesthetic appreciation: "I have seen roses damasked, red and white." But this sensibility is not applied to his mistress: "no such roses see I in her cheeks" (lines 5–6). "See I," with its spondaic structure and insistence on the speaker's distinctness, might suggest that another, less "tough-minded" viewer might indeed see roses in this woman's cheeks.[52] The poet then seems to turn from "realism" to denigration: "And in some perfumes there is more delight / Than in the breath that from my mistress reeks" (lines 7–8). The octave ends on a word that, despite the valiant efforts of various annotators, cannot, in its

48. Helen Vendler, *The Art of Shakespeare's Sonnets* (Cambridge: Harvard University Press, 1997), 451.

49. Dubrow, *Echoes of Desire*, 123–24.

50. Compare Donald L. Guss's claim with regard to Donne that "a number of themes whose charm was once attributed to their anti-Petrarchism, are now understood to be Petrarchan" (*John Donne, Petrarchist: Italianate Conceits and Love Theory in the "Songs and Sonnets"* [Detroit: Wayne State University Press, 1966], 22). Fineman cleverly prefers to use "para-Petrarchan" rather than "anti-Petrarchan" (*Shakespeare's Perjured Eye*, 29, and see note 1 above).

51. The parenthetical description is from Cornwall's brilliant parody of the exaggeratedly plain speaking that Kent adopts in his role as Caius. See *King Lear: A Parallel Text Edition*, ed. Weis (see chap. 1, n. 57), Q 2.2.90; F 2.2.92 (identical in both texts).

52. Vendler, *Shakespeare's Sonnets*, sees the poem as a whole as responding to some other hypothetical love sonnet (which she composes), but does not see the poem as establishing any distance from its speaker's self-characterization and self-valuation in the octave.

connection with breath and its emphatic placement, be perceived as anything but negative.[53]

The sestet, however, does not continue in this mode. It moves, for the first time, as Vendler notes, into the realm of affect, and it is entirely positive, almost naively so.[54] The speaker straightforwardly expresses "delight" in his mistress—"I love to hear her speak" (line 9a). We might now have to go back and revisit the opening of line 7. In the miasma of "reeks," we might well have overlooked "in *some* perfumes there is more delight." The critics, when they have noted this qualification, have tried to find ironies in it, but the plain meaning of the line is that while some perfumes provide more delight than the breath of the speaker's mistress does, some don't.[55] Her breath provides more delight than "some [other] perfumes." The point seems to be that love and appreciation do not require hyperboles or absolutes. That this is the meaning of the poem is fully established by the end of this quatrain and by the couplet, which is semantically continuous with the quatrain. The final negation of an absolute in the poem seems to be in direct dialogue with Petrarch's "Erano i capei d'oro" (poem 90). There, we recall, Petrarch said of his beloved, "Her walk was not that of a mortal thing." Shakespeare's speaker, continuing his "plain man" debater's mode, tells us "I grant I never saw a goddess go; / My mistress when she walks treads on the ground" (lines 11–12). But this speaker's point is not that his beloved is inferior, but that she is in fact quite special. He uses a word that comes close to asserting absolute value. His mistress is "as *rare* / As any she belied with false compare."[56] "False compare" has already been seriously critiqued in the sequence (see sonnet 35), but the point is that sonnet 130 is a love poem (Stephen Booth, who thinks the poem "a trifle," has to

---

53. Duncan-Jones's edition of the sonnets (130) provides the obvious analogue: Coriolanus's comparison of the breath of the multitude to "reek o' th' rotten fens." In his edition, Booth cautions the modern reader against reading "reeks" as we normally would, but then wisely notes that commentators often "over-caution modern readers" against experiencing the word as negative (454).

54. Vendler, *Shakespeare's Sonnets*, 557.

55. Booth sees the speaker's qualification giving the line "a tone of wry irony" (he does not say directed at what); Duncan-Jones argues that Shakespeare did not think that all perfumes were pleasant-smelling. Vendler entirely misses the qualification.

56. That "rare" is an extremely strong value term in Shakespeare is easily demonstrated. After Enobarbus's astonishing description of Cleopatra's self-presentation of the river Cydnus, Agrippa says, "O rare for Antony." The word is crucial to the romances. See, for instance, *Pericles*, ed. Suzanne Gossett (London: Thomson Learning, 2004), 3.3.103, 105; 5.1.152.

concede that it is a "winsome" one).[57] When we put this poem in the context of Petrarch's treatment of mortal things, and of Petrarch's own recantation in the nightingale sonnet ("Quel rosigniuol," poem 311) of "Her walk was not that of a mortal thing"—"I did not believe that Death reigns over goddesses"—we can see Shakespeare's sonnet 130 as continuing Petrarch's stress on what it means for his beloved to be a "mortal thing."

The continuity is deeper in Shakespeare's sonnets numbered 104 and 108. These sonnets pick up on the most extraordinary moment in "Erano i capei d'oro," the ending in which, as we have seen, Petrarch, having allowed himself the thought that Laura may not be, in the present, as she was in the epiphanic moment evoked in the first twelve lines of the sonnet (*se non fosse or tale*), then dismisses this thought as irrelevant, for "a wound is not healed by loosening of the bow." Shakespeare fully develops the idea that his beloved is "a beautiful mortal thing" (recall Petrarch's "Chi vuol veder," poem 248). Shakespeare's sonnet "To me, fair friend, you never can be old" (numbered 104) echoes Petrarch's habit of precisely recording the time that has elapsed between the onset of the speaker's love for the beloved and the moment of the poem's composition: "Three winters cold . . . three beauteous springs."[58] But sonnet 104 is distinctively Shakespearean in its grand sense of natural development—"process of the seasons"[59]—and, in the sestet, in its evocation of the uncanny way that time seems both to move and to stand still: "Ah yet doth beauty, like a dial hand, / Steal from his figure, and no pace perceived." The poem ends with a gesture like that on which Petrarch's "Chi vuol veder" ends, addressing persons who may miss (in Petrarch) and who definitely will miss (in Shakespeare) the beloved in full bloom—or, in Shakespeare, almost in full bloom, since "yet art green" suggests the last moment of youth (late summer).[60]

In "What's in the brain that ink may character" (numbered 108), Shake-

57. Booth, *Sonnets*, 452.

58. For poems in the *Rime* that do this, see numbers 30 (seven years), 62 (eleven years), 79 (fourteen years), 118 (sixteen years), 122 (seventeen years), 212 and 221 (twenty years), 364 (twenty-one years up to her death; ten years since).

59. On the way in which Shakespeare's sonnets open up grand cosmic vistas, see C. S. Lewis, *English Literature in the Sixteenth Century Excluding Drama* (Oxford: Clarendon, 1954): "In Shakespeare each experience of the lover becomes a window through which we look out on immense prospects" (549). Lewis is contrasting this movement of mind with what he finds in Donne's greatest (love) lyrics, in which the movement of mind is "centripetal."

60. The difference in the temporal distances from the present imagined for the generalized audiences of Petrarch's entire poem and Shakespeare's couplet, Petrarch's short—it is possible to "come in time" (*s'arriva a tempo*), and Shakespeare's long ("Ere you were born")—accounts

speare focuses not on the poignancy of the beloved's beauty but on the ability of love to maintain the illusion of the permanence of this beauty, an idea that was prefigured in line 11 of sonnet 104, "your sweet hue, which methinks still doth stand," with its prominent "methinks" and its pun on "still." The octave of "What's in the brain that ink may character" figures timelessness in terms of repetition—the poet has no "new" things to say to his beloved (Vendler's postulation of the beloved's demand for novelty may be helpful, but may also give to the opening quatrain a petulant tone rather than the meditative one that seems equally possible).[61] The analogue to the timeless repetitiveness of love-language ("thou mine, I thine," line 7b) is that of religious ritual (perhaps suggested by "merit" in line 4). The permanence of what one prays for ("like prayers divine," line 5b) allows for the mental state, in its context, of "Counting no old thing old" (line 7a). The sestet, picking up on the continuity of the erotic and the religious asserted in "hallowed thy fair name" in the final line of the octave, applies the idea of an "old thing" not being "counted" as such to the physical being of the beloved.

Pretending to complete sequaciousness (which may be true, emotionally), the sestet begins: "So that eternal love, in love's fresh case, / Weighs not the dust and injury of age." Enduring love has its own mystical body that remains permanently "fresh" (taking "case" to mean something like "external appearance"), and it sustains what sonnet 65—now taking "case" in its legal sense— calls the "action" of beauty against the "injury of age" by not considering the evidence ("Weighs not the dust," line 10). But, of course, this evidence is there, and the point is not to deny its existence but rather to assert the loving mind's refusal to take this evidence into account or, as the next line suggests, to give it any "place," that is, honor, or to decide the "case" in its favor. "Nor gives to necessary wrinkles place" is a line in which the key phrase, "necessary wrinkles," combines realism with tenderness in a way related to but much deeper than that taken in sonnet 130.[62] The next line, finishing the third quatrain, goes further, and instead of merely ignoring "age," transforms it and "makes

---

for the plangent urgency of Petrarch's sonnet as compared with the defiant fatalism of Shakespeare's.

61. Vendler, *Shakespeare's Sonnets*, 460.

62. The social meaning of "giving place" is stressed by Colin Burrow in his edition of William Shakespeare, *The Complete Sonnets and Poems* (Oxford: Oxford University Press, 2002), 596; in his edition, Booth (350) suggests the legal meaning. Vendler (*Shakespeare's Sonnets*, 461) takes "necessary" here to mean "fated;" but I think that the valence of the word here is exactly as we find it in *The Merchant of Venice*, ed. John Russell Brown (London: Methuen, 1955),

antiquity for aye his page" (line 12)—permanently transforming the codger into an aristocratic youth.[63] The first line of the couplet explains how "eternal love" does this: "Finding the first conceit of love there [in antiquity] bred," it hearkens back to the past, to the moment when the sight of the beloved first entered the poet's consciousness. But the final line of the poem redescribes the operation. Instead of "there" referring backward to "antiquity," it refers forward: "Where time and outward form would show it dead." Eternal love finds in the body of the beloved "the first conceit of love," despite what physical reality would show.

Assertion of the power of the lover's mind to contradict or contravene external reality is one of Petrarch's great themes, as in "Di pensier in pensier" (poem 129), and it is developed by Shakespeare in ways that show both the continuities and the differences between the poets. "Since I left you, mine eye is in my mind" (sonnet 113) develops the Petrarchan motif directly. Whatever external things the poet's eye takes in, he tells the beloved, the poet's mind "shapes them to your feature" (line 12). As does Petrarch's in "Di pensier in pensier," Shakespeare's soul "approves its own deception": "My most true mind thus makes mine eye untrue" (line 14).[64] The sonnet (114) that follows "Since I left you" continues with some self-mockery—"my great mind most kingly drinks it up"—this approving stance, echoing Petrarch's praise of "sweet poison" in "Ben mi credea" (poem 207, line 84).

The approving stance toward the power of the "true mind" over reality culminates in the famous sonnet 116: "Let me not to the marriage of true minds / Admit impediments."[65] This expository sonnet (not a Petrarchan mode) has caused a great deal of critical confusion, since its opening praise of mutual-

---

4.1.55—"a harmless necessary cat"—in which the word is neutral (or even positive) rather than negative.

63. There is certainly a pun on "page" here, but I am not sure how to read the line in terms of that secondary meaning. Perhaps Vendler is correct that it would mean that the poet draws upon the great timeless exemplars of past love poetry.

64. There is a textual crux here. In the 1609 Quarto, the final line of sonnet 113 reads, "My most true minde thus maketh mine untrue." Most editors since Malone have emended as in my text above—adding "eye" after "mine," and changing "maketh" to "makes"—but Booth cleverly changes "mine" to "m'eyne," thus getting the meaning of the emendation while keeping the sound of the line as it is in the 1609 Quarto, while Duncan-Jones prints the line (in modern spelling) just as it appears in the Quarto. I think the emendation is justified by the logic of the poem (contrasting eye and mind), and that Booth's suggestion is too clever by half.

65. As Booth explains (384), this sonnet appears between 115 and 117 in the thirteen surviving copies of the 1609 Quarto, but in twelve of these, it is misnumbered 119.

ity seems to be inconsistent with the rest of its development, which praises autonomous and self-contained constancy in the face of all possible sorts of change. This problem disappears, however, when one recognizes that the poem is, throughout, a philosophical account of the nature of the "true mind" in love. The plural of the opening line does not refer to two persons in a relationship but rather to how all persons of a certain sort ("true minds") conduct themselves in love; it is not, despite how the famous opening line and a half sounds, about how such persons love each other.[66] Shakespeare seems to want to trick us into thinking that the poem is a simpler and more easily adoptable statement than it in fact is (why Shakespeare wants to do this is a deep and interesting question).[67]

In context and on rereading, "Let me not to the marriage of true minds" should be seen as a grander, more "credal" version of "What's in the brain that ink may character." The third quatrain of sonnet 116, focusing as it does on "rosy lips and cheeks" (line 9), is entirely familiar. The difficulty is in the ringing second half of the opening quatrain. Here the "alteration" that the poem discounts seems to be behavioral as well as physical. The love felt by a person of "true mind" not only does not "alter when it alteration finds" but also does not "bend with the remover to remove" (lines 3–4). It withstands betrayal as well as physical deterioration, emotional as well as physical change.[68] The second quatrain seems to forget the issue of betrayal and simply to provide an image of constancy in an emotionally unstable environment; the "true mind" is a sea mark, "an ever-fixed mark," and has the detachment of the Lucretian sage who famously (and happily) "looks on tempests" and wanderings "and is never shaken."[69] The very difficult final lines of this quatrain, meditating on

---

66. Braden is, I think, getting at this when he notes that "the true minds being celebrated are not necessarily marrying each other" ("Shakespeare's Petrarchism," 175).

67. Booth's puzzlement about this (387–90) seems to me utterly appropriate.

68. Propertius, in *Elegies* 2.9A.43–44, enacts this position, but does not theorize it: "No one in all my life has ever been dearer to me than you; nor will anyone be so now, for all your unkindness to me" (*te nihil in vita nobis acceptius umquam: / nunc quoque erit, quamvis sis inimica, nihil*). See *Propertius Elegies*, ed. and trans. G. Goold, Loeb Classical Library (Cambridge: Harvard University Press, 1990). I am not claiming this is an influence, only an analogue, since it is unlikely that Shakespeare knew Propertius's poetry. But the connection is intriguing.

69. Lucretius, *De Rerum Natura* 2.1–19, trans. W. H. D. Rouse, rev. Martin F. Smith, Loeb Classical Library (Cambridge: Harvard University Press, 1992). Whether the speaker of the sonnet feels the kind of *joie* here (*Suave . . . suave . . . nil dulcius*) that the Lucretian sage does is a very interesting question. That he does so might account for some of the extreme rhetorical confidence of the speaker.

the image of "the star to every wand'ring bark," are, to paraphrase Stephen Booth, perfectly clear until one asks what they actually mean. They seem to be returning to imagining the true (faithful, integral) in relation to the untrue (unreliable, betraying).

The picture seems to be that—as in the image of the compass in Donne's "A Valediction: Forbidding Mourning"—in every such relationship, the "wand'ring" figure somehow remains dependent on the constancy of the "true" one. In Shakespeare's poem, the faithful partner of a philandering one seems, given the opening lines, to be the relevant model.[70] The "true mind" turns Stoical in a Christian context, and "bears it out even to the edge of doom" (line 12). The final couplet—"If this be error, and upon me proved, / I never writ, nor no man ever loved"—is to be seen, I think, as an act of defiance against anyone who would deny the difference between the true and the untrue mind: "error" is, after all, the same as "wand'ring." "Upon me proved" is to be seen, as Duncan-Jones partly suggests, in terms of trial by combat. "There's my gauntlet, I'll prove it on a giant" says Lear in his madness (4.6.89–90), but Shakespeare can also use the phrase seriously, as in the duel at the end of *King Lear*: "I'll prove it on thy heart," Albany says to Edmund, as does Edgar a bit later (5.3.90/135). This is the context that brings this sonnet, and especially this couplet, close to bombast.[71] But its special intensity can be seen to derive from the pressure that the particular kind of "alteration" imagined in the poem (along with the physical) brings to bear on the speaker. Changes in the "outward form" of one's beloved do not produce comparable pressures on the moral identity of the lover. Compare, for example, Emilia's discussion of this issue—of altering when one "alteration finds"—with Desdemona, who ends up, like the speaker of the sonnet, making a claim that sounds like "bluster": "Beshrew me if I would do such a wrong / For the whole world" (4.3.77–78). "Love's not Time's fool" regardless of what "time and outward form" show—or do.

The distinctive way that Shakespeare develops the "mind over matter" theme—a basis for Joel Fineman's claim for Shakespeare's uniqueness—seems to emerge in the sonnet beginning "In faith I do not love thee with mine eyes"

70. In making the analogy to Donne's poem, I do not mean to suggest that the departing lover in "A Valediction: Forbidding Mourning" is expecting to be unfaithful. He isn't ("Thy firmness makes my circle just"). But there is an oddness in him seeing himself as having to "obliquely run." Freccero's brilliant cosmological reading of the poem (see note 4 above) provides a coherent metaphysical context for this and many of the other unsettling moments in Donne's poem (especially the gender and geometrical confusions), but does not, to my mind, eliminate them.

71. Duncan-Jones thinks it crosses over; Booth thinks that it seems to but doesn't (or perhaps that it does so rhetorically, but not poetically).

(number 141). This line could open a sonnet like "What's in the brain" or "To me, fair friend." But "In faith I do not love thee with mine eyes" goes on to note not merely that the beloved is aging, but that the beloved is flawed. The poet's eyes "in thee a thousand errors note." These "errors" seem, once again, to be physical rather than moral. The poet loves what his eyes "despise" (line 3), and he insists, in the second quatrain of the octave, that not a single one of his senses (systematically enumerated) is pleased by his beloved. In this sonnet, however, the inner item that prevails over the senses is not the "mind" but the heart—" 'tis my heart that loves what they [mine eyes] despise." The sestet is entirely taken up with describing the hopelessly enslaved condition of "one foolish heart" (line 10). The hard question here is the speaker's attitude toward the picture of the self that he is providing in the poem. This sonnet is clearly not self-approving in the way "Since I left you mine eye is in my mind" and "Let me not to the marriage of true minds" are, but is it unequivocally self-hating? If so, it does break with Petrarch, who, as we have seen, always presents his self-condemnations ambivalently.

The question is whether Shakespeare always does so. "In faith I do not love thee with mine eyes" ends with the following couplet:

> Only my plague thus far I count my gain,
> When she that makes me sin awards me pain.

Obviously this is bitter, and plays off the appropriateness of "pain" to "sin"— the speaker is either in hell or in purgatory—but does the speaker accept his condition? Petrarch presents himself, in the *Rime*, as having lived most of his life in something like this condition. But his use of a verb like "awards" would not, as here, be sarcastic. Petrarch would have added his characteristic *dolce* to the mention of pain—that is probably the most prevalent of all his oxymorons—and Shakespeare does not. Yet are we, in reading the couplet of Shakespeare's sonnet, to forget that his heart "is pleased to dote" in line 4 of the sonnet? And the tone of the lines that constitute the "turn" of the sonnet— "But my five wits, nor my five senses can/Dissuade one foolish heart from loving thee" (lines 9–10)—is at least indulgent, if not approving; it is certainly not straightforwardly self-condemnatory.[72]

72. My colleague Robert von Hallberg, who is working on the relation between "high" poetry and popular-song lyrics in the twentieth century, has pointed out to me that the history of the phrase "foolish heart" bears out the "indulgent" reading. He notes that "the phrase was taken up by songwriters Ned Washington and Victor Young for a great tune, 'My Foolish Heart,'

The speaker of sonnet 148, "O me! what eyes hath love put in my head," pretends to be puzzled by the problem of subjective erotic perception, but drops the issue for a mock explanation in the sestet—tears distort "Love's eye"—and ends the poem with a couplet that seems to be truly bitter, both self- and other-reproaching: "with tears thou keep'st me blind,/Lest eyes, well seeing, thy foul faults will find." Yet the couplet begins, "O cunning love." Is it possible that the speaker actually, in some sense, admires this "cunning"? A poem that almost immediately follows this one returns to the puzzled mode—"O from what pow'r hast thou this pow'rful might . . . ?" (number 150). Here the speaker seems to accept as a fact that love has the power to overcome both sensory and moral perception, both to "give the lie to my true sight" (line 4) and to present as "becoming . . . things ill" (line 5).[73] After ten lines of questions—which start to become descriptive rather than interrogatory—the speaker seems to accept, although not happily, that he loves "what others do abhor" (line 11). This acceptance—if that is what it is—connects to Petrarch's most scathing self-analyses, as in "I' vo pensando" (poem 264). Again, the question is whether Shakespeare is able to transcend, or at least to complicate, self-loathing. The ending of "O from what pow'r" seems to do something of this sort. The couplet consists of this syllogism:

> If thy unworthiness raised love in me,
> More worthy I to be beloved of thee.

There is, of course, irony and bitterness here. But is there also a picture of some sort of community based on insufficiency and radically subjective vision, something like Folly's vision of sociality?[74]

The great sonnet " 'Tis better to be vile than vile esteem'd" (number 121) is one in which Shakespeare refuses to be abhorred, and militantly refuses to accept what and how "others" see. In this poem, it is the lover and not the beloved who is the object of the world's negative judgment, and in this poem, Shakespeare (or his "speaker") is able, as Lars Engle well puts it, to clear an

---

which was also the title tune for a successful 1949 movie." As he says, "the point is that later poets/lyricists have understood the line as indulgent or affectionate."

73. On Shakespeare's development of the idea of "things ill" as "becoming," see the discussion of *Antony and Cleopatra* in chapter 3 below.

74. On Folly and sociality, see chapter 1 above.

autonomous "evaluative space" for himself.[75] Petrarch had something of this autonomy—he flees the "Babylon" of the papal court, for example, in poem 114—but he never approximates the blasphemous boldness of "I am that I am" (sonnet 121, line 9a), where Shakespeare seems to be asserting a self beyond morality rather than merely a moral self.[76] But could Shakespeare establish such a realm in relation to his own moral judgments on himself, as opposed to repudiating the views of "others"?

The famous sonnet beginning "When my love swears that she is made of truth, / I do believe her" (number 138) seems to exist purely in the realm of moral and psychological self-loathing, but a closer reading reveals it to be more complex than that. All the best readers of this poem have seen this, and indeed, the most extended reading of this poem—and one of the best readings that exists of any of the sonnets—sees the poem as a great triumph of transcending negative judgment and establishing an autonomous evaluative space for an erotic relationship rather than for a militantly assertive self.[77] If this reading, that of Edward A. Snow, is correct, then the sonnet moves out of the Petrarchan dialectic or dynamic or impasse on the positive, so to speak, rather than the negative side. Given the way the sonnet has been taken—as unrelievedly dark on the one hand, or trivial on the other—one would certainly want to err, with Snow, on the side of humanity and acceptance. Nonetheless, I think it wrong

75. Lars Engle, "'I am that I am': Shakespeare's Sonnets and the Economy of Shame," in Schiffer, *Shakespeare's Sonnets*, 195; compare Vendler, *Shakespeare's Sonnets*, 515: "recognition of independent moral self-identity"—both contra Booth's attack on the line (410).

76. For the "beyond morality" idea, see chapter 3 below, along with G. Wilson Knight, *The Mutual Flame: On Shakespeare's Sonnets and 'The Phoenix and the Turtle'* (London: Methuen, 1955), 49–52. The blasphemy is in Shakespeare's appropriation of the astonishing verse in Exodus in which (depending on how one reads it) God either names or refuses to name himself (Exod. 3:14). For Shakespeare's use of this, see Harold Bloom, *How to Read and Why* (New York: Scribner, 2000), 113. Hilton Landry in *Interpretations in Shakespeare's Sonnets* (Berkeley: University of California Press, 1967), 92–93, pointed out a striking parallel between Shakespeare's "I am that I am" and the refrain and entire stance of a poem (probably) by Wyatt that Shakespeare may have had access to in manuscript. The poem in question begins, "I am as I am, and so will I be, / But how that I am none knoweth truly: / Be it evil, be it well, be I bond, be I free, / I am as I am, and so will I be" (Sir Thomas Wyatt, *Collected Poems*, ed. Joost Daalder [London: Oxford University Press, 1975], 179). I am not sure whether Wyatt is to be seen as playing off the Exodus passage.

77. I have in mind Christopher Ricks, "Lies," *Critical Inquiry* 2 (1975): 121–42; Booth's commentary in his edition of the sonnets, 476–481; and Edward A. Snow, "Loves of Comfort and Despair: A Reading of Shakespeare's Sonnet 138," *English Literary History* 47 (1980): 462–83.

to view the poem as an entirely positive presentation, in however complex and Montaignian a mode.[78] I think that this poem points us right back to Büdel's claim that Petrarch's great contribution to the love tradition is "to acknowledge illusion and consciously live by it—even though he clearly perceives it as self-deception."[79] The poem is not about a "Petrarchan" relationship, but it is fully in the Petrarchan mode. It presents *errore* as in some sense *dolce*, but, as Yeats would say, not without vacillation.

Where Snow and Booth are clearly right is that this sonnet is focused fully on a relationship, and not on an individual psyche—or rather, as we will see, it focuses on a relationship as happening between parallel and complexly self-conscious psyches. That is its extraordinary achievement. The tone of the opening line and a half of the sonnet is extremely difficult to capture. The hyperbolic nature of the action and asseveration described—"swears . . . is made of truth"—seems to point toward comedy, or a kind of amused indulgence (especially with regard to "my love"), as does the speaker's reported regular response, "I do believe her," which is, as Snow says, "closer to a pledge or an enactment than a passive acceptance."[80] On the other hand, these lines could register disgust. The conclusion of the second line intensifies the problem, making the psychological situation even more complicated—"though I know she lies." "Know" is very strongly stressed here, and seems to move the line toward serious self-critique. We are given a picture of a radically divided consciousness, in which belief functions entirely independently of knowledge—indeed, as perhaps in some religious contexts, in the face of it. Knowledge seems to be empirical, where belief seems to be something else. But the contrast is very strong, and the paradox emphasized. The situation is more complicated, if perhaps less painful, than that described in sonnet 93: "So shall I live, supposing thou art true, / Like a deceived husband."[81]

---

78. For the analogy with Montaigne, see Snow, "Loves of Comfort and Despair," 462 (epigraph), 473. Snow's major analogy, however, is with *Antony and Cleopatra*, which I believe he reads correctly (471). Our disagreement is about the extent of the overlap between the sonnet and the play, not about the play.

79. Büdel, "Illusion Disabused," 129.

80. Snow, "Loves of Comfort and Despair," 465.

81. Another sonnet that should be considered in relation to 138 is sonnet 72, also about lying. The relation between 72 and 138 is remarkably interesting and complex. Sonnet 72 is, on the face of it, an argument against any sort of "virtuous lie" (line 5), since it associates lying with shaming oneself and with love unmotivated by the merit of its object. But the argument is so weak that it could easily be turned into support for its opposite, especially when the poem

Snow is surely right that to eliminate the paradox in the second line of sonnet 138 by glossing "I do believe" as "I do pretend to believe" is to fail to confront what the line is saying.[82] As Fineman remarks, the odd thing about the sonnet is that "it seems to mean precisely what it says."[83] The second half of the opening quatrain seems, however, to eliminate the paradox itself by treating the speaker's mental act as if it were a mere rhetorical ploy—"That she might think me some untutored youth / Unlearned in the world's false subtleties" (lines 3–4). If, however, we treat these lines as fully continuous with "I do believe her," rather than as undercutting this assertion, then we can see the entire quatrain as giving a picture of the speaker's mental state in the situation described. "That she might think" directly modifies "I do believe"—this is still within the mind of the speaker. This is the motive for the speaker's belief; it is internal to it, so to speak. We are still in the world of psychology, not of rhetoric. Lines 3 and 4 give us the core fantasy of the quatrain. The emphasis in the lines is not on the speaker wanting to be thought young as on his wanting to be thought naive—"untutored . . . Unlearned"—where naiveté means innocence, not knowing the serpentine, "the world's false subtleties."[84] He wants to be someone who does not have to ignore knowledge to have belief.

One of the strange and interesting features of the picture presented in this opening quatrain is that what is imagined in it is a meeting of minds, if not exactly of "true" ones: "I do believe . . . That she might think." Mental states, emotional and epistemological ones, seem to influence one another directly. After the initial "swearing," no verbal action is mentioned. This emphasis on "mind-meld" is continued in the next quatrain, where the way the speaker presents himself—"Thus vainly thinking that she thinks me young" (line 5)— shows "thinking" on both sides to be the activity in question. "Thinking" here turns out to be part of what we might call "normal" epistemology. It connects directly to knowing. The speaker "vainly thinks" (arrogantly, but mostly uselessly) that his partner shares or accepts his fantasy because "she knows my

---

makes it clear that the space that one would be occupying in accepting the argument would be that of "niggard truth" (line 8).

82. Snow, "Loves of Comfort and Despair," 472, and his notes 11 and 13. I am not sure, however, that the distinction that Snow insists on—between believing an assertion by a person and believing a person (implicitly, "I do believe her" versus "I do believe it") is as sharp as he wishes it to be. Invoking this distinction might actually function as another way of softening "I do believe."

83. Fineman, *Shakespeare's Perjured Eye*, 166.

84. I think that to see a possible positive dimension in "subtleties" here, as Snow does ("Loves of Comfort and Despair," 469), is mistaken.

days are past the best" (line 6). The beloved is in exactly the same epistemological and psychological state that the speaker presented himself inhabiting in
line 2—she "knows" something unambiguously, and yet that does not seem to
matter. Belief, the key term, is not mentioned here, but returns in the next line,
when the speaker returns to his own state of mind, "Simply I credit her false
speaking tongue" (line 7), and continues to enact his fantasy of innocence.[85]

What has become clear now, where the participants' consciousnesses have
been essentially equated—as Snow says, "somewhere in the course of the first
six lines we lose our sense of which side of the relationship we are on"[86]—is that
the participants' fantasies are logically and psychologically interrelated. If her
fantasy comes true, his does, and vice versa: in order for her fantasy of being
believed to come true, the speaker must enact his fantasy of being innocent—
which turns out to be the same fantasy as hers. Instead, however, of celebrating
this as achieved mutuality (as Snow does), the speaker moves outside of the
participants' consciousness(es) and presents it as complicity: "On both sides
thus is simple truth suppressed" (line 8). The speaker's simplicity is revealed
to be an artifice. The content of the line is damning, but its tone seems more
reportorial than judgmental. I do not, with Snow, think that the line means to
contrast simple with more complex truth, but I do think that it means to be
stating the "simple truth"-something that we can truly "know." The octave
comes to rest on the outside perspective ("the view from nowhere"), as if the
speaker were not a participant.[87]

An interesting feature of this description however, and part of what keeps
it from being as damning as it might be, is that it presents the participants not
as denying the truth, but rather as suppressing it—their crime, so to speak (if
that is what it is), is a social and ethical one, not a deep epistemological one.
The oddly exterior perspective continues at the beginning of the sestet, as does
the social/behavioral focus. The speaker, suddenly assuming the position of a
Martian, is concerned now not with what the lovers think but with what they
say (or do not say); he purports (like one of Swift's Houyhnhnms) to be unable

---

85. I have eliminated the hyphen between "false" and "speaking" here that all modern editors that I know of insert. The hyphen (not in the original) seems to me to eliminate an important
ambiguity. "Simply I credit her false" seems to me to make perfect sense—and to reiterate the
substance of the opening quatrain—before we get to "speaking" and have to reorient the syntax.
Eliminating the hyphen also has the value of keeping "false" and "speaking" as two separate
qualities.

86. Snow, "Loves of Comfort and Despair," 470.

87. See Thomas Nagel, *The View from Nowhere* (New York: Oxford University Press,
1986).

to understand "saying the thing which is not" (or not saying the thing which is): "But wherefore says she not she is unjust? / And wherefore say not I that I am old?" (lines 9–10). The second half of the quatrain returns, as it must, to human reality, but it does so in an extremely complex way. Instead of coming out with something like T. S. Eliot's "human kind / Cannot bear very much reality"[88]—which is obviously the point—the speaker's declaration, here an exclamation, is a generalization about love-relationships: "O love's best habit is in seeming trust" (line 11).

The strong pun on "habit" is startling here—the language of the poem has been quite straightforward so far (the pun on "vainly" is very weak)—and one truly does not know how to take it. Both meanings seem equally apt—love's best way of appearing and love's best kind of long-term behavior. But since the meanings run together, the question the phrase immediately raises is not about itself but about what the implied contrast is. What is love's worst habit? The answer, in context (and perhaps in general) would seem to be something like suspicion or jealousy, nonbelief. But the explication the poem offers for "love's best habit" is not trust but the appearance of it ("seeming trust"). Again the implied contrast is pressing: why not actual trust? I think that the answer here is that the sestet has given up on the kind of internal knowledge that the octave displayed. "Seeming trust," behavior, is all that is available to this perspective (just as love without any "habit" is unavailable to it). The line seems to accept psychological opacity—again, with a kind of lucid calmness that invokes but stays just on the hither side of moral judgment. The final line of the quatrain comes back to a simpler point—"age in love loves not t' have years told"—and makes it seem as if the previous line referred to the woman (wanting to be deemed trustworthy) just as this line refers to the speaker. But the complexity has already been introduced, and the final line of the third quatrain returns to the issue of suppression, of the importance of what is not said (and perhaps thought, since the mild pun on "told" allows for the meaning of "counted" as well as "spoken").[89]

The couplet introduces the biggest surprise in the poem: "Therefore I lie with her, and she with me" (line 13). Everything in the poem has led us to expect "Therefore I lie to her, and she to me." The sexual pun on "lies" has not previously been activated, and I think it is important to see how thoroughly this pun reorients the poem (to see sexual meanings earlier, as Booth very

88. *Four Quartets*, "Burnt Norton," lines 44–45, in T. S. Eliot, *Collected Poems, 1909–1962* (New York: Oxford University Press, 1970), 176.

89. Booth notes this pun in his edition of the sonnets (480).

characteristically does, and as other critics have followed him in doing, seems to me to diminish the force and calculated development of the poem).[90] Suddenly the relationship between the lovers is sexual as well as mental and verbal. And as Christopher Ricks has so brilliantly shown, "lying with" does not map directly onto "lying to." As Ricks says, the lie/lie pun "disconcerts, while it nevertheless does not simply overturn or deny, the widespread association of the upright with the strong and good, and of the prostrate or supine with the weak and bad."[91] The sexual meaning seems, perhaps oddly, to eliminate the moral dimension of the word. One cannot, after all, make a direct moral judgment on a physical posture. And the line, as Booth and Snow both note, emphasizes the mutuality of the couple that the octave had presented in so complex and compromised a psychological, epistemological, and ethical fashion.

This line seems to have something of the celebratory quality that Snow sees in it—the release from the verbal and mental seems powerful—but the final line of the sonnet returns to the ethical, the verbal, and the psychological: "And in our faults by lies we flattered be." "Our faults" perhaps has a physical dimension comparable to that in "lie with," but if this is present in the line, it tends to move it in the direction of disgust rather than of acceptance or neutrality. As Janet Adelman and others have noted (though, surprisingly, Booth does not), "fault" was both "a slang term for the female genitals"—which would interestingly make the sonnet an imaginatively lesbian one (not at all impossible)—and could also "carry the more general suggestion of sexual intercourse" (with the French *foutre* playing into it).[92] Here the moral and the physical do seem to coincide, since the sexual use is always negative. And "by lies" brings us back to the unrelenting plainness of line 8. The poem thus seems to be tipping, in its final moment, toward the unequivocal condemnation of both self and other, the blended unit ("our faults")—a condemnation that it has been working to

90. One might think that the effect I have described would be available only on a first reading of the poem, that on rereading, once one had gotten to the pun in line 13, one would then read it into line 2. But I do not think that this is inevitable, since line 2 insists very strongly on the verbal rather than the sexual meaning of "she lies."

91. Ricks, "Lies," 131.

92. Janet Adelman, *Suffocating Mothers: Fantasies of Maternal Origin in Shakespeare's Plays, "Hamlet" to "The Tempest"* (New York: Routledge, 1992), 252n26, and elsewhere (see her subject index). On sexual lability (or, if there is a difference, imagined sexual lability) in the sonnets, see, inter alia, Bruce R. Smith, "I, You, He, She, and We: On the Sexual Politics of Shakespeare's Sonnets," in Schiffer, *Shakespeare's Sonnets*, 411–29, and also in Schiffer, Naomi J. Miller's "Playing 'the Mother's Part': Shakespeare Sonnets and Early Modern Codes of Maternity," 347–67.

avoid, defuse, or mitigate all along. But the penultimate word seems to soften this, and to move us into a realm close to Petrarch's—recall "Laura's" characterization of Petrarch's poetry as "these sweet deceptive chatterings of yours" (poem 359, line 41). "Flattered" is something of a surprise here. We were surely expecting something harsher, something like "smothered" in the *Passionate Pilgrim* version: "Since that our faults in love thus smother'd be."[93]

"Flattered," moreover, is not merely a softer and less violent word than "smothered"; flattery, in various nominal and verbal forms, has played a number of roles in the sonnets. It has been used in contexts of purely negative self-deception, as it is here and perhaps in sonnet 114, which speaks of "the monarch's plague, this flattery" (line 2), and develops this conceit with nonhumorous self-mockery in lines 9–10: " 'tis flattery in my seeing, / And my great mind most kingly drinks it up." But the word is also used in the context of providing genuine beauty: "Full many a glorious morning have I seen / Flatter the mountain tops with sovereign eye" (sonnet 33). And, perhaps most hauntingly, the word is used in the evocation of a joy that is brief and delusive, but potent while it lasts:

> Thus have I had thee as a dream doth flatter:
> In sleep a king, but waking no such matter.
>   (sonnet 87, lines 13–14)

"As a dream doth flatter"—this resonates with Petrarch's sense, in *Rime* 1, that all earthly joy is like this: *quanto piace al mondo è breve sogno*. So, to return to the final couplet of sonnet 138, these lines on "lying with" and being "flattered" may point to some genuine accommodation with the human condition.[94]

---

93. "When my love swears that she is made of truth" is one of two sonnets in the 1609 volume that was published earlier, and in a different version. It appeared, with a version of "Two loves I have, of comfort and despair" (number 144 in 1609) and with two sonnets and a lyric from *Love's Labor's Lost* (and fifteen non-Shakespearean poems) in an octavo volume published in 1599 by William Jaggard entitled *The Passionate Pilgrime*, and said on its title page to be entirely by "W. Shakespeare." For the 1599 versions of the two sonnets that appear in altered form in 1609, see Booth's edition, 476–77 and 496. It should be noted that in the final line of the 1599 version, the aural pun on "mothered"—where "thus smothered" absorbs the initial "s" of "smothered"—might itself mitigate the harshness of this line, and be another psychologically deep pun. On the presence and meaning of mothering in the sonnets, see again Miller, "Playing 'the Mother's Part.'"

94. Snow notes that "flattered" comes "as a final clinching grace," but does not offer much by way of analytical support for this intuition ("Loves of Comfort and Despair," 478).

And—picking up on Ricks's perception of the way in which the physical meaning of "lies" resists complacent moral application, and on Snow's reminder of the etymologically physical meaning of "flatter"—I have to confess that I cannot keep from hearing "flattened" in the final line.

So in sonnet 138 Shakespeare can be seen as adding sex and companionship to Petrarch's solitary commitment to *dolce error*, producing a *folie à deux*, if not something grander. But surely Shakespeare's sonnet on lust (numbered 129) is absolute in its loathing and self-condemnation. This is another poem that is easily classified as "anti-Petrarchan." Certainly Petrarch never wrote a sonnet about the horrors of compulsive copulation. But he did write a poem about self-destructive pleasure that has become deeply habitual, and about the impotence of knowledge in the face of such a condition ("I' vo pensando," *Rime* 264, lines 125–36).[95] We must see whether Shakespeare's sonnet is indeed darker and more monolithically negative than this.

Helen Vendler notes of the opening of Shakespeare's sonnet 129 that the poem "initially mimics a philosophical or homiletic tone."[96] I'm not sure that "mimics" is the right word, since the poem simply does seem to start out in such a mode. The opening line is completely abstract. The first thing to say about this line—though I do not recall anyone ever saying it—is that it is completely puzzling. It is impossible to know what "Th' expense of spirit in a waste of shame" is or refers to. Obviously it has something to do with waste, but the focus seems to be psychological or spiritual—we are speaking of "expense *of spirit*." The poem would seem to be about wasted aspirations, and it seems to be introducing some sort of very generalized allegory in which aspiration is misguided or degraded; we are perhaps intended to have some sort of wasteland image. The continuation of the line into the beginning of line 2 is a complete surprise; it is only in retrospect that we "recognize," as we think, puns in "spirit" and "waste."[97] The opening of the sonnet is, in fact, a kind of riddle: "Th' expense of spirit in a waste of shame/Is"—what? Answer: lust. The poem is a definition poem, one that opens with a puzzle and then solves it. So far, the action of the poem, so to speak, is purely intellectual. The opening line turns out to be a definition not merely of lust but of "lust in action," of the very moment of sexual climax.

But instead of continuing this definition, the poem turns to the immediately prior state, that of lust before "action," and sets out to define that. The enjamb-

---

95. Compare Braden, "Shakespeare's Petrarchism," 178.

96. Vendler, *Shakespeare's Sonnets*, 550.

97. For these puns see Booth's commentary on the sonnets (442–43).

ment of line 2 duplicates that of line 1. We get another riddle: "till action, lust / Is"—what? But here, instead of being given another grand and abstract definition (of what lust is "till action"), we get a series of characterizing adjectives. And the list is a very strange one.[98] Even if we knew that we were supposed to supply such a series instead of a definition, it is impossible to imagine that one would have come up with "perjur'd" as the first of these. The only explanation that I can offer is that somehow the repeated mention of the word "action" triggered in Shakespeare's unconscious the legal meaning of the term, so that lust (or the lustful person) is categorized as a kind of crazed litigant: "perjur'd, bloody, murd'rous, full of blame" (line 3).[99] Lust seems to produce the criminal mind (*mens rea*), or at least a deeply angry and censorious one—"full of blame." The line seems to diminish rather than build in strength of negative characterization, with the last item the weakest, as if Shakespeare were trying to pull back from the intensity of the increasingly repetitive list and regain some sort of intellectual control. But the next line, the final one of the opening quatrain, duplicates rather than transcending the structure of line 3. It adds a new series of adjectives that alternate between the anthropological ("savage," "rude") and the moral ("extreme," "cruel"), culminating in yet another weak, referentially ambiguous phrase with a preposition in the middle—"not to trust."

This last phrase seems to give the speaker some sort of outside perspective—"not to trust" seems to mean "not to be trusted" (by others). The first quatrain moves from characterizing "lust in action" to the state of mind of the lustful prior to "action." The second quatrain moves in the other direction. The moment of "action" seems almost to disappear: "Enjoyed no sooner but despised straight" (line 5). The remainder of the quatrain focuses on the role of reason in this process. That reason does not fully control the movement toward "action" is not surprising. Line 6 begins, "Past reason hunted." But the

---

98. Vendler is certainly right that any adequate reading of this poem must ask "why its initial contained scholastic and individual definition hurtles into a spate of adjectives of social trespass" (*Shakespeare's Sonnets*, 554).

99. It is perhaps significant that when Shakespeare uses the term in the legal sense, "action of battery" is the "action" most frequently mentioned. In the Quarto of *II Henry VI* (*The First Part of the Contention betwixt the Two Famous Houses of York and Lancaster*), the term is used in a combined legal and (nasty) sexual sense. A sergeant appeals to Jack Cade for justice against a butcher. "Alas, sir he has ravished my wife," says the sergeant. The butcher, in his defense tells Cade, "Why, my lord, he would have 'rested me and I went and entered my action in his wife's proper house" (2:4.7.129–32, in Stephen Orgel and A. R. Braunmuller, *Shakespeare: The Complete Works* [New York: Penguin, 2002]). There also seem to be sexual undercurrents swirling about Mistress Quickly's "action" against Falstaff in the second *Henry IV* (2:2.1.1–17).

next lines, to the end of the octave, do contain a surprise. One would think that the retrospective self-disgust of "despised straight" would represent the role of reason in the process under description, but this is not what Shakespeare gives us.[100] After the experience (or the person) in question is "had"—again the moment of the experience disappears—the experience is "Past reason hated" (line 7a). This is a key recognition in the poem. The speaker realizes that the intensity of his hatred for the experience is exactly as far out of control as was his initial desire for the experience. And the rationale that "reason" provides for its excessive hatred of the orgasmic experience is presented. The experience is hated "as a swallowed bait, / On purpose laid to make the taker mad" (lines 7–8). Reason is presented as a sort of egotistical faculty that can only see experience in terms of itself—as if the sole purpose of sexual activity were to obliterate reason.

Instead, however, of taking this opportunity to gain perspective on this tendency within "reason," the speaker plunges right on, obliterating the break between the octave and the sestet. He seems to want to make sure that the view at which he has arrived—"to make the taker mad"—will be applied to the entire temporal sequence described in the octave. The first half of the ninth line, "Mad in pursuit," seems to add little to what has already been said about lust "till action," but the second half of the line seems to want to make sure that the missing term, so to speak, the moment of orgasm, is included in the characterization: "mad in pursuit, and in possession so" (line 9). The speaker wants to have a single term to characterize all the phases. He continues with the enumeration of the phases in the following line, but another term that will characterize them all replaces "mad." He is careful now to include the term between before and after, giving it extra metrical emphasis: "Had, having, and in quest to have, extreme" (line 10). This final word seems to rescue the speaker from the madness of reason in the poem. It is a word, as Vendler rightly notes, that implies a particular philosophical model, one in which revulsion against a vice can itself be a vice.[101] In line 4, the word functioned merely as one of the series of negative

100. I say "self-disgust" here because I do not see the presence of an object of lust in the poem, and I think that Booth, Vendler, and others are wrong to import one. The poem seems to me to be entirely self-directed, a critique of a state of mind.

101. Vendler, though, does not pause over the content of the position (*Shakespeare's Sonnets*, 551). In the *Nicomachean Ethics*, Aristotle actually does (very briefly) consider the case of the negative extreme toward sexuality, the person who enjoys sex too little, but he notes that this is rare and that it is one of the rather many vices in his scheme for which there is no name (see *NE* 1107b5–7 and 1119a6–11).

characterizations—"Savage, extreme, rude, cruel"—but here, in a culminating syntactical and prosodic position, it seems to allow the speaker both to summarize and conclude in a satisfactory way the critique that he has been making, and also to pull back from it, to stop from being merely "full of blame." For the first time, the tiny hint rushed over at "Enjoyed" is allowed a bit of expansion. Line 11 begins, "A bliss in proof." Almost a whole half-line is devoted to positive characterization before that is undercut, and the undercutting—"and proved, a very woe"—is now much less savage, extreme, rude, and cruel. "Proved" is much less abrupt and vulgar than "had," and seems almost neutral after "in proof"; and "a very woe" is itself rather soft—mournful rather than lacerating.

Shakespeare knows that if he wants to present the poem as something more than a soliloquy by a madman or a self-hating puritan, he needs to provide some intelligible account of the inward dynamism of the psychological and temporal process that he is describing. He knows that, like Petrarch, he must acknowledge, however ruefully, the existence and importance of pleasure in the process—recall "a pleasure so strong in me by habit that it dares to bargain with Death" in "I' vo pensando."[102] Suddenly, in the final line of the third quatrain, we get a sequence of delights, and, surprisingly, these are illusory and mental rather than gross and physical: "Before, a joy proposed; behind, a dream" (line 12). What a different sort of word "dream" is than "extreme"! The line even allows for pleasure in retrospection.[103] We are back to Petrarch's *breve sogno*. But before we have a chance to assimilate the effect of "a dream" on the whole picture, the poem moves to its resolving couplet, which turns out not to offer any sort of resolution but simply to characterize the whole picture the poem has presented as the essence of impotent reason:

> All this the world well knows, yet none knows well
> To shun the heaven that leads men to this hell.

The couplet equivocates on the Platonic conception of moral knowledge in just the way that Aristotle does: "all this" is well known to us and we do not know

---

102. Poem 264, lines 125–26 (*un piacer per usanza in me sì forte / ch'a pattegiar n'ardisce co la Morte*).

103. This is noted by Richard Levin, "Sonnet CXXIX as a 'Dramatic' Poem," *Shakespeare Quarterly* 16 (1975): 179. Giorgio Melchiori credits Levin with being the first to notice "the progressive toning down of the [negative] connotative features" of the poem's language (*Shakespeare's Dramatic Meditations: An Experiment in Criticism* [Oxford: Clarendon, 1976], 147).

it "well," in the sense of being able to put it into practice.[104] *Akrasia*, weakness of the will, is seen as the universal human condition (I am not sure that the lines allow for the possibility of human beings not included in "the world"). This would seem like a vast overstatement were it not for the sense of personal involvement on the part of the speaker. The poem would be quite different if its last words were "that hell" rather than "this." The speaker is there. These last lines are not a sober reflection but a cry of desperation from someone who is still "past reason." The speaker is in exactly the situation of the speaker of "I' vo pensando"—"I see the better and I lay hold of the worse"—though he offers his self-portrait in the guise of a generalization. And he knows that the problem is that what has led him into this situation, and keeps him there, where he is, is something experienced as a "heaven." It is not clear, moreover, that the summarizing couplet actually takes account of where the body of the poem has gotten. Behind, a dream still lingers.[105]

For an utterly bleak picture, one must turn to "My love is as a fever" (numbered 147). Here, pleasure is fully devalued and there is no autonomy or nobility in error (Michael Schoenfeldt takes this poem as normative).[106] The madman who hates "past reason," and who is not allowed to speak the whole of sonnet 129, is allowed to speak the whole of "My love is as a fever." The extremity of the praise that the speaker has (in the past) lavished on his beloved is presented as proof of his madness, whereas the extremity of his current condemnation of her (and himself) is not seen as such. Although the speaker states, "My thoughts and my discourse as madmen's are," he shows no awareness of the possibility of this characterization being applied to the thoughts and discourse expressed in the poem. Here, there is only hell, and no "heaven" whatever. And there is—thinking back to sonnet 138—no mutuality, only a self-loathing "I" and a loathed "thee." Yet "Love is too young to know what conscience is" (numbered 151), the other poem that ranks with sonnet 129 as the most direct expression of sexual self-disgust in the volume, does return to the evocation

104. In book 7 of the *Nicomachean Ethics*, Aristotle criticizes the view that no one knowingly does the wrong thing as "plainly at variance with the observed facts" (*NE* 1145b27). As an analogy to someone who "repeats the formulae [of moral knowledge]" without having internalized their meanings, Aristotle speaks of the way "an actor speaks his lines" (1147a23).

105. Melchiori, in *Shakespeare's Dramatic Meditations*, 152–58, comes to a view somewhat close to this, but like Snow on "When my love swears" ("Loves of Comfort and Despair," 462–83) seems to me to move too far from the element of loathing. But again, if one has to err in a direction, this seems to me the better one.

106. See Schoenfeldt, *Bodies and Selves*, 78–79 (see intro., n. 20); Schoenfeldt's general approach and views in this book are discussed at some length in my introduction.

of a relationship, and ends, for all its phallic comedy and self-revulsion, on an oddly tender note—despite (or perhaps because of) the continuation of the dirty joke: "No want of conscience hold it that I call / Her 'love,' for whose dear love I rise and fall." The poem might actually be hinting at an alternative notion of conscience, one that might allow for some accommodation between "my nobler part" and "my gross body" that amounted to something other than "treason."

In general, then, we can say that Shakespeare's sonnets are most Petrarchan when they are most psychologically complex and attitudinally balanced. The one religious poem in Shakespeare's strikingly secular volume, "Poor soul, the center of my sinful earth" (numbered 146), is not, for the most part, Petrarchan. It revels in the harsh body-soul dualism that, as we have seen, Petrarch—and perhaps, at times, Shakespeare—tried to soften. "Poor soul, the center of my sinful earth" attains what can properly be called a Petrarchan note only when it sees the body not as dross or as food for worms but as, in a phrase worthy of and reminiscent of Petrarch, a "fading mansion."[107]

---

107. In *Rime* 251, Laura's body is the "beautiful inn" (*bell'albergo*) from which Petrarch has the dreadful vision (*orribil visione*) that her soul has risen.

CHAPTER 3

Against Morality: From *Richard III* to *Antony and Cleopatra*

Moral judgments and condemnations constitute the favorite revenge of the spiritually limited against those less limited.

Should moralizing not be—immoral?

NIETZSCHE, *Beyond Good and Evil*, sections 219 and 228

One of our most important recent moral philosophers, Bernard Williams, devoted a good deal of his career to distinguishing between the terms "morality" and "ethics," arguing that the second identifies a much larger domain than the first, and that the first identifies a very limited and peculiar realm indeed. Williams denied that there is a single standard against which all human activities can or should be measured; he denied that the things that we value can be arranged into a coherent system and shown to be compatible with one another; and he specifically faulted "morality" for its commitment to the ubiquity and priority of its own relevance.[1] This might all seem distinctively "modern" or "postmodern," and certainly seems to us distinctively post-Nietzschean.[2] But Bernard Williams drew his inspiration more from Homer than from Nietzsche (though Williams was increasingly interested in Nietzsche), and Nietzsche

---

Friedrich Nietzsche, *Beyond Good and Evil: Prelude to a Philosophy of the Future*, trans. Walter Kaufmann (New York: Random House, 1966), 147, 158.

1. See Bernard Williams, *Morality: An Introduction to Ethics* (New York: Cambridge University Press, 1972), esp. the chapters (not numbered) entitled "Moral Standards and the Distinguishing Mark of Man" and "God, Morality, and Prudence," 59–67 and 68–78 respectively; and Williams, *Ethics and the Limits of Philosophy* (Cambridge: Harvard University Press, 1985), esp. chap. 10, "Morality, the Peculiar Institution."

2. Peter Holbrook, in a book to which I am quite sympathetic, claims that "Shakespeare anticipates the Romantic revolution in morals" (*Shakespeare's Individualism* [Cambridge: Cambridge University Press, 2010], 12–13).

himself drew his inspiration from Aristotle and from Homer.[3] In short, Williams's "Nietzschean" perspective might not have been unavailable to an early modern person like Shakespeare. Indeed, my argument in this chapter is that Shakespeare shared Williams's sense of the irrelevance of the moral to much of what we value, and that as Shakespeare's career proceeded, he developed more and more fully and explicitly his sense of the limitation of the moral perspective.

THE HAPPY CRIMINAL

Shakespeare's commitment to the theater, perhaps especially to the popular theater, is part of what allowed him to attain this peculiar perspective on morality. Something like this perspective is, I think, required by the theater. Aristotle, after all, invented the notion of the aesthetic in the context of seeking to account for theatrical pleasure (we enjoy seeing things represented that we do not enjoy seeing).[4] But we need not go so far from Shakespeare to locate the conditions of possibility for an attitude of the sort that I have schematically described and will attempt to fill in. We only need to remind ourselves of the first great "hit" of the Elizabethan popular theater as a vehicle for serious poetry: Marlowe's *Tamburlaine* plays (1587–88). In these plays, we are invited to enjoy the magnificence of Marlowe's writing—"high astounding terms"—and to view the "picture" of a powerfully compelling figure to whom moral terms seem, at best, trivially relevant. After all the cruelties that we have witnessed Tamburlaine performing, part 1 of the play ends with his happy marriage, and part 2 with his quiet death and successful passing on of his kingdoms to his sons.

Marlowe was a notorious iconoclast and freethinker. Can we assume that Shakespeare followed him into the realm beyond (moral) good and evil? A way into this question might be to spend a bit of time on one of Shakespeare's first and most enduring "hits," *The Tragedy* (as it is called in both the Quarto and the Folio texts) *of King Richard III*. This is a play that manifests an extraordinary degree of metatheatrical awareness. Shakespeare wants his audience to

3. For the depth of Williams's interest in Homer and in Greek tragedy, see his *Shame and Necessity* (Berkeley: University of California Press, 1993); for his increasing interest in Nietzsche, see his *Truth and Truthfulness* (Princeton: Princeton University Press, 2002), esp. chaps. 1–2. For Nietzsche and Homer, see *Beyond Good and Evil*, 151 et passim; for Nietzsche and Aristotle, see Kaufman's notes on 138 and 228.

4. See Aristotle, *Poetics*, 1448b5–20, in *Introduction to Aristotle*, ed. Richard McKeon (New York: Modern Library, 1947), 625–26.

think about their pleasure in watching this play.[5] In the second scene, Lady Anne asks Richard Aristotle's question about tragedy. She wonders whether he delights "to view [his] heinous deeds" (1.2.53).[6] Delight is indeed the question. We delight in seeing Richard play the villain—in a number of senses of "play." In this tragedy, the character who is Richard says that he "can counterfeit the deep tragedian" (3.5.5). Even more startlingly, Shakespeare has his title character remind the audience of his native theatrical lineage—that is, of the theatrical pleasure they have received from a stage villain. Richard states that in playing with words, he is acting "like the formal Vice, Iniquity" (3.2.82).

But Shakespeare has already given Richard a special intimacy with the audience by opening the play with Richard's soliloquy.[7] Richard's "villainy" is never in question; he says he is "determinèd to prove a villain"—which makes it sound, oddly and significantly, as if the endeavor might be difficult. The audience's interest is in watching his will (which, in "determinèd," he punningly presents as fate) work itself out. The energy that might have gone into moral judgment is preempted—"I am subtle, false, and treacherous," says Richard (1.1.37). So what we get to do is to watch his villainy—announced as such—unfold. It is hard not to feel that we are witnessing an exercise in skill and superior intelligence. Clarence speaks powerfully and eloquently to the two murderers Richard has set upon him, but it is (again) hard not to feel some contempt for "simple plain Clarence," as Richard calls him (1.2.118), for being so utterly taken in by Richard. It is hard not to side with the witty and intelligent, hard to avoid being seduced by cleverness and audacity.[8]

Many of the memorable scenes in the play have the quality of co-opting us into enjoyment. There is no mystery about the moral dimension of these scenes, and no interest in it. The scene with Richard as zealous contemplative "enforced" to take the throne is a major (and hilarious) set piece—a coup de théâtre staged as a coup de théâtre that is also a coup d'état. Can anyone in the theater keep a straight face when Richard thanks God for his humility (2.1.73

5. In a recent review, William Fitzgerald wonders whether "our moral revulsion at figures like [Seneca's] Atreus [is] compromised by our commitment to the aesthetic pleasures of the plays" (*Times Literary Supplement*, September 24, 2010, 7). If we substitute "Shakespeare's Richard III" for Atreus here, I suggest answering "yes," and seeing this as intended. Shakespeare may well have recognized this in Seneca's tragedies.

6. All quotations are from *King Richard III*, ed. Antony Hammond (London: Methuen, 1981).

7. On the hero-villain's "startling intimacy" with the audience, see Harold Bloom, *Shakespeare: The Invention of the Human* (New York: Riverhead, 1998), 70.

8. On Richard's seduction of Lady Anne in act 1, scene 2, see appendix 1 to this chapter.

and elsewhere), or when he points to his withered arm as proof that he has been "bewitch'd" (3.4.68–72)? And Shakespeare enjoyed the outrageous wooing scene so much that he repeats it later in the play. He has Richard seduce (or at least apparently seduce) Queen Elizabeth, the widow of Edward IV, into securing her daughter for Richard as his second wife (Anne has already "bid this world good night"). Here, the means of seduction are distinctively Marlovian. Shakespeare has Richard appeal to the imagination of earthly power—"The high imperial type of this earth's glory" and "th' aspiring flame of golden sovereignty" (4.4.245, 328–29).[9]

The mention of "this earth's glory" and the claim that Richard's arm has been "bewitch'd" raise the issues of Providence and the supernatural in the play. Whether or not the audience is meant to share Richard's mockery of witchcraft beliefs (or his superstition about curses), the awareness of a world beyond this life surely adds a moral dimension to the play. Or does it? Shakespeare gives Richard a favorite joke. He uses it twice in the opening scene and again in the next (and he, and other wicked characters, keep using it). This joke has an unsettling effect because it works by apparently taking a standard moral and religious belief with unusual seriousness. Richard says of simple and plain Clarence, "I do love thee so / That I will shortly send thy soul to Heaven" (1.1.118–19). This form of the joke recurs almost identically in scene 2, but the second occurrence of the joke in scene 1 adds another dimension.[10] "God take King Edward to his mercy," says Richard, "And leave the world for me to bustle in" (1.1.151–52). This sense of enjoyment of the world seems to place known experience over and against an abstract belief in someplace beyond. "Heaven" seems some place offstage that doesn't matter, while the word associated with "the world"—"for me *to bustle* in"—is full of humorous and delighted energy.[11]

But, of course, Richard does get his comeuppance. The representative of God in this world is not the priesthood (which Shakespeare seems to see as part of the political world), but what Milton in *Paradise Lost* calls God's "Umpire, Conscience" (3.195). Villainy is punished here. Almost all the villains in the play have attacks of conscience: the second murderer of Clarence; the two

9. Compare "The sweet fruition of an earthly crown" in *Tamburlaine*, part 1, 2.7.29 (Christopher Marlowe, *The Complete Plays*, ed. J. B. Steane [Baltimore: Penguin, 1969]).

10. For commentary on the role of the joke in the second scene, see appendix 1 to this chapter.

11. Bloom advises, "Think of Falstaff as the author of *Richard III*, and you cannot go too far wrong" (*The Invention of the Human*, 66).

men suborned by Sir James Tyrrell to kill the young princes; and, of course, Richard himself. On the eve of the battle with the invading Richmond, Richard finds himself without what he wonderfully calls "that alacrity of spirit" that (as we have indeed seen) he was wont to have (5.3.74–75). He interprets the experience of being visited by the ghosts of his victims as a troubled dream, an attack of "coward conscience" (5.3.180). He falls into a state close to the despair to which all the supposed ghosts have called him. But he does not, contrary to their instructions, "despair and die." His "alacrity of spirit" returns.[12]

He rouses himself to stir his army powerfully to nativist and aristocratic contempt for the invaders—"A scum of Bretons and base lackey peasants"— and he renounces the idea of an objectively valid internal moral arbiter:

> Conscience is but a word that cowards use,
> Devis'd at first to keep the strong in awe.
>
> (5.3.310–11)

This is desperate, of course, and meant to be seen as such. I am not suggesting that Shakespeare accepted this analysis—one that we would call Nietzschean and that Shakespeare would trace to Machiavelli and Machiavelli's classical sources.[13] But what is important to see is that this is Richard's final word on the matter. His conscience does not, finally, affect him. He loses his kingdom not, famously, for want of virtue or out of mortification, but for want of a horse. When we last see Richard, he is still "bustling," and his famous last line is wonderfully unplaceable in terms of genre. Is it comedy or pathos—or some mixture that allows us to leave the theater with a smile that is not simply (or primarily) that of moral satisfaction. The line reminds us of the solidity and reality and value of the ordinary physical, animal, social (and military) world.[14]

---

12. This is downplayed by Kerrigan and Braden, *The Idea of the Renaissance*, 66–68 (see intro., n. 7). They give a lovely account of "the crisp cheerfulness" that "gives the early acts of the play its unforgettable spirit," but as the mention of "the early acts" suggests, they finally adopt a moralistic reading—"the ultimate business of the play . . . is to bring Richard to account"—although in psychologized terms.

13. See Niccolò Machiavelli, *The Discourses*, ed. Bernard Crick, trans. Leslie J. Walker, rev. Brian Richardson (New York: Pelican, 1974), 1:xi. The ultimate classical source might be the speeches of Callicles in Plato's *Gorgias*, esp. 483b–c (see *The Complete Dialogues of Plato*, ed. Edith Hamilton and Huntington Cairns (Princeton: Princeton University Press, 1961), 266.

14. A review of Dominic Lieven's *Russia against Napoleon* notes that the author is "very good on how the availability of horses could win or lose a war" (*New York Times Book Review*, June 20, 2010, 17).

OLD MEN BEHAVING BADLY

The critique of moralism in *Richard III* is largely implicit; it is implicit primarily in the audience's experience (the discussion of conscience is an exception). Obviously one could leave the play imagining that one had witnessed a moral (or a pro-Tudor) spectacle. In what follows, I will argue that, as Shakespeare's career developed, he sought to make it more and more difficult to be like the melancholy Jaques in *As You Like It* and "moralize the spectacle" of his plays (2.2.44).

The role of Falstaff in the *Henry IV* plays is, I believe, a crucial turn in this development, perhaps the crucial turn. Like Richard III, Falstaff is another self-conscious descendent of the Vice of the old Moralities—in part 1, he threatens Hal at one point with the "dagger of lath" that was apparently the emblem of this figure (1:2.4.134).[15] As with Richard, Falstaff's moral status is never in doubt; he is, as we are told, a "vice," an "iniquity," a "vanity" (1:3.4.447). Also as with Richard, Falstaff's deviation from the moral norm is as marked as his deviation from the physical norm. Falstaff's moral, like his physical, condition is "gross as a mountain, open, palpable" (1:2.4.220–21). The interesting question, then, is why this is not all there is to say about Falstaff. Again, our pleasure betrays us. What Erasmus's Dame Folly (one of Falstaff's other ancestors) says about herself is true of Falstaff as well; like Dame Folly, Falstaff merely has to appear and "the faces of all of [us]" immediately brighten up "with a strange, new expression of joy."[16] To echo Falstaff himself in part 2, persons of all sorts "take pride to gird at" both these characters (2:1.2.5). Dr. Johnson, a serious and professional moralist, gave some thought to the problem. He put the question in terms of Falstaff's appeal to Hal. After listing a number of Falstaff's faults, Johnson stops and notes that "the man thus corrupt, thus despicable, makes himself pleasing to the prince that despises him, by the most pleasing of all qualities, perpetual gaiety."[17] Johnson does not explain why "perpetual gaiety" should have this remarkable status, but again, Dame Folly can enlighten us. This "gaiety" is, as she constantly says, the opposite of and antidote for

15. I use the A. R. Humphries editions of the plays: *I Henry IV* (1960; London: Routledge, 1988); *II Henry IV* (1966; Walton-on-Thames, Surrey: Thomas Nelson, 1999).

16. Desiderius Erasmus, *The Praise of Folly* (see chap. 1, n. 10), 9. For this connection, see Walter Kaiser, *Praisers of Folly: Erasmus, Rabelais, Shakespeare* (see chap. 1, n. 14).

17. *Selections from Johnson on Shakespeare*, ed. Bertrand H. Bronson with Jean M. O'Meara (New Haven: Yale University Press, 1986), 188.

taedium vitae, weariness of life—what the first line of part 1 calls "care."[18] Johnson attributes this power to Falstaff's "wit." But Johnson cannot allow himself to remain at this level of appreciation. He has to diminish both Falstaff's wit, "not of the splendid or ambitious kind," and Falstaff's wickedness, "stained with no . . . sanguinary crimes," and he has, finally, to moralize the spectacle:

> The moral to be drawn from this representation is, that no man is more dangerous than he that with a will to corrupt, hath the power to please; and that neither wit nor honesty ought to think themselves safe with such a companion when they see Henry seduced by Falstaff.[19]

But does Shakespeare want us to moralize the spectacle even in this way, even in a way that acknowledges Falstaff's power and charm? After all, we do not see "Henry seduced by Falstaff." As Auden, Empson, and Falstaff himself suggest, the situation seems more the other way around.[20] Shakespeare's Falstaff might be more wicked than Johnson allows—he is, in fact, stained with "sanguinary crimes" in getting his ragamuffins "peppered"(1:5.2.36–38)—and he might be more totally independent of the moral realm. The gaiety and the wit are certainly part of the answer, but they must also be related to the most striking feature of Falstaff, certainly on stage: his fatness. Falstaff first significantly enters the play not in his own first speech, but in the first speech about him—he is, as he says in the equivalent scene in part 2, "not only witty in [him]self, but the cause that wit is in other men" (2:1.2.8–9). As we would expect, the opening speech about Falstaff gives us many clues. His own first words seem innocuous enough—intimate and loving, but not especially noteworthy: "Now, Hal, what time of day is it, lad?" (1:1.2.1). Hal's response, however, is noteworthy. He rebukes Falstaff (also familiarly) for asking the question:

> What a devil hast thou to do with the time of the day? Unless hours were cups of sack, and minutes capons, and clocks the tongues of bawds, and dials the signs of leaping-houses, and the blessed sun himself a fair hot wench in a flame-

18. See *Praise of Folly*, 21, 30, 48, 109.

19. *Johnson on Shakespeare*, 188.

20. In part 1, Falstaff says, "[T]hou hast done much harm upon me, Hal, God forgive thee for it" (1.2.89–90), and he repeats this claim often. For William Empson, see *Some Versions of Pastoral* (1935; New York: New Directions, 1960), chap. 3, "They That Have Power"; for W. H. Auden, see "The Prince's Dog," in *The Dyers Hand and Other Essays* (1948; New York: Random House, 1962), 182–208.

colored taffeta, I see no reason why thou shouldst be so superfluous as to demand the time of the day.

So the time of the day is an abstraction; it has no physical existence and is, therefore, "superfluous" to Falstaff. As Hal tells him later, "there's no room for faith, truth, nor honesty in this bosom of thine; it is all filled up with guts and midriff" (1:3.3.152–54). But Hal's opening vision does not merely substitute the physical for the abstract; it transforms the abstract into the physical. Hal imagines Falstaff living in a kind of Land of Cockayne, where, as is typical of such visions, cooked chickens (here capons) fly through the air.[21] The transformation aspect of the vision culminates in its final item, in which the symbol of reason, lucidity, kingship, spirituality, and masculine authority is transgendered, transformed, and made much more approachable— "the blessed sun himself a fair hot wench in a flame-colored taffeta." This is imagination at work—Hal's imagination stimulated and tutored by Falstaff. Such a faculty has the power not to be tied to abstractions, to cares, to duties, and, ultimately, to the reality principle. It offers, as Bacon says poetry does, "satisfaction" to the mind of man where "the nature of things doth deny it."[22]

Falstaff soon himself gives an example of this capacity (thieves as "Diana's foresters"), but the most important case is his response to the trick that Hal and Poins play on him. Dr. Johnson underestimates the significance of Falstaff's "easy escapes and sallies of levity." Poins assures Hal that the sole purpose behind robbing Falstaff of the goods he has robbed from the travelers is to hear what "incomprehensible lies" Falstaff will tell (1:1.2.180–81). But the further point, after the lies have been exposed, is the important one. Can Falstaff be "put down" by "a plain tale" (1:2.4.25)? Can he be forced to "face the facts"? His first response is to refuse to be bullied by "the facts"—"Give you a reason on compulsion?" he asks (1:2.4.231). He uses the technique for dealing with abstractions that Hal borrowed for the opening speech—"If reasons were as plentiful as blackberries, I would give no man a reason on compulsion." But simply resisting "compulsion" by the facts is not enough. The bullying

21. For a Middle English Land of Cockayne, see *Early Middle English Verse and Prose*, 2nd ed., ed. J. A. W. Bennett and G. V. Smithers (Oxford: Clarendon, 1969), 138–44. For an Italian version in which it rains ravioli, see Carlo Ginzburg, *The Cheese and the Worms: The Cosmos of a Sixteenth-Century Miller*, trans. John and Anne Tedeschi (Baltimore: Johns Hopkins University Press, 1980), 82.

22. Francis Bacon, *The Advancement of Learning*, ed. G. W. Kitchin (London: Dent, 1973), 2.4.2, 82.

reality principle must be defeated, not simply refused. The "facts" must be transformed—which is what happens when the low-comic scene in the forest becomes, in Falstaff's account, a high romance tale in which "the lion will not touch the true prince" (1:2.4.267).

None of this has anything to do with morality—unless, of course, one wants to take the view that Falstaff (like the poets) is simply a liar. The realm that Falstaff inhabits is a realm of freedom, of indifference to time, and most of all, of play.[23] Hal might be taken to be saying something fundamentally true when he says, "If all the year were playing holidays, / To sport would be as tedious as to work" (1:1.2.199–200), but it is important to recognize these lines as expressing Hal's perspective.[24] For him, playing is work. But for Falstaff, it is not. "If all the year were playing holidays," Falstaff would happily play away. It is worth spending a moment on one of Falstaff's favorite roles. His special favorite might be that of repentant Puritan; the only competitor would be the role of lusty young man. Both are important for our purposes, but I want to focus on the latter. Falstaff's stance as Juventus is an especially astonishing and important denial of the reality principle. His age competes with his girth as his most notable physical characteristic. He is a "*reverend* vice," a "*gray* iniquity," a "vanity *in years*." In a gerontocracy like the Elizabethan world, age was supposed to bring with it not only the diminution of physical power but, more important, the accession of moral gravity.[25] In the second scene of part 2, the Lord Chief Justice is especially outraged at this role of Falstaff's—"Do you set down your name in the scroll of youth, that are written down old with all the characters of age," the Justice asks, before enumerating these "characters." Falstaff responds—no doubt completely accurately—"My Lord, I was born about three of the clock in the afternoon, with a white head and something of a round belly" (2:1.2.186–88). It is as impossible to imagine Falstaff young as it is to imagine him slim or virtuous. Part of his identity is to refuse the gravity, decorum, and proper "wisdom" of age.

This aspect of Falstaff's identity is thrust into the foreground in Hal's rejection of him at the end of part 2. When Falstaff addresses the newly crowned

23. On "the bliss of freedom gained in humor" as "the essence of Falstaff," see A. C. Bradley's wonderful essay, "The Rejection of Falstaff," *Oxford Lectures on Poetry* (1909; London: Macmillan, 1959), 262; see also 269, 273

24. I am not sure whether C. L. Barber, *Shakespeare's Festive Comedy: A Study in Dramatic Form in Relation to Social Custom* (Princeton: Princeton University Press, 1959), 196, sees these lines as expressing Hal's or Shakespeare's perspective (or a general truth).

25. See Keith Thomas, "Age and Authority in Early Modern England," *Proceedings of the British Academy* 62 (1976): 205–48.

monarch as "My King, my Jove," and says, "I speak to thee, my heart," Hal begins his rejection thus:

> I know thee not, old man. Fall to thy prayers.
> How ill white hairs becomes a fool and jester.
> (2:5.5.47–48)

Hal speaks here for decorum, for morality, for responsibility. It is impossible not to know that he is doing the right thing in rejecting Falstaff. Yet it is equally impossible for Shakespeare not to have known that a great deal of his audience would experience this prudence and moralism as a form of cruelty. And recognizing the biblical reference does not help. The exultantly rigorous Jesus whose surrogate in the parable of the shut door says to those who claim to have eaten and drunk in his presence, "I know you not" (Luke 13:27), is difficult to recognize as the sacrificial proponent of mercy and undifferentiating love. Shakespeare, by committing himself to writing a series of plays that would follow Prince Hal on his well-known route from Eastcheap to Agincourt, committed himself also to the rejection of the comic character that he had created in part 1 and had eventually, after the Oldcastle debacle, named "Falstaff."[26] The equipoise of part 1—with Hotspur heroically dead and Falstaff comically resurrected—could not be maintained.[27] Prudence, order, and morality had to prevail, and as I will suggest, Shakespeare never forgave himself for that. He never again put himself in a position of seeming to favor (as Falstaff puts it) "Pharaoh's lean kine" (1:2.4.467).

The next time in Shakespeare's career that we see an old man told to act his age, we are not in any doubt as to how to feel about this judgment. The entire confrontation between Lear and Goneril in which Goneril first begins her personal assault on Lear's dignity is structured as a confrontation between prudence and folly. Goneril cannot abide Lear's Fool:

26. On Shakespeare having substituted the name "Sir John Falstaff" for the name of the character originally named "Sir John Oldcastle," see, inter alia, Jonathan Goldberg, "The Commodity of Names: 'Falstaff' and "Oldcastle" in *I Henry IV,*" *Bucknell Review* 35 (1992): 76–88, and David Kastan, "'Killed with Hard Opinions': Oldcastle, Falstaff, and the Reformed Text of *I Henry IV,*" in *Textual Formations and Reformations,* ed. Laurie E. Maguire and Thomas L. Berger (Newark: University of Delaware Press, 1998), 211–30.

27. For a recent study that emphasizes (rightly, to my mind) the profound thematic and tonal differences between parts 1 and 2 of *Henry IV,* see Hugh Grady, *Shakespeare, Machiavelli, and Montaigne: Power and Subjectivity from "Richard II" to "Hamlet"* (New York: Oxford University Press, 2002), esp. 128, 182–83.

Not only, sir, this your all-licensed fool,
But other of your insolent retinue
Do hourly carp and quarrel, breaking forth
In rank and not-to-be-enduréd riots. Sir,
I had thought by making this well known unto you
To have found a safe redress, but now grow fearful,
By what yourself too late have spoke and done,
That you protect this course, and put [it] on
By your allowance; which if you should, the fault
Would not scape censure nor the redress[es] sleep,
Which in the tender of a wholesome weal,
Might in their working do you that offense
That else where shame, that then necessity
Must call discreet proceedings.[28]

(1.1.5.188–201)

There is no doubt that Goneril is speaking, very grandly and precisely, for decorum and for a proper, morally (or at least socially) sanctioned punitiveness.
Goneril "know[s] [Lear] not" in his "foolish" state—"I would you would make
use of that good wisdom / Whereof I know you are fraught, and put away /
These dispositions that of late transform you / From what you rightly are."
Lear takes up the theme of not being known—"Does any here know me?"—
and develops it with comic hyperbole: "Why, this is not Lear. / Doth Lear walk
thus? Speak thus?" (1.4.213–14). Goneril is not amused. She sees Lear's mock
wonder—"This admiration"—as "much of the same savor" of Lear's other
"pranks." Her final extended speech to him in this scene explains to Lear how
ill white hairs become a fool and jester—"As you are old and reverend," she
tells Lear, "[you] should be wise."[29]

This scene is no anomaly in *King Lear*. Goneril and Regan always speak
with the voice of decorum. At the end of scene 1, they tell Cordelia, in perfectly
good faith, that she has "obedience scanted" (1.1.267).[30] In act 2 of the play,

28. Quotations from *King Lear* are from the Quarto text in René Weis's *Parallel Text Edition* (see chap. 1, n. 57). Departures from this text, as in the interpolation of "it" in line 195 here
(which does appear in the Folio text), will be noted.

29. See William Empson, "Fool in *Lear*," in *The Structure of Complex Words*, 2nd ed. (London: Chatto and Windus, 1964), chap. 6.

30. On the paradoxes of obedience and disobedience in the play, see Strier, *Resistant Structures*, chap. 7 (see intro., n. 15).

Kent (in his role as Caius) is another irreverent old man who must be taught to behave. Cornwall is now the voice of "reverence" and decorum, and Cornwall characterizes Caius in terms borrowed from the condemnation of Falstaff—"You stubborn ancient knave, you reverend braggart" (2.2.118). With the true voice of moral authority (as well as political power), Cornwall tells Kent/Caius, "We'll teach you." Kent answers, "I am too old to learn" (2.2.119a–119b). This is a wonderful protest against what Bernard Williams calls the presumed ubiquity and priority of the moral perspective. Kent's line implies a model of acceptance rather than of teaching and reformation. It is related, on the one hand, to Kent's earlier assertion of the "privilege" of anger (2.2.64), and on the other, to Lear's later assertion of the privilege of "need" (2.4.234). At the end of act 2, when Goneril, Regan, and Cornwall are all seconding and congratulating each other on the decision to leave Lear out in the storm, the unmistakable note of punitive moral superiority returns. Goneril explains the exact moral propriety with which they are acting. Lear is getting what he deserves. It would be wrong to interfere with the punitive (and, presumably, reformative) precision of the moral universe: " 'Tis his own blame hath put himself from rest, / And needs must taste his folly" (2.4.260–61). When Gloucester points out the actual circumstances to which they are condemning Lear—"Alack, the night comes on, and the bleak winds / Do sorely [rustle]. For many miles about / There's scarce a bush"[31]—Regan assumes the task of moral explication: "O sir, to willful men / The injuries that they themselves procure / Must be their schoolmasters" (2.4.271–72). Cornwall agrees that Regan "counsels well" (278). Lear must "learn."

Interestingly, this is the view of many critics. Shakespeare has set up *King Lear* so as to invite moralizing. Lear is an old fool; he makes a disastrous set of mistakes; his men might be as unruly as Goneril says they are.[32] Yet must he "taste his folly"? Does he have to be made to "learn"? Gloucester is a credulous old fool and has had a child out of wedlock. Does this mean—as Edgar asserts and many critics from Heilman to Cavell have argued—that there is

31. I have departed from Weis's text here because he departs from the Quarto text without, I believe, sufficient reason for doing so. He substitutes the Folio reading, "ruffle," for the Quarto's "russel" (rustle). No other recent editor of the Quarto agrees with Weis in making this substitution. See William Shakespeare, *The Complete Works: Original-Spelling Edition*, gen. eds., Stanley Wells and Gary Taylor (Oxford: Clarendon, 1986), 1044; *The First Quarto of "King Lear,"* ed. Jay Halio (Cambridge: Cambridge University Press, 1994), 74; *The History of King Lear*, ed. Stanley Wells (Oxford: Oxford University Press, 2000), 177.

32. The text(s) leave this matter genuinely open. Peter Brook's 1971 film decisively accepts Goneril's view, as do many productions.

a beautiful logic to Gloucester's blinding?[33] The play certainly provides the
materials for these views. But before moralizing about Lear's follies and need
for reformation, we should notice the characters in the play with whom this
perspective associates us. The problem with moralizing the represented experiences of Lear and Gloucester is not that it is difficult to do so. It could hardly,
in fact, be easier. The problem is that it seems irrelevant to do so. Their sufferings are such as to make the whole question of "desert" seem irrelevant—or,
as in the case of Goneril and Regan's moral certainty, both niggling and cruel.
Perhaps moral judgment, however precise, is not the way to approach even
some situations to which, it seems, such judgment should apply. That, I would
suggest, is one of the "messages" of *King Lear*.

STRUMPET AND FOOL

Yet even after *Lear*, Shakespeare had still not finished atoning for the high-
minded ending of the second part of *Henry IV*. There is another character in
the canon who plays the fool and refuses to act with the dignity and solemnity
suitable to his age. I am referring, of course, to "the old ruffian" and reprobate
Mark Antony, in *Antony and Cleopatra* (4.1.4).[34] But, of course, in that play,
Shakespeare adds another aged reprobate, developing the full implications of
"Falstaff as Mom" as well as a full range of other erotics—one would not know
from Shakespeare's play, in which Cleopatra describes herself as "wrinkled
deep in time" (1.5.30), that she died at the age of thirty-nine.[35] *Antony and Cleopatra* can be seen as Shakespeare's final apology for the rejection of Falstaff,
his final refutation of the claims of the moral perspective to ubiquitous priority
and relevance. My reading of the play might sound oddly "Nietzschean"—to

33. See Robert Bechtold Heilman, *This Great Stage: Image and Structure in "King Lear"*
(Baton Rouge: Louisiana State University, 1948), chap. 2, "I Stumbled When I Saw"; Stanley Cavell, "The Avoidance of Love: A Reading of *King Lear*" (1969), reprinted in *Disowning
Knowledge in Six Plays of Shakespeare* (New York: Cambridge University Press, 1987), 44–50,
esp. 49: "Gloucester suffers the same punishment he inflicts."

34. Except where otherwise indicated, I am using the John Wilders's third series Arden edition (London: Routledge, 1995).

35. "Falstaff as Mom" was the title of an MLA talk given, I believe, by Sherman Hawkins in
1977, and not published. For Falstaff's "femininity," see Auden, "The Prince's Dog," 196; and
Valerie Traub, "Prince Hal's Falstaff: Positioning Psychoanalysis and the Female Reproductive
Body," *Shakespeare Quarterly* 40 (1989): 456–74.

which I am willing to say, "so be it." But, before crying "anachronism," one must be sure, once again, to remember Dame Folly.[36]

In *Antony and Cleopatra*, as in *Richard III* and in *Lear*, the moral perspective—or let's call it the "standard moral perspective"—is not denied by being downplayed or excluded. As in the earlier plays, this perspective could hardly be more available. Just as *Richard III* begins with Richard describing himself as a villain, and the first act of *Lear* seems to confirm over and over again Goneril's view of Lear, *Antony and Cleopatra* begins with an elaborate speech describing Cleopatra as a strumpet and Antony as "a strumpet's fool." The very first speech of the play is an invitation to "behold and see" Antony and Cleopatra in just this way. As in *Richard III*, if the play is going to offer us anything other than the rather thin pleasure of seeing what we already think we know confirmed over and over again, Shakespeare has to offer us something other than such confirmation. But at first the speech seems unambiguous. One of Antony's soldier followers (with the wonderful name "Philo") is speaking to another such follower, and Philo is filled with moral indignation. As often, Shakespeare begins the play as if we were already familiar with the situation being described. Here is the speech:

> Nay, but this dotage of our General's
> O'erflows the measure. Those his goodly eyes,
> That o'er the files and musters of the war
> Have glowed like plated Mars, now bend, now turn
> The office and devotion of their view
> Upon a tawny front. His captain's heart,
> Which in the scuffles of great fights hath burst
> The buckles on his breast, reneges all temper,
> And is become the bellows and the fan
> To cool a gypsy's lust.
>
> (1.1.10)

Things are very clear here. Antony's passion is insanity, "dotage"; it is excessive and "overflowing." This is bad, since what is good is clearly acting and feeling with "measure"—the golden mean, or some version thereof, is at the heart of the standard moral perspective. Heroic command in war, keeping an eye on "the files and musters," is the proper "office" of a general, and "office"

---

36. On the place of *The Praise of Folly* in the general intellectual landscape of Renaissance and Reformation Europe, see chapter 1 above.

is one of the great Roman words for moral and social duty conceived as both civic and religious: "office and devotion." Antony's heroic and military capacities are now diverted, perverted—wrongly turned—upon "a tawny front," upon the charms of an immoral (and distinctly non-European, non-lily-white) female. And by perverting his vision and attention in this way, Antony is completely degrading himself, turning himself into a mere mechanical device in an oriental, low-class court: "the bellows and the fan / To cool a gypsy's lust." So we end on the word that tells the whole story.

And yet, even before we move on in the play, this speech reveals more complexity than that closing word would suggest. Ostensibly, the great value, as we have seen, is "measure"—restraint, propriety, control. And yet the description of Antony in his general's role does not exactly give us that. His eyes "glowed like plated Mars"—this is a description of godlike vehemence (or delight), not of calm and control. And the idea that the heroic virtues are not coincident with the standard moral perspective is fully developed—if somewhat against the grain of the speaker's intention—in the last third of this description. These lines focus not on Antony's discipline and coolness but rather on his "captain's heart." And we are told that the great thing about this quality of Antony's—apparently his most striking and distinctive feature as a general—is that it does not keep measure. Suddenly we are in the world of hyperbolic, almost ridiculous passion: "His captain's heart . . . in the scuffles of great fights hath burst / The buckles on his breast." This cannot literally be true, but it certainly captures the extent of Antony's martial passion and excitement. So when we are then told, at the end of the same sentence, that his heart "reneges all temper," there is more of a continuity than a contrast with Antony's military behavior, and the sharp distinction that the speaker intends essentially disappears. The focus has become Antony's "heart."

But this is all very subtle, and it is hard to imagine that Shakespeare expected his audience in the theater to pick it all up, though he might well have expected his reading audience to do so.[37] What is clear is that the speaker intends to condemn Antony and to despise Cleopatra. "Look where they come," Philo says, and he tells us what we are going to see: "The triple pillar of the world"—one of the triumvirs who rule and therefore support the whole edifice of the Roman Empire—"transformed / Into a strumpet's fool." Shakespeare is insistent on focusing our attention on these two characters, on our looking at

---

37. For the argument that, throughout his career, Shakespeare intended for his plays to be read as well as seen in the theater, see Lukas Erne, *Shakespeare as Literary Dramatist* (New York: Cambridge University Press, 2003).

them carefully. "Behold and see," Philo says again, certain of what we will be seeing, namely, a strumpet and a fool.

This is the first great moment in the play, the entrance of the title characters, and Shakespeare has, characteristically, set himself an enormous challenge. What are we in fact going to see, and hear, when they arrive on stage? What Shakespeare gives us is truly astonishing. Cleopatra speaks first, and enters saying, "If it be love indeed, tell me how much." An experienced reader or viewer of Shakespeare—or simply a fairly devoted patron of the popular theater—might register some unease here. Isn't this exactly the request that caused so much trouble, just a year or two before, in Shakespeare's version of the King Lear story: "Which of us shall we say doth love us most?" But where Lear was not sure whether he was playing or not, and he pretends that his little game is somehow serious and tied up with major state matters—the division of the kingdom(s)—Cleopatra knows that she is playing.[38] We are reminded of the opening interaction between another deeply bound pair. Cleopatra's opening question to Antony is no more serious than Hal's opening answer to Falstaff's opening question. Though one of the scenes is in low prose and the other in high verse, in both of these cases, play is the key. Cleopatra is testing Antony—not in order to publicly reward him, but for the sheer pleasure of seeing what he is going to say. Will he fall into the quantity trap—a trap that is almost impossible to get out of (though Goneril brilliantly almost does)? Antony's answer makes perfectly clear that he understands what is going on. This is a game, and he responds brilliantly, not trying (as Cordelia unsuccessfully does) to reorient the terms of the game, but resisting entirely, as he must, the quantity gambit: "There's beggary in the love that can be reckoned." This is magnificent, grand, and—dare I say it?—morally assured. But in this world of high play—a world of luxuriating in intelligent and grand statements, and mock provocation—Cleopatra will not let him off so easily. She shifts her position 180 degrees and pretends, now, to want limits: "I'll set a bourn how far to be beloved." But again, Antony has the answer, which, as he recognizes, is virtually scripted by the question. He must say that there can be no limits. He does, in a sense, say this, but Shakespeare gives him an amazing way of expressing the idea, a truly major hyperbole: "Then must thou needs find out new heaven, new earth." Whatever one wants to make of this opening interaction, it does not seem to operate in a realm where terms like temperance and "measure" do, and it is hard to think that this counts against it.

38. On the irrelevance of the love test to the (original) division of the kingdom(s), see Strier, *Resistant Structures*, 178–81.

But there is even more to be said. In Antony's second line here, Shakespeare gives his strumpet's fool a reference that no biblically literate member of the audience—of which there were no doubt many—could have missed, a reference to one of the grandest and most resonant apocalyptic promises of the New Testament. The second epistle of Peter admonishes the faithful not to listen to skeptics (Aristotelians?) who say that the world has always been and always will be as it is. These sort of people do not understand that there is a time coming when everything that we know will be destroyed, when "the heavens being on fire shall be dissolved, and the elements shall melt with fervent heat" (2 Pet. 3:10, 12). But that is not the end, for after that the faithful can expect something else, that is, "a new heaven and a new earth" (verse 13). Even more grandly, in the penultimate chapter of the final book of the New Testament, the prophetic speaker again sees, after the final judgment and the destruction of our world, "a new heaven and a new earth" (Rev. 21:1). So why would Shakespeare give Antony such a line? Perhaps the line is meant to undercut the speaker. After all, Peter's epistle explicitly condemns "they that count it pleasure to riot in the daytime" (2 Pet. 2:13)—surely that is conclusive. But Antony's line seems to accept rather than to parody the biblical perspective; its mode is quite different from Falstaff's play with laboring in his vocation. If the line is not meant to be heard as irony or parody, what does this mean? Could Shakespeare be suggesting that a morally debased character like Antony has access to spiritual wisdom, or to some equivalent thereof? From a dramatic point of view, instead of the line being undercut by some sort of gross gesture, it is allowed to hang in the air, as a vision or a prophecy, for after it, the dialogue momentarily stops, and a messenger enters.

The entrance of this messenger is, after the extraordinary opening exchange between Antony and Cleopatra, the first piece of "action" in the play. The messenger brings news, from Rome, to Antony. When Cleopatra twits Antony about his (very minimal) willingness to hear the message from Rome and especially from the most important of the other triumvirs, Octavius, "the scarce-bearded Caesar," Antony rejects the idea with another grand and apocalyptic vision:

> Let Rome in Tiber melt, and the wide arch
> Of the ranged empire fall!
> (1.1.34–35)

As in the Petrine vision, the solid is imagined as melting, but here Antony adds a geopolitical and cultural dimension. The arch, especially the wide (rounded) arch, was the great Roman architectural invention, and here it is seen as the metaphysical support of the entire empire.[39] All the sounds emphasize vastness: the open vowels of "wide" and "arch" and "ranged." These lines cannot be said quickly or sloppily; the mouth must open widely to convey this sense of vast extension. But "fall" brings the whole vision to a full stop, a stop that must be pronounced (the Folio has a colon, but one followed by a capital letter). Antony declares a separate realm of value, one that contrasts in its compactness with the "wide arch": "Here is my space" (1.1.35), he says, making, no doubt, some gesture toward Cleopatra. As in Donne's most affirmative love lyrics, perhaps almost exactly contemporary with Shakespeare's play, the grandeur of the assertion of private "space," of the world "contracted thus," as Donne says in "The Sun Rising," depends on the rejection of both the world at large—all the (secular) aspirations, ideals, and activities of "the world"—and as Donne says in "The Canonization," of large things like "half-acre tombs." Donne's (slightly) aging figure in the latter poem claims saintly status on the basis of the quality of his sexual relationship and, perhaps more seriously, on the basis of his renunciation—"We can die by it."[40] Shakespeare has his more decisively "grizzled" reprobate (3.13.17) express a *contemptus mundi* that would make any ascetic proud: "Kingdoms are clay! Our dungy earth alike / Feeds beast as man."[41]

But just at this point, Shakespeare has Antony not simply reject all public values, but reclaim and redefine one of the most important of them, one of the most "Roman" of them, in a new sense: "The nobleness of life / Is to do thus," he says, as he presumably kisses or embraces Cleopatra (compare Donne's

---

39. See Reuben A. Brower, *Hero and Saint: Shakespeare and the Graeco-Roman Heroic Tradition* (New York: Oxford University Press, 1971), 321.

40. The poems in which Donne makes this kind of assertion are probably written after the accession of James. "The Canonization" seems to refer to a male monarch reigning ("the Kings reall or his stamped face / Contemplate"). This means that these poems were probably written in approximately the same period as *Antony and Cleopatra*, in, that is, the early years of James's reign (which began in 1603). Why these strikingly similar statements of the absoluteness and transcendent value of the erotic and the private should have occurred, almost simultaneously but probably completely independently, at this time is a historical puzzle that has not, to my knowledge, been answered or even, perhaps, sufficiently meditated upon. For a suggestive attempt at something like an answer, see Jonathan Goldberg, *James I and the Politics of Literature* (Baltimore: Johns Hopkins University Press, 1983), chap. 2.

41. I am not sure why Harold Bloom finds this speech "unconvincing" (*The Invention of the Human*, 553).

"Let us love nobly" in "The Anniversarie").[42] The explanation that Antony offers for this conception of "nobleness" is as striking as his appropriation of the term: "The nobleness of life / Is to do thus, when such a mutual pair / And such a twain can do't." The meter is emphatic in its stress on "such" in both lines, and that stress seems to be the point. The way in which Antony and Cleopatra each and jointly occupy their particular identities seems to be the source of the special value that is being asserted here.[43]

This idea—that personality includes and trumps all other values, including moral ones—is explicitly thematized in the play, and constitutes one of its most original and striking motifs. When Cleopatra persists in twitting Antony about the presence of the ambassadors and about his marital status—the messenger who is prevented from speaking is to announce, among other things, the death of Fulvia, Antony's wife—Antony does not lose patience with Cleopatra, but, oddly, praises her for relentlessly teasing him. He responds to her mock insistence that he "hear the ambassadors" with an apparent rebuke that turns into praise:

> Fie, wrangling queen,
> Whom everything becomes—to chide, to laugh,
> To weep; whose every passion fully strives
> To make itself, in thee, fair and admired!
>   (1.1.49–52)

"Whom everything becomes": this does not mean that "everything" turns into Cleopatra—though there is a momentary flicker of this meaning—but that everything suits her, looks well on her, is "becoming" to her. The claim is aesthetic, not metaphysical. But what can it possibly mean? Somehow actions that are normally negative and perhaps disfiguring are flattering to Cleopatra—Katherine in *Taming of the Shrew* articulates the standard moral perspective: "a woman mov'd" is "bereft of beauty" (5.2.144).[44] The second

42. On the conception of "nobility" at work in Donne's poem, see Wilbur Sanders, *John Donne's Poetry* (Cambridge: Cambridge University Press, 1971), 81.

43. Compare Nietzsche on egoism as "belonging to the nature of the noble soul" (*Beyond Good and Evil*, 215). See also Reuben Brower on the singularity of heroic identity in *Hero and Saint: Shakespeare and the Graeco-Roman Heroic Tradition*, esp. chap. 3, "Metamorphoses of the Heroic."

44. I am not, of course, suggesting that Shakespeare necessarily agreed with the view that Katherine is expressing here (or even that she necessarily does), but only that it was an available and, as the evidence clearly shows, a dominant view. See Suzanne W. Hull, *Chaste, Silent*

half of Antony's statement ("whose every passion," etc.) is clearly meant, in some sense, to explain the first ("Whom everything becomes"). The focus is not action but passion, and the claim is that Cleopatra's being is the locus in which "every passion" seeks to be beautiful. This, however, is still quite opaque. The "explanation" seems to lie in two phrases in these lines—"fully strives" and "in thee"—phrases which, again, the poetry identifies as crucial, with an enjambment after "fully strives," and with commas (or, in the Folio, parentheses) separating off "in thee." The idea seems to be that in the completeness of their expression, Cleopatra's passions become beautiful, and that this is what her mode of being leads them, essentially autonomously, to "strive" to do. Passion is the focus. As Enobarbus says in the following scene, "This cannot be cunning in her" (1.2.157). And beauty is the focus. Antony is describing a process or a phenomenon through which—in the very realm in which morality operates, that of the passions—aesthetics trumps, transcends, and confounds the moral.

This is a truly surprising perspective, and it is not one for which I know of any direct precedent. The closest I can come to providing an intellectual-historical genealogy or context for it is in certain aspects of the Neoplatonic tradition, in the thought, particularly, of Plotinus. Plotinus is the great theorist, following Plato, of diffusiveness as an essential property of the Good.[45] Plotinus is also, unlike Plato, the great theorist of multiplicity as benign; "It is not," Plotinus says, "by crushing the divine into a unity but by displaying its exuberance . . . that we show knowledge of God" (119). Without such exuberant and diffusive energy—which, Plotinus repeatedly insists, is a matter of nature and not of deliberation—"the Good would not be Good."[46] With diffusiveness and multiplicity, for Plotinus, comes fullness as a positive aesthetic quality, and with fullness comes the desirability of lesser creatures and of imperfection: the essentially generative Reason-Principle "produces even what we know as

---

and Obedient: English Books for Women, 1475–1640 (San Marino: Huntington Library, 1982); and, inter alia, David Underdown, "The Taming of the Scold: The Enforcement of Patriarchal Authority in Early Modern England," in *Order and Disorder in Early Modern England*, ed. Anthony Fletcher and John Stevenson (New York: Cambridge University Press, 1985), 116–36; and especially Susan Dwyer Amussen, "'Being stirred to much unquietness': Violence and Domestic Violence in Early Modern England," *Journal of Women's History* 6 (1994): 70–89.

45. On the essential diffusiveness of the Good, see *The Enneads*, trans. Stephen MacKenna, abr. John Dillon (London: Penguin, 1991), 111, 354, 388, 531–33; page references in the text are to this edition.

46. For Plotinus's repeated insistence that this process is natural and necessary, and not a product of intention or deliberation, see *Enneads*, 267, 271, 294–95.

evil: it cannot desire all to be good" (147). In explaining this rather startling assertion, Plotinus resorts to an analogy with the arts: "an artist would not make an animal all eyes; and in the same way, the Reason-Principle would not make all divine." And again, Plotinus argues that those who complain that the presence of nonbeautiful aspects of the universe are a defect, "are like people ignorant of painting who complain that the colours are not beautiful everywhere in the picture" or like those who censure a drama "because the persons are not all heroes." These aspects are "part and parcel" of the total beauty of the aesthetic objects in question (147).

So, was Shakespeare echoing Plotinus in Antony's praise of Cleopatra? It is not impossible. Ficino, who translated and popularized Plotinus, was well known in England.[47] It is often hard to say where Shakespeare "got" his ideas, since his absorptive powers were obviously so remarkable. Maybe he found the Neoplatonism of Plotinus—widely echoed in many Christian and non-Christian texts—"in the air."[48] What is clear is that this motif—of seemingly negative phenomena, especially passions—"becoming" particular, very special individuals, and being part of what makes them special, is repeated and emphatic in *Antony and Cleopatra*.[49] In the next scene in which we see Antony and Cleopatra together, Antony has resolved that his "pleasure" (1.2.201) and his "business" (1.2.178–79)—with both terms being put under pressure—require him to return, as he puts it, to his many "contriving friends" in Rome. Cleopatra, of course, rebukes him for this resolve, reminds him of his erotic hyperboles ("Eternity was in our lips and eyes" [1.3.36]), calls him a liar and a cold-hearted betrayer of women ("I see / In Fulvia's death how mine received shall be" [1.3.65–66]), and then, to describe the effect that all this has produced in him, uses exactly the same vocabulary that Antony has used with regard to

47. For a useful overview, see *Platonism and the English Imagination*, ed. Anna Baldwin and Sarah Hutton (Cambridge: Cambridge University Press, 1994), part 3, "The Renaissance and the Seventeenth Century."

48. On how little Shakespeare required to absorb "all he needed" of various traditions, see T. S. Eliot, "Shakespeare and the Stoicism of Seneca," *Selected Essays* (1932; New York: Harcourt, Brace, 1950), 119; and, in the same volume, "Tradition and the Individual Talent": "Shakespeare acquired more essential history from Plutarch than most men could from the whole British Museum" (6).

49. Holbrook, *Shakespeare's Individualism*, 177, calls this defining quality "style," and supplies a quotation from Nietzsche in which "the strengths and weaknesses" of one's character are fit "into an artistic plan" such that "even weaknesses delight." This is helpful, but seems a bit too much on the side of *techné* rather than being.

her. As she continues to mock and, as he said above, to "chide" him, Cleopatra urges one of her women to contemplate the current state of Antony:

> Look, prithee, Charmian,
> How this Herculean Roman does become
> The carriage of his chafe.
> (1.3.85–86)

She suddenly and humorously takes a purely aesthetic view of Antony's anger. She enjoys the way he carries it. He "does become" it, meaning it becomes him. His "chafe" becomes fair—and also, secondarily, sexy, given a related context for "chafe."[50]

For the culmination of the "everything becomes" motif, Shakespeare returns to Cleopatra. Enobarbus's wonderful and hyperbolic account of Cleopatra's first appearance to Mark Antony—"The barge she sat in . . . Burned on the water"—reminds Enobarbus's Roman interlocutor of Cleopatra's previous erotic triumph over another Roman general, Julius Caesar. Somewhat unsequaciously, but perhaps by way of explanation of her erotic power, this leads Enobarbus to recall:

> I saw her once
> Hop forty paces through the public street
> And, having lost her breath, she spoke and panted,
> That she did make defect perfection.
> (2.2.239–41)

This is the most striking and abstract formulation yet of the principle that Shakespeare celebrates and repeatedly articulates in this play, the phenomenon of somehow, through personal charisma, making "defect perfection."[51] And if hopping and being breathless seem matters too trivial to bear the weight of this remarkable theme, Enobarbus proceeds to another formulation. Hopping may be undignified, and panting unladylike, but they are hardly serious defects,

50. On the importance of "chafing" to sexuality, see Stephen Greenblatt, "Fiction and Friction," in *Shakespearean Negotiations: The Circulation of Social Energy in Renaissance England* (Berkeley: University of California Press, 1988), esp. 85, 88–89.

51. Janet Adelman's chapter on *Timon of Athens* and *Antony and Cleopatra* is entitled "Making Defect Perfection," but she does not focus on the phrase; see *Suffocating Mothers*, chap. 7 (see chap. 2, n. 92).

and they have no moral dimension whatever. Enobarbus's next formulation is his and Shakespeare's strongest. Enobarbus does not hesitate to make the claim absolute, and to exemplify it with a seemingly impossible case:

> vilest things
> Become themselves in her, that the holy priests
> Bless her when she is riggish.
> (2.2.248–50)

Nothing could be further from traditional morality, and nothing could more clearly exalt the aesthetic over the moral. It may be proof of Shakespeare's awareness of the intellectual background to this perspective that these amazing lines are at the end of the speech that opens with Enobarbus's famous praise of Cleopatra's "infinite variety" (2.2.245–46). The praise of "variety" is a hallmark of the Plotinian tradition. The sentence in which Plotinus explains that "the Reason-Principle" produces even what we know as evil ends by explaining that the whole cosmos, with all of its creatures, is "the expression of Reason teeming with intellectual variety" (146). Whenever this tradition is invoked, variety is praised. Aquinas insisted that variety "was needful in the creation."[52] To draw closer to Shakespeare's time and place, Richard Hooker, following Aquinas, explained that "the general end of God's external working is the exercise of his most glorious and abundant virtue," where "virtue" certainly means power as well as morality. And this abundant virtue, Hooker says, "doth shew itself in variety."[53]

Hooker wants the two senses of "virtue" to go together, but that the motif we have been examining is meant, in Shakespeare, to flout or transcend traditional morality should by now be clear. As I have already suggested, this is true with regard to Antony as well as with regard to Cleopatra. At the end of act 1, Alexas reports that in Rome Antony was manifesting something like an Aristotelian mean in his emotions—"between the extremes / Of hot and cold, he was nor sad nor merry" (1.5.54–55). Cleopatra approves of this in the situa-

---

52. Quoted in A. O. Lovejoy, *The Great Chain of Being: A Study of the History of An Idea* (1936; New York, 1960), 76; Lovejoy's book, to which I am deeply indebted, is the great study of the influence of such ideas in the Western tradition. For the quoted passage, see "The True First Cause of the Distinction of Things," chap. 45 of *Summa Contra Gentiles*, book 2, *Creation*, trans. James F. Anderson (Notre Dame: University of Notre Dame Press, 1956), 137.

53. Richard Hooker, *Of the Laws of Ecclesiastical Polity*, books 1–4, intro. Christopher Morris (1907; New York: Dent, 1965), 152.

tion—"O well divided disposition"—but when she really starts to think about him, Cleopatra praises him not for his avoidance but for his manifestation of extremes. She says, to her mental image of him, "Be'st thou sad or merry, / The violence of either thee becomes, / So does it no man else" (1.5.63–64). This returns us directly to "such a mutual pair / And such a twain." The quality of being released from the moral into the aesthetic is unique to these characters.[54]

The motif is so deeply embedded in the play that it surfaces even in contexts that are meant to be morally condemnatory. In responding to Caesar's characterization of Antony as "the abstract of all faults / That all men follow" (1.4.9–10a), Lepidus says:

> I must not think there are
> Evils enough to darken all his goodness.
> His faults, in him, seem as the spots of heaven,
> More fiery by night's blackness.
> (1.4.10b–13)

Lepidus means to say that Antony's faults do not completely overwhelm his virtues, and that the faults are made more obvious by the presence of the virtues. But within the simile, the faults are glowing and energetic stars that light up the night. Instead of wasting the lamps of night in revel, as Caesar has just said (1.4.4–5), Antony's faults suddenly become the lamps of night in revel. We even get the characteristic interjected clause of uniqueness, "in him" (compare "To make itself, in thee, fair and admired"). Caesar rebukes Lepidus for being "too indulgent" to Antony, and mocks the idea that Antony's low pleasures are somehow redeemed by being his. It is as if Caesar has heard the passages on what "becomes" Antony and Cleopatra. About Antony's lustfulness, foolish generosity, and low pleasure in standing "the buffet / With knaves that smell of sweat," Caesar sarcastically challenges Lepidus to "say this becomes him— / As his composure must be rare indeed / Whom these things cannot blemish" (1.4.20–23). But "rare indeed" seems to be exactly the idea. Even the final use of the word that signals the "defect perfection" motif is complex in this way. Again, the usage is Caesar's. Here it is probably meant to be neutral rather than

---

54. Nietzsche sees the problem with the moral perspective as precisely its lack of discrimination; moral laws are unreasonable because they are general, because "they address themselves to all" and "generalize where one must not generalize" (*Beyond Good and Evil*, sec. 198, 109). Without the special cases that matter, Cleopatra notes, "the odds is gone" (4.15.68). Compare Williams, *Morality*, 74–77.

condemnatory. After Antony's defeat and disgrace at Actium, Caesar sends one of his captains to "[o]bserve how Antony becomes his flaw" (3.12.34). The presumption, of course, is that his defeat has humbled and lowered Antony, but in the next scene, we see Antony, after some false moves, become himself again. It turns out that this flaw too "becomes him."[55]

Even apart from the "becoming" motif, moral condemnation has a way of turning into praise in this play. We have already seen that the opening lines of the play, meaning to condemn Antony's lack of "measure," praise the heroic extremity of his heart. The description of Antony as "ne'er lust-wearied" functions equally ambiguously (2.1.53). Even Maecenas's biblically inflected condemnation of "th' adulterous Antony" presents him as "most large / In his abominations" (3.6.95–96). The most "puritanical" speech in the play, the one most assured in its punitive moralism—like Edgar's analysis of the reason for Gloucester's blindness—is spoken by Antony himself. After calling Cleopatra a "boggler ever," he offers a generalized reflection on how utterly precise the "justice" of the gods is: "[W]hen we in our viciousness grow hard . . . the wise gods seel our eyes, / In our filth drop our clear judgments, make us / Adore our errors" (3.13.115–19). This is a powerful evocation of the curse of moral blindness, and yet in the context of this play, it is not clear that it is such a bad thing to adore our errors. And the speech is part of the post-Actium interaction between Antony and Cleopatra before Antony becomes himself (in all senses). The turning point of this scene is worth noting. Instead of trying to answer Antony's insults, Cleopatra asks him a completely different sort of question, one that has nothing to do with the moral or even practical register. She asks him, "Not know me yet?" (3.13.162). She does not point to any list of qualities, but urges him to consider and address himself to the full particularity of the person that she is.[56] Instead of saying to her "I know thee not," and turning against his heart—"I speak to thee, my heart," was Falstaff's cry to Hal/Henry—Antony asks himself, "Where hast thou been, my heart?" (3.13.177). He regains his identity by recognizing Cleopatra's, and by throwing himself into rather than rejecting what Hal-turned-King Henry terms "gormandizing"—"one other gaudy night" (3.13.188).

55. It must be said that in Caesar's awed description of Cleopatra's corpse, he too finally subscribes to the "defect perfection" motif in speaking of her "strong toil of grace" (5.2.346)—a phrase in which the negative and the positive exist simultaneously, or rather, are fused, and in which the aesthetic becomes paradoxically spiritual.

56. See Snow, "Loves of Comfort and Despair," esp. 471 (see chap. 2, n. 77).

There is another rewriting of the rejection of Falstaff in *Antony and Cleopatra*, and this one seems on the edge of being conscious. In the rejection, after Hal/Henry has declared, "How ill white hairs becomes a fool and jester"—emphatically not seeing Falstaff as one whom "everything becomes"—the new king describes his relationship to Falstaff as having had an oneiric quality:

> I have long dreamed of such a kind of man,
> So surfeit-swelled, so old, and so profane.
>
> (2:5.5.49–50)

Hal/Henry notes that "the grave doth gape / For [Falstaff] thrice wider than for other men." Cleopatra, in act 5 of *Antony and Cleopatra*, has a different dream of an old and "surfeit-swelled" man, a dream of a different kind of colossus. In Cleopatra's "dream," there was "an emperor Antony" whose "legs bestrid the ocean" (5.2.77–93). In this dream, prodigality has turned into a "bounty" with "no winter in't," and similarly, negligence has turned into a kind of behavior in which "realms and islands were / As plates dropped from his pocket." But what is most important, and most characteristic of this play, is what has happened to "gormandizing." It has turned into a general sense of "delights," and these are seen as especially "becoming" to Antony, though here that particular motif is not employed. Antony's "delights" are seen as having a special value and status, as conferring on him a special distinction: "his delights / Were dolphinlike, they showed his back above / The element they lived in." These very lively "delights" are presented, in this dream, as a source of transcendence. And where the young king "being awake" does "despise his dream" (2:5.5.51), Cleopatra cherishes hers and desires to reenter its world through, as even Caesar recognizes, a special kind of "sleep."

This last point brings me to a final link between Antony and Cleopatra and Falstaff: they are the only characters in Shakespeare for whom a happy postmortem existence is evoked. Postmortem existence is mostly imagined as terrifying in Shakespeare, so that oblivion—sleep without dreams—becomes a positive term.[57] The angels that Horatio postulates for Hamlet are in the optative mode. But Falstaff, we are quite confidently told in *Henry V*, is "in Arthur's bosom, if ever man went to Arthur's bosom" (2.2.9–10).[58] Shakespeare gives Falstaff a strikingly and unironically "christom" death, a highly "reformed"

---

57. For horrifying visions of postmortem existence, see *Measure for Measure*, 3.1.120–27; *Hamlet*, 1.5.10–22.

58. *Henry V*, ed. J. H. Walter, Arden 2 (1954; New York: Routledge, 1990).

one (he cried out against sack, and against women).[59] This is perhaps Shakespeare's direct apology to him, but Shakespeare saves Falstaff's death from piety and moralism by Mistress Quickly's urgings (that "a' should not think of God") and by her wonderful malapropism, that puts him in the realm of myth rather than that of orthodox religion—in Arthur's rather than Abraham's bosom.

The deaths that Shakespeare gives Antony and Cleopatra do not need to be saved from piety or moralism. They are entirely within a different realm. Both Antony and Cleopatra see death as "a consummation / Devoutly to be wished," but they do not see this "consummation" merely as sweet oblivion. In deep consonance with their characters, and with the play as a whole, they add an explicitly erotic dimension to this "consummation"—he as a bridegroom (4.14.101), she in three roles: as erotic connoisseur ("the stroke of death is as a lover's pinch / Which hurts and is desired"), as sexually satisfied wife ("Husband, I come"), and as blissed-out nursing mother ("my baby at my breast / That sucks the nurse asleep" [5.2.293–94, 284, 309–10]).[60] The two, moreover, are also given a less metaphysical and more social vision of the afterlife. Antony imagines them as continuing to be, in a symposiastic pastoral, the sinecure of all eyes: "Where souls do couch on flowers, we'll hand in hand / And with our sprightly port make the ghosts gaze" (4.14.52–53).[61] Cleopatra imagines meeting Antony in the afterlife as she did at Cydnus—"I am again for Cydnus" (5.2.227). There Antony had been "barber'd ten times o'er" (2.2.234), and in the afterlife Cleopatra will meet and kiss "the curled Antony" (5.2.300). The *contemptus mundi* of the sensualists is rewarded with an erotic and "sprightly" paradise. These "green fields" have nothing to do with the Lord. Shakespeare

59. For a wonderful note on the theological meaning of Falstaff's heart being "fracted and corroborate" (*Henry V*, 2.2.124), see Walter's edition (37).

60. On the significance of Cleopatra's "Husband, I come," see Stanley Cavell, *Disowning Knowledge*, 28–33, esp. 31.

61. In the line that continues this vision, Antony asserts that when he joins Cleopatra there, "Dido and her Aeneas shall want troops." It makes perfect sense, in this context, that Antony should see Aeneas not as the founder of Rome but as the lover of Dido. He is "her Aeneas," not Rome's. And I believe, contrary to Stephen Orgel's note on this passage in the 2002 Penguin edition of the complete works (see chap. 2, n. 99), that Aeneas's betrayal of Dido is entirely suppressed here. The idea, I think, is that until the arrival of Antony with Cleopatra, Dido and Aeneas held the place of most magnificent and admired couple. For a similar vision of an "Elysium" where historically unhappy pairings are rectified, see Thomas Carew's "A Rapture."

here gives the idea of rewards in the afterlife an entirely nonmoralistic dimension. Greatness and pleasure trump wisdom and prudence once again.[62]

APPENDIX 1

Shakespearean Seduction

Shakespeare seems to have recognized, from early on in his theatrical career, that showing something happening on stage—quite literally, in front of the audience's eyes—does not make the process that is being represented any less mysterious. We can watch every step of an interaction and still be puzzled as to how it happened—or even as to what happened. The great central scene of *Othello* (act 3, scene 3) is the most important example, but the two earliest and clearest cases of seduction in Shakespeare are of this sort. They are "garden variety" cases, the seduction of a woman by a man, but they are also cases in which it seems extremely unlikely for the seducer to succeed, and in which, therefore, his success seems quite mysterious. Easy cases—a very handsome, rich, or politically powerful seducer—would not be especially mysterious. The success of the seduction would raise few questions. But in the Shakespearean cases, mysteries abound. I will try to resolve some of them, but as we will see, one feature of this kind of analysis is that when one mystery is resolved, it merely gives way to another, deeper one—an effect, I believe, that is exactly what Shakespeare wanted.

Perhaps the earliest, and certainly the strangest, seduction in Shakespeare is that of Lady Anne (Neville), the Earl of Warwick's daughter, in the second scene of *Richard III*. Even apart from the practical difficulties of the situation (to which I will return), Richard has already gone on record, in the first scene, with his contempt for the entire realm of the erotic. He sees this realm as the alternative to that of war (*eros* versus *eris*, one might say). In his opening soliloquy, Richard presents "Grim-visaged War" as turning (through "smoothing") into a dandified courtier. This figure, instead of properly exercising itself by generating fear, now "capers nimbly in a lady's chamber / To the lascivious pleasing of a lute" (1.1.12–13). Unlike "War," however, Richard himself, he tells us, does not have the option of such a turn to "smoothness." He is physically incapable, he says, of participating in the eroticized pastimes of courtiership.

---

62. On "greatness," see Nietzsche, *Beyond Good and Evil*, sec. 212, 139, and the whole of part 9, "What Is Noble." On "the recognition of greatness" as "a feat more difficult" for us than for the Elizabethans, see Brower, *Hero and Saint*, 1–2.

He is a brilliant satirist of these; he calls them "sportive tricks," and sees (male) lovers as posing as much for themselves as for their ladies: "I . . . am not shap'd for sportive tricks, / Nor to court an amorous looking glass" (lines 14–15). He seems to drop the satire in speaking of "love's majesty" (or "Majesty"), but continues it in seeing this figure or activity as strutting before a female who is, as the looking glass suggests, the mirror image of the arrogant, capering, lascivious courtier, "a wanton ambling nymph."

Richard's contempt for women and the erotic continues through the first scene past his opening soliloquy. It surfaces in his attitude toward Edward IV. Of Edward's hearkening, as Clarence says in line 54, "after prophecies and dreams," Richard concludes, rather surprisingly, "This it is, when men are rul'd by women" (1.1.62). Part of Richard's contempt for the erotic has to do with its relative indifference to class and status. Edward being "rul'd by women" would, in Richard's eyes, be bad enough, but the disgrace is compounded, as Richard sees it, through Edward's involvement with non-noble women—with "the jealous o'erworn widow" (Lady Grey, his queen) and "herself" ("Jane" Shore, his mistress) —who, Richard notes with disgust, are dubbed "gentle-women" (line 82). Class contempt mingles nicely with misogyny here. It is therefore something of a surprise to find that Richard's plans, to which we are, of course, made privy, include not only the death of his brother Clarence, but an erotic project as well. No significant social descent is imagined—"then I'll marry Warwick's youngest daughter"—but there do seem to be some practical impediments to the union. These Richard acknowledges, but dismisses as trivial: "What though I kill'd her husband and her father?" (line 154). He proposes a "logical" solution to this problem, a solution that he cannot possibly take seriously, nor expect us to:

> The readiest way to make the wench amends
> Is to become her husband, and her father.
>
> (1.1.155–56)

This seems quite clearly a joke, but it expresses Richard's contempt for women—"the wench" will accept this plan of substitution—and may well express Richard's actual view that human beings and relations are thoroughly fungible. Moreover, in case we have made the mistake of thinking there an actual erotic component to this plan, Richard assures us that he will do this "not all so much for love"—a wonderful and mocking understatement—"As for another secret close intent" (lines 157–58).

So, the scene is set for the seduction. But how can Shakespeare make it work? Anne is accompanying the corpse of her would-be father-in-law (Henry VI) and contemplating the loss of her fiancé ("her husband and her father"). The first thing to recognize, in answering the "how possible" question, is that in presenting Anne thus, Shakespeare shows how totally this situation focuses her thoughts on Richard, the murderer of these (would-be) relations. Not only does Anne imagine Richard's agency in detail—"the hand that made these holes ... the heart that had the heart to do it" (1.2.14–15)—but she spends a great deal of imaginative energy hypothesizing a future erotic life for him: "If ever he have child, abortive be it" (line 21). Even more oddly, she projects herself into the psyche of the imagined future wife of Richard; she and this imagined figure are psychologically continuous:

> If ever he have wife, let her be made
> More miserable by the death of him
> Than I am made by my young lord.
> (1.2.26–28)

When Richard appears at this point (a lovely piece of theater), and Anne asks or exclaims, "What black magician conjures up this fiend" (line 34), it is clear that Shakespeare wants us to recognize that she herself, through her concentration on Richard, has already done this "conjuring."

She continues with her conceit of Richard as "fiend"—"Avaunt, thou dreadful minister of hell" (1.2.46)—but Richard responds by at once appealing to positive Christian, non-magical values, and by characterizing her treatment of him not in religious or moral terms but in ordinary anti-feminist ones: "Sweet saint, for charity, be not so curst" (line 49).[1] Anne is being, in Richard's view, not merely anti-Christian but shrewish ("curst" functions as something like a complex pun here).[2] It could seem as if Anne pays no mind whatever to Richard's interjection—she continues her "Richard as fiend" conceit—but the form of her line following his exactly echoes his line. Where he began, "Sweet saint," and made a request "for charity," she begins "Foul devil," and makes a request —"trouble us not"—"for God's sake" (lines 49–50). We will see the significance of this shortly, but it is worth pausing over the beginning of her full-scale speech of denunciation here. She tells Richard, "Thou hast made the happy earth thy hell, / Fill'd it with cursing cries and deep exclaims" (lines 51–52).

---

1. I have restored the comma after "charity" here; it appears in the Folio, but not in Hammond's edition (see chap. 3, n. 6).

2. Hammond's note on the line attempts to capture this (138–39).

She then makes some sort of gesture that turns the scene into dramatized theater: "If thou delight to view thy heinous deeds, / Behold this pattern of thy butcheries." What is striking about Anne's premise—"If thou delight"—is how easily and fully Richard could accept it. She is evoking his consciousness with uncanny accuracy in the process of condemning it. As we have seen, "the happy earth" is exactly Richard's point of view.

After Anne's aria calling for vengeance (1.2.62–67), Richard again reminds her of "charity." She denies his right to make such an appeal, claiming (rightly) that he knows "no law of God nor man" (line 70). She adds, however, the observation that "[n]o beast so fierce, but knows some touch of pity" (line 71). Richard picks this up, following out the logic: "But I know none, and therefore am no beast." She accepts this, having claimed all along that he is a devil. But what is interesting here is how they are collaborating in the development of the conceit now. Their minds are tracking perfectly, as are their words. The echoing of the syntax and phrasing that we noted earlier continues and is intensified as the speeches get shorter and the pace of the dialogue quicker: "Vouchsafe, divine perfection . . . Vouchsafe, diffused infection" (lines 75, 78); "By circumstance [Richard] . . . by circumstance [Anne]" (lines 77, 80); "t' accuse [Anne] . . . to excuse [Richard]" (lines 80, 82). They are rhyming and locked in a duet. And Richard's flattery of her is not contradicted by her insults of him.[3] The dialogue continues in this mode, including discussion of murder in this banter, until Anne makes a direct charge that does not seem cooptable into the game: "Didst thou not kill this King?" (line 103).

Richard's answer completes her line metrically; but it does not rhyme with her words or echo her syntax. "I grant ye, yea," he says. But she continues the dialogue as a kind of contest by picking up not on the content of what he has said, but on the nature of the speech-act that he has performed: "Dost grant me, hedgehog!" ("Hedgehog," is, of course, meant to be insulting, but it comes across as oddly intimate and funny.) And she continues to play on the speech-act—"Then God grant me" (1.2.104). Shakespeare shows how deeply and oddly in harmony they are at this point by having Anne provide the setup that allows Richard to make his favorite joke. In her speech about "granting," Anne asks God to grant her that Richard may be damned for killing Henry VI, and bursts out, with regard to Henry, "O he was gentle, mild, and virtu-

---

3. I cannot resist quoting here a wonderful comment from one of the Press readers for this book: "The rapid-fire stichomythia in [this] scene is like the centerpiece dance in an Astaire-Rogers movie: in the very choreography of countering the man's advances, the woman finds herself dancing with him."

ous"—which perfectly sets up Richard's response: "The better for the king of Heaven that hath him" (1.2.107).

It is no accident that this bit of dialogue exactly foreshadows an interaction between a male character and a young gentlewoman in mourning that occurs in one of Shakespeare's later plays—significantly, in a comedy. The first important interaction in the culminating scene of the first act of *Twelfth Night* is between the Lady Olivia, veiled and in mourning, and her father's Fool, Feste. Olivia initially refuses to have anything to do with the Fool, twice commanding that he be taken away. But Feste refuses to leave and insists that she is the fool. He asks for her permission to "prove" this: "Good madonna, give me leave to prove you a fool." And suddenly Olivia is interested rather than aloof. She asks: "Can you do it?" After being granted leave to proceed, Feste makes his "proof" by "catechizing" her:

CLOWN: Good madonna, why mourn'st thou?
OLIVIA: Good fool, for my brother's death.
CLOWN: I think his soul is in hell, madonna.
OLIVIA: I know his soul is in heaven, fool.
CLOWN: The more fool, madonna, to mourn for your brother's soul, being in heaven.[4]
(1.5.61–66)

This is exactly Richard's joke. Olivia is delighted by it, and she utters her splendid rebuke to Malvolio when the latter fails to find the above interaction delicious.

This tiny but significant moment in *Twelfth Night* gives us a lens through which to see more clearly what is going on in scene 2 of *Richard III*: Richard is playing the Fool to an aristocratic lady—who enjoys it. Olivia's "Can you do it?"—the moment at which she, in Malvolio's precise phrase, "minister[s] occasion" to Feste is exactly duplicated at the moment of parodic transcendentalism in this scene of *Richard III*. When Anne, quite predictably, follows suit and immediately answers Richard's "he was fitter for that place than earth" with "thou unfit for any place but hell" (1.2.10–111), Richard makes a new move. In continuing the ongoing discussion of the "fitness" of various persons for various places, Richard claims that he is "fit" for "one place else" (other than hell—or earth). But suddenly he is curiously deferential. This is exactly a

4. I quote the Arden 2 edition of *Twelfth Night*, ed. J. M. Lothian and T. W. Craik (London: Methuen, 1975).

moment like Feste's "Give me leave, good madonna." Richard speaks of "one place else, *if you will hear me name it*" (line 112; emphasis mine). At this point, Anne is hooked. She is interested; she is curious; she wants to know what he is going to say. This is Olivia's "Can you do it?" Instead of professing lack of interest, Anne continues the game by guessing a "place" for which Richard is "fit." "Some dungeon," she says, clearly inviting him to go on. So he makes his big move: "Your bedchamber" (line 114). And instead of being shocked, Anne continues the game. At this point, Richard knows that he is more than halfway to his goal, and he names for us what has been going on, in case (one can see Shakespeare worrying slightly) we haven't gotten it. The conversation has progressed to Richard envisioning them sleeping together, and Lady Anne has all but explicitly shared the fantasy—her "I hope so" refers ambiguously to "ill rest" for him and to his lying with her (lines 115–17). Richard decides to alter his mode of attack somewhat for the rest of the scene, but here he names what has thus far been occurring. "But gentle Lady Anne," he says, "To leave this keen encounter of our wits" (line 119).

"This keen encounter of our wits"—this is the major means of seduction in Shakespeare. "Keen," in this phrase seems to mean sexually excited as well as verbally sharp, as in Hamlet's exchange with Ophelia ("You are keen, my lord, you are keen," says Ophelia; to which Hamlet responds, "It would cost you a groaning to take off my edge" [3.2.239–40]).[5] Shakespeare seems to have believed (or perhaps recognized) that intense, playful verbal interaction—even if its content is ostensibly hostile—is a form of sexual interaction, of foreplay. In this, as in so many insights of this sort, Shakespeare is following Marlowe. In *Hero and Leander*, Marlowe's narrator observes, "Women are woon [*sic*] when they begin to jarre" (the old spelling here creates a pun on "won" and "wooed').[6] I am not at all sure that we need any particular Renaissance theory of sexual physiology to explain this view.[7] What is certain is that understanding this premise about verbal interaction explains the mystery of the strange successful seductions in Shakespeare. At the end of the scene in *Richard III*, Richard professes amazement at his success—"Was ever woman in this hu-

5. Since the Second Quarto and the Folio are virtually identical on these lines (Q2 has "mine" for "my"), I have cited from Harold Jenkins's Arden 2 edition (London and New York, 1982).

6. Christopher Marlowe, *Hero and Leander*, 1.332, in *Elizabethan Narrative Verse*, ed. Nigel Alexander (Cambridge: Harvard University Press, 1968), 64.

7. Stephen Greenblatt in "Fiction and Friction" (see chap. 3, n. 50) suggests that this view of witty interaction is undergirded by Renaissance theories of sexuality, especially the "one-sex" theory that male and female genitalia are mirror images of each other.

mour won?"—and masks his narcissistic pleasure in mocking narcissistic pleasure ("I'll be at charges for a looking-glass"). But it is clear that he does, in some sense, understand his success, and that we do as well.

Let us look at one other, more or less contemporary, Shakespearean seduction: the scene in *The Taming of the Shrew* in which Petruchio apparently gains the "special thing" that Baptista insists is prior to all "specialties," Katherine's love (2.1.128–29).[8] This is another unconventional seduction, and it works in one of the ways that the first half of the scene in *Richard III* does. The role of wit and of what Petruchio calls "spirit" (2.2.169) is clear in the scene. Once we have taken these into account, the only important thing to note is the way in which Kate, or, as we should say, Katherine, ministers occasion to Petruchio. She calls him, somewhat to his puzzlement, a "movable," and then it is she who specifies that the "movable" in question is a "joint-stool" (2.1.197–98). This opens the way for Petruchio's invitation: "Thou has hit it: come sit on me." When Petruchio calls Katherine a wasp, it is she who brings up the wasp's sting, and it is she, moreover, who invites him to "find it where it lies" (line 212). The result of this verbal collaboration cannot help but be sexual. Petruchio's joke about "my tongue in your tail" (line 216) was equally created by both of the interlocutors. That Kate/Katherine hits him at this point suggests a climax. It is perhaps true that when Kate says, "I'll chafe you if I tarry" (line 243), there is a specifically sexual suggestion.[9] In any case, that we are encountering a "keen encounter" of wits that is a form of courtship and seduction is unmistakable. Energy, "spirit," is what succeeds—in the face of all social and moral proprieties. Machiavelli sometimes called it audacity (*audacia*), sometimes ferocity (*ferocità*) and often being spirited (*animoso*).[10] It was part of *virtù* but not of virtue.

8. I have used the Arden 2 edition of *Shrew*, ed. Brian Morris (London and New York: Methuen, 1981).

9. On erotic chafing, see Greenblatt, "Fiction and Friction."

10. For *audacia*, see *Machiavelli's "The Prince": A Bilingual Edition*, trans. and ed. Mark Musa (New York: St. Martin's, 1964), 214; for *ferocità*, see, inter alia, 60, and for *animoso*, 68, 94, et alia.

APPENDIX 2

Morality and the Happy Infant: The Case of *Macbeth*

Macbeth is perhaps the Shakespearean play most committed to "normal" moral and political values. Recent criticism has shown its politics not to be merely absolutist—it certainly seems to allow for, perhaps promote, tyrannicide—but its moral position seems to be entirely conventional, and its political position is deeply committed to the support of proper, virtuous kings (of kings, that is, as opposed to tyrants).[1] I want to demonstrate what Shakespeare had to do, in

---

1. In *The Royal Play of Macbeth* (New York: Macmillan, 1950), Henry N. Paul argued persuasively that Shakespeare made use of George Buchanan's history of Scotland, as well as of Holinshed's. Paul did not, however, take Buchanan's political views into account. The argument that Shakespeare was quite aware of the republican politics of James's former tutor, was made by David Norbrook in "*Macbeth* and the Politics of Historiography," in *Politics of Discourse: The Literature and History of Seventeenth-Century England*, ed. Kevin Sharpe and Steven N. Zwicker (Berkeley: University of California Press, 1987), 78–116. At virtually the same time, Alan Sinfield questioned the assumption that what he calls "the Jamesian reading of *Macbeth*" is "necessary on historical grounds," and suggested a "Buchananite disturbance" of this reading ("*Macbeth*: History, Ideology, and Intellectuals" [1986]; reprinted in *Faultlines: Cultural Materialism and the Politics of Dissident Reading* [Berkeley: University of California Press, 1992], 100). Arthur F. Kinney, in "Imagination and Ideology in *Macbeth*," *The Witness of the Times: Manifestations of Ideology in Seventeenth Century England*, ed. Katherine Z. Keller and Gerald J. Schiffhorst (Pittsburgh: Duquesne University Press, 1993), saw resistance theory as relevant to the play (165–66). Earlier, in an essay entitled "History, Politics and *Macbeth*," Michael Hawkins had noted that "increasingly, in the sixteenth and seventeenth centuries, political theory became concerned with the right of resistance" (in *Focus on "Macbeth*," ed. John Russell Brown [London: Routledge, 1982], 172. William C. Carroll includes a section on resistance theory in his *Macbeth: Texts and Contexts* (Boston: Bedford St. Martin's, 1999), 231–49. In *Treason by Words: Literature, Law and Rebellion in Shakespeare's England* (Ithaca: Cornell University Press, 2006), Rebecca Lemon reverts to the view that Shakespeare's position on resistance to tyrants—that it is never permissible—was the same as King James's (99ff.). Andrew Hadfield's *Shakespeare and Republicanism* (Cambridge: Cambridge University Press, 2005) presents a strong case that resistance theory and various aspects of "republican" thought, ancient and modern, were widely known in Renaissance England, but sees the "republican moment" as being over with the death of Elizabeth, and so, extremely oddly, he barely touches upon the plays written after 1603, including *Macbeth*. The current fashionable view seems to be that the politics of the play are indeterminate. David Kastan, in *Shakespeare after Theory* (New York: Routledge, 1999), sees the play as swerving toward James's position (Lemon sees Kastan as supporting this view), but ultimately remaining indeterminate (179), while Peter C. Herman, in "*Macbeth*: Absolutism, the Ancient Constitution, and the *Aporia* of Politics," in *The Law in Shakespeare*,

the value structure of the play, to get this result. He had to buy into a very tight version of "the Elizabethan world picture," a version in which all the realms of value line up together rather than, as we have seen in many of the other plays, exploiting and exploring (and celebrating) tensions between value systems. There is no positive realm "against morality" in *Macbeth* (though, oddly and interestingly, Nietzsche thought there was).[2] The play lines up social hierarchy and ordinary morality with ordinary perception and cognition and basic biological functioning. Disruption of the first two results in disruption of the second two. It is this concatenation of values, especially the blending of the hierarchical with the biological, that especially defines the world of this play, and makes it, as I suggested above, so deeply conservative despite its awareness of tyranny and its support of tyrannicide. My reading of the play, therefore, while wholly secular, may be seen, in some basic ways, to fall in with the "orthodox" one promoted by G. Wilson Knight and others; but I see this orthodoxy as special to this play rather than as normative for Shakespeare (or "the Elizabethan mind"), and as needing to be created by the systematic suppression of alternative conceptions or realms of value to which Shakespeare elsewhere—as we have seen—gave powerful expression.[3]

Duncan is, I think, rightly taken as the locus of positive social life in the play. The language that is associated with him includes, as many critics have noted, some traditionally "feminine" terms and attributes. Shakespeare takes this from his sources; in Holinshed, Duncan is overly "soft and gentle of nature," and his enemies call him a "millkesop."[4] But Shakespeare's treatment

---

ed. Constance Jordan and Karen Cunningham (New York: Palgrave Macmillan, 2007), 208–32, sees the play as swerving toward legitimating resistance but ultimately remaining indeterminate (see 224–26).

2. For Nietzsche's comment on *Macbeth*, see note 28 below. As my use of Nietzsche in the main part of this chapter suggests, I think him right in general about Shakespeare's theater, just wrong in this case—which points to what I am interested in exploring in this case.

3. For Knight's influential reading of *Macbeth*, see *The Imperial Theme* (1931; London: Methuen, 1965), chap. 5. For identification of this as the orthodox reading, see Harry Berger, "The Early Scenes of *Macbeth*: Preface to a New Interpretation" (1980); reprinted in Berger, *Making Trifles of Terrors: Redistributing Complicities in Shakespeare*, ed. Peter Erickson (Stanford: Stanford University Press, 1997), chap. 5.

4. See the selections from Holinshed's *Chronicle of Scotland* in appendix A of Kenneth Muir's edition of *Macbeth* (London: Methuen, 1984), 167–68; unless otherwise noted, citations of the play are from this edition, identified hereafter by the editor's name. See also Geoffrey Bullough, ed., *Narrative and Dramatic Sources of Shakespeare* (New York: Columbia University Press, 1978), 7:488–89.

of Duncan is much more positive, and I do not agree with Janet Adelman and many others that, in Shakespeare's play, Duncan's "feminine" attributes suggest weakness.[5] The play seems, rather, to see masculine androgyny as entirely good—King James, after all, instructed his son to be a loving "nourish-father" to the church.[6] In contrast, feminine androgyny, ambiguity, or gender-neutrality (as in the witches and in Lady Macbeth's desire to be "unsexed") is bad, as is hypermasculinity—who would be more than a man "is none" (1.7.46–7).[7] The first time that we see Duncan, he is admiring a swashbuckling bridegroom (Macbeth as Bellona's) and speaking of his "bosom interest" (1.2.55, 66). It is easy to fault Duncan for having been fooled by the original Thane of Cawdor, as well as by this thane's successor, but I am not sure that this is meant to count against Duncan. Believing well of people in general seems to be a virtue in Shakespeare. It makes the virtuous especially vulnerable to deception, but that does not mean that the quality in question is not part of virtue. The virtuous may simply be, by their nature, especially vulnerable to deception.[8] That Duncan was wrong in placing "an absolute trust" (1.4.14) in the original Cawdor, and in the following one, may be thought to speak badly of them,

5. Adelman, *Suffocating Mothers*, 132 (see chap. 2, n. 92).

6. See *Basilikon Doron, or His Maiesties Instructions to this dearest sonne, Henry, the Prince* (1599), in *The Political Works of James I*, intro. Charles Howard McIlwain (Cambridge: Harvard University Press, 1918), 24. The idea comes from Moses's protest to God in Numbers 11:12, and the phrase "nursing father" appears in the King James Bible of 1611; it is not in the Geneva Bible. The translators may have been influenced by the king's use of the phrase.

7. The play's problems with hypermasculinity are apparent in the odd treatment of Macbeth's military heroism in the opening few scenes, on which see Berger, "The Early Scenes of *Macbeth*." On "exaggerated masculinity" in the play, see Adelman, *Suffocating Mothers*, 130ff. Masculine androgyny is morally positive in the play even when it is forced on an agent; Macbeth's experience of being "cowed" by Macduff (5.8.18) leads him, momentarily, to try to avoid further offence against Macduff. On "cow'd, see Coppélia Kahn, *Man's Estate: Masculine Identity in Shakespeare* (Berkeley: University of California Press 1981), 191, though I think that Kahn is wrong to take this as negative. One of my Press readers pointed out that the reading of Macbeth's line at 1.7.47 that I have accepted ("Who dares do more is none") is an emendation, a very early one by Nicholas Rowe, of the Folio's "Who dares no more is none" (through-line numbering, 525). The Rev. Joseph Hunter, in *New Illustrations of the Life, Studies, and Writings of Shakespeare, Supplementary to All the Editions* (London: J. B. Nichols, 1845), 2:178–80, supports the Folio reading, and thinks that the line should be assigned to Lady Macbeth. No modern edition of which I am aware has adopted this suggestion.

8. See Marjorie Garber's comparison of Duncan to Desdemona in *Shakespeare after All* (New York: Pantheon, 2004), 704.

not of him. As Wilbur Sanders says, "There is no hint that this trustfulness is reprehensible; rather the reverse."[9]

Duncan is a figure of munificence and of gratitude; the first words that Macbeth hears about Duncan in the play are that "His wonders and his praises do contend, / Which should be thine" (1.3.91–92). The bestowal of favors and titles is "a marked feature" of Duncan's kingly style.[10] He is aware of the problems inherent in the cycle of debts and rewards, and he seeks to work out of such problems. His compliment to Macbeth, the new Thane of Cawdor, is quite magnificent: "[W]ouldst thou hadst less deserv'd, / That the proportion both of thanks and payment / Might have been mine" (1.4.18–20). Macbeth knows what the proper response to such grand courtesy and, in the best sense, condescension, ought to be. It is Satanic to see gratitude as an endless and burdensome debt (see Satan's soliloquy in *Paradise Lost*, 4:52–53). Macbeth has already spoken the first words of *politesse* in the play, and they are lines about the pleasure and non-opprobriousness of obligation. At the end of the previous scene, Macbeth had said to Angus and Rosse, "Kind gentlemen, your pains / Are register'd where every day I turn / The leaf to read them" (1.3.151–53). With regard to Duncan, Macbeth professes to stand outside of the whole system of debt. He claims that his acts exist in an emotional/political context that eliminates the issue of compensation: "The service and the loyalty I owe, / In doing it, pays itself" (1.4.23–24). He gives voice to a vision of political allegiance as a strong version of kinship: "Your highness' part / Is to receive our duties: and our duties / Are to your throne and state children and servants" (1.4.23–25).[11]

I am afraid that I do not see, with Harry Berger, a "carefully measured and even guarded tone" here.[12] I think that it is right to say that "this pledge of

---

9. Sanders, *The Dramatist and the Received Idea: Studies in the Plays of Marlowe and Shakespeare* (Cambridge: Cambridge University Press, 1968), 257.

10. See Lisa Hopkins, "Household Words: *Macbeth* and the Failure of Spectacle," in *Shakespeare and Language*, ed. Catherine M. S. Alexander (Cambridge: Cambridge University Press, 2004), 255. Hopkins speculates that there might be here "an unusually favorable imaging of James I's notorious openhandedness with knighthoods and other titles." Simon Forman's notes on seeing *Macbeth* at the Globe in 1611 include a recollection of Dunkin's "kindly wellcome" of Mackbeth and Bancko (see *The Norton Shakespeare*, gen. ed. Stephen Greenblatt [New York: Norton, 1997], 3336).

11. I have eliminated the comma after "state" in line 25 here. The Folio puts commas before and after "and State," which does not break the flow of the line the way that the single comma after "state" does.

12. Berger, *Making Trifles of Terrors*, 88.

loyalty is not simply a precursor to duplicity."[13] The conception is of absolute commitment as ordinary; such "children and servants"—the "duties" flow into the persons—do "but what they should by doing everything / Safe toward your love and honour" (1.4.26–27)—a sentence that could well have ended before the enjambment. Duncan, for his part, sees his sociopolitical beneficence as a form of natural process. He says to Macbeth, quite remarkably, "I have begun to plant thee, and will labour / To make thee full of growing"; to Banquo he speaks of "infold[ing]" him in his heart. The elevation of Malcolm (like, I suppose, the elevation of the Son in book 5 of *Paradise Lost*) is meant to raise the entire court circle.[14] The honor of Malcolm's designation as heir to the throne is meant "Not unaccompanied [to] invest him only, / But signs of nobleness, like stars, shall shine / On all deservers" (1.4.41–42). The scene ends, after some overt courtesy and covert rumination by Macbeth (including "Stars, hide your fires"), with Duncan saying of Macbeth that "in his commendations I am fed" (1.4.55)—which seems to mean that Duncan takes social and psychological sustenance from the praise that he gives to Macbeth (not from what Macbeth gives to him). And Duncan insists on the nourishment aspect of this relation, elevating the kind of eating imagined in both social and alimentary terms—"It is a banquet to me" (1.4.56)[15]

When we next see Duncan, outside of Macbeth's castle, he is commenting on the benignity of the natural setting—an observation that Banquo brilliantly extends by adding a connotation of numinousness and procreation to it ("the temple-haunting martlet . . . Hath made his . . . procreant cradle")—and Duncan is, once again, manifesting gracious condescension (now to Lady Macbeth): "The love that follows us sometime is our trouble" (1.6.11)—which I take to mean that he is aware that his followers put themselves out in accommodating him, and that he finds this troubling.[16] He speaks the language of high

13. Sharon Alker and Holly Faith Nelson, "*Macbeth*, the Jacobean Scot, and the Politics of Union," *Studies in English Literature* 47 (2007): 386.

14. For commentary on the lines in *Paradise Lost* (5.841–45), see Richard Strier, "Milton's Fetters, or, Why Eden is Better than Heaven," in *John Milton: The Author in His Works*, ed. Michael Lieb and Albert Labriola, *Milton Studies* 38 (2000): 179.

15. Muir's note here (25–26) discusses the ambiguous meaning of "a banquet" in the period. It can mean either a sumptuous meal in general, or a dessert course. Muir argues for the former against another scholar who argued for the latter meaning, but from my point of view, the ambiguity is welcome.

16. Elizabeth Fowler's interesting suggestion that Duncan is on a "progress" here (à la Queen Elizabeth) would fit in perfectly with this worry, though I must say that there is no explicit indication that this is what Duncan is doing. See "*Macbeth* and the Rhetoric of Political Forms,"

courtesy. Lady Macbeth, like her husband, is also able to speak this language. Just as Macbeth, earlier, had denied that service to Duncan is effort—"The rest is labour, which is not us'd for you" (1.4.44)—Lady Macbeth insists that she and her husband are not actually giving anything to Duncan but merely restoring things to him: "Your servants ever / Have theirs, themselves, and what is theirs in compt . . . Still to return your own" (1.6.25–28).

We find out at the beginning of act 2 that Duncan was, not surprisingly, in a state of "unusual pleasure" at the hospitality of the Macbeths (2.1.13). He "sent forth great largess to your offices"—which may refer to the household staff (Rowe suggested that the word should be "officers"), but seems to me, more probably (and without need for emendation) to refer, in the grand Roman sense, to the "offices" that the Macbeths have performed for him; Duncan specifically, as Banquo tells Macbeth, with "[t]his diamond . . . greets your wife" (2.1.15). Duncan is a figure of happiness and generosity, representing the possibility of happy service, of service that truly "pays itself" psychologically—but is also abundantly and happily rewarded. This is "a culture of gifts and feasting which ties the participants into a network of obligation and recompense."[17] When Banquo says, in a very rich phrase, that he intends to keep his "bosom franchis'd, and allegiance clear" (2.1.28), his language suggests the combination of freedom and willing duty appropriate to Duncan's service. Macbeth notes, in another wonderful phrase, that Duncan has been "so clear in his great office" (1.7.18)—guiltless and transparent, but also perhaps, just (as in "clearing an account"). After the murder, Macbeth speaks the language of willing service for the last time, telling Macduff, in regard to hosting Duncan, "The labour we delight in physics pain" (2.3.49)—another vision of happy service, however hypocritically intended. As Sharon Alker and Holly Faith Nelson wisely remark, "the discourse of loyalty and kinship is still active in his being."[18]

Interestingly, in this play, among the forces that work against keeping one's "bosom franchis'd, and allegiance clear" are all the mental faculties that detach one from the present and from ordinary functioning. When the witches—who seem themselves both to exist and to be figures that one imagines ("fantastical" ones)—address Macbeth, he is "rapt" (1.3.57); when the first of their prophecies

in *Shakespeare and Scotland*, ed. Willy Maley and Andrew Murphy (Manchester: Manchester University Press, 2004), 75.

17. Kathleen McLuskie, "Humane Statute and the Gentle Weal: Historical Reading and Historical Allegory," *Shakespeare Survey* 57 (2004): 7.

18. "*Macbeth*, the Jacobean Scot, and the Politics of Union," 387.

comes true (Macbeth as Thane of Cawdor), he is again described as "rapt" (1.3.143). This term is the signal for the detachment from present reality and ordinary functioning that characterizes Macbeth's potential evil. The first mention of murder in the play is as an imagined phenomenon—a "thought" that is "but fantastical" (1.3.139)—and this thought detaches Macbeth from normal behavior: "function is smother'd in surmise." When asked about it, Macbeth claims that he "was wrought / With things forgotten" (1.3.151)—one of those wonderful lines that turns out to reveal more than the speaker intends. "Things forgotten" seem to have the exact status of what we would call "things repressed"; they are "thoughts" not immediately relevant to the present, but present somewhere in the mind. These "things forgotten" seem to occupy exactly the same mental place as what are later called "desires" (1.4.51), which, in this play, are only sinister. When Macbeth falters in his resolution to do the murder, "desire" is the term to which Lady Macbeth appeals: "Art thou afeard / To be the same in thine own act and valour, / As thou art in desire" (2.7.41).

It is in relation to "desires" that Macbeth first commits himself to a willed renunciation of ordinary seeing. Light and ordinary eyesight in the play are always morally benevolent. Since Macbeth recognizes his desires as "black and deep" but still cherishes them, he must rant, "Stars, hide your fires"—this just after Duncan has imagined his whole court as shining stars—and he must wish for the eye to "wink at the hand," and for the hand to do what the eye fears to see (1.4.50–55). In the great "naked new-born babe" speech, in which Macbeth expresses all his reservations about the murder, the eye is seen as a cosmic moral force, though now through its capacity to weep rather than to see: "tears shall drown the wind" (1.7.25). And in the speech in which Macbeth finally resolves to do the murder, he is led to it by a "vision" that has nothing to do with ordinary sight and is entirely detached from reality. Imagination, in this play, works exactly as Francis Bacon (in reality) or Shakespeare's Theseus (in *A Midsummer Night's Dream*) states that it does: it has nothing at all to do with reality, "being not tied to the laws of matter"; it shows only "the forms of things unknown."[19] As Macbeth says, with complete philosophical precision, of the imaginary dagger, "There's no such thing" (2.1.47).

A feature of the realm of the imaginary in this play, however, is that it is seen not merely as an aberration from "cool reason" that is characteristic, at its most benign, of lovers and poets, and at its least benign, of mad people; rather, the

19. See Francis Bacon, *The Advancement of Learning*, ed. G. W. Kitchin (London: Dent, 1973), 2.4.1; *A Midsummer Night's Dream*, ed. Harold F. Brooks (London: Methuen, 1979), 5.1.15.

realm of the imaginary is seen as outside of the realm of "nature"—which is imagined as entirely benign—and, most significantly, as connected to the realm of the demonic. Just before the imaginary dagger speech, Banquo is presented as not wanting to fall asleep, even though it is after midnight and he is tired. Sleep is a central concern of this play, and it is presented in a complex way—as both benign and sinister. It is benign, as we shall see, when it is connected to biological processes; it is sinister when it is connected to psychological ones. The unconscious is feared in the play; it is the realm of "desires." Banquo does not want to go to sleep because he fears the realm of mental detachment from ordinary reality, from the realm of light. He invokes "merciful Powers"—which may be as specific as Walter Clyde Curry would have us see them as being ("that order of angels . . . concerned especially with the restraint and coercion of demons")—and implores these Powers, "Restrain in me the cursed thoughts that nature / Gives way to in repose" (2.1.8–9).[20] Banquo understands the danger of nonordinary "thoughts," ones that are not restrained by the controls that operate in normal waking consciousness, controls associated with "nature." These "thoughts" that need to be "restrained" are clearly "desires." Nature is somehow imposed on, supervened upon, by these "thoughts" that occur in dreams.

Macbeth has exactly the same understanding. He says of midnight that "now o'er the one half-world / Nature seems dead, and wicked dreams abuse / The curtain'd sleep"—dreams that he explicitly associates with witchcraft, murder, and lust (2.1.49–56). "Wicked dreams" are not part of "nature," and they "abuse" the otherwise benign world of sleep. As Banquo recognizes, the ideal state is to be firmly rooted in the world of light, which is the world of "nature" (of "living light" [2.4.10]), which is the world of ordinary sense-perception, of ordinary emotional and moral responses, and also the world of present attention—not that of "things forgotten," or of "desires," or, to use the play's most general term for this dangerous realm, of "thoughts."[21] If "fancies" are one's companions, one has lost one's human ones (see 3.2.8–10). Detachment from the world—the ordinary and the immediate—is not only mad and desocializing but potentially demonic.

20. Curry is quoted in Muir's note on this passage (45).

21. In a fascinating account of playing Macbeth (and Leontes), Antony Sher writes: "Think: it's the clue to playing the part [of Macbeth] . . . I've never played a character who thinks so much" ("Leontes in *The Winter's Tale*, and Macbeth," in *Players of Shakespeare 5*, ed. Robert Smallwood [Cambridge: Cambridge University Press, 2003], 111).

The great plea for detachment from the ordinary world in the play is also the greatest moment of invocation of the demonic. When Lady Macbeth invokes the "Spirits / That tend on mortal thoughts"—these are the first sinister "thoughts"—and asks these Spirits to "unsex" her, she is not asking to be made into a man. She is asking to be made into a woman who is impervious to nature. She is not asking for any special powers, to be Circe or Medea.[22] She is only asking that her fundamental biological and psychological constitution be altered in such a way that she is not oriented toward natural feelings. This requires a fairly major overhaul of her internal plumbing—"make thick my blood, / Stop up th' access and passage to remorse" (1.5.43–44).[23] What is striking is how much effort and work this is seen as requiring. Her breasts are filled with milk—has she recently given birth?—and she wants it to serve as nourishment for perverse creatures ("take my milk for gall, you murth'ring ministers").[24] This is not seen as easy or certain (the "murth'ring ministers" seem to have to come from far away; they are "wherever"). She too has to ask

22. As Muir's note observes, the speech is based on the opening of Seneca's *Medea*. My student Elizabeth Hutcheon points out, in the Medea chapter of her dissertation on female rhetorical models in Tudor drama, that "unlike Seneca's Medea, whose capacity for cruelty is increased by her identity as a mother, Lady Macbeth wants to suppress her maternal potential."

23. This passage is filled with biological and gynecological allusions. "Thick" blood is, of course, unhealthy (see "thin and wholesome blood" in *Hamlet*, ed. Harold Jenkins [London, 1982], 1.5.70); both the menstrual flow and the neck of the womb were often called a "passage"; and "visitings of nature" (1.5.45) was a way of describing menstruation. For these details, see Jenijoy La Belle, "'A Strange Infirmity': Lady Macbeth's Amenorrhea," *Shakespeare Quarterly* 31 (1980): 381–86. I think, however, that the passage means rather to allude to the physiological than directly to describe it, since I take the mixture of the physiological, the ethical, and the psychological to be deeply characteristic of the play: "compunctious visitings of nature." La Belle seems to me to mistake allusion and parallel for direct description. Her title phrase does not, in fact, refer to Lady Macbeth (Macbeth uses it to describe his behavior at the banquet [3.4.85]), and the medical doctor in the play does not see Lady Macbeth's symptoms as physiologically derived. He speaks of "infected minds," which more need "the divine than the physician" (5.1.69–71), and Macbeth's fantasy of a physical cure for her, an "antidote" that will purge her "stuff'd bosom," is seen as truly a fantasy (5.2.39–46).

24. If the infant to which Lady Macbeth gave birth died of what Nicholas Culpeper called "ill milk," the request to "take my milk for gall" has even more resonance, envisioning a condition that Lady Macbeth might see as already, in a sense, having occurred. Culpeper is quoted in Alice Fox, "Obstetrics and Gynecology in *Macbeth*," *Shakespeare Studies* 12 (1979): 128. Holinshed comments on the determination of Scottish women to nurse their infants themselves (Muir edition, 180; Bullough, *Narrative and Dramatic Sources*, 7:506).

to be freed from eyesight and from light, that "my keen knife see not the wound it makes / Nor Heaven peep through the blanket of the dark."

In the follow-up speech, in which she claims actually to be the mother without remorse and "visitings of Nature" that she asked the "Spirits" to make her, what is striking is the detailed evocation of the pleasure that she says she is willing to destroy: "I have given suck, and know / How tender 'tis to love the babe that milks me" (1.7.55–56).[25] This remembered pleasure is contrasted with a fantasy of cruelty and murder, of violent infanticide—plucking "my nipple from his boneless gums," and dashing "the brains out"—but not with any other pleasure. This is what I want to explore further—the lack in the play of pleasures that contrast with virtuous ones. There do not seem to be wicked pleasures in the play. Instead, wickedness seems to have the effect of detaching its perpetrators from the only sources of pleasure that there are. William Kerrigan is right to see Macbeth (and Lady Macbeth) as having "murdered the pleasure principle," but we must look into how this principle operates in the play.[26]

There are in the play, as far as I can see, only a handful of brief moments that approach Marlovian gusto. These include Macbeth's contemplation of "happy prologues to the swelling act / Of the imperial theme" (1.3.128–29)—though this contemplation immediately leads into stupefyingly "horrible imaginings" (1.3.138); Macbeth's harping on "greatness" in his letter to Lady Macbeth (1.5.11, 13); Lady Macbeth's reference to "the golden round" (1.5.28); and her assertion that, if the Macbeths succeed in the murder of Duncan, "this night's great business . . . shall to all our nights and days to come / Give solely sovereign sway and masterdom" (1.5.68–70).[27] She speaks to Macbeth of "that /

---

25. I agree with Stanley Cavell that it seems perverse "to deny or to slight the one break in Lady Macbeth's silence on the subject of her childlessness, her assertion that she has suckled a (male) child" (*Disowning Knowledge in Seven Plays of Shakespeare* [Cambridge: Cambridge University Press, 2003], 239). I would argue—following, apparently, the director Glen Byam Shaw (quoted in Fox, "Obstetrics and Gynecology," 127)—that the evidence is that Lady Macbeth has done so very recently, still having milk in her breasts. This would help explain, as Alice Fox points out, the shared obsession of the Macbeths with infants, and with gynecological references.

26. See William Kerrigan, "*Macbeth* and the History of Ambition," in *Freud and the Passions*, ed. John O'Neill (University Park: Pennsylvania State University Press, 1996), 20.

27. Arthur F. Kinney has argued that Macbeth's use of the word "imperial" denotes something grander, more topical, and potentially more sinister than the word "regal" would. See "Scottish History, the Union of the Crowns and the Issue of Right Rule: The Case of

Which thou esteem'st the ornament of life"—presumably, the crown—but the phrasing is oddly oblique and weak, and there is little evidence in Macbeth's own language to support such a claim (1.7.41–42).

We never see the Macbeths enjoying either their crime or its aftermath.[28] Freud considers Lady Macbeth under the rubric of "Those Wrecked by Success."[29] Contrast Aeschylus's Clytemnestra glorying in her crime and, as Yves Peyré points out, some of Seneca's murderers: Atreus, who "gleefully anticipates" and then celebrates Thyestes's sufferings; and Medea, who, despite misgivings, feels a *voluptas magna* come over her, and increase, when she can show Jason what she has done.[30] By contrast, as soon as Macbeth has "done the deed," he is worried about his inability to participate in prayer ("I could not say, 'Amen'"), and he then goes into an aria about how he has ruined for himself one of the most fundamental biological processes—which is seen, oddly enough, in terms of an even more basic, pleasurable, and necessary biological process. Sleep is not only "sore labour's bath" and, more pertinent to

---

Shakespeare's *Macbeth*," in *Renaissance Culture in Context: Theory and Practice*, ed. Jean R. Brink and William F. Gentrup (Aldershot: Scolar, 1993), 22–28. I am not convinced that this is the case. The term is certainly grander than "regal"—and this is relevant, I think, to Macbeth's use of it—but I am not at all sure that Shakespeare intended the term to have specific or (especially) sinister connotations, or to be aimed at King James. The description of Queen Elizabeth as "the imperial votress" in *A Midsummer Night's Dream*, 2.1.164, would seem to suggest otherwise.

28. Nietzsche did think that Macbeth had such enjoyment, or at least that the play could provide it: "He who is really possessed by raging ambition beholds this its image with *joy*; and if the hero perishes by his passion this precisely is the sharpest spice in the hot draught of this joy." See *Daybreak: Thoughts on the Prejudices of Morality*, trans. R. H. Hollindale (Cambridge: Cambridge University Press, 1982), no. 240, p. 140; quoted in Bloom, *The Invention of the Human*, 519 (see chap. 3, n. 7). Nietzsche seems to me to see the play as more Marlovian than it is.

29. This essay is a subsection of "Some Character Types Met with in Psychoanalysis" (1916), in *The Standard Edition of the Complete Psychological Works of Sigmund Freud*, trans. James Strachey (London: Hogarth Press and Institute for Psychoanalysis, 1957), 14:316–24. Freud's assertion that "the forces of conscience which induce illness in consequence of success . . . are closely connected with the Oedipus complex" (331) seems appropriate to *Macbeth*.

30. Yves Peyré, " 'Confusion now hath made his masterpiece': Senecan Resonances in *Macbeth*," in *Shakespeare and the Classics*, ed. Charles Martindale and A. B. Taylor (Cambridge: Cambridge University Press, 2004), 150. See Aeschylus, *Agamemnon*, 1380–94, in *Oresteia*, trans. Richmond Lattimore (1953; New York: Washington Square Press, 1967), 89; also Seneca, *Thyestes*, 902–7, 1096–99; *Medea*, 990–94; Seneca, *Tragedies*, 2:306, 320; *Tragedies*, 1:428, ed. and trans. John G. Fitch, Loeb Classical Library (Cambridge: Harvard University Press, 2002). When she is joying in them, Seneca's Medea also feels that she has attained her identity through her crimes: *Medea nunc sum* (line 910).

Macbeth, the "Balm of hurt minds," but also the "chief nourisher in life's feast" (2.2.36–39). Macbeth's speech of mock grief for Duncan—"The wine of life is drawn" (2.3.93)—turns out to be exactly true for Macbeth, and its continuation of the image of lacking pleasure in a foodstuff that normally brings pleasure is nonaccidental.

Aside from two very negative instances, "Tarquin's ravishing strides" (2.1.55) and Malcolm's imagined and counterfactual bottomless "voluptuousness" (4.3.61), sex is never directly evoked or considered in *Macbeth*.[31] What is focused upon is the inability of the Macbeths to enjoy happy hierarchical sociability. The only pleasures fully imagined in the play are not physical (or imperial or psychological) but social—exactly the pleasures that Duncan enjoyed and enabled. Macbeth does have a moment of imagining himself enjoying the pleasures of self-containment, of being "perfect"—"Whole as the marble, founded as the rock" (3.4.20–21)—but most of the pleasures to which he seems to wish access are more ordinary social ones. At the beginning of act 3, the Macbeths announce that they are planning a major dinner party—"our great feast . . . a solemn supper" (3.1.12, 14), with "solemn" here meaning "high style," not gloomy.[32] Banquo agrees to attend, and either gives or pretends to give to Macbeth something like the kind of allegiance that Duncan generated. He says, "Let your Highness / Command upon me, to the which my duties / Are with a most indissoluble tie / For ever knit" (3.1.15–18)—this is something like "Duncan language," though perhaps, while strong, more duty oriented. Macbeth speaks as the grand, benign, philosophical host, dispersing his followers for the afternoon in order "[t]o make society the sweeter welcome" at suppertime (3.1.42).

Instead, however, of following this prescription for enjoyment himself, Macbeth spends the time working hard and rather demeaningly ("I to your assistance do make love") at convincing two murderers that they have their own reasons for killing Banquo (3.1.75–114)—in this play, the promise of advancement is, apparently, not sufficient to suborn a murder or two—and explaining

---

31. Malcolm purports to "grant" to Macduff that Macbeth has "every sin / That hath a name," including being "luxurious" (4.3.57–60), but there is no evidence that this is true of Macbeth—and in any case, Malcolm, as Muir suggests (125), may not mean it. The connection to Tarquin, and to Shakespeare's *Rape of Lucrece* (noted by Muir, 49 [from Warburton]), is more in terms of violation and guilt than sex. Shakespeare's Tarquin, who knows he will repent his crime, and does, is an early avatar of Macbeth.

32. Muir (73) has a useful note on the term; for a wonderful commentary on it, see C. S. Lewis, *A Preface to "Paradise Lost"* (1942; New York: Oxford University Press, 1961), 17.

to them that his community of well-wishers gets in his way.[33] He could, he says, "with bare-fac'd power sweep him [Banquo] from my sight . . . yet I must not, / For certain friends that are both his and mine, / Whose loves I may not drop" (3.1.117–21). The "loves" of his "friends" are an obligation and a burden to him. In the next scene, we first encounter Lady Macbeth in the role of contemplating joylessness and, in doing so, using the exact term that stands in for their shared motive—"our desire is got without content" (2.2.5). Macbeth then gives a full picture of their joyless state, focusing on biological disruption. He does not wish to (but presently does?) "eat our meal in fear, and sleep / In the affliction of these terrible dreams, / That shake us nightly" (3.2.17–19). Duncan, it turns out, is still, in his present, postmortem existence, the model of happiness. He is imagined as having the greatest of privileges: "he sleeps well," just as he did in life (3.2.23).[34]

Both the Macbeths want to be able to manifest sociability. "Be bright and jovial among your guests tonight," says Lady Macbeth (3.2.30); and in turn, "be thou jocund," Macbeth says to her (3.3.40). "Bright and jovial . . . jocund"—these are the terms of their fantasy. They attempt a grand dinner party. Of Macbeth's first words to his guests, "You know your own degrees, sit down" (3.4.1), Charles Ross writes, "As Macbeth welcomes his guests, he makes his banquet the image of former, untroubled times . . . some noncompetitive golden age, when guests know their 'own degrees,'" and "no keeper of the castle is needed to seat them."[35] With sublime condescension, Macbeth announces, "Ourself will mingle with society / And play the humble host" (3.4.3–4). Lady Macbeth gives a brilliant, high-style speech about the importance of graciousness as what distinguishes a true feast from a purchased meal, on the one hand, and from merely eating, on the other: "[T]he feast is sold / That is not often vouch'd while 'tis a making: / 'Tis given with welcome; to

33. As Michael Hawkins remarks, "Whether or not the murderers accept Macbeth's proffered justification for Banquo's murder—that [Banquo] has wronged them—it is interesting that [Macbeth] makes it and does not simply pay them to kill him" ("History, Politics and *Macbeth*," 164). I take the point to be that the play primarily conceives of motivation as personal.

34. So Stanley Cavell's observation that "the opposite of thinking in Macbeth's mind is sleep" (*Disowning Knowledge*, 235) needs to be modified to say that the opposite of thinking in Macbeth's mind is sleeping "well"—that is, without "terrible dreams—or perhaps any dreams, or unconscious processes, at all.

35. Charles Ross, *The Custom of the Castle: From Malory to "Macbeth"* (Berkeley: University of California Press, 1997), 124.

feed were best at home; / From thence, the sauce to meat is ceremony, / Meeting were bare without it" (3.4.32–36).[36]

But the ghost of Banquo ruins the party. Every time Macbeth attempts to enter properly into the social scene, the ghost interferes. A while after the ghost's first entry, Macbeth gathers himself, confessing to "a strange infirmity"; he steps back into his role as grand and gracious host, pledging "love and health to all," and commanding, "Give me some wine: fill full; / I drink to th' general joy o' th' whole table" (3.4.83–86). But of course, Banquo's ghost appears again. As Lady Macbeth says, Macbeth has "displac'd the mirth" (3.4.107). Moreover, it turns out that the appearance of ordinary grand social life was not available to the Macbeths. The feast was a political test, recognized as such, and not truly a social event at all.[37] Macduff did not attend, as is resentfully noted by Macbeth (3.4.127), and in the last scene of the act, an unnamed Scottish lord notes that because Macduff "fail'd / His presence at the tyrant's feast," Macduff lives "in disgrace" (3.6.22–23). This is the same lord who announces the presence of Duncan's son and of Macduff and others at the English court, and from this lord we hear for the first time of the possibility of a combined Anglo-Scottish war against Macbeth. The aim of this war, as the unnamed lord sees it, is to restore biological and social pleasures to Scotland; the war will be fought in order that

> we may again
> Give to our tables meat, sleep to our nights,
> Free from our feasts and banquets bloody knives,
> Do faithful homage, and receive free honours,
> All which we pine for now.
> (3.6.33–37)

The Scottish nobility "pine" to do willing and happy service and to receive proper (generous and unforced) rewards for such just as much as they desire food and sleep. All these needs go together.[38]

36. For the sake, I believe, of clarifying the meaning, I have altered the punctuation from that provided by Muir. I have followed the Folio in enjambing line 32 and placing a colon after line 33 and a comma after line 35. I have departed from both Muir and the Folio by omitting a comma after "vouch'd" in line 33 and by placing a semicolon rather than a colon after "welcome" in line 34.

37. Compare Hopkins, "Household Words," 258.

38. Hopkins, focusing on homeliness and the *unheimlich* in Macbeth, notes, "It is little wonder that the Lord who converses with Lennox should figure the rule of Macbeth precisely in

The rest of the play confirms Macbeth's lack of all pleasures. Two of the apparitions that he sees, the bloody child and the crowned child with a tree, represent the mingling of the biological and the political that characterizes the play. The detachment from biology that Macbeth is led to believe that these portend is, of course, mistaken—no human being is "not of woman born," and nature will continue to function normally. Macbeth's political aim becomes to eliminate biology. He failed with Banquo, leaving Banquo's line in "the seeds of time" to "grow" (1.3.58–59), but Macbeth succeeds with Macduff, where his aim is, explicitly, to destroy all of Macduff's biological and social attachments: Macbeth will "give to th' edge o' th' sword / His wife, his babes, and all unfortunate souls / That trace him in his line" (4.1.151–53). The totality of Macbeth's attack on Macduff's domus is stressed—"wife, children, servants, all" (4.3.211)—another great enjambment.

Act 5 brings us back to the Macbeth household. While Macbeth cannot sleep, or cannot sleep "well," and therefore cannot be nourished "in life's feast" by it or flavored and preserved by it—"the season of all natures" (3.4.140)— Lady Macbeth can sleep, but is deprived of all the positive features that are normally associated with sleep, especially rest and the "Balm of hurt minds." Having committed herself to "black and deep desires" that are normally repressed—"the cursed thoughts that nature / Gives way to in repose"—she becomes entirely a victim of unconscious mental process, of "stopped up" remorse ("a great perturbation in nature, to receive at once the benefit of sleep, and do the effect of watching!" [5.1.9–10]).

Macbeth has no functioning attachments in his domus. We have seen Lady Macbeth, and he has no children. He also has no loyal servants or followers. It is repeatedly and insistently noted that the bonds by which his followers are tied to him are purely political; they are not attached to him in any positive affective way. This is seen as unusual, and as being as telling about the nature of his rule as is the fact that there are regular uprisings against him. Each time the "revolts" are mentioned—and they seem to be viewed as quite legitimate— what immediately succeeds is a comment about the nature of the following that Macbeth does have: "Now minutely revolts upbraid his faith-breach" is succeeded by the observation, "Those he commands move only in command, / Nothing in love" (5.2.18–20). "Both more and less have given him the revolt" is succeeded by "none serve with him but constrained things, / Whose hearts

---

terms of the subversion of the domestic" (ibid., 259). McLuskie, "Humane Statute and the Gentle Weal," speaks rightly of the "deep desire for peace" and "social harmony" in this speech, and connects this to feasting (8), but does not quite bring the biological and domestic into focus.

are absent too" (5.4.12–14). There is no doubt that armed resistance to tyranny is considered legitimate in the play, but much more important to it is the idea that, normally, and in the proper course of things, service to a king is accompanied by love.[39] Service for any other reason but love is almost unimaginably contemptible (see Macduff's disdain for "wretched Kernes, whose arms / Are hir'd to bear their staves" [5.7.17–18]).[40]

As always, Macbeth is fully aware of his condition and his situation.[41] He knows not only that "the Thanes fly from me" (5.4.49) and that his enemies are reinforced "with those that should be ours" (5.5.5.), but also that what he receives from those who do follow him is "mouth-honour, breath / Which the poor heart would fain deny" (5.3.27–28). And he is fully and painfully aware of what the advanced life of a great nobleman or king should look like; he has, after all, seen it in Duncan:

> that which should accompany old age,
> As honour, love, obedience, troops of friends,
> I must not look to have.
> (5.3.24–26)

What is striking here is how oddly and wonderfully social and peaceable this vision is for a great warrior-king. It belongs to the *Odyssey* rather than the *Iliad*. But these are the only positive values available in the play.[42] Macbeth dies a

---

39. The idea of hierarchical subordination as normal and nonoppressive is so deeply part of the texture of the play that even the witches seem to share this social-psychological formation. Shakespeare presents the witches as servants (rather than masters) of their demons, and they seem to accept this as unproblematic. At the end of the opening scene, two of the witches apparently respond to their familiars' summons—"I come, Graymalkin! / Paddock calls"—and at the beginning of the fourth act, when Macbeth seeks out the witches for information about the future, they ask him, quite neutrally, whether he would prefer to "hear it from our mouths, / Or from our masters" (4.1.62–63).

40. The play takes a very negative view of straightforwardly monetary transactions. Recall Lady Macbeth's contempt for feasts that are "sold," and Macbeth's interaction with the murderers of Banquo, where Macbeth tells them not only, as we have seen, that "the execution takes your enemy off" but that it "grapples you to the heart and love of us" (2.1.105). Again, what is important is not the truth of the assertion but the terms in which it is made.

41. Compare Sanders, *The Dramatist and the Received Idea*, 301, though I don't agree with Sanders (following G. Wilson Knight) that this kind of "scrupulous fidelity" to "the realities of his situation" is new to Macbeth at this point in the play.

42. Steven Greenblatt seems to be getting at this when he speaks of Duncan's language and life representing a vision of "what it would be like to be at home in the world" ("In the Night

heroic death, crying "damn'd be him that first cries, 'Hold, enough!'" (5.7.34),
but the play seems to invite us to see this as some kind of madness—"Some
say he's mad; others, that lesser hate him, / Do call it valiant fury" (5.2.13–14)—
rather than as nobly heroic—"fury/ Signifying nothing." This contrasts with
Antony and Cleopatra, in which to see Antony's determination to go on fight-
ing after Actium as "furious" is presented as a low and unworthy view (see
Antony and Cleopatra, 4.1.200–206).

In the final speech of the Scottish play, the proclaimed king restores love
and gratitude to the political realm. Sounding exactly like his father, Malcolm
assures his followers:

> We shall not spend a large expense of time,
> Before we reckon with your several loves,
> And make us even with you.
> (5.9.26–28)

He promotes them all: "My Thanes and kinsmen, / Henceforth be Earls."[43]
There is very little difference in the play between being a subject of and being
a kinsman to a proper king; Macbeth, when he was contemplating his original
relationship to Duncan, counted being a subject and being a kinsman as a single "trust."[44] The presumption at the end of the play is that ordinary social and
biological functioning—"to our tables meat, sleep to our nights"—will follow
the restoration of an order in which political ties are also those of love. This,
we recall, is what all the Scottish lords were "pining" for—"To give obedience

---

Kitchen," *New York Review of Books*, July 17, 2008: 28). It might be even more faithful to the play
to say that its ideal is to be at home at home, where "chambers will be safe" (5.4.2). Hopkins
("Household Words," 261) notes that when Macbeth calls the English "epicures" (5.3.8), this
suggests that he "identifies himself with simple produce"—and, I would add, simple pleasures—
but this identification is ironized by Macbeth's alienation. Douglas Burnham suggests that since
"the condition of exile and of being at home are opposites, apparently mutually defining," then
"the most unnerving" form of exile must be "*exile in the home*," and he sees Macbeth as the para-
digmatic case of this ("Language, Time, and Politics in Shakespeare's *Macbeth*," in *Displaced
Persons: Conditions of Exile in European Culture*, ed. Sharon Oudit [Aldershot: Ashgate, 2002],
21; the phrase is emphasized in the original.

43. On the significance of this, see John Kerrigan, *Archipelagic English: Literature, History,
and Politics, 1603–1707* (Oxford: Oxford University Press, 2008), 111.

44. Macbeth notes that Duncan, at the time of the murder, was in Macbeth's home "in double trust": first, Macbeth was Duncan's "kinsman and his subject"; second, "his host." For this
arithmetic to work, kinsman and subject have to count as one item (1.4.12–14).

where 'tis truly ow'd" (5.2.26). This vision responds, in the world of the play, to a much deeper need than the lust for power (or for anything else) does. It is the deepest pleasure available, and the one that guarantees the others that are available.[45] Ordinary pleasures are the highest goal, and are enabled by loving service to one's king that is lovingly accepted and rewarded by him. Despite the tracks of Buchanan in the play, King James had to be pleased.

45. See McLuskie, "Humane Statute and the Gentle Weal," on social order in the play being imagined as producing "an almost magical assurance of security" (10). Fowler argues that Malcolm revises "the social practices of Duncan's . . . modes of governance," but notes that the psychological effects of these (supposed) new modes would be equivalent to those of the older ones ("*Macbeth* and the Rhetoric of Political Forms," 82).

* 2 *

In Defense of Worldliness

CHAPTER 4

Sanctifying the Bourgeoisie: The Cultural Work of *The Comedy of Errors*

HONEST MERCHANTS

The Comedy of Errors is Shakespeare's most wholehearted evocation and celebration of bourgeois life. *The Merry Wives of Windsor* might reasonably be seen as a competitor, but it is not, like *Errors*, thoroughly committed to the happy evocation of an urban and specifically commercial context; it might be called a suburban (or town) rather than an urban (or city) drama.[1] Closer in spirit and in time of composition to *Errors*, *The Taming of the Shrew* evokes a bourgeois urban context, but does not seem especially interested in it, and *Shrew* vividly evokes other contexts as well: a very grand Renaissance aristocratic household in the "Induction"; Petruchio's midlevel gentry country household after the wedding.[2] *The Merchant of Venice* certainly touches intensely on monetary and commercial matters, but it can hardly be seen as celebratory in its presentation of them (except perhaps in its fanciful evocation of mercantile shipping), and there is, of course, the contrasting presence of the other world of Belmont, a

---

1. Compare Lena Cowen Orlin, "Shakespearean Comedy and Material Life," in *A Companion to Shakespeare's Works*, ed. Richard Dutton and Jean E. Howard, vol. 3, *The Comedies* (Oxford: Oxford University Press, 2003), 160: "Windsor is not London, nor is it even a city." Orlin goes on, however, to treat *Merry Wives* as the closest thing Shakespeare produced to a city comedy.

2. The first two scenes have normally been referred to, from Pope's edition (1725) on, as the "Induction," but Leah Marcus has pointed out to me that they are not so designated in the Folio, and suggests that they should simply be treated as the first two scenes of the play.

completely nonurban world of vast, stable, inherited, and, presumably, landed wealth.[3]

In *Errors*, on the other hand, there is no representation of aristocratic or nonurban life.[4] The Duke in the play is a figure conceived in terms of juridical power rather than social status. *The Comedy of Errors* gives us, uniquely in Shakespeare, a world of merchants—every one of whom is honest, generous, and admirable. The mistaken identity plot is perfect for such a vision, for conveying, as Eric Auerbach would say, "this view of things"; it allows Shakespeare to attain maximal dramatic energy without the need to put into the plot either a malicious or a manipulative character.[5] Despite the city of Ephesus's supposed reputation for being "full of cozenage," there is not a single lie or deception, not a single crooked, devious, or dubious business or monetary dealing in the play.[6] Contracts are honored, and it is a matter of shame not to do so. Money in

3. For the positive evocation of mercantile shipping, and of wealth in *Merchant*, see Mark Van Doren, *Shakespeare* (Garden City, N.Y.: Doubleday, 1939), 79–87, esp. 80, built on by C. L. Barber, *Shakespeare's Festive Comedy: A Study of Dramatic Form and Its Relation to Social Custom* (Princeton: Princeton University Press, 1959), chap. 7, esp. 170–72. For some of the complexities that the economic issues bring into *Merchant*, see, inter alia, W. H. Auden, "Brothers and Others," in *The Dyer's Hand and Other Essays* (see chap. 3, n. 20), 218–37.

4. Anne C. Christensen in "'Because their business still lies out a' door': Resisting the Separation of the Spheres in Shakespeare's *Comedy of Errors*," *Literature and History* 5 (1996): 19–37, notes that "the action of *Errors* depends on the bustle of monetary trade, and thus Ephesus resembles Tudor London" (19), and that Shakespeare's play highlights "market activities" in a way that his source does not (21). In "*The Comedy of Errors*: A Modern Perspective," Arthur F. Kinney recognizes the commercial nature of the social world depicted in the play, and the closeness of this world to that of early modern London (see *The Comedy of Errors*, ed. Barbara A. Mowat and Paul Werstine [New York: Washington Square Press, 1996], 179–93, esp. 183–85). Peter Holbrook's useful effort to place the genre of the play in the actual social world of Shakespeare's time—*Errors* as showing that Shakespeare could "do" the classics—largely ignores the social world represented in the play ("Class X: Shakespeare, Class and the Comedies," in Dutton and Howard, *A Companion to Shakespeare's Works*, 3:67–89, esp. 74–79).

5. See Eric Auerbach, *Mimesis: The Representation of Reality in Western Literature*, trans. Willard R. Trask (Princeton: Princeton University Press, 1953), 29. I owe my awareness of the closeness of my approach here to that of Auerbach to the dissertation of my student Rana Choi. In *The Invention of Suspicion: Law and Mimesis in Shakespeare and Renaissance Drama* (Oxford: Oxford University Press, 2007), Lorna Hutson also stresses the absence of intrigue in the play (150–57).

6. Quotations of the play, unless otherwise indicated, are from *The Comedy of Errors*, ed. R. A. Foakes (see chap. 1, n. 44); hereafter identified by the editor's name. For "They say this town is full of cozenage," and reference to "cheaters" and "mountebanks," see the soliloquy by Antipholus of Syracuse that ends the first act (1.2.97–105). Martin Van Elk's attempt to con-

the play is neither filthy nor corrupting. No one is self-conscious about it, and no one is either greedy or miserly. It is taken as perfectly normal not to cheat and to expect not to be cheated. One might think that in presenting such a context, Shakespeare is merely celebrating the secular or responding to the spirit of Roman comedy (Plautus's *Menaechmi* is the major source for *Errors*). But we will see that the play reminds us that to establish the "secular" as a positive realm involves competition with a religious perspective that would demonize or at least subordinate this realm. My argument is that in *Errors*, Shakespeare presents a consciously humanist and Protestant conception of what, following Max Weber, we might call "inner-worldly" holiness.[7]

The "frame" story establishes the context. The geopolitical setting of the play is a war that seems to be based on a commercial rivalry. The "envy and discord" that has arisen between the polities of Syracuse and Ephesus derives from what the Duke of Ephesus calls the Duke of Syracuse's "rancorous outrage" directed "[t]o merchants, our well-dealing countrymen" (1.1.5–7). The epithet here seems to mean something like "both prosperous and upright" (doing well and doing good; doing well by doing good?).[8] The enmity between the cities not only arises from an attack on merchants, but is officially decreed ("in solemn synods") to take the form of a mutual commercial ban—"To admit no traffic to our adverse towns"—and the temptation to go to the other city is seen in commercial terms, in terms of attending the other city's "marts and fairs" (1.1.15–17).[9] The "stranger" Antipholus, Antipholus of Syracuse, in announcing how he intends to spend his first hour in Ephesus, states that he will not only view "the manners of the town" and its "buildings," but also "peruse the traders" (1.2.12–13). The "hapless" figure whose plight provides the frame of the play is a "merchant of Syracusa"—in the Folio, his speech heading throughout the scene, although we know his name (Egeon, given in line 140),

---

nect the play to the Elizabethan rogue ("cony-catching") pamphlets founders, as he periodically acknowledges, on what he rightly calls "Shakespeare's choice to make misidentification unintentional," in "Urban Misidentification in *The Comedy of Errors* and the Cony-Catching Pamphlets," *Studies in English Literature* 43 (2003): 333; see also 337 and 339.

7. See Max Weber, *The Protestant Ethic and the Spirit of Capitalism* (1904–5), trans. Talcott Parsons (1930; New York: Scribner's, 1958), esp. chap. 3.

8. The best gloss on the line that I have found is "Honest-trading; more generally, civil or well-behaved," in *The Norton Shakespeare* (see chap. 3, app. 2, n. 10), 690. The Folger edition sees the richness of the phrase, but is oddly diffident: "Well-behaved, perhaps with reference to business dealings" (*The Comedy of Errors*, ed. Barbara A. Mowat and Paul Werstine [New York: Washington Square Press, 1996], 6).

9. As Foakes (4) points out, "traffic" is a synonym for trade.

is some variant of merchant ("Marchant," "Mer," or "Merch")—and he is an entirely sympathetic character.[10] Even the Duke who is sentencing him to death finds him so. The character who apprises the stranger Antipholus of the situation between the cities, and therefore the danger to Antipholus as a Syracusan, is another merchant, an Ephesian who apparently does not care about the official "enmity and discord" between the cities.[11] This merchant is not only kindly in warning Antipholus, but is also—for no plot reason whatever—explicitly presented as completely honorable and trustworthy. His speech ends with the line: "There is your money that I had to keep" (1.2.8).[12] This merchant leaves the scene (and the play) with a description of his own plan for the afternoon, a plan in which the social and the mercantile mingle, and in which economic gain is presented in a term that seems to transcend the economic, and that suggests public as well as private gain: "I am invited, sir, to certain merchants, / Of whom I hope to make much benefit" (1.2.25–26).

10. For the Folio text of the play, I have used *The First Folio of Shakespeare*, prepared by Charlton Hinman (New York: Norton, 1968).

11. Although this character is designated "First Merchant" in all modern editions that I know of, in the Folio, after his first speech (where he is designated only as "Mer."), he is designated as "E.Mar." This is obviously "Ephesian Merchant," and I am not sure why Foakes professes uncertainty on the matter (12). The New Cambridge edition of *Errors*, ed. T. S. Dorsch, revised and with a new introduction by Ros King (Cambridge: Cambridge University Press, 2004), takes note of this merchant's indifference to the enmity (63).

12. This financial trustworthiness extends to the servants in the play as well. The (large amount of) money that the Ephesian merchant gives back to Antipholus (of Syracuse), Antipholus gives to his Dromio, who explicitly calls attention to the possibility of dishonesty that he is rejecting. When Antipholus tells him to "Get thee away," the Syracusan Dromio says, "Many a man would take you at your word, / And go indeed, having so good a mean" (1.2.17–18). Foakes (13) notes that T. W. Baldwin glossed "mean" here as "means," that is, wealth. Despite the worries that the encounter with the wrong Dromio has raised in Antipholus of Syracuse (1.2.54, 70), and despite the final line of the scene ("I greatly fear my money is not safe"), at the beginning of the next scene, we are immediately assured by this Antipholus, "The gold I gave to Dromio is laid up / Safe" (2.2.1–2). Dromio of Ephesus is, presumably, similarly trustworthy—since the other Dromio, mistaken for him, is entrusted with money (4.3.63)—although the Ephesian Dromio is not, as the "errors" develop, actually entrusted with any. While Douglas Bruster, *Drama and the Market in the Age of Shakespeare* (Cambridge: Cambridge University Press, 1992), notes the anxiety that Antipholus of Syracuse suffers with regard to his money (74), and Shankar Raman, "Marking Time: Memory and the Market in *The Comedy of Errors*," *Shakespeare Quarterly* 56 (2005): 176–205, notes that in *Errors*, as in the Florentine *libri da famiglia*, "monetary transactions seem surrounded by the possibility of deception and fraud" (200), neither of them acknowledge that, in the play, such anxiety is unfounded, and that the "possibility of deception and fraud" never materializes.

These, however, are only hints. The evocation of happy bourgeois life primarily enters the play through the presentation of the at-home Antipholus (Antipholus of Ephesus) and the representation of his experience—even when he is not the one having it. Shakespeare's fictional world of commercial (Renaissance?) Ephesus corresponds remarkably precisely to many features of the actual world of Elizabethan business depicted by a recent social-economic historian.[13] The first time that we meet Antipholus of Ephesus, at the beginning of act 3, scene 1, he is coming home somewhat late for dinner—the socially crucial midday meal—in the company of two friends whom he has invited to dine with him.[14] The friends are both identified as commercial types, "Angelo the Goldsmith" and "Baltha[za]r the Merchant" (F).[15] There is no suggestion that this is exactly a "business dinner," but Antipholus's home is also his shop, "The Phoenix" (1.2.75), and the two functions seem to blend together.[16] Anne Christensen notes that the family dwelling being above the business is "an arrangement resembling the situations of sixteenth century urban tradesmen"; to this should be added Craig Muldrew's observation that because of the generally "low intensity of business" (in the sense of number of transactions), Elizabethan shopkeepers could spend a great deal of time "mixing business and hospitality."[17] The normal explanation for Antipholus not coming home for dinner would be that "some merchant" has invited him instead: "And from the mart he's somewhere gone to dinner" (3.1.4–5). Antipholus of Ephesus certainly

13. I am referring to Craig Muldrew's *The Economy of Obligation: The Culture of Credit and Social Relations in Early Modern England* (New York: Palgrave, 1998). This chapter could be seen as an exemplification of many of Mudrew's views, but I would prefer to see my chapter and Muldrew's book as providing independent confirmation for a similar picture of the ideals (and in his case, some of the realities) of Elizabethan commercial and social life, since my analysis was worked out before I had consulted his book. I believe Ted Leinwand first sent me to Muldrew—for which I am, obviously, grateful.

14. On the status and function of the midday meal, see Joseph Candido, "Dining Out in Ephesus: Food in *The Comedy of Errors*," in *The Comedy of Errors: Critical Essays*, ed. Robert S. Miola (New York: Garland, 1997), 206–8, and the references there given.

15. Interestingly, "the merchant" of Ephesus (like that of Venice) is introduced to us as, for unexplained reasons, "sad" (3.1.19). Curtis Perry notes that even in his younger days, Egeon, the commercial traveler, was oddly ready to embrace death at the first "tragic instance" he experienced. See "Commerce, Community, and Nostalgia in *The Comedy of Errors*," in *Money and the Age of Shakespeare: Essays in the New Economic Criticism*, ed. Linda Woodbridge (New York: Palgrave, 2003), 39–51, esp. 42.

16. Foakes's note on "The Phoenix" as a business establishment is helpful (16).

17. Christensen, " 'Because their business still lies out a' door,' " 24; Muldrew, *Economy of Obligation*, 93.

does not, contra one recent critic, have "the mistaken belief that the private and public sides of social existence can be separated from one another."[18]

Muldrew also argues for the importance of humanism to mid- and late-Tudor conceptions of business and of civil life,[19] and the verbal exchanges between the merchant-friends in *Errors* are a textbook model of humanist dialogue and graciousness. Antipholus of Ephesus pretends to doubt his ability to be properly hospitable: "[P]ray God our cheer / May answer my good will, and our good welcome here" (3.1.21). Balthazar, in good humanist fashion, values the intention over the realization: "I hold your dainties cheap, sir, and your welcome dear." Antipholus, as the host who will be providing whatever "cheer" there is, then makes the materialist point that, as Hamlet says, "one cannot feed capons so": "A table full of welcome makes scarce one dainty dish"(we know that, as they are speaking, "[t]he capon burns, the pig falls off the spit" [1.2.44]—perhaps manifesting the humanists' "new appreciation for pork").[20] Balthazar, as the nonmaterialist merchant-guest, disparages the importance of mere food: "Good meat, sir, is common; that every churl affords" (poverty does not seem to occur to these people). Antipholus continues to disparage mere words, and this set-piece dialogue ends with each of the interlocutors getting off one final good line. As in any well-developed humanist dialogue, both sides acquit themselves well:

BAL: Small cheer and great welcome makes a merry feast.
EPH. ANT: Ay, to a niggardly host, and more sparing guest.
   (3.1.26–27)

Ben Jonson would have been pleased with this exchange. It shows, like his own (and Martial's) epigrams "Inviting a Friend for Supper," a proper regard for both material and nonmaterial values.[21] Clearly both goodwill and good food

18. Jessica Slights, "The 'Undividable Incorporate': Householding in *The Comedy of Errors*," in *Domestic Arrangements in Early Modern England*, ed. Kari Boyd McBride (Pittsburgh: Duquesne University Press, 2002), 81. Christensen, " 'Because their business still lies out a' door,'" sees the play as both asserting and resisting this separation. Slights too sees the play as ultimately rejecting this separation, though her emphasis is on its assertion of it.

19. Muldrew, *Economy of Obligation*, 132–47.

20. Ken Albala, *Eating Right in the Renaissance* (Berkeley: University of California Press, 2002), 252.

21. Epigram 101, in *The Complete Poetry of Ben Jonson*, ed. William B. Hunter, Jr. (New York: Anchor Books, 1963); Martial, epigrams 5.78 and 11.52, in *Epigrams*, trans. Walter C. Ker, Loeb Classical Library (1919; Cambridge: Harvard University Press, 1968).

are desirable and, in this context, expected. This is the world that the "errors" interrupt. The expected experience of hospitality is aborted, and the goldsmith notes that they have ended up with "neither cheer . . . nor welcome." Balthazar the merchant, ever wise and witty, observes of "cheer" and "welcome" that "[i]n debating which was best, we shall part with neither" (3.1.67).

It is worth looking at some other evocations of the normal life of Antipholus of Ephesus. The most striking and lyrical of such evocations occurs at the beginning of act 4, scene 3, where Antipholus of Syracuse muses on the nature of the urban experience that he has been having. He is, of course, having the experience of Antipholus of Ephesus:

> There's not a man I meet but doth salute me
> As if I were their well-acquainted friend,
> And every one doth call me by my name;
> Some tender money to me, some invite me,
> Some other give me thanks for kindnesses,
> Some offer me commodities to buy.
> Even now a tailor call'd me to his shop,
> And show'd me silks that he had bought for me,
> And therewithal took measure of my body.
>
> (4.3.1–9)

This is truly an urban pastoral, and unlike the urban pastoral in act 4, scene 6, of *Coriolanus*—"our tradesmen singing in their shops and going / About their functions friendly"—this vision is not in any way ironized.[22] It is a vision in which "kindnesses" and commercial transactions are completely compatible and interwoven. Money is "tendered," money is owed; commodities are offered, appreciated, and individualized. Luxury items are accepted as normal, as connected to businesses, and as part of happy commercial and social life.[23] The experience of all this is weird to Antipholus of Syracuse, but it is part

---

22. In *Coriolanus*, this vision is ironized by the military context.

23. For the view that early modern Europeans were happily and eagerly buying manufactured goods, and did not experience anxiety in doing so, see Jan de Vries, *The Industrious Revolution: Consumer Behavior and the Household Economy, 1650 to the Present* (Cambridge: Cambridge University Press, 2008). De Vries's study begins slightly later than Shakespeare's period, and deals with people perhaps of somewhat lower status than Antipholus of Ephesus and his friends, but the view it presents is certainly relevant to Shakespeare's play. De Vries's view of consumer behavior complements Muldrew's view of commercial.

of what it means to be Antipholus of Ephesus.[24] This is clearly a picture, as Stephen Greenblatt says of Duncan in *Macbeth*, of "what it would be like to be at home in the world," but here "the world" in question is commercial and bourgeois rather than aristocratic.[25]

But perhaps I am painting too rosy a picture of business transactions in the play. Act 4 begins with a scene that seems to suggest less amiable business relations. Angelo, the goldsmith to whom the Ephesian Antipholus owes money for the making of a chain, himself owes money to another merchant (not Balthazar). This merchant has an "officer" with him to arrest Angelo if he does not pay the debt. As was normal in the period, apparently, the creditor has not (as he says) "much importun'd" Antipholus for timely payment, but at this moment he has a pressing need for his money (4.1.1–4).[26] It is probably significant that this merchant, who thinks that he will need an officer to collect his debt, is not a native of Ephesus.[27] In fact, Angelo has a totally plausible plan for payment; he will get the money from Antipholus of Ephesus, who owes him "just the sum" (4.1.7) that is in question. This will allow Angelo, as he explains to the merchant, to be able to act perfectly in this world—that is, with both probity and graciousness: he will be able to "discharge my bond, and thank you too" (4.1.13). The transaction should work out not only with no need for legal enforcement but with complete goodwill. When first given the gold chain, Antipholus of Syracuse offers to pay instantly lest something go awry if he delays; instead of simply accepting the chain and walking away rejoicing, he offers eagerly, even importunately, to pay for it: "I pray you sir, receive the money now" (3.2.175). Angelo takes Antipholus (of Ephesus, as he thinks) to be joking in suggesting that he needs to pay up on the spot: "You are a merry man, sir: fare you well" (3.2.177).[28] This is not the way things are done

---

24. On weirdness, see G. R. Elliott, "Weirdness in *The Comedy of Errors*," *University of Toronto Quarterly* 9 (1939): 95–106; reprinted in Miola, *Critical Essays*, 57–70.

25. Greenblatt, "In the Night Kitchen," 28 (see chap. 3, app. 2, n. 42).

26. On "the willingness to tolerate unpaid debts for long periods of time before going to law," see Muldrew, *Economy of Obligation*, 200.

27. For evidence that this merchant is non-native, see Foakes's comment (61n). Matthew Steggle points out that the officer evokes the fear of punishment for debt, a fear that haunts the urban world of this play as an alternative to its normal workings—and as a reminder of one of the darker aspects of the commercial world of contemporary London ("Arrest for Debt in *The Comedy of Errors*," Shakespeare Association of America [SAA] seminar paper, Bermuda, 2005).

28. Andrew Zurcher's claim that Angelo here "fears he would be dishonouring his patron" in suggesting that he is worried about being paid seems to me to be on the right track but to imply a misleading level of anxiety. Angelo's response is lighthearted, not nervous or fearful. Zurcher

in Ephesus. When the true Antipholus of Ephesus does not receive the chain, he says to Angelo, "Belike you thought our love would last too long / If it were chain'd together, and therefore came not" (4.1.25–26). This is indeed joking and sarcastic, but it is striking that he speaks of their "love." Antipholus of Ephesus is fully willing to pay for the chain; he does not have the cash on him, but tells Angelo: "[W]ith you take the chain, and bid my wife / Disburse the sum on the receipt thereof" (4.1.37–38). Everything is straightforward, honest, and good-humored. No one wishes to cheat anyone or to avoid either payment or delivery. When the "errors" manifest themselves here, and Angelo insists that he has already delivered the chain, Antipholus of Ephesus is indignant to be accused of nonpayment: "You wrong me much to say so" (4.1.66).

This is a world where lack of complete transparency in business dealings is considered almost unthinkably dishonorable, a matter, as Angelo says, of "shame" (4.1.85). When, at the beginning of the fifth act, Angelo is asked (by the nonresident merchant) to describe Antipholus of Ephesus's status in the city, Angelo mentions the excellence of Antipholus's "reputation" and that he is "highly belov'd." But I have skipped over the phrase that comes between "reputation" and "belov'd"—Antipholus, Angelo says, is of "credit infinite." And just in case Angelo's merchant interlocutor might be under the impression that the goldsmith is speaking of "credit" only in a general sense, Angelo states that Antipholus's word "might bear my wealth at any time" (5.1.4–8). And the other Antipholus is as straightforward and honest as everyone else in the play. We have already noted that he offers to pay for the chain as soon as he has received it; he is horrified to be accused of denying that he has received the chain. "Who heard me to deny or to forswear it," he asks (5.1.25), and he upbraids Angelo's creditor for bringing such a charge against him. "Thou art a villain to impeach me thus," he asserts, using technical legal language (5.1.29). He draws his sword (or rapier) to defend "mine honour and mine honesty"—the bourgeois as well as the aristocratic code, "honesty" as well as "honour."[29] As Muldrew has demonstrated at length, "credit" in the period

---

seems to me mistaken in seeing "a heavy penumbra of distrust" in the play's portrayal of commercial relations. See "Consideration, Contract and the End of *The Comedy of Errors*," in *Shakespeare and the Law*, ed. Paul Raffield and Gary Watt (Oxford: Hart, 2008), 26–27. Antipholus of Syracuse's anxiety is understandable, but it is, unsurprisingly, general, and has nothing in particular to do with commercial relations.

29. On honor in the period, see Mervyn James, "English Politics and the Concept of Honour, 1485–1642," in *Society, Politics and Culture: Studies in Early Modern England* (Cambridge: Cambridge University Press, 1986), 308–415; on the different valence of "honesty," see Joshua Scodel, *The English Poetic Epitaph: Commemoration and Conflict from Jonson to Wordsworth*

was both a financial and a moral term, and the two meanings were intimately interrelated: one's reputation for honesty and reliability was crucial to one's business and social standing.[30]

Even the character "Courtesan" in this play seems to be an upright citizen. She is a direct descendant of Erotium in *Menaechmi*, but she does not play nearly as important a role in Shakespeare's play as Erotium does in Plautus's. The Courtesan figures in Shakespeare's plot as an object of sexual jealousy for Antipholus of Ephesus's wife, but, as this Antipholus insists—in a context in which we are pretty clearly intended to believe him—he has been accused "without desert" (3.1.112). Plautus's Erotium is presented as a kind of sex goddess (or at least she strikes the infatuated at-home Menaechmus as such); her first appearance on stage is heralded with the astonishing line by Menaechmus, "Oh, see how the sun is dimmed beside the radiance of that lovely body" (*oh, solem vides / satin ut occaecatust prae huius corporis candoribus*).[31] In Shakespeare, the first thing that Antipholus of Ephesus says about the Courtesan is that she is "a wench of excellent discourse" (3.1.109). This precedes the mention of her being "pretty"—an observation that is immediately balanced by "and witty" (3.2.110). This might mean that she is to be seen as a *cortigiana* rather than merely a prostitute, an unconscious revival, as Wolfgang Riehle (following Burckhardt) puts it, of "the tradition of the cultivated *hetairai* of Menandrian comedy,"[32] but in the play, the Courtesan, despite her designation, seems less a courtesan than the proprietress of an inn, "the Por-

---

(Ithaca: Cornell University Press, 1991), chap. 5, "Praising Honest Men: Social and Religious Tensions in the Mid-Seventeenth-Century Epitaph." On rapiers versus swords here and elsewhere in the play, see the updated New Cambridge *Comedy of Errors* (52). The ambiguity about the weapon matches the class ambiguities.

30. This is a major thesis of Muldrew's book (*Economy of Obligation*, 34–49, et passim).

31. Plautus, *The Brothers Menaechmus*, in *The Pot of Gold and Other Plays*, trans. E. F. Watling (London: Penguin, 1965), 109 (translation slightly emended: "body" for "person"); for the Latin, see *Menaechmi: The Two Menaechmuses*, in *Plautus*, trans. Paul Nixon, Loeb Classical Library (Cambridge: Harvard University Press, 1917), 2:382 (lines 179–80). See also Wolfgang Riehle, *Shakespeare, Plautus and the Humanist Tradition* (Cambridge: D. S. Brewer, 1990), 57.

32. Riehle, *Shakespeare, Plautus and the Humanist Tradition*, 58. See Burckhardt, *The Civilization of the Renaissance*, 2:394 (see intro., n. 2): "Even the intercourse with courtesans seems to have assumed a more elevated character, reminding us of the *hetairae* in classical Athens." On the complexities of the figure of the *cortigiana*, see Margaret F. Rosenthal, *The Honest Courtesan: Veronica Franco, Citizen and Writer in Sixteenth-Century Venice* (Chicago: University of Chicago Press, 1992).

pentine" (3.1.116). Obviously, these roles can run together (as, perhaps, they do in Mistress Quickly), but *Errors* seems to insist not only on Antipholus's lack of sexual involvement with the Courtesan, but also on her status as the "hostess" of the Porpentine (3.1.119). Her business does not, at least primarily, seem to be that of selling herself.

The Courtesan's other function in the plot is in relation to the chain that tracks and generates so many of the "errors' in the play.[33] The gold chain was originally commissioned, with great insistence—it was "bespoke . . . [n]ot once, nor twice, but twenty times" (3.2.172)—by Antipholus of Ephesus for his wife, but after being barred from his own house for dinner, he decides to "bestow" the chain on the Courtesan instead (3.1.117).[34] This would seem to be a fairly direct parallel to the valuable dress which, in Plautus, the at-home Menaechmus gives to Erotium, but even here the differences are striking. In Plautus, this Menaechmus has, with great delight in his own cleverness—he is wearing the dress under his cloak—stolen the dress from his wife to give to his "girl" (*ad scortum fero*); his wife's resentment over this theft of a valuable from her is a major issue in Plautus's play.[35] In Shakespeare, as we have seen, the decision to give the chain to the Courtesan is a reaction to the locking-out scene, as is Antipholus of Ephesus's purchase of a "rope's end" with which to scourge his wife and her "confederates" (4.1.16-17). Adriana knows that the chain is being made for her, but she asserts that she values Antipholus's fidelity

33. On the chain as a symbol of the marital bond and of social solidarity in general, see Richard Henze, "*The Comedy of Errors*: A Freely Given Chain," *Shakespeare Quarterly* 22 (1971): 35–41; for the claim that the chain is related to Protestant theological discourse, especially to William Perkins's *A Golden Chain, or The Description of Theology* (1591), see Donna B. Hamilton, *Shakespeare and the Politics of Protestant England* (Lexington: University Press of Kentucky, 1984), 84.

34. It is interesting to reflect on how richly detailed the "social life" of this chain is in the play. We know what it is made of, who made it, who commissioned it, why it was commissioned, and what it cost, as well as who came to have it, how it was finally paid for, and so forth. See *The Social Life of Things: Commodities in Cultural Perspective*, ed. Arjun Appadurai (Cambridge: Cambridge University Press, 1986).

35. See *The Brothers Menaechmus*, 107; for the Latin, *Plautus*, 2:376 (line 130); hereafter English and Latin page references are cited together, with the English preceding the Latin. For the wife's resentment about the dress, see especially *The Brothers Menaechmus*, 126–27/2:428, 430. In Plautus, we do not know who made this dress, or how it came into being, though we do that Menaechus bought it for his wife, and what it cost (110/2:386 [line 205]). Anne Christensen notes that "the Roman husband procures his gifts to the courtesan from his wife's closet, thereby obscuring actual economic transactions" (" 'Because their business still lies out a' door,' " 22).

much more than the material object: "[W]ould that alone . . . he would detain, / So he would keep fair quarter with his bed" (2.1.106–8).[36]

It turns out, moreover, that Antipholus of Ephesus does not actually intend to "bestow" the valuable chain on the Courtesan; he actually intends to trade her for it. When she (as she believes) confronts him later, she says, "Give me the ring of mine you had at dinner, / Or for my diamond, the chain you promised" (4.3.66–67). This is still a diversion of the chain from Antipholus of Ephesus's wife, and it is still a good bargain for the Courtesan, since the chain is worth a good deal more than the ring (it is notable that we are given the exact value of each—the ring is worth forty ducats (4.3.80, 94), the necklace two hundred (4.4.132). The Courtesan did not ask for the chain, and when (through the errors) she does not get it, all she wants is her ring back, because, as she sensibly says, "forty ducats is too much to lose." Faced with the possibility of loss of her ring, the Courtesan unhesitatingly resolves to go to Antipholus's home and report his bizarre behavior to his wife (4.3.89–92). The Courtesan does redescribe Antipholus's dinnertime behavior—"He rush'd into my house and took perforce / My ring away" (4.3.91–2)—and this may qualify her for being "the only deliberate deceiver" in the play.[37] But she might well think him "mad," on the basis of the preposterous "tale he told to-day at dinner / Of his own doors being shut against his entrance" (4.3.85–86), and her motive in redescribing his behavior is only to recover her property. In the next scene, the wife and the Courtesan seek Antipholus (of Ephesus) together, and they agree, with the Courtesan's story in mind, that he must be mad.[38] Antipholus of Ephesus's wife describes her husband as "[d]oing displeasure to the citizens" (4.1.142). The Courtesan is fully in this category. The wife's belief that her husband must be mad is based, as she says, on his strange and unwonted "incivility" (4.4.44)—a very strong negative term in this play (and in the early modern business world).[39] Antipholus of Ephesus is not behaving like a proper citizen; and he is offending other citizens, other property owners, in the city. He must

36. There is some textual corruption in Adriana's speech here. See Foakes (25), although the emendation he accepts has not been adopted by other editors. There is, it should be noted, also a chain in *Menaechmi*, but it too was stolen from the wife (line 537).

37. See Laurie Maguire, "The Girls from Ephesus," in Miola, *Critical Essays*, 369.

38. Hutson, *The Invention of Suspicion*, points out how the courtesan's "little fib" feeds into the wife's perception (153).

39. For the significance of "civility"—and the shock of "incivility"—in early modern English business dealings, see the quotations in Muldrew, *Economy of Obligation*, 201–2. Camille Wells Slights, in *Shakespeare's Comic Commonwealths* (Toronto: University of Toronto Press, 1993), recognizes the importance of the term for the play (28).

be mad because he is behaving weirdly—that is, apparently dishonestly—with regard to property: stealing rings, not paying debts, and so forth.

A COMPANIONATE MARRIAGE

The mention of Antipholus of Ephesus's wife brings us to the other half of the celebration of bourgeois life in this play: its celebration, exposition, and demonstration of companionate marriage.[40] This was anticipated, as was the positive treatment of commerce, in the "frame" of the play. The condemned Syracusan merchant (Egeon) tells the story of how he was "severed from [the] bliss" (1.1.118) of a happy marriage, a marriage in which emotional and material prosperity coincided. He unites the two kinds of happiness in a single spectacularly paratactic line of verse: "With her I liv'd in joy; our wealth increas'd" (1.1.39). There is no irony here. These things are meant to go together.[41] Tragedy becomes possible when they are pulled apart. When laudable and completely intelligible "care of goods at random left" (1.1.42) leads the happily married merchant from "kind embracements of [his] spouse" [1.1.43]), he is forced to leave his city and expose himself to the (potentially) tragic world of seafaring (1.1.63). The worst that an apparently hostile universe can inflict on him—"We were encounter'd by a mighty rock" (1.1.101)—is to foist upon him "an unjust divorce" (1.1.104). The play does not investigate "the competing roles of the household and the marketplace," and then finally come to reconcile the two arenas, because the play never sees these arenas as competing, but presents them as ideally compatible all along.[42] It is not "business trouble" that leads to Egeon's tragic voyage, and his stay at Epidamnum is not "fatefully

40. I have been anticipated in this claim by Thomas Hennings in "The Anglican Doctrine of Affectionate Marriage in *The Comedy of Errors*" (see chap. 1, n. 53).

41. Perry notes the "affective connection between the familial and the economic" here ("Commerce, Community, and Nostalgia," 41). What is odd about Perry's essay is that he then goes on to contrast "commercialized relationships" with "more meaningful kinds of affective bonds" (49)—exactly the polarity that Muldrew seeks to deconstruct in *Economy of Obligation* (see his introduction, "Deconstructing Capitalism," 148–50, et passim). Perry quotes Muldrew on the anxiety involved in "webs of credit and obligation in the period" (Perry, 44; Muldrew, 95) but brushes aside the idea that these networks were "of course in some sense socially binding"— which is, again, Muldrew's major point. Kinney, "*The Comedy of Errors*: A Modern Perspective," also sees the business world of the play in pseudo-Marxist terms, and therefore as negative, in terms of "commodification" (187).

42. Jessica Slights, "The 'Undividable Incorporate,'" 74.

protracted."[43] His wife prudently "made provision" to join him there—"And soon, and safe, arrived where I was" (1.1.47–48)—where she became a "joyful mother of two goodly sons." The family was prospering in all respects in Epidamnum. It was only Egeon's wife's constant insistence on the couple's returning back to Syracuse—her "daily motions for our home return" (1.1.59)—and his acquiescence to this demand, that led to the fatal voyage.

But, again, for the real development of the theme of the companionate marriage—and of the happy continuity between the domestic and the commercial—we must look to the life of the central Ephesians. As we have already noted, Shakespeare goes out of his way to give Antipholus of Ephesus's house a name, making it clear that, like the Porpentine, it is as much an establishment as a home; Adriana, Antipholus of Ephesus's wife, is fully the mistress of both house and establishment—"my mistress at the Phoenix," Dromio of Ephesus calls her (1.2.88). She is surprised at the thought that there is an aspect of her husband's financial life with which she is unacquainted: "[T]his I wonder at, / That he unknown to me should be in debt" (4.2.48–49). But that is only a small part of the evocation of this marriage in the play. Nowhere does Shakespeare depart more sharply from his major Plautine source than in his treatment of the at-home twin's marriage and in his handling of the character of the at-home twin's wife. In *Will in the World*, Stephen Greenblatt has claimed that Shakespeare was incapable of imagining "what it would mean fully to share a life."[44] Yet this, as I have suggested and will develop further, is exactly what is imagined in *The Comedy of Errors*.

The wife, in Shakespeare's play, is, as we will see shortly, a remarkable character, but before focusing on her, there is a question that must at least briefly be considered: does Shakespeare create an image of companionate marriage by upgrading the woman while leaving the character of the husband basically unreconstructed? We have already noted the rejection of actual sexual infidelity on the part of the husband in the play. We should also take seriously the fact that he is having the chain made for his wife—"Go home with it, and please

43. Ibid., 78.

44. Stephen Greenblatt, *Will in the World* (New York: Norton, 2004), 131. Greenblatt sees this (supposed) incapacity in Shakespeare as having both personal and cultural sources. With regard to the latter, his suggestion that the idea of a "companionate" marriage is anachronistic when applied to Shakespeare (128–29) is misguided, as the example of Spenser's poetry and life shows, as does (perhaps) the life and some of the poetry of Donne. Emma Lipton has shown that the idea (and practice) was developing in the fifteenth century. See *Affections of the Mind: The Politics of Sacramental Marriage in Late Medieval English Literature* (Notre Dame: University of Notre Dame Press, 2007).

your wife withal" says the goldsmith (4.2.172)—and we should take seriously not only Adriana's assumption of Antipholus's candor about business, but also his assumption that she will immediately and unquestioningly "bail" him after he is arrested. It is in this latter context that we get the lovely household detail of "the desk / That's covered with the Turkish tapestry" (4.2.105–6).[45]

This is a home that is truly a home. Shakespeare's Courtesan never says to Antipholus what Plautus's Erotium says, with apparent justice, to Menaechmus: "[T]his house is more of a home to you than your own" (*magis quam domus tua domus quom haec tua sit*).[46] Antipholus is looking forward to entertaining his friends and colleagues at home. When he asks the goldsmith to "excuse us all" for coming late for dinner, and notes, "My wife is shrewish when I keep not hours" (3.1.20), this may seem to be moving toward low comedy, but his complaint is mild ("shrewish") and limited ("when I keep not hours"). This request can also tell us some things about the nature of Antipholus's marriage. He is apparently not prepared simply to assert his "right" to do as he pleases, and his request can perhaps also be seen as showing some concern for his wife's feelings: at least he feels compelled to offer an excuse (or have his friend do so).[47] And after Antipholus and his companions are locked out, and Antipholus is threatening to break into his house, Balthazar reminds him not only of "the unviolated honor of your wife," but also of what an impressive person she is, and is apparently known to be. He reminds Antipholus of "your long experience of her wisdom" (3.1.89), and this seems, together with worry about "vulgar comment" on his behavior, to work on him—"despite of wrath" (3.1.108).[48] When the Syracusan Antipholus is (naturally) puzzled at and unresponsive to Adriana's address to him—she gives an extraordinary speech that we will examine later—Luciana asks him, "When were you wont to use my sister thus?" (2.2.153). So, if the at-home Antipholus is not as distinct from the at-home Menaechmus as Adriana is from Matrona in *Menaechmi*, Antipholus

45. With regard to household finances, it may be significant that Antipholus of Ephesus seems to hold the only key to this desk. This is pointed out by Mario di Gangi, "Shakespeare's Comic Households," in Dutton and Howard, *A Companion to Shakespeare's Works*, 3:100, though I am not sure where di Gangi gets the idea that this key could open a private study.

46. *The Brothers Menaechmus*, 115/2:400 (line 363).

47. For an entirely negative view of the Ephesian Antipholus's behavior here, see Jessica Slights, "The 'Undividable Incorporate,'" 81.

48. Like some earlier editors (see Foakes, for example, 48n), I have accepted Theobald's emendation of "wrath" for the Folio's "mirth" in this line, since "despite of mirth" makes no sense, despite various editors' attempts to explain it. Foakes, it should be noted, prints "mirth," as do all recent editions.

of Ephesus is still a very long way from the husband in *Menaechmi*, and the marriage evoked in *Errors* is very far—even when considering the husband's depicted and implied feelings and behavior—from the loveless, purely social arrangement evoked in Plautus's play.[49]

Even the most bizarre moment in Shakespeare's play, Luciana's advocacy of marital hypocrisy—of the husband concealing his infidelity—is part of the play's emphasis on the companionate aspect of marriage.[50] In response to Antipholus's apparently odd behavior in relation to Adriana, Luciana asks him a wonderful question:

> And may it be that you have quite forgot
> A husband's office?
> (2.2.1–2a)

"A husband's office" here is much more than a matter of keeping the wife "in clothes, jewelry, and all the servants and provisions you could possibly need"—the account of husbandly duty given to Matrona in *Menaechmi* by both her husband and her father.[51] "A husband's office" in Shakespeare's play is a

49. My major disagreement with Candido, "Dining Out in Ephesus," has to do with his treatment of Antipholus of Ephesus. Candido views Antipholus as "repudiating" his marriage (200 et passim), yet Candido himself notes Antipholus's assumption that his wife will be perfectly happy for him to bring unannounced guests home to their midday meal, and will be perfectly ready—as she indeed is—for him to do so (207). Candido's animus against Antipholus of Ephesus leads him to present the "refined humanist discourse" about food that we have examined as somehow meant to exclude Adriana, and this animus leads Candido to downgrade this discourse itself as "somewhat precious" (211). But this discourse is pretty clearly coded as noble and learned, and we have already seen that Adriana is well-spoken as well as outspoken, and that her intelligence is recognized by those who know her (recall "your long experience of her wisdom"). Jessica Slights's indictment of Antipholus of Ephesus's "neglect of his household" ("The 'Undividable Incorporate,'" 91) seems somewhat ludicrous in light of his being locked out of it; elsewhere she acknowledges his dependence on his household and his wife. For a defense of the character of Antipholus of Ephesus, see Riehle, *Shakespeare, Plautus and the Humanist Tradition*, 60–61.

50. I would be interested in seeing the sermons of the period that Kinney sees this speech as "echoing almost verbatim." "*The Comedy of Errors*: A Modern Perspective," 181. Riehle recognizes the oddness of this speech (205).

51. *The Brothers Menaechmus*, 106, 132 / 374, 444. The lists in the two passages are not identical, but are very similar. That the wife's speech heading in Plautus is "Matrona" perhaps suggests a higher social status than the generic "Wife" (*uxor*).

matter of showing affection. The couple are quite young, and relatively newly married. This is apparent from the amazement with which Luciana asks of the (apparent) young husband, "shall Antipholus, / Even in the spring of love, thy love-springs rot?" (3.2.2b-3). She is desperate for Antipholus (of Ephesus, of course) to show affection to his spouse, to show, as she says "kindness" (3.2.6). She wants this under all possible circumstances. "If," she says with straight-forward realism, "you did wed my sister for her wealth," then "for her wealth's sake use her with more kindness." This desperate concern for her sister's husband to show "kindness" is what leads Luciana to her very odd and passionate recommendation of hypocrisy: "[I]f you like elsewhere, do it by stealth. . . . Let not my sister read it in your eye." The point is that he should "look sweet, speak fair" to his wife (3.2.7-11). This is "a husband's office": "Comfort my sister, cheer her, call her wife" (3.2.26). The companionate aspect of marriage, on this account, is even more important than sexual fidelity. This is all irrelevant, of course, since we know that sexual infidelity is not an issue, and since the apparent husband is acting coldly for an entirely different reason, but the fact that this position is articulated in the play is significant.

In *Menaechmi*, the wife's "pestering" of Menaechmus about his comings and goings is not directly presented; we only hear his protest against it and the wife's father's rebuke to her for such behavior, given the husband's proper provision for her (quoted above).[52] Adriana, on the other hand, while she shares the Roman wife's concerns with her husband's comings and goings, enters the play in her own voice and offers a philosophical defense of her position (it is perhaps significant that in Plautus's play, the "other woman" has a name and the wife does not, whereas in Shakespeare the situation is reversed). Adriana first appears onstage in what is essentially a formal debate about gender roles within marriage. Her sister, Luciana, serves as the voice of patriarchy, and of good-humored submission to it. "Good sister," she says, "let us dine and never fret"; there is no point in or justification for worrying about what husbands do, since "[a] man is master of his liberty" (2.1.6-7). This is essentially what the wife's father in Plautus says to his daughter.[53] In Plautus, this is unquestionably seen as common sense and common wisdom (though the wife is not expected to put up with having her accoutrements stolen). The wife in Shakespeare

---

52. For the husband's protest, see *The Brothers Menaechmus*, 106/2:344-45. Menaechmus says that his wife acts as if she were a *portitor*, a customs-house officer (*portitorem domum duxi*); Watling cleverly translates this "an immigration officer."

53. See *The Brothers Menaechmus*, 132/2:444 (lines 793-97).

rejects all of Luciana's premises. We have already considered Adriana's critique of patience; our focus here is her conception of marriage.[54] She sees her marriage as what we would call a "relationship." She expects it to be fun, sexy, and intellectually interesting. She protests that her husband's "company must do his minions grace, / While I at home starve for a merry look" (2.1.87–88). She expects her marriage to be "merry"; she expects to be recognized as beautiful, asking rhetorically whether "homely age [has] th' alluring beauty took / From my poor cheek?"; and she expects to be, and to be valued for being, a fine conversationalist. Again rhetorically, she asks, "Are my discourses dull, barren my wit?" (2.1.91).[55]

In the next scene, when Adriana and Luciana confront Antipholus (of Syracuse) in the street, Adriana evokes the norm of her marriage to Antipholus (of Ephesus). Speaking ironically, as if the "time" in question were the distant past, she notes (with her typical verbal accomplishment):

> The time was once when thou unurg'd wouldst vow
> That never words were music to thine ear,
> That never object pleasing to thine eye,
> That never touch well welcome to thy hand,
> That never meat sweet-savour'd to thy taste,
> Unless I spake, or look'd, or touch'd, or carv'd to thee.[56]
>
> (2.2.113–18)

This is a vision of a very high degree of domestic pleasure and intimacy. Anne C. Christensen, following Karen Newman, speaks of "the special nearness of wives" in early modern England, and explains the social and cultural significance of the item on which the list ends—"carv'd to thee." Christensen notes that in describing herself as taking on this task, Adriana "aligns herself with

54. On patience, see chapter 1 above.

55. Women in the play, in order to be valued, are consistently expected to be intelligent and eloquent. We have already noted Antipholus of Ephesus's description of the Courtesan as "a wench of excellent discourse" (3.1.109). Antipholus of Syracuse is struck by Luciana's eloquence at least as much as her appearance. He tells her, "Less in your knowledge and your grace you show not / Than our earth's wonder," and implores her to teach him "how to think and speak" (3.2.31–33). If Francis Douce was right that "our earth's wonder" refers to Queen Elizabeth, the point is reinforced (see Foakes, 51).

56. Candido misses the irony in this speech, and so is deceived into thinking that Adriana is actually referring to "an earlier stage" in their marriage ("Dining Out in Ephesus," 209).

[the] special brand of service, skill, and trust newly designated to middle-class wives."[57]

Most interesting of all, Adriana protests against the sexual double standard. "Why should," she asks, "their liberty than ours be more?" (2.1.10). She rejects the pragmatic argument for greater male "liberty"—"their business still lies out o' door" (2.1.11)—an argument to be developed by Katherine in her final speech in *Shrew*—and she also rejects the metaphysical argument for female restraint: "There's nothing situate under heaven's eye / But hath his bound" (2.1.16–17]).[58] Adriana's point, however, as becomes clear later in this dialogue and in the continuation of it in the scene following, is not that she wants greater "liberty." What she wants is for her husband to have to play by the same rules that she does. She is perfectly happy to accept the ideal of chastity—here, of course, meaning not virginity but marital fidelity—but she rejects the notion that this ideal does not apply equally to married males. Construing her marriage partner as an ideal classical friend (another self), and adding to that the idea of husband and wife as "one flesh" (Gen. 2:24), Adriana sees distance within marriage as "estrangement from oneself" (2.2.120). She then goes on, quite brilliantly, to use the intensity of male sexual possessiveness as an argument for mutual marital faithfulness.[59]

She accepts the force and validity of male possessiveness, asking (to the wrong Antipholus, as it happens):

> How dearly would it touch thee to the quick,
> Shouldst thou but hear I were licentious?
> And that this body, consecrate to thee,
> By ruffian lust should be contaminate?
>
> (2.2.130–33)

---

57. Christensen, " 'Because their business still lies out a' door,' " 30, quoting Karen Newman, *Fashioning Femininity and English Renaissance Drama* (Chicago: University of Chicago Press, 1991), 17.

58. On the outdoor-indoor contrast as an argument for male dominance, see the discussion of the classical source (Xenophon) and Renaissance adaptations of this argument in Lorna Hutson, *The Usurer's Daughter: Male Friendship and Fictions of Women in Sixteenth-Century England* (London: Routledge, 1994), chap. 1. On the metaphysical argument, see 46 above.

59. Greenblatt notes the passion in Adriana's speech (he quotes 2.2.119–29), but does not consider the ideal from which this passion springs, and to which it gives voice (*Will in the World*, 130). Camille Wells Slights observes that Adriana's speech here is hardly "the tirade of a comic virago bent on mastery" (*Shakespeare's Comic Commonwealths*, 19).

She accepts that, were she to be "contaminate" in this way, it would be completely appropriate for Antipholus to issue "a deep-divorcing vow." She then goes on to play her trump card. She asserts that she is so "contaminate." "I am," she says, "possess'd with an adulterate blot." She claims, continuing this vehement and intense language, that her very blood is infected: "My blood is mingled with the crime of lust" (2.2.141). But this is not because of her behavior, but of his. In a triumphant and completely unassailable syllogism, she concludes:

> For if we two be one, and thou play false,
> I do digest the poison of thy flesh,
> Being strumpeted by thy contagion.
>
> (2.2.142–44)

So, if Antipholus does not want his wife to be "adulterated," he must keep "fair league and truce with [his] true bed" (2.2.145).

Adriana is not at all silent, is not inclined to be obedient, but she is most definitely chaste. Lena Cowen Orlin has shown that the three items in the famous supposed triumvirate of virtues for the ideal woman ("chaste, silent, and obedient") were not all on the same plane, and that violations of the second two were not necessarily taken, and should not be taken, as violations of the first.[60] Just as Shakespeare keeps Antipholus of Ephesus chaste in his relations with the "Courtesan," Shakespeare carefully keeps Adriana from sleeping with the wrong Antipholus. In the scene of the Plautus play from which Shakespeare borrowed the idea of the husband locked out while his "twin" was with the wife within—*Amphitryo*, rather than *Menaechmi*—the wife does sleep with the figure who is identical to her husband: "You had dinner with me and went to bed with me," she says to this figure.[61] The wife in *Amphitryo* is

60. Orlin, "Shakespearean Comedy and Material Life," 171–77. Orlin demonstrates that if one consults documents other than sermons and treatises (church court records, in particular), it becomes clear that actual women in the Elizabethan world, including "ordinary" (nongentry) women, were much less "constructed" and constricted by patriarchal ideology than the official formulations of this ideology would lead one to believe (and has led many scholars to believe). To the assertion in *The Merry Wives of Windsor*, "Wives may be merry and yet honest too," we must add the notion that wives may be assertively eloquent and freethinking, and yet honest too. See *The Merry Wives of Windsor*, ed. H. J. Oliver (London: Methuen, 1971), 4.2.96. In *Merry Wives*, there is, oddly, virtually no representation of positive relations between spouses.

61. Plautus, *Amphitryo*, in *The Rope and Other Plays*, trans. E. F. Watling (London: Penguin, 1964), 258.

held blameless (she could not have known that she was not with her husband, and the identical figure turns out to be Jupiter, in any case), but in *The Comedy of Errors*, Shakespeare does not even allow the hint of such a development.[62] He might have done so when Antipholus of Syracuse speaks of entertaining "the offer'd fallacy" (2.2.186), and when Adriana insists on the intimacy and privacy of the dinner that she (and her sister) will have with her husband—they will dine "above," and Dromio is strictly enjoined to "keep the gate . . . and let no creature enter (2.2.207–10).[63] But in the scene with the double within and the husband without—the *Amphitryo* situation—Shakespeare makes Antipholus of Syracuse emphatically disclaim any attraction to (the no doubt beautiful) Adriana: "She that doth call me husband, even my soul / Doth for a wife abhor" (3.2.157–58).[64]

This talk of the "soul" is significant. Marriage, in this play, is indeed a matter of finding a "soul-mate." Antipholus of Syracuse's "soul's pure truth" (3.2.37) is what leads him, he says, to the choice of Adriana's unmarried sister (whom Shakespeare pretty clearly invented to serve this role in the plot).[65] This Antipholus sees himself as already spiritually married to Luciana, since he addresses her in exactly the terms in which Adriana addressed him (as her husband). Adriana spoke of herself in relation to Antipholus of Ephesus as "thy dear self's better part" (2.2.123). Antipholus of Syracuse speaks of Luciana as "mine own self's better part" (3.2.61).

Males and females in this play seem to have the same idea of marriage and to manifest (more or less) the same high level of chastity. Even the servants seem (more or less) to keep to this level. Muldrew notes that "the honesty, fidelity and modesty of a wife, and the honesty and diligence of servants, all

---

62. Alcmena, the wife in *Amphitryo*, is eloquent, unafraid, outspoken, and completely virtuous: "An innocent woman is not afraid to speak out boldly for herself," she says (264). She, rather than the unnamed wife in *Menaechmi*, is the model for Adriana (compare Riehle, *Shakespeare, Plautus and the Humanist Tradition*, 41, 56). I confess that I cannot follow Hutson's argument about the audience's supposed "uncertainty about [the female characters'] sexual intentions and desires" in *Errors* and other Shakespearean plays (*Usurer's Daughter*, 190, 204–8).

63. On the way in which Adriana imagines and arranges this meal, see Candido, "Dining Out in Ephesus," 210.

64. Whether Adriana has sexual relations with the wrong Antipholus is not, contra Maguire (and the productions she cites), "a moot point" in the play ("The Girls from Ephesus," 367).

65. Hennings, "Affectionate Marriage," seems to be confused about what Antipholus of Syracuse is saying here, taking the "unknown field" that Antipholus does not wish to "wander in" as incest, rather than Adriana (99–101).

contributed to the credit or reputation of a family."[66] When Luce (or Nell) acted seductively to the wrong Dromio, she apparently did so in the context of an engagement, since he speaks of her as "a wondrous fat marriage" (3.2.92).[67] As Emma Lipton has shown, the idea of the companionate—or, as she calls it, "sacramental"—marriage was strongly emerging in the later Middle Ages, and served the function of giving the lay "middle strata," as opposed to the clergy on the one hand and the aristocracy on the other, "its own discourse of legitimation."[68]

The rejection of the double standard followed a similar trajectory and is related to the "companionate" or "sacramental" idea. Keith Thomas's article on the double standard is mainly devoted to documenting and trying to explain the surprising longevity of this arrangement in the British legal system—male, as opposed to female, adultery was declared a legal cause for divorce only in 1923—but Thomas does devote some space to opposition to the double standard.[69] He notes that in the course of the Middle Ages, "the idea that unchastity was as much a sin for the one sex as for the other steadily gained ground."[70] But with the Reformation, this idea gained greater momentum. Here, as with the development of the idea of the companionate marriage, the so-called Puritans took the lead.[71] However, as Thomas P. Hennings points out, the idea of a single standard is explicit in the government-sponsored and required Homily on Matrimony, in which the first point of marriage is that man and woman should live lawfully in a "perpetuall friendship"; the second is "to bring foorth fruite"; and the third is "to avoide fornication" so that "a good conscience might bee preserved *on both parties*."[72] Thomas sees "the other main source of

---

66. Muldrew, *Economy of Obligation*, 158.

67. On the name uncertainty here (Luce or Nell), see Foakes's note on 3.2.107 (56).

68. Lipton, *Affections of the Mind*, 3.

69. Keith Thomas, "The Double Standard," *Journal of the History of Ideas* 20 (1959): 195–216.

70. Ibid., 203.

71. On the "Puritan" role in developing the idea of the companionate marriage, see ibid.; William and Malleville Haller, "The Puritan Art of Love," *Huntington Library Quarterly* 5 (1942): 235–72; Frye, "The Teachings of Classical Puritanism on Conjugal Love," discussed above in the introduction (see intro., n. 34), and James Grantham Turner, *One Flesh: Paradisal Marriage and Sexual Relations in the Age of Milton* (Oxford: Oxford University Press, 1987), chap. 2.

72. Hennings, "Affectionate Marriage," 96–97; "An Homilie of the state of Matrimonie," in *Certaine Sermons or Homilies Appointed to be Read in Churches In the Time of Queen Elizabeth . . . I*, facsimile reproduction of 1623, intro. Mary Ellen Rickey and Thomas B. Stroup (Gainesville: University Presses of Florida, 1968), the second tome, 239 (emphasis mine).

opposition" to the double standard as what he calls "the ever-growing current" in the early modern period, of "what can only be described as middle-class respectability."[73]

MARITAL "OFFICES"

Both Reformation and respectability operate in *The Comedy of Errors*. It might seem that the latter is clearer, but the two (as Weber and others have suggested) are related, and *Errors* must be seen as consciously Protestant as well as consciously committed to "middle-class respectability." The skepticism in the play, especially with regard to fairies and witches, is a recognizably Protestant skepticism; the medical doctor / exorcist who is mocked in the play, Dr. Pinch, is marked as a specifically Catholic figure.[74] When attempting, at the request of Adriana and the Courtesan, to "conjure" the apparently mad Antipholus (in this case, of Syracuse) back into "his true sense again," Pinch utters a formal adjuration:

> I charge thee, Satan, hous'd within this man,
> To yield possession to my holy prayers,
> And to thy state of darkness hie thee straight;
> I conjure thee by all the saints in heaven.
>
> (4.4.52–55)

While the reference to "my holy prayers" could have been said by a Puritan exorcist—though even this is doubtful, for the phrase bears a suggestion of set or ritual prayers, which the Puritans opposed—the last line of this "conjuration" could only have been spoken by a Catholic. No Protestant, however High Church, would have conjured (meaning "adjured") "by all the saints in heaven."[75] There is a famous episode with exorcists—"Or, conjurers," says the Genevan gloss—that takes place in the biblical Ephesus in Acts 19:12–16, but as T. W. Baldwin noted, "it was not the exorcists of [ancient] Ephesus, but those of the Roman Catholic Church who 'conjured' with 'holy prayers,' and 'by all

---

73. Thomas, "The Double Standard," 204.

74. On both of these points, see Richard Strier, "Shakespeare and the Skeptics," *Religion and Literature* 32 (2000): 171–96.

75. For the Church of England position on "the saints in heaven," see George Herbert's "To all Angels and Saints." I have discussed this poem at length elsewhere (Richard Strier, " 'To all Angels and Saints': Herbert's Puritan Poem," *Modern Philology* [1979]: 132–45).

the saints in heaven.'"[76] Contra Ros King, Pinch is not an all-purpose "fanatic"; he is a Catholic.[77] He is also a figure of fun—totally misguided, as are all the references in the play to supernatural forces.[78] The one event that is described in the play as "past thought of human reason" and as a "miracle" is clearly and evidently neither (5.1.189, 265). In this play, as in normative Protestantism, "the working of miracles is ceased."[79]

76. T. W. Baldwin, *On the Compositional Genetics of The Comedy of Errors* (Urbana: University of Illinois Press, 1965), 54. In insisting that Pinch is surely a Puritan, Aaron Landau has to omit line 55 from his treatment, and in insisting that when *Errors* was produced, "exorcism was largely identified with Puritan sectarianism," Landau must fail to mention Samuel Harsnett's attack on "Egregious Popish Impostures," and treat the association of exorcism with Catholics as somehow a later development, which is false (see " 'Past Thought of Human Reason': Confounding Reason in *The Comedy of Errors*," *English Studies* 85 (2004): 203). For exorcism in late Elizabethan England, see F. W. Brownlow, *Shakespeare, Harsnett, and the Devils of Denham* (Newark: University of Delaware Press, 1993).

77. See the introduction to the updated New Cambridge *Comedy of Errors*, 12–14. Baldwin (*Compositional Genetics*, 40) cites a Protestant attack on Catholic exorcism from a treatise of 1550 (reprinted in 1590) called *The Epiphanie of the Church* by one Richard Phinch. King seems to suggest that Pinch is meant to recall Phinch (obviously pronounced "Finch"), but it is hard to see how this helps her case. I am not sure why Arthur Kinney thinks Dr. Pinch an "unbeliever" ("Shakespeare's *Comedy of Errors* and the Nature of Kinds," in Miola, *Critical Essays*, 158).

78. If the note by Malone that is adopted by Foakes (96) and others is indeed apropos, then Pinch's ultimate fate in the play, beard "sing'd off with brands of fire," and so forth (5.1.170–75), suggests further anti-Catholic satire, since the note suggests a connection between the haircut that Pinch is given—"[Antipholus of Ephesus's] man with scissors nicks him like a fool"—and the tonsure of monks: "They are shaven and notcht on the head, lyke fooles."

79. The quotation is from Reginald Scot, *The Discoverie of Witchcraft . . . Whereunto is added An excellent Discourse of the Nature and Substance of Devils and Spirits*, ed. Brinsley Nicholson (Totowa, N.J.: Rowman and Littlefield, 1973), 39, but, as I have indicated, the position is normative. On Shakespeare's apparent rejection of this position in a speech by Lafew in *All's Well that Ends Well*, see Strier, "Shakespeare and the Skeptics," 177–80. While Landau, " 'Past Thought of Human Reason,' " is correct that Montaigne's Pyrrhonism led him to rely on institutional Catholicism, Montaigne was scarcely, as his essay "On Repentance" shows, a normative Catholic, and it hardly helps Landau's argument that, as he ruefully notes, "English Catholics like Allen, Parsons, Fitzherbert, or Verstegan hardly ever resort to skeptical arguments" (192). The epistemological skepticism of the play—as opposed to its skepticism about miracles and exorcism—does not have any clear denominational orientation and, if one wishes to read it theologically, seems to call more for direct divine intervention—"Some blessed power deliver us from hence" (4.3.42)—than for reliance on an authoritative religious institution. For detailed discussion of the peculiar religious position of Montaigne's "On Repentance," see chapter 5 below.

But the strongest indication of the play's conscious commitment not just to worldliness but to what I have called the Protestant conception of inner-worldly holiness occurs in the final act of the play. Suddenly, at the beginning of the fifth act, the figure of the Abbess enters the play, an explicitly Catholic and, in specifically Catholic and institutional terms, an officially "religious" figure. What is important to see is that this entire section of the scene is staged as a competition between the Abbess and the wife (Adriana) for the right to take charge of Antipholus (supposedly of Ephesus) and his "treatment."[80] In this scene (as opposed to that with Pinch, which takes a mixed approach), Adriana views Antipholus's supposed condition purely naturalistically. She refers to him as "my poor distracted husband," and she wishes to treat him in the normal way that mad persons were treated—placed, as he has already been (5.1.247–49), and as the supposedly mad Malvolio will be, "in a dark room and bound" (*Twelfth Night*, 3.4.136); compare Pinch's own prescription: "They must be bound and laid in some dark room" (4.4.92). Adriana has no doubt as to the proper locus for such treatment. "Let us come in [to the abbey]," she requests or commands the Abbess, "that we may bind him fast / And bear him home for his recovery" (5.1.40–41). The Abbess, however, views Antipholus's condition as more than natural—exactly as Dr. Pinch had. "How long," she asks, "hath this possession held the man?" And the Abbess immediately recognizes that she is in direct competition with the wife. Through clever and seemingly neutral questions, the Abbess tricks Adriana into presenting herself as obsessed with her husband's (supposed) infidelity, and as allowing this obsession to color their entire domestic life (eating, sleeping, *à deux*, and in company). The Abbess then produces a grand vision of how this behavior has poisoned and unhinged Antipholus—a Burtonian vision, we might say, of how lack of "recreation" leads to madness and melancholy (5.1.69–86).[81]

---

80. Christensen, " 'Because their business still lies out a' door,' " 31, sees this as a struggle between a wife and a mother. This is true, of course, but it is not how the play stages the conflict, since at the moment of this contention, the Abbess does not know that she is (in the present) a mother, and is speaking entirely in her official role.

81. I owe to Carole Schuyler, another member of the '05 SAA seminar, the observation that the Abbess's position here is undercut not only by Luciana's defense of Adriana—"She never reprehended him but mildly" (5.1.87)—but by the fact, available through either reading or reseeing the play, that in her former life, as a wife, Egeon presents Emilia (now the Abbess) as having treated Egeon in much the same way that the Abbess presents Adriana having treated Antipholus of Ephesus. As we have already noted, Emilia and Egeon were doing fine in Epidamnum, but Emilia "[m]ade daily motions for our home return" (1.1.59), and this is what put them at the mercy of the sea (Schuyler, "The Comedy of Eros / Erring: Much Ovid and More Paul," SAA

Adriana is momentarily silenced by this maneuver, but the Abbess's apparent triumph is merely a rhetorical one, and Adriana perseveres in her practical endeavor, commanding her followers to enter the abbey and "lay hold" on her (supposed) husband.[82]

At this point, the Abbess takes a different tack. She appeals to the special status of her locale and, in particular, to the special legal status that this locale affords: "He took this place for sanctuary, / And it shall privilege him from your hands" (5.1.94–95). "Privilege" is precisely the legal meaning of sanctuary. Sanctuary "privileges" those who claim it (by physical entrance) from the reach of the secular laws of the land or realm. With regard to religious buildings as sanctuaries, the "privilege" is entirely a matter of the asserted or assumed sacredness of the physical space; those who seek sanctuary or asylum in an ecclesiastical building enjoy immunity not for its own sake, but for the honor of the church (*gaudent immunitate non propter se, sed propter honorem ecclesiae*).[83] Yet Adriana is unmoved by this as well. She asserts her own special position with regard to Antipholus—"I will attend my husband"—and continues to refer to his condition in purely medical terms; she will be "his nurse" and "[d]iet his sickness." She justifies her position thus:

> it is my office,
> And I will have no attorney but myself.
>
> (V.i.99–100)

She will have no mediator in her relation to her husband, and she invokes the great Roman term for social duties, for duties that define the polity and the social order, and that may even have divine sanction: it is her office. Muldrew has

---

Seminar paper, Bermuda, 2005). Dorothea Kehler, "Shakespeare's Emilias and the Politics of Celibacy," in *In Another Country: Feminist Perspectives on Renaissance Drama*, ed. Dorothea Kehler and Suysan Baker (Metuchen, N.J.: Scarecrow, 1991), 157–78, seems to have been the first to point out Emilia's culpability, but seems to exceed the (classical/pagan) framework of Egeon's narrative in seeing the interaction between Emilia and Egeon in this regard as replicating the biblical Fall (159).

82. Puzzlingly, Valerie Wayne accepts the view that "the Abbess does finally convince Adriana" ("Refashioning the Shrew," 168). This is perhaps because Wayne is committed to seeing Adriana as some sort of (by the end, reformed) shrew. Candido takes the Abbess's speech entirely at face value, and entirely ignores its status as a trick. He mistakenly sees Adriana as "merging" with the Abbess rather than in competition with her ("Dining Out in Ephesus," 219).

83. Quoted in Richard Helmholz, *The "Jus Commune" in England: Four Studies* (Oxford: Oxford University Press, 2001), 27n43.

argued that the humanist revival of ancient conceptions of civil society contributed to the Elizabethan business and social context, and did so largely through the revival and wide dissemination of Cicero's treatise on "offices."[84] This term is used in the play primarily with regard to marital roles.[85] We recall Luciana's attempt to remind the apparent Antipholus of Ephesus of "a husband's office" (3.2.2). In answer to Adriana's claim, the Abbess first tells her, "Be patient"—a piece of advice that, as we have seen, has been subject to critique throughout the play—and then lays out what we might call an expanded "Pinchian" approach to Antipholus's supposed condition. The Abbess will use, she says, "wholesome syrups, drugs, and holy prayers" (Pinch, we recall, attempted to feel Antipholus's pulse before adjuring the devil within Antipholus to "yield possession to my holy prayers"). Finally, in response to Adriana's appeal to her special "office" as a wife, the Abbess appeals to her special (that is, Catholic) religious and institutional status; she sees treatment of Antipholus as "a branch and parcel of mine oath, / A charitable duty of my order" (5.1.106–7).

In response to this, Adriana reasserts her own sense of duty—"I will not hence and leave my husband here"—and she makes a sharp critical comment:

> ill it does beseem your holiness
> To separate the husband and the wife.
>
> (V.i.110–11)

This can be seen as merely saying that the Abbess is acting badly, but "holiness" is such a powerful word here, and the situation is so generically described—"To separate *the* husband and *the* wife"—that it is hard not to feel, especially in the light of Adriana's earlier reference to her body as "consecrate to" her husband (2.2.132), that she is here asserting a competing notion of "holiness," a conception that would see the relation between "the husband and the wife" as itself a form of holiness, as indeed, a higher form of holiness, and one that it would be unholiness, sacrilege, to interfere with.[86] The Abbess

---

84. For the dissemination and importance of *De Officiis*, in the Erasmus-Melanchthon edition (1520), and in English translation (first edition, 1556), see Muldrew, *Economy of Obligation*, 132–33.

85. The one exception occurs in the locking-out scene, when Dromio of Ephesus protests that the other Dromio has "stol'n both mine office and my name" (3.1.44). Here too, the context is domestic, though not marital.

86. Luther asserted, "If the institution of marriage had stood firm, monasticism wouldn't have amounted to anything" (*Table Talk*, ed. and trans. Theodore G. Tappert, in *Luther's Works*, American Edition, gen. eds. Jaroslav Pelikan and Helmut Lehmann (Philadelphia: Fortress, 1967), 54:328 (*Tischreden* 4, no. 4322).

responds by telling Adriana, once again, to be quiet; once again refusing to hand her supposed husband over; and, finally, by exiting into her "privileged" place. At this point, the newly bold and activist Luciana again steps in. She introduces a new factor into the situation. The former rebuker of complaining suggests to Adriana: "Complain unto the duke of this indignity" (5.1.113). The "dignity" of a wife is suddenly at issue. Adriana eagerly accedes to this suggestion, stating that she will prostrate herself before the Duke until her "tears and prayers / Have won his grace" to come to the abbey and deal with the Abbess (5.1.115–17).

This is quite strange. Suddenly the language of devotion, "tears and prayers," is being used in a secular context—although the reference to the Duke as "his grace" suggests that perhaps "secular" is not quite the right term. This suggestion is further developed when Adriana addresses the Duke (who turns out to be on the spot in any case, since the place of Egeon's execution is "[b]ehind the ditches of the abbey here") in the following manner: "Justice, most sacred Duke, against the Abbess" (5.1.133). Clearly there are two versions of "sacred" figures in competition here, and clearly there is a matter of jurisdiction at issue. Adriana explains the situation (as she understands it) to the Duke, who apparently has a special interest in her marriage—Adriana married Antipholus of Ephesus, she reminds the Duke, "at your important letters"— and she concludes, with regard to her supposed husband: "Therefore, most gracious duke, with thy command / Let him be brought forth, and bore hence for help" (5.1.159–60). Adriana assumes that the Duke has jurisdiction over the abbey, that his "command" will govern the Abbess. And it turns out that she is right in this assumption. The Duke delays his intended business (the execution of Egeon) to deal with the situation that Adriana has brought to his attention, and he sees the matter as indeed a legal one, a case. Adriana has, after all, asked for "justice." The Duke assumes his right to command the Abbess, and jurisdiction in the case: "[B]id the lady abbess come to me. / I will determine this before I stir" (5.1.166–67).[87] When Antipholus of Ephesus emerges onto the scene, he too petitions the "most gracious" Duke for justice (5.1.190).

Each character then tells his or her story, with complete probity and with fully competent eye-witnesses (see 5.1.255, 260).[88] Each complainant claims

---

87. Steggle, "Arrest for Debt," rather understates the matter when he says that the Duke "undertakes to negotiate with the Abbess."

88. Muldrew notes that "witnesses rather than account books were the most important form of security for debts and other agreements, throughout all levels of society" (*Economy of Obligation*, 63).

to be—and is—telling the "simple truth," and each group accuses the other of perjury (5.1.212, 227). Antipholus of Ephesus complains, quite rightly, of the "deep shames and great indignities" that he has suffered, including being publicly arrested for debt (5.1.254). Muldrew notes that "the legal process of arrest or attachment . . . if it became public knowledge, could severely damage a householder's reputation."[89] The Duke recognizes the situation as a legal conundrum—"what an intricate impeach this is" (5.1.270)—a situation of legal claims and cross-claims (compare "Thou art a villain to impeach me thus" in line 29 of this scene). What has happened is in doubt. What is not in doubt is the Duke's jurisdiction.

The Abbess appears at the Duke's command, but as it turns out, the confrontation between the Duke and the Abbess does not have to take place.[90] It is obviated by the great surprise that Shakespeare springs on the characters and on the (at least the first-time) audiences of the play: the Abbess turns out to be Emilia, Egeon's long-lost wife.[91] The conflict between abbess and wife, Catholic and Protestant sanctity, holy place and holy (secular) "office" disappears when the Abbess turns out not only to have been a wife but to be ready, without a moment's hesitation, to resume that role—something that canon law might not have encouraged (and perhaps not have allowed).[92] Emilia is happy to "gain a husband" by Egeon's freedom (5.1.340). Although redemption by money does not seem terribly ironic in this play—merchants in the trade war die for "wanting guilders to redeem their lives" (1.1.8)—Egeon, the Epidamnian merchant, is not actually "redeemed" by money. His "bonds" are loosed through the reestablishment of his marriage: "I will loose his bonds, / And

89. Ibid., 202.

90. Nothing in the text supports James L. Sanderson's claim that the Abbess "brings forth Antipholus and Dromio of Syracuse" at a moment that she knows will be "truly propitious for the immediate resolution of the disputes" ("Patience in *The Comedy of Errors*," 618 [see chap. 1, n. 48]). She emerges from the abbey as one of the disputants addressing the Duke, saying: "Most mighty Duke, behold a man much wrong'd" (5.1.330).

91. On how unusual it is for Shakespeare to surprise his theatrical audience in this way, see Evans, *Shakespeare's Comedies*, 9 (see chap. 1, n. 46).

92. "Presumption of death" cases were normally concerned with the issue of a husband's reappearing after the wife had remarried, not after she had entered into a cloistered religious community, but in such cases, James Brundage has opined that "if the matter came before the courts, the abbess (assuming that both her marriage and her religious profession were valid) would have been required to remain in her monastery and the husband would have been required (or at least strongly pressured) to enter a male religious community" (personal communication with the author, August 2007, quoted by permission).

gain a husband by his liberty," says Emilia, the former Abbess (5.1.339–40).[93] To enter into these bonds is, apparently, to be free.[94]

Equity, the special prerogative (and virtue) of a ruler, prevails, without the need for further familial piety—though the Duke in this play suspends the law only after it is clear that it has been fulfilled: "These ducats pawn I," says Antipholus of Ephesus; "It shall not need," says the Duke (5.1.389–90).[95] The "errors" are cleared up without the need for supernatural intervention, everyone's property is graciously restored, and the family units are reassembled. There is, it is true, as Greenblatt says, no "scene of reconciliation" between Antipholus of Ephesus and Adriana, but there is a defined moment of reconciliation.[96] When Adriana turns toward Antipholus of Syracuse, and asks, "Are not you my husband," Antipholus of Ephesus steps vigorously in to say: "No, I say nay to that" (5.1.371). This is certainly short and proprietary, but equally certainly a reassertion of the marital bond; it is a strong statement, and a director could

93. Landau somehow sees these lines as affirming the papal prerogative of "binding and loosing" ("'Past Thought of Human Reason,'" 201), and seems to confuse Emilia's renunciation of her Catholic institutional status with an affirmation of it.

94. This is a paraphrase of line 31 of Donne's elegy "To his Mistris Going to Bed." It was this line that apparently led one seventeenth-century reader of the poem to associate the poem with marriage, and to consider it the poet's self-epithalamium (see *John Donne: The Elegies and the Songs and Sonnets*, ed. Helen Gardner (Oxford: Clarendon, 1965), 132. Kehler's vision of Emilia continuing her celibacy through the resumption of her marriage is entirely projected ("Shakespeare's Emilias," 160). Emilia seems to be truly happy to "gain a husband."

95. On the significance of this—that the Duke's action is not actually necessary—see Oliver Arnold, "The King of Comedy: The Role of the Ruler and the Rule of Law in Shakespeare's Comedies," *Genre* 31 (1998): 13. It is a nice touch that the offer to ransom Egeon is made by the Ephesian Antipholus, who, as he says, has never—until this moment—laid eyes on his father (5.1.319). A cynical reading would suggest that this speaks badly of the Syracusan Antipholus, but I think that the point is what the Ephesian brother does, not what the Syracusan one does not. Perry, "Commerce, Community, and Nostalgia," takes the nonmonetary nature of this "redemption" to signal a "nostalgia for pre-commercial community" in the play (50); this conclusion relies on the negative view of the commercial community that Perry adopts (see note 41 above). The exercise of equity by the ruler seems to me to be more germane. On the special relation of equity to the ruler in England, see Andrew J. Majeske, *Equity in English Renaissance Literature: Thomas More and Edmund Spenser* (New York: Routledge, 2006), 4–5, 32–33. In *The Merchant of Venice*, Portia asserts the special appropriateness of "mercy" to rulers: "'Tis mightiest in the mightiest" (4.1.184–93).

96. Greenblatt, *Will in the World*, 130.

(and perhaps should) add appropriate physical action.[97] The entire cast of honest bourgeois folk receive their due, including the Courtesan, who gets back her ring along with thanks for her hospitality (presumably, the second merchant also gets his money from the goldsmith), and the Abbess invites the whole cast into the abbey.

Suddenly the abbey is no longer sacred through being a place apart from ordinary social life; rather, it becomes a place that will be a locus for a high form of ordinary social life, a feast. And it will, moreover, be sacred for being that. Arthur Kinney rightly notes that Emilia "gives up her long life of service to the priory," but I am not sure that it is exactly true to say that she does so "for a secular existence with her family."[98] What triumphs is not, as Kinney thinks, the spirit of capitalism, but rather the Protestant ethic. We recall Luther's celebration of the holiness of "the works of a farmer labouring in the field, or of a woman looking after her home."[99] The abbey is not violated but, apparently, sanctified by the family reunion being celebrated there.

The religious language of the Abbess's final speech is unmistakable, but this does not mean that such references "emphasize her former religious identity."[100] Still indeed in her nun's garb—there has been no time for her to change—the Abbess asserts that to all of those who "by this sympathized one day's error / have suffer'd wrong," we "shall make full satisfaction" (5.1.397–99). This is a startling phrase if one is theologically or ecclesiologically attuned. "Satisfaction" is the central feature of the Catholic sacrament of penance, the feature that produced much of the institutional and devotional structure of the medieval church, and that generated the realm of purgatory.[101] The "satisfaction" that the Abbess and other characters will "make" here is of an entirely different sort. Nor is it the purely monetary "satisfaction" that the foreign merchant demanded of Antipholus (4.1.5). What Emilia offers is intellectual and

---

97. Contrast the *Menaechmi*, where the happy ending involves the husband and his twin planning to return to "their own country" (*in patriam redeamus*), Syracuse, after the brother who has been living in Epidamnum auctions off his household, including, as his brother's freed slave asserts, and as part of the dream of freedom in the play, "a wife, should there be any purchaser" (*Brothers Menaechmus*, 146).

98. Kinney, "*The Comedy of Errors*: A Modern Perspective," 193.

99. See *The Babylonian Captivity*, in *Selections from His Writings*, 311 (see intro., n. 55). For further references (and some theological explanation), see chapter 1 above.

100. Kehler, "Shakespeare's Emilias," 160.

101. For an account of the conflicting doctrines of penance, see Richard Strier, "Herbert and Tears," *English Literary History* (Summer 1979): 221–47.

emotional, not penitential or monetary. But her language becomes even more charged. She presents the entire story that began in the opening narration and culminated here as an elaborate process of birth; her identity all along, as she now sees it, has been that of a biological mother. Her "oath" and her "order" are forgotten:

> Thirty-three years have I but gone in travail
> Of you, my sons, and till this present hour
> My heavy burden ne'er delivered.
> (5.1.400–402)

Lewis Theobald pointed out long ago that the number here, "Thirty-three years," cannot be correct; the actual number of years that Emilia (formerly known as the Abbess) was separated from members of her family is twenty-five.[102] Theobald emended the line to reflect this, but there is, as all modern editors agree, no need for emendation. Shakespeare clearly wanted the mystical and Christological number, regardless of the "facts" of the matter. Emilia's / the Abbess's speech concludes by inviting the whole cast, designated by their social and familial roles, to a rather grand version of a feast celebrating a baptism. She does so in language that seems to merge the "rebirth" into their family of the Antipholus and Dromio twins with the birth that defined Christianity:

> The duke, my husband, and my children both,
> And you, the calendars of their nativity,
> Go to a gossips' feast, and joy with me,
> After so long grief, such nativity.
> (5.1.403–6)

This is the Folio reading of the Abbess's last line, and it is the reading adopted by most modern editors (though not by Foakes, who adopts "felicity" to end the line, or the Oxford editors, who adopt "festivity"). Even if one believes that the final "nativity" here is a mere eye-slip by the compositor, and that the word must therefore be emended, the idea is present nonetheless.[103]

---

102. See the note on 5.1.400 in the Foakes edition (106).

103. Foakes borrows "felicity" from Hanmer; Johnson suggested "festivity," which is adopted by the Oxford and Norton Shakespeares, and (oddly, for an edition supposedly of the Folio) by Jonathan Bate and Eric Rasmussen in their *Shakespeare: Complete Works* (New York: Mod-

One must remember what a "gossips' feast" was. It was not an ecclesiastical event. It was the secular aftermath of a baptism. As David Cressy puts it, "Removed from the solemnity of the church, it was hard to tell whether christening parties were more famous for their food or their drink."[104] A "gossips' feast" could also be a party at the end of the "churching" period for a woman, and these too were notorious—"as drunk as women at a gossiping" was a common expression.[105] The collective joy being imagined at the end of the play is sacred, but decidedly not ecclesiastical.[106]

One must ask, finally, what Shakespeare's audience might have made of all this. Perhaps there were persons in the audience who would have been shocked at the play's casualness about sanctuary and its lack of regard for the "oath" and "order" of the Abbess. Perhaps. But I am not sure that such persons, devoted to the old religion and to the Counter-Reformation, would have been numerous at the public theater (or even at a performance at Gray's Inn).[107] What is certain is that many in Shakespeare's audience were not even born when the abbeys were appropriated by the crown and laicized in 1539, and surely few, if any, could remember them as functioning institutions in England.[108] Most (or at least many) in Shakespeare's audience would have been

---

ern Library, 2007). The old and new Pelicans accept the Folio reading, as do Bevington, New Cambridge, and Folger. The unique capitalization of the final word (adopted by the Pelicans) is editorial and interpretive, since, in the Folio, the word is also capitalized two lines before, so there is no difference between the two instances.

104. David Cressy, *Birth, Marriage, and Death: Ritual, Religion, and the Life-Cycle in Tudor and Stuart England* (Oxford: Oxford University Press, 1997), 167. Cressy notes that "a London tradesman provided two gallons of French claret and two quarts of Spanish canary wine for a christening party" (ibid., 166).

105. Ibid., 202.

106. Candido seems to confuse this "gossip's feast" with an actual, sacramental one, and he entirely misses the cultural significance of the fact that what is going to happen "inside the Abbey" is, as he says, "a family feast" ("Dining Out in Ephesus," 220).

107. On the early stage history of the play, see Foakes (xxxiv–xxxix). On the denominational makeup of the constituency of Gray's Inn, see the judicious treatment in Wilfrid R. Prest, *The Inns of Court under Elizabeth and the Early Stuarts, 1590–1640* (London: Longman, 1972), chaps. 8–9. Prest concludes that while Catholics were certainly present in the Inns, they "never comprised more than a small, impotent minority" (186). Given the recorded behavior of the students at the Gray's Inn performance, one is not surprised that Prest also finds that the Puritan presence at the Inns has been exaggerated (190).

108. For "An Act for the Dissolution of Abbeys" (1539; 31 Henry VIII, c. 13), see *The Tudor Constitution*, 2nd edition, ed. G. R. Elton (Cambridge: Cambridge University Press, 1982), 388–91.

used to the idea of the ruler of the realm as the Supreme Governor (if not the Supreme Head) of the church.[109] And the general privilege of sanctuary was holding on by a thread in Elizabethan England, and was finally to be abolished in 1623.[110] Interestingly with regard to *The Comedy of Errors*, merchants, from the late medieval period on, were generally negative toward sanctuary, since debtors made use of it to escape payment, and certain areas in London continued to be "pretended privileged places" for debtors at least until 1723.[111]

There is no reason, therefore, not to trust the play—which I would be inclined to do in any case. The ending is meant to be a happy one, and even, in its way, a holy one. I think that most of Shakespeare's audience would have agreed with Adriana that it ill beseems holiness to separate the husband and the wife. With regard to the abbey, they might well have agreed with Andrew Marvell, a half century or so later, who, when considering a historical situation parallel to that which confronted Adriana early in act 5, asserted strongly that spousal rights trumped Catholic ones, and that the nunnery in which a would-be spouse was being kept was spiritually transformed for the better when it was made into a private estate. Of the moment of laicization, Marvell wrote: "Though many a Nun there made her vow, / 'Twas no religious house till now."[112] In *The Comedy of Errors*, at least, it seems that Shakespeare would have agreed.

109. On Henry as "Supreme Head" of the Church of England, see ibid., 364–65; for Elizabeth and her "heirs or successors" as Supreme Governor, 372–77.

110. See Isobel Thornley, "The Destruction of Sanctuary," in *Tudor Studies Presented to A. F. Pollard*, ed. R. W. Seton-Watson (1924; New York: Russell and Russell, 1970), 182–207.

111. See Thornley on merchants and sanctuary (ibid., 188–95); also James R. Hertzler, "The Abuse and Outlawing of Sanctuary for Debt in Seventeenth-Century England," *Historical Journal* 14 (1971): 467–77; and Steggle, "Arrest for Debt." Steggle—following Nigel Stirk, "Arresting Ambiguity: The Shifting Geographies of a London Debtors' Sanctuary in the Eighteenth Century," *Social History* 25 (2000): 316–29—shows that the privilege of sanctuary for debt continued to be invoked into the eighteenth century. For the quoted phrase, see Hertzler (473) and Stirk (318). None of the cases cited, it should be noted, involved functioning religious institutions.

112. "Upon Appleton House, to my Lord Fairfax," lines 279–80. For contextualization, see Gary D. Hamilton, "Marvell, Sacrilege, and Protestant Historiography: Contextualizing 'Upon Appleton House,'" in *Religion, Literature, and Politics in Post-Reformation England, 1540–1688*, ed. Donna B. Hamilton and Richard Strier (Cambridge: Cambridge University Press, 1996), 161–86.

APPENDIX

Sanctifying the Aristocracy: From Ignatius Loyola to François de Sales (and then to Donne and Herbert)

Luther's revolution, according to Weber, was to declare the fulfillment of worldly duties "the highest form which the moral activity of the individual could assume."[1] Luther broke down the distinction between the layperson and "the religious." This was the point of his exaltation of baptism, which produced the revolutionary doctrine of "the priesthood of all believers," in which "we who have been baptized are all uniformly priests by virtue of that very fact."[2] "A shoemaker, a smith, a farmer, each has his manual operation and work; and yet, at the same time, all are eligible to act as priests and bishops."[3] All legitimate worldly activity was sacred when done in the proper spirit—thus, "the term 'spiritual is often applied to one who is busy with the most outward of works," and "the common work of a serving man or maid is more acceptable [to God] than all the fastings and other works of monks."[4] Luther can be seen as responding to one of the great challenges for late medieval and early modern spirituality in Western Europe: the increasing wealth, urbanization, and literacy of the lay population. The religious status of ordinary Christians, of persons living in "the world," outside of monastic or religious orders needed to be rethought. The *devotio moderna* and the popularization of Rhineland mysticism were responses to this problem, as were the confraternities in Italy and, in part, the Lollard movement in England.[5] At the beginning of the sixteenth century, Erasmus preceded Luther in seeing baptism as the essential

1. Max Weber, *The Protestant Ethic and the Spirit of Capitalism* (see chap. 3, n. 7 above), 80.

2. Luther, *The Babylonian Captivity*, in *Selections from His Writings*, 345 (see intro., n. 55).

3. Luther, *An Appeal to the Ruling Class of German Nationality as to the Amelioration of the State of Christendom*, in *Selections from His Writings*, 410.

4. Luther, "Preface to Romans" and *The Babylonian Captivity*, in *Selections from His Writings*, 25 and 311 respectively.

5. See, for instance, Preserved Smith, *The Reformation in Europe* (1920; rpt. ed., New York: Collier, 1962), chap. 1; A. G. Dickens, *The English Reformation* (New York: Schocken, 1964), chaps. 1–2; Albert Hyma, *The "Devotio Moderna" or Christian Renaissance (1380–1520)*, 2nd ed. (Hamden, Conn.: Archon, 1965); and Steven Ozment, *The Age of Reform, 1250–1550* (New Haven: Yale University Press, 1980), chap. 5. On the confraternities, see Richard Trexler, *Public Life in Renaissance Florence* (New York: Academic Press, 1980).

Christian "vow" and "the holiest of ceremonies."[6] His was another attempt to break down the barrier between the layman and the "religious." "I would have all Christians," said Erasmus, live in such a way that those who alone are now called 'religious' appear not religious enough."[7] The Puritan movement in England and America can be seen as continuing the Protestant version of this endeavor.[8]

As the example of Erasmus shows, this endeavor was not, in the early modern period, confined to Protestants. Although Weber distinguishes Luther's position from what he calls "the liberal utilitarian compromise with the world at which the Jesuits arrived," the Jesuit movement must be seen as part of the same large cultural movement.[9] The Jesuits were the spearhead of the Roman Church's attempt to recapture the laity as, in some significant sense, "religious." The Jesuit schools "offered genuine opportunities for upward social mobility, which were taken up by the sons of the merchant, professional, and artisan classes."[10] But the idea was for such persons to become *honnêtes hommes*—persons who could behave as, formerly, only aristocrats had done. One important Jesuit pedagogue referred to education as the means for turning oneself into "a *galant homme* in little time."[11] It was out of this emphasis that the movement known primarily in France as "devout humanism" took its

---

6. See *The Enchiridion of Erasmus*, trans. Raymond Himelick (Bloomington: Indiana University Press, 1963), 40, 116, and passim.

7. Letter to Paul Volz (1518), in *Christian Humanism and the Reformation*, ed. and trans. John C. Olin (New York: Harper and Row, 1965), 128.

8. See Weber, *Protestant Ethic*, chap. 4, and R. H. Tawney, *Religion and the Rise of Capitalism* (1926; New York: Mentor, 1954). The distinctiveness of "Puritan" economic views has been questioned by Charles H. and Katherine George, *The Protestant Mind of the English Reformation, 1570–1640* (Princeton: Princeton University Press, 1961). The Georges argue that the sermon literature of English Protestantism in general in the earlier seventeenth century incorporates "the most outgoing and positive view of work which exists in the Christian tradition" (143).

9. Weber, *Protestant Ethic*, 81. H. M. Robertson's *Aspects of the Rise of Economic Individualism: A Criticism of Max Weber and His School* (Cambridge: Cambridge University Press, 1933) argued that the Jesuits were more favorable to capitalist practices and attitudes than was any Protestant group. Robertson was, in turn, immediately critiqued by J. Brodrick, S.J., *The Economic Morals of the Jesuits: An Answer to Dr. H. M. Robertson* (Oxford: Oxford University Press, 1934).

10. Judi Loach, "Revolutionary Pedagogues? How Jesuits Used Education to Change Society," in *The Jesuits II: Cultures, Sciences, and the Arts, 1540–1773*, ed. John O'Malley et al. (Toronto: University of Toronto Press, 2006), 66.

11. Ibid., 70.

orientation.[12] Devout humanism might be described as a movement that set out to show Christianity to be fully possible within the bounds of ordinary and recognizable elite social life. Its class orientation is essential to it.[13] For the Catholics, "devout humanism" was a way of capturing the part of the laity that mattered, from the artisans upward, and keeping the lay elite from either Protestantism or "libertinage."[14] But there were also Protestant forms of this movement.[15] The major text of "devout humanism" is François de Sales's *Introduction to the Devout Life* (first edition, 1609). Pascal's *Provincial Letters*, later in the century (first edition, 1656), is the great attack on both the Jesuit and the Salesian movements. George Herbert has been claimed for "devout humanism" in England, as has John Donne.[16]

With regard to François de Sales, it is important to see that he was building on a development already underway in the great foundational text of Jesuit

12. The phrase seems to have been coined by Henri Bremond in *A Literary History of Religious Thought in France*, vol. 1, *Devout Humanism* (1914), trans. K. L. Montgomery (New York: MacMillan, 1928). For a more recent treatment, see Aldo Scaglione, *The Liberal Arts and the Jesuit College System* (Philadelphia: J. Benjamins, 1986).

13. Bremond's presentation of the movement obfuscates its essential social elitism. This elitism is noted, in somewhat metaphysical form, in Paul Benichou, *Morales du grand siècle* (Paris: Gallimard, 1948), chap. 3 (*Man and Ethics*, trans. Elizabeth Hughes [New York: Doubleday, 1971]), and very clearly in A. W. S. Baird, *Studies in Pascal's Ethics* (The Hague: Martinus Nijhoff, 1975), chaps. 3–4.

14. For "libertinage," see Antoine Adam, *Les libertins au XVIIe siècle* (Paris: Buchet-Chastel, 1964).

15. In a fascinating article, Abel Athouguia Alves compares the social teachings of an early sixteenth-century (Catholic) Christian humanist (Vives) with those of Ignatius and Calvin. The continuities are striking. In particular, they all had programs for poor relief but they all distinguished between the deserving and the undeserving poor. As Alves rather bemusedly notes, "the resulting practices of those [all three reformers] who assumed the Christian discourse [of charity] were quite mixed" with regard to their actual treatment (or plans for treatment) of the poor. See "The Christian Social Organism and Social Welfare: The Case of Vives, Calvin, and Loyola," *Sixteenth Century Journal* 20 (Spring 1989): 13.

16. For Herbert, see Louis L. Martz, *The Poetry of Meditation: A Study of English Religious Literature of the Seventeenth Century*, rev. ed. (New Haven: Yale University Press, 1962), 249–59; for Donne, *John Donne: The Divine Poems*, rev. ed., ed. Helen Gardner (Oxford: Clarendon, 1956), xxvi. Neither Martz nor Gardner claim direct influence, though it seems that Martz would have liked to do so. Martz's distinctions between Jesuit and Salesian spirituality (144–52) have some plausibility, but Martz overlooks the deep historical continuity between the two movements. For a treatment of the two saints that perhaps overstates this continuity, see F. Charmot, S.J., *Ignatius Loyola and François de Sales: Two Masters, One Spirituality*, trans. Sister M. Tenelle (St. Louis: B. Herder, 1966).

spirituality, the *Spiritual Exercises* of Ignatius Loyola (published 1548, but completed earlier).[17] Despite a good deal of confusion and obfuscation on the matter, the exercises are not ascetic in orientation. They are addressed neither to the cloistered nor the adept. Early in the text, in its "Introductory Observations," the director who is administering the exercises is admonished not to urge the exercitant "to embrace poverty or to make any other promise [vow] rather than its contrary; neither should he encourage him to embrace one state of life or way of living [*un estado o modo de vivir*] rather than another."[18] This is very striking; in the exercises, the normal Catholic valuations of "states of life" are to be suspended. As Roland Barthes says, "the Ignatian tree [of binaries] has the paradoxical purpose of *equilibrating* the objects of choice, and not, as one would have expected, of preferring one of them."[19]

Ignatius is fully aware of the oddity of this, but he insists on it. "Apart from the Exercises," he quickly goes on to say, "it would be both lawful and meritorious to urge all who are probably fitted for it"—even this is interestingly careful—"to choose continence, virginity, religious life, and all other forms of evangelical perfection."[20] But the stance of the *Exercises* is to be completely neutral to all possible (nonsinful) ways of life. The one who gives the exercises should be "like a balance at equilibrium" (*estando en medio como un peso*), not leaning in any direction (sec. 15). The aim of the exercises is to produce exactly this state of mind in the exercitant, so that he too is to be "like a balance at equilibrium" (sec. 179). The aim is not rejection of the world but "indifference" to it (*hacemos indiferentes a todas las cosas criadas*); the exercitant should come

17. For a useful chronology of Ignatius's life, within the context of general political and religious developments in the period, see *The Spiritual Exercises of St. Ignatius*, trans. Louis J. Puhl (New York: Random House, 2000), xxv–xl.

18. For the translation, I have used and sometimes, as here, combined the Puhl translation (ibid., 8) with that in *The Spiritual Exercises of St. Ignatius*, trans. Anthony Mottola (New York: Doubleday Image, 1964), 40. The Puhl translation, like the Spanish editions, numbers the sections throughout the text, and I will refer to passages by section numbers. For the Spanish, I have used *Exercicios spirituales de San Ignacio de Loyola*, 9th ed. (Madrid: Editorial Apostolado de la Presa, 1956); the quotation is from section 15. In section 14, promises and vows are equated (*no haga promessa ni voto alguno inconsiderado*); see note 20 below.

19. Roland Barthes, *Sade, Fourier, Loyola*, trans. Richard Miller (New York: Hill and Wang, 1976), 57–58; for the French I use the original edition (Paris: Editions de Seuil, 1971).

20. Ignatius's nervousness about vows perhaps reflects the influence of Erasmus. For Erasmus on monastic vows, see the Colloquy "On Rash Vows," in *The Colloquies of Erasmus*, trans. Craig R. Thompson (Chicago: University of Chicago Press, 1965), 4–7; and his letter to Volz, 130–32. For a general treatment of Erasmus and Ignatius, see Ricardo Garcia-Villoslada, *Loyola y Erasmo: Dos almas, dos epocas* (Madrid: Taurus, 1965).

"not to prefer health to sickness, riches to poverty, honor to dishonor" (sec. 23). He should be made into a vacuum in which the spirit of God can work directly, without any internal interference.[21] The exercises are meant to help the individual discover "in what kind of life or in what state His Divine Majesty wishes to make use of us" (sec. 15). This is what leads Barthes to speak of the *Exercises* as a divinatory or "mantic" text.[22] The aim is to "arrive at perfection in whatever state or way of life God our Lord"—and here the phrasing gets very careful, and perhaps paradoxical—"may grant us to choose" (*nos diere para eligir*; sec. 135).

"Perfection" can be attained in any "state or way of life." If we are to be "indifferent" with regard to all such matters, then not only are we not to prefer riches to poverty and honor to dishonor, but we are also, conversely, not to prefer poverty to riches or sickness to health. The ideal is "only to will and not will as God our Lord inspires" (sec. 155), and to serve God in whatever state of life he has led us to believe that he wishes us to be in—"in either alternative" (sec. 166). Marriage and benefices, for instance, can be used in the service of God (sec. 169), and can, the logic of the position requires, be forms of "perfection." In the "Rules for Thinking with the Church" that Ignatius added to the *Exercises* in 1535, in a specifically polemical (anti-Protestant) context, Ignatius held that vows are only appropriate for a specific kind of life, the life of renunciation; that only this sort of life is capable of "perfection"; and that other sorts of life "may not be made the object of a vow, for example, a business career, [or] the married state" (sec. 357).[23] However, earlier in the *Exercises* (sec. 38), Ignatius had stated that oaths should be used in situations of importance "either for the

21. The immediacy with which divine action is invoked here has troubled many commentators, but, as Karl Rahner notes: "[It is] clear that Ignatius thought such a personal vocation to be the normal thing for those who are fitted to make the whole of the Spiritual Exercises—and not only for such rare cases [as] mystics. Furthermore, the fact that the excesses of Illuminism have shown the dangers of misinterpreting this concept is not sufficient reason for denying that Ignatius believed in genuine guidance by the Holy Spirit." See Karl Rahner, "The Ignatian Process for Discovering the Will of God in an Existential Situation," epitomized by Harold E. Weidman in *Ignatius of Loyola: His Personality and Spiritual Heritage, 1556–1956* (St. Louis: The Institute of Jesuit Sources, 1977), 283.

22. Barthes explains: "[Mantic art is] the art of divine consultation. A language of interpellation, mantic art is comprised of two codes: that of the questions addressed by man to the divinity, [and] that of the response sent by the divinity to man" (*Sade, Fourier, Loyola*, 46; following the French text, I have not capitalized "Divinity," as Miller's translation does).

23. On the dating and context of the "Rules for Thinking with the Church," see the introduction by Robert W. Gleason, S.J., to the Mottola translation of the *Spiritual Exercises*, 16.

welfare of the soul or of the body, or with regard to temporal interests" (*algún momento cerca el provecho del ánima o del cuerpo o de bienes temporales*). Those who possess great wealth can live a godly life (sec. 189). Alms are to be given in the right amount, "neither more nor less" (sec. 339). In general, with regard to oneself and one's household, "it is better to retrench and reduce expenses as much as possible"; the Third Council of Carthage is adduced for the principle that "the furniture of a bishop should be cheap and poor" (sec. 344). Ignatius asserts that "the same consideration applies to all stations in life." But he then adds the highly important qualification that, nonetheless, "attention must be given to adapting it [this consideration] to each one's condition and rank" (*mirando y proporcionando la condición y estado de las personas* [sec. 344]). Moreover, in doing good deeds, one should not be troubled by worry about the issue of vainglory (sec. 351).

Yet Ignatius's text is haunted by the ascetic ideal. He distinguishes between interior penance—"sorrow for one's sins and a firm purpose not to commit them or any others"—and "exterior" penance, which has a bodily component (secs. 82–86), and he does not seem to be satisfied (as Erasmus and the Protestant reformers were) with only the former.[24] He considers the denial of food and of sleep, and the self-infliction of physical pain. One is to deny oneself food up to the point of causing harm to oneself; the same is true of sleep, but here Ignatius insists, interestingly, that "we should not deny ourselves a suitable amount of sleep." On self-inflicted pain, he seems to take a severe line, recommending causing one's body pain by "wearing hair shirts, cords, or iron chains on the body, or by scourging or wounding oneself" (sec. 85). But he then adds a paragraph limiting this to "superficial pain," and concludes that "it would seem more suitable to chastise oneself with light cords [*lastimarse con cuerdas delgadas*]"—a sentence that beautifully expresses his ambivalence.

With regard to poverty, Ignatius makes a distinction similar to the one he makes concerning penance. Just as there is interior and exterior penance, there is spiritual and actual poverty. Everyone is called to the former (spiritual poverty); the latter (actual poverty) is religiously higher, but is only appropriate for those who have been granted a specific call to it (sec. 146). Of the three kinds of humility—Ignatius certainly does have the *obsession numérative*[25]—the state of indifference is only the second kind. The first and lowest kind is fear of committing mortal sin; the third and highest consists not of indifference to wealth

24. For an account of the great controversy over penance in the sixteenth century, see Strier, "Herbert and Tears," 221–47 (see chap. 4, n. 101).

25. Barthes, *Sade, Fourier, Loyola*, 3 (French text, 7).

but of actively choosing poverty (sec. 167). Yet in the next section, the crucial "Introduction to Making a Choice of a Way of Life," the pivot of the entire text at the end of the exercises for the second week, the emphasis is again on living holily in whatever choice one has made: "[N]othing must move me to use such means [marriage or benefices], or to deprive myself of them, save only the service and praise of God."[26]

In the discussion of eating and sleeping, Ignatius placed penance, which involves depriving oneself of "what is proper for us to have," over temperance, which involves merely doing away with what is superfluous, and there is to be no confusion of the one with the other (*quando quitamos lo superfluo no es penitencia, mas temperancia* [sec. 83]). Yet when, in the exercises for the third week, he returns to "Rules with Regard to Eating," the ideal is to "arrive at the mean" (sec. 213). To whip oneself with light cords turns into "if delicacies are taken, to eat of them only sparingly" (sec. 212). In fact, the exercises in general are meant to move away from penance, and toward temperance. This is the tenth and final "additional direction" for the fourth (and final) week (sec. 229). We recall the rhetoric of finding the mean ("neither more nor less") with regard to alms. One of the final "rules" in the text before the "Rules for Thinking with the Church" is pure classical philosophy—Aristotelianism with a Stoic tint (sec. 350):

> A soul that wishes to make progress in the spiritual life must always act in a manner contrary to that of the enemy. If the enemy seeks to make the conscience lax, one must endeavor to make it more sensitive. If the enemy strives to make the conscience delicate with a view to leading it to excess, the soul must endeavor to establish itself firmly in a moderate course, so that in all things it may preserve itself in peace.

One can have excess of conscientiousness, and this seems to be exactly equivalent in spiritual weight to having a lack of it. Certainly Ignatius was right to distinguish temperance from asceticism. Temperance is an ideal of worldly appreciation, not of world-renunciation. The state of mental indifference (close to Stoic *ataraxia*) is the distinctive ideal of the *Spiritual Exercises*. In this state of mind, one can rightly—holily—take earthly glory, as well as leaving it.

---

26. On the pivotal nature of the end of the second week of the exercises, see Barthes, *Sade, Fourier, Loyola*, 47 (citing Gaston Fessard, *La Dialectique des Exercises spirituels de Saint Ignace de Loyola* [Paris: Aubier, 1956]).

In the ninth epistle of the *Provincial Letters*, Pascal's Jesuit interlocutor notes that "men of the world are generally deterred from devotion by the strange idea[s] they have been led to form of it"; to counter these strange ideas, he especially praises one Father Le Moine for drawing a "perfectly charming" picture of devotion in his work entitled *Devotion Made Easy.*[27] This is not parody. Le Moine and his book exist, and Le Moine's treatise "does little more than paraphrase some chapters of the *Introduction à la vie dévote.*"[28] As Henri Bremond rather dryly notes, "Port Royal, too prudent to attack the master [de Sales], gladly delivered the disciple [Le Moine] over to the scourge of Pascal."[29] Devotion made easy—the fundamental premise of François de Sales's book is that "the way to heaven is not as difficult as the world makes it out to be."[30] The aim, as Pascal's Jesuit (following Le Moine and others) says, is to produce "genteel saints" (*saints polis*) and "well-bred devotees" (*devots civilisés*) (438/159), Christian versions, as we have seen, of the *hônnete-homme.*[31] For a course in the town college of Lyon run by the Jesuits, Claude-François Menestrier produced a syllabus called "L'idee de l'estude d'un honneste homme."[32]

For François de Sales, the devout life can happily include a remarkable range of behavior—of leisure-class behavior, that is—sports, banquets, parties,

---

27. Blaise Pascal, *The Provincial Letters*, trans. Thomas M'Crie, in *"Pensées" and "The Provincial Letters,"* Modern Library (New York: Random House, 1941), 438; *Les Provinciales*, intro. Louis Cognet (Paris: Garnier, 1965), 158 (the plural in "strange ideas" is not in the original). Page references are hereafter cited parenthetically in the text, first to the translation, second to the original.

28. Bremond, *Devout Humanism*, 296.

29. Ibid. For attempts to rescue Le Moine from Pascal's critique (the first more measured than the second), see Elfrieda Dubois, "Le Père Le Moyne et *La devotion aisée*," and Richard Maber, "Spiritualité et mondanité chez le Père Le Moyne," both in *Les Jésuites parmi les hommes aux XVIᵉ et XVIIᵉ siècles* (Clermont: Faculté des Lettres et Sciences Humaines de l' Université de Clermont-Ferrard II, 1987), 153–62, 163–171.

30. St. Francis de Sales, *Introduction to the Devout Life*, trans. John K. Ryan, Image Books (Garden City: Doubleday, 1950), 68; *Oeuvres de Saint François de Sales*, book 3, *Introduction à la vie devote*, ed. Dom B. Mackey (Annecy: Niérat, 1893), 53. Page references are hereafter cited parenthetically in the text, first to the translation, second to the original.

31. For a precise seventeenth-century formulation of the conception of the *honnête-homme*, see Chevalier de Méré, "De la vraïe honeteté," in *Oeuvres complètes* (Paris: Fernand Roches, 1930), 3:69–84, esp. 70: "Si quelqu'un me demandoit en quoi consiste l'honnêteté, je dirois que ce n'est autre chose que d'exceller en tout ce qui regarde les agréments et les bienséances de la vie." I owe this reference to my colleague, Philippe Desan.

32. See Loach, "Revolutionary Pedagogues," 68.

and balls (77/65) as well as hunting and games of skill played for (modest) stakes (208/247). Cleanliness is seen, by virtue of a remarkable use of a passage in Isaiah, as "to a certain extent" (*en quelque façon*) next to godliness (192/226). Most characteristically perhaps, de Sales "would have devout people, whether men or women, always the best dressed in a group" (193/227). The premiere courtly virtue, *sprezzatura*—the appearance of not making an effort—is the key to proper social and Christian behavior: "If beauty is to have good grace, it should be unstudied [*négligée*]" (133/143).[33] The devout are not only to be the best dressed but also "the least pompous and affected." One can, as one should, maintain the dignity due to one's rank "without damage to humility"—if this is done *négligemment* (134/145). But there is more here than accommodation of Christianity to *le beau monde*. Unaffectedness also extends to the spiritual and emotional realm. One must speak of one's sufferings only "in a natural, true, and sincere way," and not exaggerate them in order to get sympathy (130/137). This latter case, in which Saint Paul becomes the perfect model of a gentleman, shows the way in which this perspective can offer something more than mere accommodation. The critique of affectation captures "very subtle and refined ambition and vanity" in its diagnosis of ostentation in suffering.

With similar sensitivity to the manipulation of (virtuous) appearances, the aristocratic ethos is itself at times subject to moral criticism in the *Introduction to the Devout Life*. Yet the drive toward accommodation is always present. In speaking of the way in which everyone can take and keep his proper rank without damage to humility, François de Sales notes that his defense of this assertion might seem to pertain "to [worldly] wisdom rather than [to] humility" (134/145). But he then provides a brilliant critique of the sort of strategic humility that Castiglione discusses. One of Castiglione's speakers recommends that the courtier refuse favors and honors, but do so "in such a way as to give the donor cause to press them upon him more urgently."[34] De Sales knows all about this. He specifically designates humility as false when "we make a show of flying away and hiding ourselves so that people will run after us and seek us out," when "we pretend to want to be last in the company and to be seated

33. For *sprezzatura*, see Baldesar Castiglione, *The Book of the Courtier*, trans. Charles S. Singleton (New York: Doubleday, 1959), 43-45. For discussion, see, inter alia, Frank Whigham, *Ambition and Privilege: The Social Tropes of Elizabethan Courtesy Theory* (Berkeley: University of California Press, 1984), 93-95, and Harry Berger, Jr., *The Absence of Grace: Sprezzatura and Suspicion in Two Renaissance Courtesy Books* (Stanford: Stanford University Press, 2000).

34. Castiglione, *The Book of the Courtier*, 113. In the dialogue, another interlocutor jokingly provides Gospel ratification for this strategic advice, using Luke 14:8-10 (the parable of the wedding guest).

at the foot of the table, but it is with a view toward moving more easily to the upper end" (135–36/147). True humility is either hidden or, when expressed, sincere. Yet de Sales cannot end the discussion at this point. The position he has been developing is overly rigorous with regard to the ordinary interactions of polite social life. He goes on to add that while the devout person must (perhaps) not play the game himself, "sometimes good manners require us to offer precedence to those who will certainly refuse it," and he insists that "this is neither duplicity nor false humility" (136/147). The same is true of employing "certain words of honor which do not seem to be strictly true," but which ordinary social decorum requires. It is certainly "not always advisable to say all that is true" (206/244).[35]

For François de Sales, sociability is the essence of charity. It even covers sins. In discussing games, de Sales initially makes a clear distinction between games of skill and games of chance, allowing games of skill and prohibiting those of chance (208–9/247–48). Yet a few pages later, participation in games of chance is declared allowable to the devout "when prudence and discretion direct you to be agreeable," since "to be agreeable [*la condescendance*] is part of charity, and makes indifferent things good and dangerous things permissible."[36] *La condescendance* even "removes harm from things in some way evil [*aucunement mauvaises*]" (212/253). We are inevitably—but perhaps improperly—reminded of Pascal's discussion of the Jesuit relaxations of the conception of "proximate occasions of sins" (457–58/181–82). De Sales's appeal to the image of Ignatius Loyola at genteel card parties (212/253) hardly removes the discomfort.

For François de Sales, this image is exactly parallel to that of Saint Catherine of Siena "turning the spit" in her father's kitchen (214/255). The difference in the nature and social meaning of the activities is irrelevant. De Sales does not see Christian values as exerting very much pressure on the class orientation of his text. Concern for reputation—one of the great aristocratic obsessions—is upheld because "good name is one of the bases of human society [*l'un des fondemens de la societè humaine*]" (143/155). There is no conflict between humility and concern for one's honor. At times, de Sales does seem to allow biblical

---

35. One of my Press readers made the wonderful and, I believe, both profound and historically significant point, that de Sales sounds here "remarkably like Erasmus's Folly." For the relevant passage in *The Praise of Folly*, see 33–34 above.

36. "To be agreeable" (*la condescendence*) seems like a weak translation here. The French term is much richer and more complex, involving the rejection or overcoming of snobbery, but without the modern connotation of distaste and contempt.

testimony to threaten social norms, as when he speaks of David and Saint Paul bearing shame in the service of God. "Nevertheless [*J'excepte neanmoins*]," he immediately adds, certain reproaches cannot be borne, and certain persons, "on whose reputations the edification of many others depends," should not bear reproaches at all (144/160). It is neither necessary nor desirable to be a fool for Christ's sake (138/150); if certain servants of God have pretended to be fools in order to render themselves abject in the eyes of the world, "we must admire but not imitate them" (compare the Utopians on their ascetic priests).[37] Again, Christ and the biblical exemplars are to be followed—but with prudence and discretion (*mais sagement et discretement* [145/159]).

Sociability is the essence of charity, and sociability requires participation in and mastery of the forms, fictions, and practices of polite society. *Eutrapelia*, "which we call pleasant conversation" (196/231), is redeemed from its Pauline status as a vice and returned to its Aristotelian standing as a virtue.[38] The seemingly dour virtue of mortification is brilliantly adapted to the demands of social life. De Sales builds on the Ignatian conception of "indifference," but is more consistent than Ignatius in placing indifference above denial. With regard to food, de Sales concedes that although "always to choose the worst" may seem more austere, the truest kind of mortification is to eat whatever is put before you, *even if you like it* (186/219; emphasis mine). In this way—and the point is quite a brilliant one—we renounce our choice as well as our taste, since the austere-seeming form of mortification involves continuous assertions of will. The proper exercise of mortification—mortification through adaptability and acquiescence—"doesn't show in public, bothers no one, and is well-adapted to social life [*est uniquement propre pour la vie civile*]." At a moment like this, it is difficult to distinguish ingenuousness from disingenuousness in the text.[39]

The biblical conceptions of humility and mortification are sticking points for "devout humanism," as for any world-affirming version of Christianity. The Gospel condemnations of wealth are particularly unsettling. De Sales's way around this is to stress Jesus's praise of "the poor in spirit" (Matt. 5:3). He therefore distinguishes—again, building on but extending Ignatius—between

37. See the extended discussion of More's *Utopia* in the introduction.

38. For Paul's condemnation of *eutrapelia*, see Ephesians 5:4 (George Ricker Berry, *The Interlinear Greek-English New Testament* [Grand Rapids: Zondervan, 1897], 508); for Aristotle's praise of *eutrapeloi*, see *NE* 1128a10 (*Nicomachean Ethics*, ed. and trans. H. A. Rackham, Loeb Classical Library [Cambridge: Harvard University Press, 1932], 246).

39. As we have seen, the issue of "accommodation" in civil life tends to produce these sorts of aporias. See the discussion of "performing the play of life" in *The Praise of Folly* and *Utopia* above in chapter 1.

spiritual and material poverty. A whole section of the third part of the *Intro-duction* is devoted to the claim that "[p]overty of spirit can be observed in the midst of riches" (sec. 14). You can possess riches without being spiritually hurt by them "if you merely keep them in your home and purse, and not in your heart" (162/185). Moreover, "you may take care to increase your wealth and resources"—through just means, of course (163–64/187). One can be poor "in effect" through *any* experience of inconvenience, as when "our best clothes are in one place and we need them in another" or—the one that strikes closest to my wine-collector's heart—when "the wines in our cellar ferment and turn sour" (166/190).

De Sales tells us that Saint Elizabeth, daughter of the king of Hungary, some-times, for recreation among her ladies, "clothed herself like a poor woman, say-ing . . . 'If I were poor, I would dress in this manner'"—and thereby manifested poverty of spirit. The ideal is to have "the advantages of riches for this world and the merit of poverty for the world to come" (162/185). The asserted con-nection to poverty is what is distinctive here (as opposed, for instance, to the celebration of earned wealth as a sign of God's favor).[40] The happy harmony of worldly riches and "the merit of poverty" is exactly what Pascal sought to disrupt. A. W. S. Baird cogently argues that the reason why casuistical argu-ments legitimizing aristocratic pastimes are so frequently singled out in the *Provincial Letters* is not merely because such arguments represent the most vulnerable point in the Jesuit armor but also "for the more basic reason that the aristocratic way of life requires more numerous and more serious attenuations than any other in the standard of Christian conduct."[41]

Much Protestant writing and preaching on social and economic matters in England was devoted to exalting the spiritual status of "the industrious sort of people," and downgrading the status of beggars and aristocrats (often lumped together), and of course, monks.[42] Yet, in the introduction to his volume, Bremond mentions that if time and space had allowed he "would fain have shown" how among the "Anglicans" of the first half of the seventeenth century a temper was produced "analogous to French devout humanism."[43] There is some truth to this. A number of English Protestant texts in the early seven-

40. On the (Protestant) celebration of earned wealth, see Tawney, *Religion and the Rise of Capitalism*, building on Weber, *Protestant Ethic*.

41. Baird, *Studies in Pascal's Ethics*, 42.

42. See Christopher Hill, "The Industrious Sort of People," in *Society and Puritanism in Pre-Revolutionary England* (New York: Schocken, 1967), 124–44.

43. Bremond, *Literary History of Religious Thought*, xiii.

teenth century did share the attitudes and the elitism of *l'humanisme dévot*. Donne's "A Litanie" may well have been one of those works that Bremond would have treated; George Herbert's "The Church-porch" may well have been another.

Helen Gardner, citing Bremond, links "A Litanie" to the movement.[44] In this poem, Donne professes heroic willingness not to suffer for God, crying, "Oh to some / Not to be Martyrs, is a martyrdome" (lines 89–90). The poem seems to pray for a balanced view of worldly splendor: to be kept "from thinking that great courts immure / All, or no happinesse" (lines 129–30). But the dramatic enjambment and punctuation of "All" betrays the balance; "or no" is rushed over—to think that is not really an option for the speaker in the way that thinking courts "immure / All . . . happinesse" is. The rest of the stanza is devoted not to finding a mean between the excesses of over- and undervaluing courtly life but exclusively to the problem of undervaluation. The "or" clauses become additive rather than antithetical as Donne prays to be delivered from thinking "that this earth / Is only for our prison fram'd," or "that they are maim'd / From reaching this worlds sweet, who seek thee thus" (lines 129–34).

The God of this poem is not a jealous God (to think "that thou art covetous / To them whom thou lov'st" is a mistake). With regard to wealth, Christians are "to both waies"—riches and poverty—"free" (line 162). This exactly recapitulates Ignatian indifference. Donne finds the Gospels perfectly balanced on the matter of wealth. In a colloquy with Christ, Donne does concede that "through thy poore birth . . . thou / Glorifiedst Povertie" (lines 158–59). But the next line begins "And yet." Donne notes that "soone after" his birth, Jesus "riches didst allow" by "accepting Kings gifts in the Epiphanie" (lines 160–61). As in the stanza on princely courts, the balanced treatment falls away. Poverty is seen as merely punitive or dangerous, whereas plenty is seen as not only "Gods image" but also his "seale" (line 185). Most of all, as in François de Sales's view, God does not demand antisocial behavior. In a moment very close to de Sales, Donne stresses "our mutuall duties," and prays to be delivered from "indiscreet humilitie" that might scandalize "the world" (lines 149–51). Discretion is the commanding virtue (in a later poem Donne asserts, "Wicked is not much worse than indiscreet").[45] Again, we must follow the Gospels, *mais sagement et discretement*.

44. See note 16 above.

45. "The First Anniversarie," line 338, in *The Complete Poetry of John Donne*, ed. John T. Shawcross (Garden City, N.Y.: Doubleday Anchor, 1967).

Helen Gardner noted the lack of balance in "A Litanie," its "rather exaggerated stress" on "the compatibility of the service of God with 'this worlds sweet.'"[46] Gardner offers some plausible biographical reasons why Donne may have fallen into such exaggeration in 1608, when he may have been tempted to see renunciation as desirable (as he purports to do, for instance, in "The Canonization"), but John Carey has shown that Donne's perspective stays the same in his sermons (after 1615) when his worldly position (through the church) was much better.[47] In a characteristic moment, Donne assures his auditors in 1621: "Salvation it selfe being so often presented to us in the names of Glory, and of Joy, we cannot thinke that the way to that glory is a sordid life affected here, an obscure, a beggarly, a negligent abandoning of all wayes of preferment, or riches, or estimation in this World."[48] Donne explains that "the glory of Heaven shines downe in these beames" of preferment, riches, and worldly comforts.

Like the Protestant reformers, François de Sales, and Father Le Moine, Donne is worried lest "men thinke, that the way to the joyes of Heaven, is a joylesse severenesse, a rigid austerity." Donne is part of the devout humanist tradition in his special concern for the rich and aristocratic. He makes use of the distinction between the two kinds of poverty that was adumbrated in Ignatius Loyola and flowered in François de Sales. Poverty of spirit, Donne explains, "is humility; it is not beggary." And therefore, of course, it follows that "a rich man may have it" (4:303). God, Donne explains, "weares good cloathes, silk, and soft raiment, in his religious servants in Courts, as well as Cammels haire, in *John Baptist* in the Wildernesse"; and God manifests himself to man "as well in the splendor of Princes in Courts, as in the austerity of *John Baptist* in the Wildernesse" (9:328).

Donne's version of "the devout life" is even more splendid than that depicted by François de Sales. But, as Carey has shown, it comes from the deepest springs of Donne's sensibility.[49] What is striking about Herbert's "The Church-porch" in relation to the texts of both Donne and François de Sales

---

46. Introduction to Donne, *Divine Poems*, xxv.

47. John Carey, *John Donne: Life, Mind and Art* (New York: Oxford University Press, 1981), 113–14. For "The Canonization" in the context of Donne's life, see Arthur F. Marotti, *John Donne, Coterie Poet* (Madison: University of Wisconsin Press, 1986), 157–65.

48. *The Sermons of John Donne*, ed. George R. Potter and Evelyn M. Simpson (Berkeley: University of California Press, 1957), 3:270 (further references in text).

49. Carey, *John Donne*, 113–25.

is that Herbert's poem can hardly be seen as offering any vision or version of "devout life." The poem participates much more fully in the elitism than in the piety of devout humanism. The addressee of "The Church-porch" is a young person (only male) whose prospects and social position make him especially valuable: "Thou, whose sweet youth and early hopes inhance / Thy rate and price, and mark thee for a treasure" (lines 1–2).[50] The idea that "[k]neeling ne'er spoil'd silk stocking" (line 407) would certainly have been endorsed by François de Sales, as would the charmingly expressed injunction, "Dress and undress thy soul" (line 453). Aside from a few moments like this that call for introspection, itself put in prudential terms—"Since thou shalt be most surely judg'd / Make thy accounts agree"—Herbert's poem is not concerned with the service or love of God at all.[51] Insofar as it has a "religious" dimension, the poem is concerned with Christian behavior—almsgiving, tithing, and church attendance—and with proper behavior in church (not flirting, and, especially, not making fun of the preacher, to which Herbert devotes four stanzas [72–75]). There is no equivalent in "The Church-porch" to Donne's conception of "splendor" or to François de Sales's sustained attempt to transform sociability into an actual version of charity. Unlike the *Introduction to the Devout Life*, "The Church-porch" does not attempt a transformation of the courtesy-book tradition. The poem merely places a distinct version of that tradition—addressed to the *gentiluomo* rather than the *cortegiano*—in a behaviorally Christian framework.[52] The courtesy book to which the poem is closest is Bacon's

50. All citations of "The Church-porch" and other writings of Herbert are from *The Works of George Herbert* (see intro., n. 54). Citations from "The Church-porch" will be followed by line numbers. There is some confusion in the scholarship about the social status of the addressee. One critic sees the poem as addressed to "simple parishioners" (Valerie Carnes, "The Unity of George Herbert's *Temple*," *English Literary History* 35 [1968]: 512). Stanley Fish sees the poem as addressed to universalized catechumens. His argument for the catechistical character of "The Church-porch" leads him to deny the class orientation of the poem and to obfuscate the particular nature of many of its precepts (*The Living Temple: George Herbert and Catechizing* [Berkeley: University of California Press, 1978], 126–28).

51. On the prudential perspective of the entire poem, see the analysis in Strier, *Resistant Structures*, 98–107 (see intro., n. 15).

52. John Lievsay, *Stefano Guazzo and the English Renaissance, 1575–1675* (Chapel Hill: University of North Carolina Press, 1961), chap. 1. Whigham (*Ambition and Privilege*, chap. 3, n. 29) questions the propriety of this distinction, pointing out that both figures were members of the gentry, but the distinction, nonetheless, remains useful (the *gentiluomo* is not oriented toward serving a prince).

Essays, a collection of "counsels, civil and moral," in which, as in the poem, the "civil" bulks large.[53]

The attempt has been made to read "The Church-porch" as moral. Louis L. Martz sees the poem as falling "into three general divisions," reprehending in turn "sins related to individual conduct (stanzas 1–34); sins related to social behavior (stanzas 35–62); and finally, sins related to specifically religious duties (stanzas 63–77)."[54] The central section of the poem, however, on social behavior, is concerned not with sins but with strategies, and it takes up five-sixths rather than one third of "The Church-porch." By the fifth stanza, Herbert is already dealing with the negotiation (mostly the dangers) of sociability. At the opening of stanza 5, there is a striking and typical descent in level of discourse; the speaker moves from the high moral ground of stanzas 2 through 4—from "O what were man, might he himself displace" in line 23 to "Drink not the third glasse" in line 25 (virtually repeated at line 41). Despite Martz's neat scheme of sins, the high moral ground is basically abandoned after stanzas 2 through 4. Another critic's scheme is more nuanced. Joseph H. Summers sees the poem as proceeding "by skilful use of traditional methods" through the seven deadly sins, from lechery, "the least important," to "the greatest spiritual sins" of anger, envy, and pride.[55] This is, again, perfectly plausible, but there is no indication in the poem that its author considers lust and drunkenness the "least important" of sins. In fact, the stanzas treating these are the most horrified and horrifying in the poem—"He that is drunken may his mother kill" (line 31). These stanzas are, to repeat, the high moral ground of the poem. The poem does offer critiques of anger and envy, but these critiques are anything but "traditional."

The problem with anger, according to "The Church-porch," is that it inhibits calculation. "Calmnesse is great advantage"; one must model oneself on "cunning fencers," who keep their cool, and "suffer heat to tire" (stanza 53, lines 313–16). Similarly, envy is reprehended not because it is a "spiritual

53. For Bacon's *Essays* as a courtesy book, see Whigham, *Ambition and Privilege*, 28. For "Civil Knowledge" as distinct from moral, see book 2, sec. 23 of Bacon's *The Advancement of Learning* (see chap. 3, n. 22 above), 179–209. For the two kinds of "counsels" in Bacon's *Essays*, see Jacob Zeitlin, "The Development of Bacon's *Essays* and Montaigne," *Journal of English and German Philology* 27 (1928): 496–512.

54. Martz, *The Poetry of Meditation*, 291.

55. Joseph H. Summers, *The Heirs of Donne and Jonson* (New York: Oxford University Press, 1970), 90. Summers is more accurate on the social dimension of the poem, seeing it as addressed to "a worldly young man of the contemporary ruling class" (89), and he recognizes, very uncomfortably, its strongly prudential cast (see note 51 above).

sin" but because it implies self-deprecation and is, moreover, socially coun-terproductive. Envying "great persons"—persons, that is, holding positions of power—is counterproductive because "thou mak'st thereby / Thy self the worse," and so "the distance [between them and you] greater" (lines 259–60). Toward such persons, Herbert recommends the complex stance that he calls "respective [respectful] boldnesse," since "[t]hat temper gives them theirs," while, at the same time, it "doth take / Nothing from thine" (lines 253–56). "Be not thine own worm," Herbert advises (line 261). Canon Hutchinson rightly glosses this advice as "do not disparage yourself and your qualities," and he rightly connects this advice to that which Herbert gave to his younger brother in a letter: "Be proud," Herbert advised, "not with a foolish vaunting of your-self . . . but by setting a just price on your qualities."[56] "It is the part of a poor spirit," Herbert continues, "to undervalue himself."

There is a version of Christianity that continued on the road of "proper pride"; we will see it in Milton.[57] It is not the theological path that Herbert himself ultimately took.[58] "The Church-porch" presents the least attractive vision of Christian life in the world among those—Catholic or Protestant, aris-tocratic or bourgeois (or, in Luther, occasionally peasant)—that we have seen. Its worldliness is very wary.[59]

56. In *Works of George Herbert*, 480; for the letter, see 365–66. Amy M. Charles, *A Life of George Herbert* (Ithaca: Cornell University Press, 1977), 78, 82–84, has convincingly redated this letter to 1614 (when Herbert was twenty-one). Hutchinson had dated it 1618. The date of the letter is probably an indicator of the original date of composition of the poem.

57. This matter in Milton is discussed in chapter 6 below.

58. For Herbert's theological development away from "The Church-porch," see Strier, *Resistant Structures*, 107–17.

59. On Herbert's attitude toward worldly pleasures throughout his career, see the introduc-tion above.

* 3 *

In Defense of Pride

CHAPTER 5

Self-Revelation and Self-Satisfaction in Montaigne and Descartes

In general, I prefer "Renaissance" to "early modern," but one major aspect of the period to which both descriptions seem equally fruitfully applied is the centrality of the term "self" to much of our period's most important writing and thinking.[1] I have no wish, in saying this, to discount the wealth of material uncovered and studied by Georg Misch and Arnoldo Momigliano, yet it is still fair to say that autobiography is not a major ancient mode.[2] Letters contained some autobiography—Cicero's, Seneca's, Saint Paul's—but even in these cases, autobiography was not their major function. The kind of self-knowledge that the Delphic oracle so strongly commended, and that Socrates took as his goal, was not exactly the sort that led to autobiography—to providing specific, idiosyncratic details about one's own life and history. The effort in the Platonic dialogues, even in the early most "Socratic" ones, is always to move from the details of the individual interlocutor's situation to the general issues that Socrates and Plato see as underlying them.[3] The *Apology* that Plato

1. On "Renaissance" versus "early modern," see note 3 in the introduction above.

2. Georg Misch, *A History of Autobiography in Antiquity* (1907), trans. in collaboration with the author by E. W. Dickes, 2 vols. (London: Routledge and Paul, 1950); Arnoldo Momigliano, *The Development of Greek Biography* (Cambridge: Harvard University Press, 1971), esp. 57–62, 89–95.

3. See the essays on *elenchus* by Richard Robinson in *The Philosophy of Socrates* (see chap. 1, n. 9), 78–109, and for a sustained treatment of the issue in a major Platonic dialogue, see Charles L. Griswold, Jr., *Self-Knowledge in Plato's "Phaedrus"* (New Haven: Yale University Press, 1986).

puts in the mouth of Socrates is a defense of Socrates's peculiar pedagogical and philosophical beliefs and practices, not an account of his history or personality as such. Augustine's *Confessions* immediately leaps to mind as (perhaps) an ancient counterexample, but, strikingly, as the only one.[4] And although Augustine was the most widely read church father in the West from the fall of Rome in the fifth century up to and beyond the sack of Rome in the sixteenth, the *Confessions* was not the Augustine that mattered.[5] Petrarch was quite unusual in thinking of Augustine as, first and foremost, the author of the *Confessions*.[6] Yet both Montaigne and Descartes produced works in which an individualized and historical first person was the focus, and both of them had vexed relations to the self-abnegation that their religious tradition demanded. Both were self-revealing and self-satisfied. This chapter will explore the rationales that each developed for defending self-revelation and self-satisfaction.

UNREPENTANT MONTAIGNE

One of the pressures on any premodern biographer or autobiographer was to make it clear why anyone should care about the details of an individual life, especially the life of someone who was not a saint, a king, or a conqueror. The answer—if there was one—was, normally, that the details were in some

4. On the distinctiveness of the *Confessions*, see Karl Joachim Weintraub, *The Value of the Individual* (Chicago: University of Chicago Press, 1978), 1–2; for how Marcus Aurelius's *To Myself* differs from sustained autobiography, see 16–17.

5. On the surprising lack of widespread use of the *Confessions* as a model in the Middle Ages, see ibid., chap. 3. It is significant that the *Confessions* barely exists in, for instance, an overview of medieval Augustinianism like D. W. Robertson's *A Preface to Chaucer: Studies in Medieval Perspectives* (Princeton: Princeton University Press, 1962). The very interesting materials uncovered by Pierre Courcelle in *Les Confessions de Saint Augustin dans la tradition littéraire* (Paris: Institut d'Etudes Augustinnenes, 1963), 235–327, change the picture only in a small way.

6. For Petrarch's devotion to the *Confessions*, see Courcelle, *Les Confessions*, 329–51. For Petrarch's use, in the *Secretum*, of a fictional version of Augustine to interrogate Petrarch's own life, see 60–62 above, and the references there given. In the Renaissance, the use of the *Confessions* (as opposed to other works of Augustine) continues to be surprisingly sparse. Molly Murray points out that in the late sixteenth century in England, William Alabaster seems to have modeled his spiritual autobiography to some extent on the *Confessions*, but Murray also acknowledges how unusual this is (*The Poetics of Conversion in Early Modern English Literature* [Cambridge: Cambridge University Press, 2009], 49–51). For the problem of Montaigne and the *Confessions*, see note 23 below.

way exemplary.[7] When a sonneteer, for instance, following Petrarch, gave details about his (or occasionally her) life, the point was to illustrate the heights, lengths, or depths to which love had raised or degraded the author. We learn, to take a specific case, a certain amount about Sir Philip Sidney in *Astrophil and Stella* and perhaps about William Shakespeare in his sonnets, but the point is to illustrate something about the compelling power of love. The autobiographical details themselves—if that is what they are—are not the point. This recognition is exactly what makes Montaigne so interesting. He seems to want, as Milton said in an autobiographical moment in his prose, "to venture and divulge unusual things" of himself.[8]

In the preface to an ambitious collection of stories about great historical figures (*De Viris Illustribus*), Petrarch explains that he has omitted many details from his accounts because they would be of no moral use to the reader; specifically, he has omitted morally useless details such as "what slaves or dogs an illustrious man has had, what beasts of burden, what cloaks, what were the names of his servants, what was the nature of his married life, his professions, or his personal property . . . what sort of food he liked best, or what he preferred as means of transportation, as a breastplate, as a cloak, or finally, even for sauces and vegetables."[9] Yet these are exactly the sort of details that Montaigne includes in his book. We know things about him that we know about no other author in the period (with the exception of Pepys, writing over a hundred years later, and certainly not writing for publication). We know not only what classical authors Montaigne liked, and what style of writing he liked, but also what his study looked like, what his handwriting was like, how tall he was, what his complexion was like, what sports he was good at, what kind of bread he liked to eat, what utensils and linen he liked to use when eating, how he liked to eat, when he liked to eat, how he slept, when he liked to make love, what problems he had in making love, what his bowel movements were like, what diseases he

---

7. See Timothy Hampton, *Writing from History: The Rhetoric of Exemplarity in Renaissance Literature* (Ithaca: Cornell University Press 1990), chap. 1.

8. See *The Reason of Church-Government Urg'd against Prelaty*, in *The Complete Prose Works of John Milton*, vol. 1, ed. Don M. Wolfe (New Haven: Yale University Press, 1953), 808. For a discussion of this passage in its context, see chapter 6 below.

9. Quoted from Benjamin G. Kohl, "Petrarch's Prefaces to *De Viris Illustribus,*" *History and Theory* 13 (1974): 141. In "The Figure of the Reader in Petrarch's *Secretum,*" *Publications of the Modern Language Association* 100 (1985): 154–66, Victoria Kahn has shown that Petrarch's practice in other works is more complex than this, and may sometimes raise "doubts about the very possibility of the example" (164).

had in his old age (and the list could easily be extended). His body becomes as present to us as his mind.[10]

But this immediately raises the question of what Montaigne thought he was doing in his book of experiments in first-person discourse, his assays or essays—a writing activity (if not exactly a genre) that he invented.[11] In the remarkable brief address, "Au lecteur," that prefaced all the authorially produced editions of the *Essays* (1580, 1582, 1588, 1595), Montaigne disclaims having any designs on the general reader at all.[12] The Renaissance revived the great classical boasts and claims for the enduring value and power of art—more lasting than brass, as Horace famously said (*Odes* 3.30), and as Ronsard and Shakespeare and others sonorously echoed.[13] Montaigne, however, explicitly denies that he has any such hope or goal. Even more shockingly, before he renounces that aspiration, he renounces the aim that virtually all forms of Renaissance writing, from the highest to the lowest, claimed, the aim of doing the reader some good. He tells the reader point blank, "I have not been concerned to serve you, nor my reputation" (*Je n'y ay eu nulle consideration de ton service, ny de ma gloire*).[14] He claims that the goal of his book is entirely "private" and is intended only for the benefit of his "friends and kinsmen," and only for the limited purpose of helping them keep their memories of him "more full, more alive" than such memories would otherwise have been. But what does he take

10. On immodesty and the body in the *Essais*, see Jean Starobinski, *Montaigne in Motion*, trans. Arthur Goldhammer (Chicago: University of Chicago Press, 1985), chap. 4, "The Body's Moment."

11. On the nonliterariness of Montaigne's conception of the term, *essai* or *essaier*, see Hugo Friedrich, *Montaigne*, ed. Philippe Desan, trans. Dawn Eng (Berkeley: University of California Press, 1991), 340–42.

12. The 1595 edition, though posthumous (Montaigne died in 1592) is thought to include Montaigne's final revisions (see note 16 below).

13. See the chapters grouped under the heading "Poetry and Immortality" in J. B. Leishman, *Themes and Variations in Shakespeare's Sonnets* (London: Hutchinson, 1963), 27–91.

14. For ease of accessibility, quotations from the *Essays* indicate page numbers in Michel de Montaigne, *The Complete Essays*, trans. M. A. Screech (London: Penguin, 1987), but my translations often depart from this edition in favor of the more accurate *Complete Essays of Montaigne*, trans. Donald M. Frame (Stanford: Stanford University Press, 1958), distinguished hereafter by the editor's name, or sometimes in favor of a translation of my own. For the French text, and again for reasons of accessibility, I have used the three-volume Garnier-Flammarion edition by Alexandre Micha (Paris, 1969), hereafter cited as *Essais*. I have given the French whenever it seemed important to have the exact words of a phrase or passage. Quotations from the French give the volume number followed by the page number in this edition (essays are also identified in terms of their place in the three-book *Essays* by book and chapter).

their memories or their "knowledge" of him to contain? Apparently it does not have a historical or narrative component. He is not going to remind them of facts and incidents in his life. One would think that a book with an intimate memorial aim would do this, that memoir would be the mode, but that is not to be the case here.

What Montaigne's supposed intimates will find is "some traits of my character and of my humours" (*aucuns traits de mes conditions et humeurs*).[15] Moreover, they will find this nonnarrative material presented in a particular stylistic mode. Montaigne insists that his self-portrait (what he is "painting") will be realistic rather than idealized, will not censor out his "defects." He states further that he will push the edge of propriety in his self-presentation, that he will present himself as "nakedly" as "respect for social convention" (*la reverence publique*) allows—and he makes it clear that he feels this *reverence* to be an unhappy imposition on him.

Elsewhere, Montaigne expands on these claims. In "On Giving the Lie" ("Du dementir," book 2, chap. 18), he repeats that his book is "for a neighbor, a relative or a friend" who will "find pleasure in meeting me and frequenting me again" through "this portrait" (754). In the final (C) version of this essay, he skips lightly over an obvious question, stating that "the only commerce I have with the public at large is my borrowing their printing-tools, which are more ready and convenient." In the earliest (A) version, he had more directly stated, "I had to cast this portrait in print to free myself from the bother of making several manuscript copies" (754n4).[16] This is so obviously disingenuous as to be impossible to believe. Why Montaigne had his "warts and all" verbal self-portrait printed obviously bears further scrutiny—as he full well knows.

15. For Montaigne as a model of an "episodic" rather than a narrative conception of the self, see Galen Strawson, "Against Narrativity," *Ratio*, n.s. 17 (2004): 428–52, esp. 449–50. This philosophical article strikes me as extraordinarily important for understanding the project of the *Essays*. Within Montaigne scholarship, a similar perception leads Craig B. Brush to deny that what Montaigne is doing in the *Essays* is autobiography. See *From the Perspective of the Self: Montaigne's Self-Portrait* (New York: Fordham University Press, 1994), chap. 3. As his subtitle suggests, Brush sees Montaigne as doing "self-portraiture" instead.

16. For the different layers of the text, known since the 1923 edition by Pierre Villey as A, B, and C—though the Garnier-Flammarion edition does not use this system—and for the dates of each layer so designated, see the Screech edition (liii). For clear accounts of the layers, see R. A. Sayce, *The Essays of Montaigne: A Critical Exploration* (Evanston: Northwestern University Press, 1972), chap. 2, "The Text of the *Essays*"; and David Maskell, "The Evolution of the *Essais*," in *Montaigne: Essays in memory of Richard Sayce*, ed. I. D. McFarlane and Ian MacLean (Oxford: Clarendon, 1992), 13–34.

"On Giving the Lie" presents the beginning of an answer. "Somebody," he says, "will tell me that my project of using myself as a subject to write about [*ce dessein de se servir de soi pour subject* (2:325)] would be pardonable" only in "exceptional, famous men" about whom the reader was already curious, and, more pointedly, that "it is unseemly for anyone to make himself known except he who can provide some example and whose life and opinions can serve as a model" (753). Montaigne's answer is to point to the fact that his project is truly a project, that it has a sustained temporal dimension. Making a detailed "painting" of himself as an ongoing entity has served Montaigne as something like a spiritual or psychological discipline; the process has affected the object of study: "[T]he original [*le patron*] has acquired more definition and has to some extent shaped itself [*aucunement formé soy-mesmes*]" (326) in the process.[17] Moreover, the process of providing a "long-term account" (*un registre de durée* [327]) has allowed for depth: "Those who merely think and talk about themselves occasionally do not examine the basics, and do not go as deep as one who makes it his study, his work, and his business" (755).

But the pressure of exemplarity still remains. If the project is not truly a merely "private" one, a memorandum for surviving friends and family, then Montaigne will have to redefine the conception of what sort of life can serve as an example to others. He must defend the public value of the private life. His essay on glory (book 2, chap. 16) begins to do this. He has contempt for those who act worthily "only when others can know of it" (708). The moral life must be conducted in private as well as in public; if it is not, the result is hypocrisy: "Our soul must act her part not when on parade but at home within us [*chez nous au dedans*], where no eyes but our own can penetrate" (709). The private rather than the public becomes the true testing ground of character. But can it be? Montaigne must answer that question. By the end of the *Essays*, he does so in a militant fashion. In "On Experience" (book 3, chap. 13), he insists that "the life of Caesar is less exemplary for us than our own," and the reason for this is that "a life, whether imperial or plebeian, is always a life affected by everything that can happen to a person" (1218). If we were astute enough observers, we would find all the guidance that we need to moral development within our own

17. The qualification "to some extent" (*aucunement*) is extremely important here. It counts strongly against a view like that of Ermanno Bencivenga of Montaigne's conception of the self as a process rather than an object (see *The Discipline of Subjectivity: An Essay on Montaigne* [Princeton: Princeton University Press, 1990]). I discuss Montaigne's conception of selfhood and of an "inner authority" (*un patron au dedans*) below.

experience—whatever its particular content. We would be able to recognize temptations, errors, and the like. The essential claim is that "Nature, to display and show her powers, needs no great destiny: she reveals herself equally at any level of life, both behind curtains or without them" (1258).[18]

This would seem a sufficient defense against triviality and irrelevance if all the "private" matters in question were presented in the mode of ethics and exemplarity. But the urge to self-disclosure in Montaigne is deeper and more peculiar than that. He does not want to reveal himself simply as an exemplar of this or that moral truth. He wants to reveal himself as a self, as a particular individual. He wants to be a "case," fully revealed, with all its "circumstances."[19] I purposely use here what sounds like (and is) legal language, but is also the language of casuistry and of the confessional, of, that is, the technical analysis of spiritual counsel and discipline.[20] This is a framework of which Montaigne is keenly aware, and to which, in explaining his project, he points us. In this context, it must be said, before continuing, that Montaigne makes his official position within the religious spectrum of his time extremely clear: he is a supporter of the old religion, Catholicism, and finds the whole Protestant project of "reformation" mistaken, troubling, and pernicious.[21] So he is joking in "On Some Verses of Vergil" (book 3, chap. 5) when he presents himself as proceeding

18. My colleague Lisa Ruddick has commented on how interesting it is that Montaigne "does not see some external guidance as at least helpful" (personal communication).

19. Kevin Hart has pointed out that the notion that I am attributing to Montaigne here is one "of full revelation," not (as Hart himself might like to see it) as "one of revealing and re-veiling as a double movement."

20. Peter Biller notes that "'circumstances' of sin and penitent" fill the late medieval works of instruction for the confessor. See "Confession in the Middle Ages," introduction to *Handling Sin: Confession in the Middle Ages*, ed. Peter Biller and A. J. Minnis (Rochester: York Medieval Press, 1988), 13. The same is true, as we will see, for the Council of Trent. See John Bossy, "The Social History of Confession in the Age of the Reformation," *Transactions of the Royal Historical Society*, ser. 5, 25 (1975): 23, 30.

21. See, for instance, the second half of "On Habit: and on Never Easily Changing a Traditional Law" (book 1, chap. 23); "On Prayers" (book 1, chap. 56), on the inadvisability of translating the scriptures into the vernacular (359); and the mockery in "On Experience" of the idea of referring to the words of the bible for religious authority (1208). Yet at the beginning of "On Prayers," Montaigne notes that the effect of his submission to the authority of the Roman Church, is to allow him to "meddle boldly with all sorts of subjects—as here," in this essay on a devotional topic (*me remettant tousjours à l'authorité de leur censure . . . je me mesle ainsi temerairement à toute sorte de propos, comme icy* [377]). This paradox is explored in Alain Legros, "Justice divine et juges romains dans *Essais*, I.56, 'Des Prieres,'" in *Montaigne et la justice*,

in the way he does out of regard for the French Protestants (955). But the joke is a complex one. The sentence reads (in literal translation): "As a courtesy to the Huguenots [*En faveur des Huguenots*], who condemn our private and auricular confession, I make my confession in public, religiously and purely" [*religieusement et purement* (3:62)].

Even when one discounts the joke, Montaigne can be seen to be acknowledging that he is in some odd relation to sacramental confession in his writing practice. "Religiously" is a striking word in this context, as is (we shall see) "purely."[22] Montaigne's "confession" is outside the context of any institution, and yet he wants it to have the content and something of the status of sacramental confession. He notes that "St. Augustine, Origen, and Hippocrates publicly admitted the error of their opinions," but Montaigne claims that he goes beyond them by including the errors of his morals (955).[23] In strangely passionate language, he states: "I hunger to make myself known" (*Je suis affamé de me faire connoistre*). He then emends this, changing the positive desire into a fear: "Or, to put it better, I hunger for nothing, but I go in mortal fear of being taken to be other than I am [*pris en eschange*] by those who happen to know my name."[24] The fear is even stronger than the "hunger." He is in "mortal fear"—as if his soul depended on it—that he will not be properly known, that his name will not be associated with his own sense of his identity. He wants to be known in an absolute sense, virtually in a metaphysical sense. He wants to be known even as he knows, significantly reversing "then shall I know even as I am known" (1 Cor. 13:12), and locating "then" in a historical rather than a transcendental future.[25]

---

ed. Jean-Claude Arnould, *Bulletin de la Societé Internationale des Amis de Montaigne* [*BSAM*], ser. 8, 22 (2001): 251–62.

22. Friedrich, *Montaigne*, 217, downplays the significance of *religieusement* here.

23. Screech (955n19) takes this passage to suggest that Montaigne did not know Augustine's *Confessions*. For an argument that he must have known this text, together with an attempt to account for why, if he did so, he so thoroughly hid this fact (in contradiction to his normal practice of liberal quotation), see Gìsele Mathieu-Castellani, *Montaigne, ou La vérité du mensonge* (Geneva: Droz, 2000), chap. 7.

24. Frame's translation, "taken to be other than I am" (643) seems to me to capture the meaning of Montaigne's odd use of *pris en eschange* much better than Screech's more literal "being taken for another"—which, I think, misses the point.

25. My friend Jeffrey Stern, a psychoanalyst (and literary critic), has asked, "What is behind this fear and hunger?" I wish that I could answer this wonderful question. Perhaps, as hinted in my text, it is the only form of immortality that Montaigne feels is actually possible.

While Montaigne's "confession" is noninstitutional, he shares the confidence of the Catholic sacrament about the possibility of knowing the self.[26] For the Catholic, confession was one of the "parts" of the sacrament of penance. This sacrament, even more than the Eucharist, was at the center of the great conflict between the churches in the sixteenth century; Luther's "Ninety-Five Theses" were about sacramental penance (from which the indulgence matter flowed).[27] The reformers attacked all aspects of the Romanist conception, including both the practice (auricular confession to a priest) and the ideology of sacramental confession. Formal confession—to a priest—was crucial to the sacrament.[28] The whole efficacy of the sacrament depended on the fullness and accuracy of the penitent's confession, "circumstances" included, "for without them the sins themselves are neither integrally set forth by the penitent nor are they known to the judges [that is, the confessors], and it would be impossible for them [the confessors] to estimate rightly the grievousness of the crimes and to impose the punishment due to the penitents on account of them."[29] Luther and Calvin and their followers denied the need for such punishment, and denied as well that one could "integrally set forth" one's sins. Of the latter, Luther said, "This is to ask the impossible," since "we can know only the minor part of our sins."[30] Calvin pointed to David, the psalmist, as one who had "rightly pondered confession of sins," and therefore exclaimed, "Who will understand his errors? Cleanse thou me from my secret errors, O Lord"—by which David meant, according to Calvin, not sins secret from others but sins of his own secret from himself.[31]

26. Ann W. Astell has reminded me that the Catholic framework relies on a conception of prevenient grace—which is entirely absent from Montaigne.

27. On the penance controversy, and the relation of the indulgence matter to this, see Strier, "Herbert and Tears," 221–47 (see chap. 4, note 101).

28. Luther certainly believed in the efficacy and usefulness of confession; he called it "a singular medicine for afflicted consciences." But he thought that a Christian "may lay bare his sins to whomever he chooses," to "any brother or sister," since "the power of the keys" was given to all Christians (it is part of the priesthood of all believers). See *The Babylonian Captivity*, in *Selections from His Writings*, 319–21 on confession, 345 on the priesthood of all believers (see intro., n. 55).

29. See *Canons and Decrees of the Council of Trent*, trans. Rev. H. J. Schroeder (Rockford, Ill.: Tan Books, 1978), 93 (14th sess., chap. 5). For Luther's contempt for "circumstances," see *The Babylonian Captivity*, 322–23.

30. *The Babylonian Captivity*, 318.

31. *Institutes*, 3.4.16; also secs. 17–18 (see intro., n. 33).

Montaigne, on the contrary, had an extraordinary confidence in the availability of the self to a sustained effort at self-knowledge.[32] He did not believe that this was easy—any more than Ignatius Loyola or the authors of confessional manuals did. The Tridentine decree stated not only that sins must be "integrally" set forth but also that "diligent self-examination" was required to do so. Montaigne certainly believed that self-knowledge took sustained effort. "Nothing," he said, "is more difficult than the describing of oneself" ("On Practice," book 2, chap. 6, 424–25). Most people have a trivial, and therefore false, self-understanding ("On Experience," 1220). But true self-understanding is possible. Montaigne believed that he knew his virtues and his vices, and for the most part, he did not see them as the same (as Luther and Calvin sometimes did).[33] In the "courtesy to the Huguenots" passage in "Some Verses," Montaigne states that "if a man were to praise me for being a good navigator, for being very [handsome], or very chaste, I would not owe him a thank you"— because, he says, they would not actually be praising Montaigne. Similarly, "if anyone should call me a traitor, a thief, or a drunkard, I would not think that it was me he attacked."

Only persons who misjudge themselves can "feed on false approval" and be inwardly affected by false accusations. Montaigne says bluntly that he cannot be so (*non pas moy*). He sees himself and explores himself right into his innards (956; *jusques aux entrailles* [3:62])—exactly what Luther and Calvin said God uniquely does.[34] Montaigne was famously skeptical about many things and many kinds of knowledge, but not, ultimately, about this.[35] About his account of himself, he says, "nothing is wanting and there is nothing to guess" ("On Vanity," book 3, chap. 9, 1112). He is strangely untroubled by the possibility of self-deception. This seems to be because of the privacy of his endeavor on the

32. For dissenting views on this, see Hassan Melehy, "Montaigne's 'I,'" *Montaigne Studies* 3 (1991): 156–81; Jan Miernowski, *L'ontologie de la contradiction sceptique: Pour l'étude de la métaphysique des "Essais"* (Paris: Honoré Champion, 1998); and, in a slightly different vein, Bencivenga's *The Discipline of Subjectivity*.

33. For the (pagan) virtues as vices in Luther and Calvin, see chapter 6 below. Montaigne seems to adopt this view at one moment in "On Practice" (425)—"our very virtue is faulty and needs repentance"—but does not stay with it. In "On Practice" (425), he sees this moral fact as undermining all institutionalized forms of confession, which he sees as essentially identical, whether private and "our own" (Catholic) or public and that of "our neighbors" (Huguenot).

34. See Luther, "Preface to Romans," in *Selections from His Writings*, 22; Calvin, *Institutes*, 3.2.4–5.

35. Compare Peter Burke, "The Self from Petrarch to Descartes," in *Rewriting the Self: Histories from the Renaissance to the Present*, ed. Roy Porter (London: Routledge, 1997), 24.

one hand—its lack of concern for honor or glory—and its strenuousness and temporal continuity (*durée*) on the other (what Bencivenga calls its "discipline of subjectivity").[36]

Montaigne wanted to be known as a self. And we have now ascertained one feature of how he characterized the self—it is something that is available to introspective scrutiny. In this, as we have seen, he is at one with the sacramental ideology of his church with regard to confession. But what of his relation to the rest of the sacrament of penance? Confession is only the second of the three parts that constitute the "matter" of the sacrament of penance (the priest's absolution is its "form"). Repentance, contrition, is the first of these parts ("satisfaction," the performance of the punishment or "penance" imposed by the priest as judge, is the third).[37] For Erasmus, repentance was all that really mattered;[38] the Protestants, as we shall see, also believed this, though with a different underlying theology. One of Montaigne's most remarkable essays, and the one that perhaps gives us the clearest answer to the question of what he thought a "self" was, is "On Repentance" ("Du repentir," book 3, chap. 2), his essay on the sine qua non of penitence, sacramental or otherwise. A number of scholars have taken "On Repentance" to be a crucial essay.[39] It is also one that is, for Montaigne, unusually sequacious.[40] He is truly working on his topic here.

Like many of the essays, "On Repentance" has an abrupt and striking opening: "Others form man" (*Les autres forment l'homme* [3:20]).[41] These "others" could refer, literally, to sculptors or painters, but more probably refers to rhetoricians, those who would "fashion a gentleman" or otherwise form or

36. Bencivenga, *The Discipline of Subjectivity*.

37. See *Canons and Decrees of Trent*, 90–91 (14th sess., chap. 3).

38. *The Enchiridion of Erasmus*, 125–28 (see chap. 4, app., n. 6), though Erasmus is careful to say that rituals "are not condemned" (126). See Bossy, "Social History of Confession," 27.

39. See for instance, Donald M. Frame, "Observations sur le chapitre 'Du repentir' des 'Essais' de Montaigne," in *Études montainistes en hommage à Pierre Michel*, ed. Claude Blum and François Moureau (Geneva: Editions Slatkine, 1984), 103–10; Miernowski, *L'ontologie de la contradiction*, chap. 4, "Le 'Moi': Repentir et regret"; James Supple, "'Du repentir': Structure and Method," *Montaigne in Cambridge*, ed. Philip Ford and Gillian Jondorf (Cambridge: Cambridge University Press, 1989), 69–85, and Ian Winter, "Form, Reform, and Deformity in Montaigne's 'Du repentir,'" *Montaigne Studies* 3 (1991): 200–207, who asserts that "there is every reason for viewing '*Du repentir*' as the pivotal chapter of the Third Book" (200).

40. On the sequaciousness of "On Repentance," see Supple, "Structure and Method," 70.

41. The other quotations in French in this paragraph and the next are from the same page.

transform their audiences for the better.[42] Montaigne presents himself, by contrast, as sketching a picture of an individual who is "very badly formed" (*un particulier bien mal formé*). It might seem that he is saying that he is presenting a negative example, and the end of the sentence encourages that reading, stating that Montaigne is presenting "one whom I would truly make very different from what he is if I had to fashion him afresh." But he immediately brushes the issue of the negative nature of his "sketch" aside (as Jules Brody puts it, "at this precise point a shift from pejorative to meliorative occurs").[43]

Montaigne claims, in a famous phrase, to be portraying not being "but passing"—or "becoming," as Screech has it (*Je ne peints pas l'estre. Je peints le passage*). He cannot, therefore, be held to any standards of consistency; his account is contradictory "because I myself have become different" (908). This has struck many as manifesting a remarkably postmodern sense of the fluidity of the self and its nonidentity with itself over time.[44] But Montaigne immediately provides an alternative to this ontological account of his apparent contradiction of himself. His account may seem contradictory for the reason just given "or because I grasp hold of different attributes or aspects of my subjects" (*soit que je sois autre moymesme, soit que je saisisse les subjects par autres circonstances et considerations*). The latter explanation is an important alternative, since it does not contradict the consistency of the self over time. It is perceptual or functional, not ontological. And this turns out to be a picture—pace the postmodernists—that Montaigne does not wish to contradict. To quote Brody again, the "celebrated paean to human mutability takes place under the banner of constancy."[45]

After a claim to authoritative self-knowledge of the sort that we have already examined—"never did a man treat a subject that he knew or understood better"—Montaigne turns to the announced topic of "On Repentance." The sentence in which he does so is astonishing. He rejects completely the apparent

42. In the letter to Sir Walter Ralegh prefixed to *The Faerie Queene*, Spenser, in a now famous phrase, states that "the generall end" of the entire poem is "to fashion a gentleman or noble person in vertuous and gentle discipline" (*Spenser's "Faerie Queene,"* ed. J. C. Smith [Oxford: Clarendon, 1909], 2:485).

43. Jules Brody, "'Du repentir' (III: 2): A Philological Reading," *Yale French Studies* 64 (1983): 242.

44. See Jerome Schwartz, "The Deconstructive Moment in Montaigne's *Essais*," *Stanford French Review* 9 (1985): 321–33. For an overview of the development of this perspective in Montaigne studies (though the early '80s), see Richard L. Regosin, "Recent Trends in Montaigne Scholarship: A Post-Structuralist Perspective," *Renaissance Quarterly* 37 (1984): 34–54. See also the works cited in note 32 above.

45. Brody, "'Du repentir,'" 243.

humility of the opening of the essay ("one of them who is very badly formed," and so forth). Montaigne writes: "Let me justify here what I often say: that I rarely repent" (909).[46] And for the revised final addition, he compounds the felony, so to speak, by explaining that his lack of the practice or habit of repenting is a sign not of his bad but of his good character. "My conscience," he says, "is happy with itself" (*ma conscience se contente de soy* [3:22]), and he immediately presents this complacent self-regard as utterly proper—"not as the conscience of an angel, or of a horse, but as behooves the conscience of a human" (909). Quite nervously, he adds some clauses about this assertion not having practical consequences ("I . . . abide by the common lawful beliefs"), and about his claims being descriptive rather than normative (*Je n'enseigne poinct, je raconte*), but the rest of the essay is devoted to defending nonrepentance.

Yet as soon as he gets going, he seems immediately to contradict himself, presenting vice as inherently recognizable in its true nature by reason—which produces repentance. But, as James Supple notes, "Montaigne undermines the point even as he makes it" by only seeming to agree with the Platonic view ("perhaps those philosophers are right" [*à l'advanture ceux-là ont raison*]).[47] As the essay develops, it becomes clear that the point of this allusion to the supposedly self-apparent nature of vice is to get to the following paragraph on the pleasure of virtue. Montaigne, like Milton after him, fully adopts the Aristotelian conception of "proper pride": "There is a certain delight in acting well [*Il y a certes je ne scay quelle congratulation de bien faire*], which makes us inwardly rejoice; a noble feeling of pride [*une fierté genereuse*] [which] accompanies a good conscience" (910/3:22).[48] In "On Practice" (book 2, chap. 6), Montaigne gave a completely accurate account of this position: "To say that you are worse than you are is not modest, but foolish" (426), and he correctly attributed the view to Aristotle, according to whom "to prize yourself at less than you are worth is weak and faint-hearted."[49] In "Of Presumption" (book 2,

46. I strongly dissent from Donald Frame's view that in the context of the *Essays*, this statement avoids shocking the reader ("Observations sur le chapitre 'Du repentir'"), 103. Winter, "Form, Reform, and Deformity," struggles to see this sentence in the way that Frame does, though with more sense of the difficulty of doing so (205).

47. Supple, "Structure and Method," 71.

48. For Milton and proper pride, see chapter 6 below. Jeffrey Stern (see note 25 above) has pointed out to me that the psychology here resembles that of Heinz Kohut, for whom "the superego is a source of pleasure, rather than [as in Freud] of torment."

49. See book 4, chap. 3, of the *Nicomachean Ethics* (*NE* 1123b10), page 94 in the Ostwald edition (see chap. 2, n. 28). The person who underestimates himself manifests *mikropsychia*, the opposite of "proper pride" or great-souledness (*megalopsychia*).

chap. 17), he is equally against having an overly high and an overly low opinion of oneself; rather, he states, one's judgment should "perceive whatever truth presents it with," and notes that if one is Caesar, one should "frankly acknowledge that he is the greatest captain in the world" (718).

Montaigne truly and sincerely rejoices in the (relative) purity of his soul; he lists the vile things of which "anyone who could see right into my soul" would not find him guilty (910). Eric Auerbach and many other critics worry about the "element of self-satisfaction" in Montaigne.[50] They are struggling with both an essential feature of classical ethics and a feature of Montaigne's personality that he views as basic and enduring—see "On Physiognomy" on his own "righteousness that is aware of itself" (*justice qui se cognoist* [3:256]).[51] Max Gauna wisely reminds us, considering Montaigne's education, "that Greek and Latin ideals, mores and mental habits seemed to him not just infinitely better, but actually more natural for him personally than did those of his own [culture]."[52]

After discussing the "noble pride" of a good conscience, Montaigne goes on to explain how he makes judgments on himself and to assert, characteristically, that these judgments are much more accurate than anyone else can make, for "others never see you; they surmise" (*ils vous devinent par conjectures incertaines* [3:23]).[53] He speaks of the importance of establishing "an inner authority [*un patron au dedans*] by which to try our actions" (911/3:23).[54] This sounds—like the previously mentioned perception of the odiousness of vice—as if it would be a force that would lead to repentance, but that is not, again, where the essay is going. It returns to the defense of nonrepentance. After two quotations from Cicero on the importance of relying on one's own judgment and conscience, Montaigne returns to his more unusual and dis-

---

50. See Eric Auerbach, *Mimesis: The Representation of Reality in Western Literature* (see chap. 4, n. 5), 303; Winter, "Form, Reform, Deformity," 205–7; Frame, "Observations," 105–109.

51. I have given the translation in Frame (799). Screech (1183), misses (or obscures) the point by translating the phrase as "justice which knows what is what."

52. Max Gauna, "The Hard Problem," in *Le visage changeant de Montaigne*, ed. Keith Cameron and Laura Willett (Paris: Champion, 2003), 161.

53. On "the concept of judgment in Montaigne," see the book by that title by Raymond C. La Charité (The Hague: Martinus Nijhoff, 1968).

54. The sense of this phrase in French (*un patron au dedans*) hovers interestingly and perhaps significantly between an abstraction, like "model" (Screech) or "pattern" (Frame) and an active presence, like "master"; "authority" is my own attempt to mediate between the two.

tinctive claim.[55] Despite the assertions he has made about conscience and the obvious odiousness of sin, he notes that "the saying that 'repentance follows hard upon the sin' does not seem to touch sin that is fully arrayed [*en son haut appareil*], lodged in us as in its own home" (911). He sees vices that seize us at a particular moment "and towards which we are carried away by passion" as ones that can be repented or "disowned" (*desavouër*)—treated, that is, as alien from the self—but he argues (and here he is indeed arguing) that vices that "are rooted and anchored in a will that is strong and vigorous brook no denial." He sees the disowning of such as, in an existential rather than a logical sense, self-contradictory. To attempt to "repent" such a vice "is but to gainsay our will" (*n'est qu'une desditte de nostre volonté* [3:23]). How can one will not to will what one does? Devotees of Saint Paul might find this intelligible, but Montaigne does not. Montaigne sees it as giving up what it means to have a self; such "repentance" belies all stability—"it can lead us in any direction." He quotes as an example of utter nonsense two lines from a Horace ode in which a speaker laments that his inner state corresponds to his bodily one (911).

The argument of the essay becomes that one must judge selves or souls by "their settled state" (913; *leur estat rassis* [3:26]) and when they are—and this is another argument for the special status of the private—"at home" (*chez elles*), both literally (as a space imagined as free from external constraint) and figuratively ("Here in my bosom, and at home," as Ben Jonson says).[56] But how do souls or selves get their settled states? Although the earlier mention of *un patron au dedans* may have suggested something that can be intentionally constructed or willed, that is not, in fact, Montaigne's view. He is, one can fairly say, a determinist on this matter. On the great question of what education can do, on whether and to what extent art and education can change "nature"—a question on which there was a spectrum of answers from the relative pessimism of most of the Italian humanists through the extreme optimism of Erasmus and Roger Ascham—Montaigne is strongly on the pessimistic side.[57] Natural

55. Miernowski, *L'ontologie de la contradiction*, tries to show that Montaigne could not fully intend the pride and self-sufficiency in the Cicero quotes, and that they would be read ironically by the properly informed reader who recognizes their original context. This is a very clever argument with which I disagree.

56. Line 68 of "To the World: A Farewell for a Gentle-woman, Vertuous and Noble," poem 4 in *The Forrest*, from *The Complete Poetry of Ben Jonson* (see chap. 4, n. 21), 86.

57. For Italian humanists on the limits of what education can do, see Pier Paolo Vergerio, *The Character and Studies Befitting a Free-Born Youth* (*De Ingenuis Moribus*), in *Humanist Educational Treatises*, ed. and trans. Craig W. Kallendorf (Cambridge: Harvard University

tendencies (*les inclinations naturelles*), he says, "are helped and reinforced by education, but they can hardly be said to be changed and conquered" (913). You cannot, he says, "extirpate the qualities we are originally born with" (*On n'extirpe pas ces qualitez originelles* [3:26]). So Montaigne would seem pretty clearly to be a psychological determinist, with the view that psychological tendencies are inborn.

Yet the example of an inborn quality that he gives seems to complicate or destabilize this claim. Right after the assertion of the impossibility of extirpating inborn qualities, Montaigne gives the following example from his own life: "Latin is like a native tongue for me" (*le langage latin m'est comme naturel* [3:26]).[58] He gives as an example of the natural something that is "like" something natural, but he continues in a way that disregards the "like." He notes that Latin is the language that, despite his lack of use of it for most of his life, he falls into in moments of sudden distress—"nature," he says, "against long nurture, breaking forcibly out" (914). So it seems that early habituation must be considered a form of "nature," or so "like" nature that the difference disappears. This is probably to be taken as Montaigne's position, but the whole question of custom versus nature in his work is an extremely vexed matter.[59] In the essay on husbanding one's will (book 3, chap. 10), Montaigne opts for a

---

Press, 2002), 37, 39 (on Claudius and Nero), and Aeneas Silvius Piccolomini, *The Education of Boys* (*De Liberorum Educatione*), in *Humanist Educational Treatises*, 133. For the optimism of Erasmus, see *De Pueris Instituendis*, in *Desiderius Erasmus concerning the Aim and Method of Education*, trans. William Harrison Woodward (1904; New York: Teachers College, Columbia University, 1964), 190, 196, and 200; for the full Latin text and a complete and more accurate translation (into French), see Erasme, *Declamatio de Pueris Statim ac Liberaliter Instituendis*, trans. Jean-Claude Margolin (Geneva: Droz, 1966). For the optimism of Ascham, see Roger Ascham, *The Schoolmaster*, ed. Lawrence V. Ryan (Charlottesville: University Press of Virginia, 1967), 34–35. For a careful treatment of this issue in Montaigne, one that is fully aware of his pessimism, see James J. Supple, *Arms versus Letters: The Military and Literary Ideals in the "Essais" of Montaigne* (Oxford: Clarendon, 1984).

58. Screech (914), unlike Frame (615), drops the "like," and therefore obscures the complexity of the passage.

59. For a critique of the notion of the "natural" in human affairs, see "On Habit: and on Never Easily Changing a Traditional Law"—"there is nothing that custom may not do and cannot do" (129)—and "An Apology for Raymond Sebond" (book 2, chap. 12) for the assertion that nothing is "universally accepted by the agreement of all peoples" (654), and for apparent mockery of philosophers who "model themselves on their concept of Nature as she originally was" (658). But contrast Montaigne's regular appeals to "nature" and the "natural," as in "On the Cannibals" (book 1, chap. 31, 232ff.) and elsewhere. On this contradiction, see Sayce, *The Essays of Montaigne*, 188–201; Peter Burke, *Montaigne* (New York: Hill and Wang, 1981), 50–51;

definition of the natural that includes "a little more" (*quelque chose plus* [3:221]) than biology. "Let us call 'nature,'" he says, "the habits and character of each one of us" (1141; *l'usage et condition de chacun de nous* [3:222]). He notes that by long usage "this form of mine has passed into substance, and my fortune into nature" (1143; *Par long usage cette forme m'est pasée en substance, et fortune en nature* [3:223]).[60] But in any case, the point for the essay on repentance is that the inner "form" of an individual is not something subject to change by the will.

In fact, despite the accommodation of custom as "second nature," Montaigne does seem to tend toward a strong biological (rather than psychocultural) determinism. The "form" of the self does seem mainly given by nature. He sees his basic character as having been given to him by good luck ("my virtue . . . is incidental and fortuitous"); good genetics ("an excellent father" ["On Cruelty," book 2, chap. 11, 478]); and a happily healthy, well-tempered, and lower-class wet nurse ("Of Presumption," book 3, chap. 12, 1201).[61] He has, as he sees it, the same basic structure of character (*complexion*) that he had as a child ("On Educating Children," book 1, chap. 26, 197; "On Cruelty," book 2, chap. 11, 478). As Auerbach puts it, "at every moment of the continual process of change, Montaigne possesses the coherence of his personality; and he knows it."[62] Montaigne is extremely fond of a section in *De Officiis* in which Cicero explains that since "we are invested by nature with two characters as it were," one of which is universal (*communis*) and shared with all rational creatures, the other "assigned to individuals in particular," we must "resolutely hold fast to [our] own peculiar gifts, insofar as they are peculiar

---

Charles Larmore, "Michel Eyquem de Montaigne," in *Dictionnaire d'ethique et de philosophie morale*, ed. Monique Canto-Sperber (Paris: Presses Universitaires de France, 1996), 983–87.

60. For a recent discussion of this topic in Montaigne (though one that seems to me too ethically optimistic and too ready to dismiss Montaigne's determinism), see Francis Goyet, "La notion éthique d'habitude dans les *Essais*: Articuler l'art et la nature," *Modern Language Notes* 118 (2003): 1070–91.

61. For my awareness of the class dimension here, with regard to Montaigne's sense of owing his "soft" (*molle*) disposition to his wet-nurse (who has the "soft" disposition of a commoner), I am indebted to unpublished work by George Hoffmann, and to David Quint, *Montaigne and the Quality of Mercy: Ethical and Political Themes in the "Essais"* (Princeton: Princeton University Press, 1998), 9: "It becomes possible to hear in the '*mollesse*,' the softness that Montaigne attributes to commoners, women, children, and . . . himself, the technical force of *mollitia*, the Stoic Seneca's favorite term of reproach that is often translated as 'effeminacy.'" As Quint says, "Montaigne declares himself to be a softie."

62. Auerbach, *Mimesis*, 294.

only, and not vicious" (*non vitiosa, sed tamen propria*).[63] In the essay on vanity (book 3, chap. 9), Montaigne names his "master qualities," independence (*la liberté*) and sloth (1122), and he clearly sees these as inborn and definitive of his self—"matters," as he says in "On Husbanding Your Will" (book 3, chap. 10), "which by nature belong to my own being" (1135; *mes affaires essentiels, propre et naturels* [3:217]).[64]

When we return to "On Repentance" with this issue in mind, we see that Montaigne is unusually assertive in stating that "provided that he listen to himself, there is no one who does not discover in himself a form entirely his own, a master-form [*une forme maistresse*] which struggles against one's education as well as against the storm of emotions which would gainsay it" (914).[65] Moreover, "On Repentance," with its radical rejection of the possibility of personal transformation, goes beyond Cicero and defends even vices as potentially "forms" of the self that cannot be changed.[66] In a somewhat obscure passage, Montaigne speaks of some people—they sound like Aristotle's victims of *akrasia*, weakness of the will (*Nicomachean Ethics* 7.2–3)—who recognize that certain habits or pieces of behavior are vices, but who are unable to give up the

63. See Cicero, *De Officiis*, with an English translation by Walter Miller, Loeb Classical Library (Cambridge: Harvard University Press, 1913), 1.3.107, 1.31.1; cited in Montaigne's "On the Useful and the Honorable" (book 3, chap. 1, 897), where Screech gives an inaccurate reference, and in "On Vanity" (1118).

64. "Liberty" here seems to mean something like "resistance to having one's thoughts and affairs dictated by others." Montaigne's two "master qualities" balance each other nicely, producing a person with independent ideas but no inclination to act on them boldly and visibly in the world. His "sloth" is related to his softness (*mollesse*), discussed in note 61 above.

65. This phrase is an especial irritant to those who wish to deny the stability of the self in Montaigne. See, for instance, Jean-Yves Pouilloux, "La forme maîtresse," in *Montaigne et la question de l'homme*, ed. Marie-Luce Demonet (Paris: Presses Universitaires de France, 1999), 33–45; Miernowski, *L'ontologie de la contradiction*, 100–103; and Timothy Reiss, "Montaigne and the Subject of Polity," in *Literary Theory / Renaissance Texts*, ed. Patricia Parker and David Quint (Baltimore: Johns Hopkins University Press, 1986), 133–34. Patricia Eichel struggles somewhat inconclusively with the phrase in "Le démenti et la sincérité," *BSAM*, ser. 7, 10 (1987): 35–48, esp. 45–47. Gauna, "Montaigne and the Hard Problem," brilliantly characterizes the *forme maistresse* as "something like a mould of a certain shape, open at both ends, through which physical matter and mental phenomena, shifting and changing as they go, flow for as long as the spring of life determines and the mold remains intact, which is to say the same thing" (160).

66. This is recognized by Supple, "Structure and Method," 74–75.

pleasure that, quite consciously, accompanies that vice (914–15).[67] Montaigne counts himself among this number, and he repeats his distinction between sudden impulses toward vice and vices that are "rooted" in an individual. He sees the latter sorts of vices as parts of an individual's character or self: "I cannot conceive that they should be rooted so long in one identical heart without the reason and conscience of him who is seized of them being constant in his willing and wanting them to be so." Montaigne cannot understand what it would mean for such an individual to "repent" of a vice so rooted. He does not believe in what he calls the "Pythagorean" faith in the possibility of attaining through any efforts or acts of piety a "new soul" (916; *une ame nouvelle* [3:28]).

He views this desire to have an entirely different self (*en general estre autre*) as an empty fantasy—indeed, in an earlier essay, "A Custom of the Island of Cea" (book 2, chap. 3), he had shown it to be logically incoherent, for if one were changed totally, one would no longer be there to note it.[68] The fantasy (or "desire") of being entirely different is one, he says, that "should not be called repenting any more than my grieving at not being an angel or Cato" (916). Montaigne sees this sort of imagining or desiring as truly pointless, as having no more effect than imagining that "my arm or my intelligence would become stronger because I can imagine others that are so." Basically, he can only imagine himself acting, in like circumstances, exactly the way that he has acted in such circumstances (917). The essay goes on to consider two other kinds of attitude that Montaigne does not consider true repentance. One of these is being sorry that a situation turned out badly. Montaigne does not "repent" having acted in a certain way, unsuccessfully, if he has done so in accordance with his settled character. Again, to "repent" such an action would be to imagine that he could have acted differently—which he denies and basically, as we have seen, finds incoherent. Finally, in the last section of the essay, Montaigne

67. Supple (ibid., 75), seems to me correct in seeing Montaigne as rejecting the equation of knowledge and virtue that lies at the heart of Socratic ethics. See also Miernowski, *L'ontologie de la contradiction sceptique*, 122: "La conscience du mal ne résulte pas en repentir." On *akrasia*, see (among many others), Amélie O. Rorty, "*Akrasia* and Pleasure: *Nicomachean Ethics*, Book VII," in *Essays on Aristotle's Ethics*, ed. Amélie Oskenberg Rorty (Berkeley: University of California Press, 1980), 267–84. Montaigne, however, seems to conflate *akrasia* (weakness of the will, incontinence) with *akolasia*, intemperance. Aristotle sees the former as "curable," the latter as not (*NE* 1150b31; Ostwald ed., 197). Montaigne's view is darker.

68. "Anyone who wishes to be changed from man to angel does nothing at all for himself: *he* would gain nothing by it. Who is supposed to be feeling that amendment for him and rejoicing at it? *He* is no more" (Screech, 397).

considers what might be called "after the fact" repentance, the repentance that the aged have for the sins of their youth. He finds this contemptible, since it is easy to be "virtuous" when temptations or the ability to act on them have ceased. Moreover, and more in consonance with the argument of the essay, he finds the "repentance" of the aged another way of refusing to accept who you are. On Montaigne's view, one of the things that it means to be who you are is to have been who you have been.

So the essay seems to be an absolute critique of repentance—which is seen as impossible, trivial, or contemptible. One must follow one's nature. Montaigne, as we have seen, saw himself as lucky in his. He saw Socrates as even luckier, and in a remarkable late addition to another essay, Montaigne specifically denies Socrates's claim to have changed his nature through education, for "never," says Montaigne, "did so excellent a soul make itself" ("On Physiognomy," book 3, chap. 12, 1199; *jamais ame si excellent ne si fit elle mesme* [3:269]). But, and here we encounter an extremely interesting historical curiosity, Montaigne does, as Guy Mermier notes, have a conception of true repentance.[69] In the passage where Montaigne mocks the "desire to be entirely different," he at one point conceives of his entire being, his *forme universelle*, not as basically benign and fortunate—his normal self-perception—but in rather negative terms. This means, given his sense of the fixedness and consistency of an individual's character, that "it is no spot but a universal stain which soils me" (917; *un teinture universelle qui me tache* [3:29]). The repetition of *universelle* is striking; it refers both to his fundamental being and to its "stain." At an earlier point in the essay, when Montaigne was criticizing judging character by public deeds, he spoke of the difference between deeds and motives, and presented grand deeds as "no more than thin fine jets of water spurting up from the depths (which are moreover heavy and slimy)" (913).

This view of the self produces a rejection of "surface repentance, mediocre, and a matter of ceremony" (917; *repentance superficielle, moyenne, et de ceremonie*)—which sounds, as George Hoffmann argues, like a systematic critique of the Tridentine understanding of the sacrament of penance.[70] But what Hofmann does not suggest is that it sounds like a Protestant critique.[71] This

---

69. See Guy Mermier, "L'essai 'Du repentir' de Montaigne," *French Review* (1968): 485–92.

70. George Hoffmann, "Emond Auger et le contexte Tridentin de l'essai 'Du repentir,'" *Montaigne et la justice* (see note 21 above), 263–75.

71. Hoffmann's view is that Montaigne's position on penance is not a recognizable one in the period; it is, for Hoffmann, "peut-être plus radical et surtout plus insolite que l'on n'a souvent prétendu" (274).

impression is deepened by the picture of true repentance that Montaigne then presents: "Before I call it repentance, it must touch me everywhere, grip my bowels, and afflict them—as deeply as God does see me, and as totally" (917). This is, as Mermier says, "la seule forme acceptable du repentir" according to Montaigne, and it is exactly, as Mermier does not say, the Reformation view of repentance—as a gift rather than an attainment or an institutional process.[72] "Repentance," said Calvin, "is a singular gift of God"; it is the same as conversion or regeneration—the reorientation of one's whole being toward God, a change, it might be said, in one's *forme universelle* (*Institutes*, 3.3.21, 5–6). And of course, it is not something that can be willed.[73] For the reformers as for Montaigne, it did not make sense to think that one could will oneself to have a different sort of will. As Calvin said—sounding (to put things backwards) exactly like Montaigne—"it would be easier for us to create men than for us, of our own power, to put on a more excellent nature" (*Institutes*, 3.3.21). So, despite Montaigne's undoubted practical loyalty to the Catholic Church, we can see that his conception of what a self was, his psychological determinism—when seen darkly rather than benignly—linked him very deeply to the position of the reformers.[74]

This unexpected connection to the thought of the reformers leads me to a final point about Montaigne's self-presentation. He did not want to be seen only as a self—a psychological and moral character of a certain kind. He also wanted to be seen, and to present himself as, a person. This meant having a body as well as a soul, being a body as well as a soul. Many of Montaigne's

72. Mermier, "L'essai 'Du repentir.' " 491, and see also 489: Montaigne "insiste sur le fait que l'homme seul est incapable de maîtriser son repentir: il faut l'intervention de Dieu sur son coeur." Mermier, however, does not put this insight into any theological context. Montaigne puts forth this same view at the end of the "Apology for Raymond Sebond," where he insists that man can be transformed only "by abandoning and disavowing his own means," and relying on grace alone (683).

73. Supple, who sees the role of grace in Montaigne's conception, calls Montaigne "a wayward Catholic, but a good Christian" ("Structure and Method," 80). He does not explain what he means by "a good Christian," and later in the essay presents Montaigne as somehow adopting a model of sincerity or effort (83). Goyet, "La notion éthique," similarly sees Montaigne as believing in cooperation with grace (1085–86).

74. In "Rhetoric, Ethics and Reading in the Renaissance," *Renaissance Studies* 19 (2005): 1–21, Peter Mack argues that, within the humanist tradition, 'Du repentir' constitutes "a new approach to an understanding of human nature in relation to vice," but notes in passing that "at the same time, Montaigne leaves the way open for an almost Lutheran direction from God" (17). I owe this reference to Kathy Eden.

most famous and characteristic utterances are defenses of the bodily, and of the human as properly including the bodily. He had contempt for *contemptus mundi*. In "A Custom of the Isle of Cea," he asserts that "the opinion which holds our life in contempt is a ridiculous one"; and he goes on to make the strong, and characteristic, comment that "it is a sickness peculiar to Man to hate and despise himself" (397). Compare also the exclamation from "Some Verses of Vergil" (book 3, chap. 5), "What a monstrous animal, to be a horror to himself!" (994)[75]. Montaigne felt very strongly that, as he said in "On Presumption" (book 2, chap. 17), "those who wish to take our two principal pieces"—that is, body and soul—"apart and to sequester one from another are wrong" (727). In the final section of his final essay, "Of Experience" (book 3, chap. 13), Montaigne finds a way to allow for the Catholic conception of saintliness—"That endeavour is a privilege" (1267; *C'est un estude privilegé* [3:327])—but the real message is that it is "as it were God-like [*comme divine*] to know how to enjoy our being rightfully" (1268).

Again, the striking thing about these positions is how close they are to those of the reformers, especially those of Luther, and how much strain they put on traditional Catholic models. Luther, as we discussed in chapter 1, was constantly inveighing against a conception of sainthood that rejected the ordinary pleasures and obligations of life; he also vigorously denounced the idea that sexuality was sinful.[76] Against the Platonists—and all theologians influenced by them—Luther insisted on what he called the whole man (*totus homo*). When asked what he thought about Plato's view of the soul, Luther is recorded as exclaiming: "Oh no . . . what can Plato [have to] say about such a thing! I believe that God created the whole person from the mud of the earth." (*Ach nein!* . . . *wie kann Plato von dem ding reden! Ich glaub das Gott totum hominem ex limo terrae gemacht hatt.*)[77] The *Table Talk* is filled with parodies of the Platonists. Luther thought the distinction between the body and the soul was *dreck*, and that one could not tear off a part (*ein stuck*) of a person, and say "it will live"

75. The translation here is Frame's (670).

76. Dennis Costa notes that Montaigne presents "a non-elitist view of what it means to be good or even 'holy,'" and that this view contrasts sharply with both the early church and the "more modern" definition of a saint, but does not recognize his "more modern" definition as specifically Catholic, and does not make the connection between the nonelitist view and Protestantism. See Costa, "The Matter at Hand: Normative Ethics and Self-Stimulation in Montaigne's 'Du repentir,'" *Modern Language Notes* 124, no. 5., suppl. (Dec. 2009): S172. With regard to Montaigne's defense of sexuality, Costa (again) does not make the connection to Luther.

77. *WA*, *Tischreden* 5, no. 5230, 18 (see chap. 1, n. 27); my translation. Compare Calvin, *Institutes*, 2.1.9, 2.3.1.

while the rest will die.[78] Luther held this view from the time of his theological breakthrough on; he took it to be part of the breakthrough.[79] In an early disputation with a Louvain theologian (1521), Luther explained that God's love and his wrath "have to do with persons," not with "parts" of persons: "Whom therefore God receives in grace He receives wholly. . . . He does not love the head and hate the foot, nor favor the soul and hate the body."[80] Montaigne stands (again) squarely with Luther in his defense of *totus homo*, the *forme universelle* of the human being.[81]

UNREPENTANT DESCARTES

Montaigne, as we have seen, developed a genre or a mode in which he did not have to worry about idiosyncrasy or vanity, one in which he could be both self-revelatory and self-satisfied. He had a project that required (to revert again to Milton's strangely haunting phrase) that he "venture and divulge unusual things" of himself. But why would the author of a *Discourse on the Method*

78. See *WA, Tischreden* 5, no. 5534, 219; translated by Tappert in *Luther's Works*, 54 (see chap. 4, n. 86): "If one should say that Abraham's soul lives with God, but his body is dead, this distinction is rubbish [*dreck*]. I will attack it. One must say: 'The whole Abraham, the whole man, shall live' [*Es muss heissen: Totus Abraham, der gantze mensch, soll leben*]. The other way, you tear off a part of Abraham, and say, 'It lives.' This is the way the philosophers speak: 'Afterwards, the soul departed from its domicile,' etc." (326).

79. See the definitions of "spirit" and "flesh" in the "Preface to Romans" (1522), and the solemn warning against "all teachers who use these terms differently, no matter who they may be," whether church fathers or eminent contemporaries. See *Martin Luther: Selections from His Writings*, 25 (see intro., n. 48).

80. See *Against Latomus*, in *Luther's Works*, 32:228.

81. Another remarkable connection between Montaigne and Luther is Montaigne's use of the unusual and distinctively Lutheran term "consubstantial" (*consubstantiel*) to describe his self's relation to his book (see "On Giving the Lie" [book 2, chap. 18]). The word is obscured by Screech (755); see Frame, 504, and *Essais*, 2:326. The idea of Christ's bodily presence as "consubstantial" with that of the Eucharistic elements was precisely part of Luther's attempt not to split the spiritual from the physical (see Richard Strier, "Martin Luther and the Real Presence in Nature" [see intro., n. 31], 271–303). Marjorie O'Rourke Boyle, "Montaigne's Consubstantial Book," *Renaissance Quarterly* 50 (1997): 723–49, calls it "a canard" to import the Lutheran meaning of the term (724), but she then goes on to document Montaigne's detailed knowledge of the Protestant Eucharistic controversies (734–36). Montaigne uses the word again, in a context recommending not giving oneself the lie (*ne se desmentir poinct* [3:25]), in "On Repentance," with regard to deeply rooted—both physical and psychic—vices (*vices naturels consubstantiels et intestines* [3:26]).

of Rightly Conducting One's Reason and Seeking Truth in the Sciences do so? Why would Descartes, publishing this "discourse" as a preface to his own sort of "essays"—scientific ones on optics, meteors, and geometry, essays instantiating "the method"—adopt an autobiographical mode? And what are we to make of an anonymous autobiography? Montaigne's name, it should be noted, appears prominently on the title pages of all the editions of his *Essays*. With Descartes, as we will see, we are dealing with a more explicitly and obviously calculating rhetorician than we are with Montaigne; Montaigne's prose is looser and more easygoing.[82] And in Descartes's case, we are dealing with a project that has a very vexed and complex relation to both self-revelation and self-satisfaction.

Perhaps the beginning of an answer to our questions about the *Discourse on the Method* can be found in Descartes's comments on its title. He explained that a "discourse" on the method is different from a treatise on it; that in this piece—unlike, say, in his earlier but unpublished "Rules for the Direction of the Mind"—he did not intend to teach the method, "but only to describe it."[83] The piece is propaganda for the method, and not a demonstration of it, as the appended "essays" are. The *Discourse* is rhetorical, and it aims at a lay rather than an officially learned audience, being written, as Descartes puts it at the very end of the work, "in French, which is the language of my country, rather than in Latin, which is that of my teachers."[84] This decision, with its slight autobiographical component (pointing to the author's nationality and education), is itself consciously polemical. The anonymous educated French author hopes to appeal to "those who avail themselves only of natural reason in its purity [*raison naturelle toute pure*]" as opposed to those "who believe only in

---

82. See Jean Lafond, "Discours et essai, ou De l'ecriture philosophique de Montaigne à Descartes," in *Descartes: Il metodo e i saggi*, ed. Giulia Belgioioso et al. (Rome: Istituto della Enciclopedia Italiana, 1990), 63–75, esp. 70.

83. Letter to Mersenne, February 27, 1637. See Descartes, *Philosophical Letters*, trans. and ed. Anthony Kenny (Oxford: Clarendon, 1970), 30.

84. Descartes, *Discourse*, in *The Philosophical Works of Descartes*, trans. Elizabeth S. Haldane and G. R. T. Ross (Cambridge: Cambridge University Press, 1931), 1:129. Page references in subsequent citations of the *Discourse* are to this edition; nevertheless, I have also consulted and sometimes preferred the translation in *The Philosophical Writings of Descartes*, vol. 1, trans. John Cottingham, Robert Stoothoff, and Dugald Murdoch (Cambridge: Cambridge University Press, 1985), and that in *Discours de la méthode / Discourse on the Method: A Bilingual Edition*, ed. and trans. George Heffernan (Notre Dame: University of Notre Dame Press, 1994), which I have also used for the French text. The translations given are sometimes my own, and do not necessarily correspond to any of these.

the writings of the ancients" (104). As Abby Zanger wittily points out, the decision to publish in French was "a choice not to publish in [the] *lingua franca*," and thus a choice to restrict publication and not to expand it."[85] But even if we understand why "natural reason in its purity" would demand the vernacular, why would it demand autobiography?[86] I will try to provide a reading of the *Discourse on the Method* with this question in mind, and with attention to the vexed matter of humility.

The opening sentence of the *Discourse* is a wonderfully fetching one: "Good sense [*Le bon sens*] is of all things in the world the most equally distributed, for everybody thinks himself so abundantly provided with it, that even those most difficult to please in all other matters do not commonly desire more of it than they already possess" (81). It is impossible to read this sentence without thinking that it is satire—how absurd that everyone should be so self-satisfied in this regard! The temptation to read the sentence in this way is intensified when we realize that it is borrowed, all but verbatim, from Montaigne's essay on presumption, where Montaigne notes that "[i]t is commonly said that the fairest division of her favors Nature has given us is of sense; for there is no one who is not content with the share of it that she has allotted him" (746).[87]

Montaigne delights in the self-undercutting irony of the sentence, saying, "I think my opinions are good and sound; but who does not think as much of his?" Descartes, however, defeats our expectations by taking the sentence entirely non-ironically.[88] He states, "It is unlikely that this [everyone's belief

85. "I Publish Therefore I Perish . . . or Do I? Cartesian Agitations on Print and Publication." Manuscript cited courtesy of the author.

86. On the relation between "natural reason" and the vernacular, see Philippe Desan, *Naissance de la méthode* (Paris: A. G. Nizet, 1987), 138–39. For treatments of the *Discourse* that raise the question of autobiography, see Sylvie Romanowski, *L'illusion chez Descartes: La structure du discours cartésien* (Paris: Klincksieck, 1974), who wrestles with this issue at 110ff., and John D. Lyons, "Subjectivity and Method in the *Discours de la méthode*," *Neophilologus* 66 (1982): 508–24. Roger Smith notes that the *Discourse* "is remarkable not least for the directness and persistence with which sentences begin with 'I'" (see "Self-Reflection and the Self," in Porter, *Rewriting the Self*, 51 [see n. 35 above]).

87. Frame translation (499).

88. Compare David Simpson, "Putting One's House in Order: The Career of the Self in Descartes' Method," *New Literary History* 9 (1977): 85–7. C. E. J. Caldicott argues that Descartes means for this and other virtual but unacknowledged quotations from Montaigne in part 1 to be recognized as such by the reader. Caldicott sees Descartes as seeking subtly to associate himself with Montaigne (as if "by a natural convergence of minds"), whereas I see Descartes as seeking to distinguish himself sharply from his great forebear. See Caldicott, "Disguises of the Narrative Voice in *Discours de la méthode*," in *Subject Matters: Subject and Self in French*

in his own good sense] is an error on their part"; he takes it rather "to be evidence in support of the view that the power of forming a good judgment and of distinguishing the true from the false, which is properly speaking what is called good sense or reason, is by nature equal in all men" (81). The aim of Descartes's piece is not satirical and not skeptical, and it is committed to providing what it takes to be correct definitions of its key terms. He is prepared to tell us—immediately—what is properly (*proprement*) termed good sense: it is the power that defeats skepticism, that "of distinguishing the true from the false." But this runs squarely into the skeptical objection, so important and central to Montaigne's thinking, that it is hard to see any uniformity in reason when so many different things are held by different people to be reasonable.[89] Descartes answers this implied objection by arguing that the skeptic's ammunition—"the diversity of our opinions"—"does not proceed from some persons being more rational than others," but rather from the fact that we proceed with our thoughts in different manners and direct our thoughts to different topics (81–82). The phenomena that give rise to skepticism, in other words, are not caused by a defect in human reason but by the varying ways in which this faculty is used. The use of the faculty becomes the key issue, for "to be possessed of good mental powers is not sufficient; the principal matter is to use them well." What is needed, we can see, is a method—or rather, as Descartes will argue, the method.

Interestingly, just at this point, when Descartes is about to introduce "the Method," he makes use of his first humility topos. In the final sentence of the paragraph, he seems to contradict the democratic assertion of universal and equal rationality with which he began; he distinguishes between "great minds," or souls (*âmes*), and others, favoring, perhaps surprisingly, the latter: "[T]hose who proceed very slowly may, provided they always follow the straight road, really advance much faster than those who, though they run, forsake it." This leads naturally, at the beginning of the next paragraph, into the humility claim: "For myself, I have never ventured to presume that my mind [*esprit*] was in any way more perfect than that of the ordinary person" (82). Already, even having read only the few preceding sentences in the *Discourse*, it is impossible to believe this. So the question becomes why Descartes wants to say it, and whether

---

Literature from Descartes to the Present, ed. Paul Gifford and Johnnie Gratton (Amsterdam, Ga.: Rodopi, 2000), 34.

89. For Montaigne's presentations of this, see, inter alia, "On Habit: and on Never Easily Changing a Traditional Law," 126–30, and "Apology for Raymond Sebond," 653–66.

he is aware that the idea of distinction between minds seems to involve him in a contradiction.

Of course he is aware of the latter; he makes it clear that the distinctions between minds have to do with particular faculties of the mind—wit, imagination, or memory—rather than with the fundamental reasoning capacity that "distinguishes us from the brutes" and that he has already affirmed to be "equal in all persons." Descartes must claim that "the Method," which he is about to introduce, does not depend on any special endowment. It must pertain to the general structure of reason itself, which is the same in all men—or else it is a gift, and not a universal tool. Attentive readers of the *Discourse* have struggled with the question of the apparently false democracy of the opening.[90] What is important to see is that the rhetoric of modesty is required by the very idea of a method of the sort that Descartes wishes to propound, "for rightly conducting the reason" in general. But this recognition raises, in turn, another set of problems. If Descartes's mind is nothing special—and cannot be so for his method to be what he claims that it is—how can he account for his having devised the method, and for the fact that no one else has?

The answer that he gives is, as it has to be, luck. Descartes cannot, without deep self-contradiction, claim anything else. After the explanation of the sense in which all minds are the same, he states (and his adversatives are always crucial), "But I shall not be afraid to say that I have had great good fortune, from my youth up, in lighting upon and pursuing certain paths which have conducted me to considerations and maxims from which I have formed a Method, by whose assistance it appears to me [that] I have the means of gradually increasing my knowledge, and of little by little raising it to the highest possible point which the mediocrity of my talents and the brief duration of my life can permit me to reach." It is impossible to parse out the mixture of pride and humility in this account. Luck put him on the path, which led him to certain "considerations," from which (he has to admit) he "formed a Method," and through employing this method he has reached the "highest possible point"—though only as high as "the mediocrity of [his] talents" would allow.

But can he allow this characterization to stand? The next sentence states that despite his (as he claims) tendency toward self-deprecation, and his (as he says) "philosophical" awareness that most of the actions and enterprises of mankind are "vain and useless," he notes that "I do not cease to receive extreme satisfaction [*une extreme satisfaction*] in the progress which I seem

---

90. See Romanowski, *L'illusion chez Descartes*, 134; Lyons, "Subjectivity and Method," 522.

to have already made in the search after truth" (82). Although the search in question is for "truth," the focus might still seem to be on a subjective state— "extreme satisfaction." So Descartes goes on to claim that he is not only personally delighted with the progress he has made so far, but he has "such hopes for the future as to venture to believe [*j'ose croire*] that, if among the occupations of men, simply as men [*purement hommes*], there may be some one that is solidly good and important [*solidement bonne et importante*] it is the one that I have chosen" (82). This is carefully hedged—"if among the occupations" and "simply as men"—but it is impossible to miss the grandeur as well as the self-satisfaction of the claim. Yet the *purement hommes*, which Gilson, surely correctly, glosses to mean, "without divine assistance," is not merely part of a half-hearted humility topos.[91] The method cannot require inspiration any more than it can require genius. Moreover, the phrase also suggests that there is something impersonal in this glorying, something that relates to the species in general and not to any individual.

At this point, Descartes puts forth his autobiography. He acknowledges that he may be self-deceived, and that people are often so about themselves. The autobiography that he will put forth—anonymously—will allow his readers to decide whether the author has a right to the "extreme satisfaction" that he feels and to the special status that he has claimed for his choice of life. Here Descartes might be seen, like Montaigne, to be making his "confession in public." Self-examination leading to a choice of life was precisely what the most famous Renaissance book of "meditations" before the forthcoming one of Descartes's was intended to guide and enable. The *Spiritual Exercises* of Ignatius Loyola was not a method for discovering "truth in the sciences" but for "preparing and disposing the soul to free itself of all inordinate attachments, and, after accomplishing this, of seeking and discovering the Divine Will *regarding the disposition of one's life*."[92] Descartes wishes to show the reader "the paths I

91. Descartes, *Discours de la méthode*, ed. Etienne Gilson (Paris: J. Vrin, 1925), 96; hereafter identified by editor's name.

92. I quote from the first paragraph of the *Spiritual Exercises* in the Mottola translation, 37; emphasis mine (see chap. 4, app., n. 18). Ignatius's *Exercises* is treated at length in the appendix to chapter 4 above. Descartes's *Meditations* has, for obvious reasons, been related to the *Spiritual Exercises*, but the *Discourse* has generally not been so related. For a perhaps overly skeptical examination of the relation of the *Meditations on First Philosophy* to the religious tradition, see Bradley Rubidge, Descartes' *Meditations* and Devotional Meditations," *Journal of the History of Ideas* 51 (1990): 27–49. This topic is being richly (and less skeptically) explored in a study in preparation by my colleague Christopher Wild.

have followed" and, like Montaigne, to "set forth my life as in a picture." But Descartes's aim in doing this is to appeal to the reader's innate good sense—"so that everyone may judge of it for himself" (83). He claims that he is putting forth this work not as a guide for others but "simply as a history, or, if you prefer, a fable" (83; *une histoire, ou, si vous l'aimez mieux, une fable*). He is asking the reader, in other words, to draw a moral from the story or tale that he is presenting.[93] And there is no doubt what this moral is: that Descartes is right in his judgment of the supreme excellence and importance of the choice of life that he has made. Good luck seems to have fallen away.

So Descartes begins the history or "fable." He seems to echo Montaigne's self-presentation—he will not present himself as (wholly) exemplary; his primary virtue is that of "frankness" (*franchise*).[94] But his account is entirely of his intellectual life. We will not, for better or worse, learn of his eating habits or bowel movements. He presents himself almost as a pure mind. As an infant he was nourished "on letters" (83)—parents, wet nurses, and other caregivers apparently were not involved. But he was eager to pursue humanistic studies not because of this sustenance, but because he thought that through such education he could attain "a clear and certain knowledge . . . of all that is useful in life." He thus presents himself as knowing, from the beginning of his education, what he wished to get from it—knowledge that was "certain" (*assurée*) and "useful." The sentence that describes the eager beginning of Descartes's humanistic education is immediately followed by one that describes its unhappy ending. Given what he sought from education, it is not surprising that

93. See Gilson edition, 98–100, and see Jean-Luc Nancy, "Mundus Est Fabula," *Modern Language Notes* 93 (1978): 635–53; Stephen Gaukroger, *Descartes: An Intellectual Biography* (Oxford: Clarendon, 1995), 305–6. Jean-Pierre Cavaillé sees the function of the "fable" in the *Discourse* as ultimately apotropaic: "La présentation du Discours comme une fable est ainsi destinée à susciter une lecteur critique et reflexive" ("Un histoire, un discours, des meditations: Récit, eloquence et métaphysique dans le *Discours de la méthode*," in *Descartes: Il metodo e i saggi*, 197). For a deconstructive approach to the *Discourse* as a "fable," see Hassan Melehy, *Writing Cogito: Montaigne, Descartes, and the Institution of the Modern Subject* (Albany: State University of New York Press, 1997), 113–14.

94. Caldicott, "Disguises of the Narrative Voice," struck by the inaccuracy of Descartes's presentation of his earlier life and education, sees the claim to frankness (*franchise*) here as entirely rhetorical—"It is precisely with this non-candid claim to candour in Part I that Descartes launches into his false autobiography" (35). I think, however, that the challenge is to see how to take the claim seriously. And surely the invitation to take the account of the narrator's education as "a history, or, if you prefer, a fable" should dispose of the issue of falsehood.

after having "achieved the entire course of study at the close of which one is usually received into the ranks of the learned," the young Descartes "entirely changed" his opinion about the value of letters (83). On graduation, he fell into the state in which Montaigne was content to live: "I found myself embarrassed with so many doubts and errors that it seemed to me that the effort to instruct myself had no effect other than to increase discovery of my own ignorance." He then discounts a series of "morals"—other than the one he intends—that might have been drawn from his *histoire*. He asserts, in order, that the problem was not (1) that he had gone to a bad school ("I was studying at one of the most celebrated schools in Europe"); (2) that he was lazy in pursuing knowledge ("not being satisfied with the sciences that were taught," he read books treating "curious and rare" matters not covered in the curriculum); (3) that he wasn't very smart (he was not "esteemed inferior" to his fellow students); or finally, (4) that the age in which he lived was an intellectually degraded one ("our century seemed to me as flourishing and as fertile in great minds as any which had preceded"). The problem, therefore, had to be with his education itself, not with him, his particular school, or his era. That is the "moral."

Most of the rest of part 1 of the *Discourse* follows from this; Descartes offers a detailed critique of the entire school and university curriculum. Like Doctor Faustus at the beginning of Marlowe's play, Descartes goes through the disciplines and objects of study one by one, and finds them wanting. He says he esteemed the humanistic studies—eloquence and poetry—most highly, but found that they were often misleading and that, in any case, the capacities they involved were "gifts of the mind rather than the fruits of study" (85). He found philosophy merely a form of rhetoric—"it teaches us to speak with an appearance of truth on all things," and to impress the less learned—and he found the professions, jurisprudence and medicine, merely worldly: they "bring honor and riches to all that cultivate them" (84). The study of morals was vitiated by its paganism, but the truths of Christianity were not available through intellectual labor, and the benefits of Christianity did not depend on learning or intellect (85). We recall *purement hommes.* The only science that seemed promising was mathematics, which offered certainty in its demonstrations but seemed to be "of service only in the mechanical arts," and had not yet been used (as Descartes presents himself as early recognizing that it could be) for building a "loftier" intellectual edifice (85). So, he says, "as soon as age permitted me to emerge from the control [*la sujétion*] of my tutors, I entirely quit the study of letters" (86). He decided to "seek no other science than that which could be found in myself or in the great book of the world" (86). Ordinary books were laid aside.[95] He dedicated himself to travel and to gaining experience outside the schoolroom while always, he says, under the sway of his one passion, an extreme desire to learn to distinguish the true from the false (*une extreme désir d'apprendre à distinguer le vrai d'avec le faux* [22]).

In "the great book of the world," Descartes found, as Montaigne did, as much diversity in the customs of peoples as in the opinions of philosophers. He learned "to believe nothing too certainly of which I had only been convinced by example and custom" (87). But again, instead of this leading Descartes to skepticism, it led him to find that, little by little, "I delivered myself from many errors," errors which "can obscure our natural light and render us less capable of listening to reason" (87). The pronoun shift is of great interest here (the English exactly duplicates the French: *je me déliverais . . . de beaucoup d'erreurs, qui peuvent offusquer notre lumière naturelle* [24]). To be open to "our natural light" is Descartes's personal goal and exercise. His autobiography is meant to be, as he said, both a history and a fable. As Jean-Luc Nancy says, "the *Discours* is the fable of the generality of a singular and authentic action."[96] At the very end of the first section of the *Discourse*, Descartes decides to shift from studying the book of the world—here meaning the social world—to "making myself an object of study," and to devoting himself to the all-important matter of the choice of life.

The second part opens by giving us some unusually specific details: geographical ("I was then in Germany"), narrative ("I was returning from the coronation of the Emperor"), and creaturely ("a stove-heated room"). As John D. Lyons notes, Descartes gives us something like a "full" (Montaignian) subject before he introduces "the narrative of methodical doubt and of methodical solitude."[97] The whole "action" of the section takes place within the pleasantly warm room in which the autobiographer is entirely alone, and without any social, physical, or emotional distractions.[98] Before getting to this "action," Descartes provides a series of considerations on the desirability of a single

95. I owe to my student Dr. Rivi Handler-Spitz my awareness of the remarkable fact that there is not a single direct classical quotation in the *Discourse*, and, in general, not a single quotation presented as such (the relation to Montaigne discussed in note 88 above is never acknowledged).

96. Nancy, "Mundus Est Fabula," 641.

97. Lyons, "Subjectivity and Method," 521 (though he does not make the connection to Montaigne).

98. For this as a version of pastoral, see Kevin Dunn, "'A Great City is a Great Solitude': Descartes' Urban Pastoral," *Yale French Studies* 80 (1991): 93–107.

individual undertaking, all at once, a project of founding or reform, rather than a group doing so over time. He gives the examples of city planning, of legislation (where, like Machiavelli, he thinks that the best constitutions are laid down by a single "prudent legislator"), and, briefly, of religion.[99] The nondemonstrative sciences found in books are seen as the work of many persons, haphazardly accumulated, while truth can better be approached by "the simple reasonings" which—again—a person of *bon sens* can "quite naturally carry out respecting the things which come immediately before him" (88). A historical individual's set of beliefs is another composite created haphazardly over time, a structure much less reliable and coherent than would have been created, Descartes argues, had we never been children, and therefore had had "complete use of our reason since our birth" (88).

This is one of Descartes's core fantasies: to be born anew, as an adult, with one's reason fully functioning, and without preestablished beliefs.[100] As Gerald Bruns says, "Descartes constructs not merely a new philosophy but, prior to this, and as a condition of its possibility, a new Descartes: new, because this Descartes has no history."[101] To enact this kind of rebirth is what Descartes does in the warm room (womb?) in Germany: "[A]s regards all the opinions which up to this time I had embraced, I thought I could not do better than to endeavor once and for all to strip them completely away [*je ne pouvais mieux faire que d'entreprendre, une bonne fois, de les en ôter*], so that they might later on be replaced, either by others which were better, or by the same [beliefs], when I had made them conform to the uniformity of a rational scheme [89; *ajustés au niveau de la raison* (28)]." "To strip them completely away"—it is a

---

99. See *The Prince*, chap. 6. On the importance of "innovation" in *The Prince*, and of chapter 6 in particular, see J. G. A. Pocock, *The Machiavellian Moment: Political Thought and the Atlantic Republican Tradition* (Princeton: Princeton University Press, 1975), chap. 6.

100. Henri Gouhier comments on how strange it is to regret having been an infant and child before becoming an adult, but he fully recognizes its importance to Descartes, and gives an excellent account of Descartes's conception of the epistemological disaster of childhood (see "Ab infantio," in *La Pensée metaphysique de Descartes* [Paris: J. Vrin, 1962], chap. 2, part 2). On the importance of the fantasy of "rebirth" to Descartes, see Harry Frankfurt, *Demons, Dreamers, and Madmen: The Defense of Reason in Descartes' "Meditations"* (Indianapolis: Bobbs-Merrill, 1970), 16; and Susan R. Bordo, *The Flight to Objectivity: Essays on Cartesianism and Culture* (Albany: State University of New York Press, 1987), 98–101.

101. Gerald L. Bruns, "A Literary Man's Guide to the *Discourse on Method* (1637)," *Diacritics* (1980): 143.

breathtakingly radical project, another endeavor at privileged nudity.[102] But the next move that Descartes makes is to make sure that his project is not misunderstood, that it is not taken as being or conducing to radicalism of a political or social sort: "[A]lthough in so doing I recognized various difficulties, these were at the same time not insurmountable, nor comparable to those which are found in reformation of the most insignificant kind in matters which concern the public" (89). He does not intend to give the smallest encouragement to reformers in public affairs, whom he characterizes as "turbulent and restless spirits" (*ces humeurs brouillonnes et inquiètes* [30]).

In the world of reforming his own opinions, however, Descartes presents himself, and this is still within a modesty topos, as forced to proceed on his own. He could not point to "a single person whose opinions seemed preferable to those of others" (91). He found himself therefore "so to speak constrained" (*je me trouvai comme constraint*) to become his own guide (to do his exercises, one might say, without a director).[103] Through meditating in solitude on what was most indubitable in logic, ancient geometry, and modern algebra, Descartes came up with a set of general rules for direction of the mind, and he found that when he rigorously adhered to these rules, "not only did I arrive at the solution of many questions which I had hitherto regarded as most difficult, but ... it seemed to me that I was able to determine in the case of those of which I was still ignorant, by what means, and to what extent, it was possible to solve them" (93–94).

At this point, however, Descartes has a moment of self-consciousness. Directly addressing the reader, and in a syntax that expresses his anxiety, he states, "In this, I might not perhaps appear to you very vain" (94; *En quoi je ne vous paraîtrai peut-être pas être fort vain*) if the reader is able to consider the matter properly.[104] He appeals to basic epistemology. Since there is only one true answer to any particular question (*n'y ayant qu'une vérité de chaque chose*), we must recognize that when a true answer is found, "whoever succeeds in finding it knows in its regard as much as can be known." He gives

102. With regard to the connection to Montaigne, it might be worth noting that Starobinski speaks of Montaigne entertaining "the idea of a voluntary birth" in withdrawing from the world (*Montaigne in Motion*, 7).

103. The Ignatian spiritual exercises were to be done only under the guidance of a director. This is assumed throughout. See, for instance, "the one who is giving instruction in the method ... should be explicit" (37) and all of the preliminary "directions" (37–43).

104. The Haldane and Ross translation, "I might perhaps appear to you to be very vain," simplifies the syntax and the rhetorical situation.

the clever—and modest—example of a child doing sums correctly: the child knows, "as regards the sum of figures given to him, all that the human mind can know [of the sum of that addition]" (94). Still trying to appear modest, Descartes presents himself as gradually becoming more mentally acute and reliable through habituating himself to the method. Having succeeded with algebra, he began to contemplate applying the method to other domains, but he found that the difficulties in many of them sprang from general problems in philosophy—so that he saw that "it was requisite above all to try to establish some certainty" there, in philosophy (94). The section ends in a mixture of grandiosity and humility. Descartes recognizes the endeavor to find certainty in philosophy as (again) "the most important [endeavor] in all the world" (*la chose du monde la plus importante*)—compare his choice of life as, among the occupations of men, only *solidement et importante*—but he decides that at the age of twenty-three (our first detail of this kind) he should perhaps not yet attempt it, but should prepare himself further in clearing his mind and in using the method.

The third part of the *Discourse* continues the task of sharply distinguishing epistemological radicalism from any other sort.[105] While Descartes continues his total stripping—his drive toward naked rationality—he decides on a series of practical maxims by which he will live his everyday life in the world. In this, Descartes is exactly like Montaigne. The maxims are utterly conservative: "to obey the laws and customs of my country"; to adhere constantly "to the religion in which, by God's grace, I had been instructed since my childhood"; and, in practice, to adopt the "most moderate" of received opinions (95). Another of the practical maxims that Descartes adopted was "to be firm and resolute" in his actions (96). His practical attitude, therefore, was the exact opposite of the method of philosophical doubt: he would not worry in the slightest that the

---

105. Gilbert Gadoffre argued that the third part of the *Discourse* was the last part composed. See the introduction to his edition of the *Discourse* (Manchester: University of Manchester Press, 1941), and "Sur la chronologie du *Discours de la méthode*," *Revue d'Histoire de Philosophie et d'Histoire Generale de la Civilization* 11 (1943): 45–70. As Romanowski (*L'illusion chez Descartes*, 118–37) and others have noted (see the review by Alexander Koyre in *Philosophy and Phenomenological Research* 5 [1944]: 149–52), one can accept Gadoffre's genetic analysis without necessarily accepting his account of the total incoherence of the text. It should be noted that part 2's allusion to *humeurs brouillonnes et inquiètes* already anticipated the position of part 3. For work that questions the genetic analysis as well as the conclusions of Gadoffre, see Edwin M. Curley, "Cohérence ou incohérence du *Discours?*" in *Le Discours et sa méthode*, ed. Nicolas Grimaldi and Jean-Luc Marion (Paris: Presses Universitaires de France, 1987), 41–64, and the references there given.

opinions that he decided to adopt in practice were merely probable, or were no better than many others. This allows Descartes to be another person who never repents. The principle of resoluteness "was sufficient to deliver me from all the penitence and remorse [*tous les repentirs et les remords*]" (42) that can agitate the consciences of those who fall into the weakness of allowing themselves to reconsider actions they have taken (96).[106] Further like Montaigne (and with an equal commitment to a Stoical attitude toward "fortune"), Descartes was indifferent (so he says) to the matter of outcomes (97).

But the point of all this, for Descartes, was not to live a life of contented self-regard (like Montaigne or the ancient philosophers).[107] The point was to allow Descartes to put aside all questions of morality and practice, "along with the truths of religion," in order to get on with his philosophical project (98).[108] He claims to have spent the next nine years after the day in the stove-heated room in Germany as a spectator rather than an actor in the world, rooting out errors from his mind. He reminds us, however, that his aim, all along, was not the skeptical one of avoiding error but the nonskeptical one of establishing truth: "Not that indeed I imitated the skeptics, who only doubt for the sake of doubting . . . on the contrary, my design was solely to find good grounds for assurance" (99). He points to the "essays in the method" that follow the *Discourse* as examples of what he was doing while he seemed to be merely living the life of an idle but honest and law-abiding gentleman, making use of all "honest amusements" (*tous les divertissements qui sont honnêtes*). Part 3 ends with a rather tortured account of why Descartes is publishing his book. As Sylvie Romanowski says, the release of the book was more problematic for Descartes than its composition.[109] Descartes claims to be publishing in order

---

106. "And this was capable from then on of delivering me from all the repentances and regrets that usually disturb the consciences of those feeble and staggering minds that allow themselves inconstantly to go and practice, as good, things that they later judge to be bad." (*Et ceci fut capable dès lors de me délivrer de tous les repentirs et les remords, qui ont coutume d'agiter les consciences de ces esprits faibles et chancelants, qui se laissent aller inconstamment à pratiquer, comme bonnes, les choses qu'ils jugent après être mauvaises.*)

107. On philosophy as a "way of life" in the ancient world, see Pierre Hadot, *Philosophy as a Way of Life: Spiritual Exercises from Socrates to Foucault* (see chap. 1, n. 7).

108. Compare Simpson, "Putting One's House in Order," 95: "The moral code thus seems to function by announcing a superficial conformism behind and within which the real business of the method can be carried on."

109. Romanowski, *L'illusion chez Descartes*, 104: "Plus encore que l'acte d'écrire, c'est celui de publier qui présente à notre auteur un problème moral, immédiat et concret."

to try to live up to the reputation that he has unwillingly gained of being a philosopher who has reached some conclusions (100).[110] Romanowski explains that Descartes could not live with people having only the "illusion" that he was a philosopher.[111] We will come back to this.

In part 4 of the *Discourse*, Descartes gives an overview of his "metaphysical" and "uncommon" meditations (100). He will publish these under his name and at greater length four years later (in 1641) as the *Meditations on First Philosophy*. I will skip over the account in the *Discourse*, noting only that it seems to me to stress the religious rather than the philosophical aspects of the project.[112] Similarly, I will skip over the discussion of natural laws and, in particular, of the movement of the heart and blood, in part 5 of the *Discourse*. With regard to the difference between Descartes and Montaigne, however, it should be noted that the discussion of the relation between humans and animals with which this part ends is the exact contrary of Montaigne's views in his great skeptical treatise, the "Apology for Raymond Sebond," where Montaigne sees (or professes to see) many animals as superior to humans.[113] Descartes insists, as is deeply consonant with the *Discourse* as a whole, on the special ontological status and dignity of general human reason.

In the sixth and final part of the *Discourse* (probably composed first), Descartes returns to the negotiation of pride and humility.[114] He returns to the question of publication, explaining (with purposeful vagueness and without mention of Copernicanism or Galileo) why he suppressed his earlier treatise *The World*, and why he is—with a great deal of professed ambivalence and reluctance—publishing the present text.[115] He was going to publish his scientific theory because he had discovered some principles by which we could, as he

---

110. Simpson ("Putting One's House in Order," 96) sees an echo here of Socrates's report in the *Apology* of the Delphic oracle telling one of his friends that there was no one wiser than Socrates. This is an intriguing suggestion, but I am not sure I believe it.

111. Romanowski, *L'illusion chez Descartes*, 124–25.

112. Lyons, "Subjectivity and Method," 520, has some excellent remarks on the different role of the *cogito* in the *Discourse* and the *Meditations*.

113. See "Apology for Raymond Sebond," 506–41.

114. For the probable order of composition, see Gadoffre cited in note 105 above.

115. Descartes suppressed his *The World* and his *Treatise on Man* when he heard of the condemnation of Galileo by the Inquisition in 1633. See, inter alia, Gilson, 440–441. There are selections from these works in Cottingham et al., *Philosophical Writings of Descartes*, 81–108, and full texts in *Oeuvres de Descartes*, ed. Charles Adam and Paul Tannery (Paris: J. Vrin, 1964–76), vol. 11. Zanger speaks of Descartes's "almost frenetic rhetoric against and for print publication" in her essay on the *Discourse* ("I Publish Therefore I Perish").

says in an almost Baconian phrase, "render ourselves, as it were, the masters and possessors of nature" (119; *nous rendre comme maîtres et possesseurs de la nature* [86]).[116] Descartes was, he says, compelled by "the law which obliges us to procure, as much as in us lies, the general good of mankind" to make these principles known, especially with regard to medicine (119–20). Another motive that had led him to plan on publication was the necessity to carry on a great many experiments "of such a nature, and of so great a number, that neither my hands nor my income, though the latter were a thousand times larger than it is, could suffice" (121), so "all those who have the good of mankind at heart" could communicate to him "those experiments that they have already carried out," and also help him "in the investigation of those that still remain to be accomplished" (122). Descartes presents himself here as needing and desiring a community of contributors and collaborators.

But that picture is not sustained. As Kevin Dunn puts it, "if this vision seems to partake of a kind of Baconian institutionalization of science, it stalls at key moments."[117] Descartes returns to the problem of publication. Having established that he has an obligation to write up his philosophical and scientific thoughts, and even that it does him good to do so (leading him to scrutinize his thoughts more thoroughly), the issue now is not whether he is obliged to publish but whether he is obliged to do so during his lifetime. His general view is that he is not. The reason for this is that, were he to publish what he has so far found, the resultant controversies and conflicts that the work would provoke would seriously distract him from making further discoveries. With a typical mixture of humility and confidence, he states that "the little which I have learned hitherto is almost nothing in comparison with that of which I am ignorant, and with the knowledge which I do not despair of being able to attain" (122). Then, dropping the humility topos entirely, he claims that the truths he has discovered in the sciences all depend on "five or six principal difficulties which I have surmounted," and he says that he will not even fear to assert (*Même je ne craindrai pas de dire* [92]) that "I think I shall have no need

116. I am not sure why Descartes adds the un-Baconian "as it were" (*comme*) here. Perhaps to avoid *hubris*; perhaps, as Melehy would suggest, to avoid Quixotism (Melehy, *Writing Cogito*, 114). For Bacon's aspirations, see the stated goal of Salomon's House in *New Atlantis*: "the knowledge of Causes, and secret motions of things; and the enlarging of the bounds of Human Empire, to the effecting of all things possible" (Francis Bacon, *A Selection of His Works*, ed. Sidney Warhaft [New York: Collier Macmillan, 1982], 447).

117. Dunn, "'A Great City is a Great Solitude,'" 105. Dunn goes on to make the interesting observation that "Descartes never admits a truly collaborative project, only a collective one."

to win more than two or three similar victories in order to reach entirely the goal of my plans" (123).

But what of the possibilities that Descartes might learn something from the controversies that his work would stir up, and that, as he had suggested, a collectivity might advance his work further than he alone could? With regard to the first possibility, Descartes notes that he has rarely encountered an objection to his work that he "did not in some sort foresee" (124); with regard to the second, he returns to the argument of part 2 for the superiority of a single planner. On the matter of continuing his work, he again attempts to brush aside the question of pride, saying flatly, "I think I can, without vanity [*sans vanité*], say that if anyone is capable of doing this, it must be myself rather than another." He then tries to defuse the issue by advancing a humility topos—"not that there may not be [*non pas qu'il ne puisse*] in the world many minds incomparably superior [*incomparablement meilleurs*] to my own"—and then appealing to a general maxim: "[N]o one can so well understand a thing and make it his own when he learns it from another as when he discovers it himself" (124).

But this clearly will not do, as the tortured syntax of "not that there may not be" and the obvious hyperbole of "incomparably superior" make clear. In discussing objections to his work, Descartes has already rejected the possibility that there are in the world "many minds incomparably superior" to his own. Moreover, when he goes on to consider those who are most likely to attack his work, namely, the Aristotelians, he finds—and here all pretense at humility drops away—that their manner of philosophizing "is very convenient—for those who have only very mediocre minds" (125; *leur façon de philosopher est fort commode, pour ceux qui n'ont que des esprits fort médiocres* [96]). On the other hand, to those who could profit from Descartes's scientific work, "it is not necessary that I say any more than I have already said in this discourse," since, if they understand it, they will be able to duplicate his conclusions for themselves (126). And as regards the question of experiments, Descartes basically thinks that those wishing to help would in fact hinder his great progress. Speaking in general, third-person terms, he rather archly speculates that "if there were in the world someone [*quelqu'un*] known to be unquestionably [*assurément*] capable of discovering matters of the highest importance and utility to the public, and if, for this reason, other men were eager by every means to help him," no one could do anything for him except "contributing to defray the expenses" of his experiments, and making sure that he would not be "deprived of his leisure by the importunities of anyone" (127). At this point, as Dunn says, Descartes suggests "that his fellow workers might best serve as fund-raisers and security guards."[118]

After this amazing display of hubris—hardly disguised by hypothetical and third-person phrasing—Descartes immediately claims that he does not "esteem himself so highly as to be willing to promise anything extraordinary," and then solemnly avers that he would find it debasing to accept from anyone "a favor which it might be supposed that I did not merit" (127; *aucune faveur, qu'on pût croire que je n'aurais pas méritée* [98]). He leaves open the question of whether he does actually merit it; his fear is that someone might believe that he does not. Insofar as Descartes wants to be known, he wants, like Montaigne, to be known on exactly his own terms. One could certainly say about Montaigne's *Essays* what Zanger says about Descartes' *Discourse*, that "his book, then, is about controlling his self-presentation."[119] At the end of part 3, Descartes had explained his decision to live in urban solitude as resulting from his desire to live up to his reputation because, in a strikingly affect-oriented phrase, he saw himself as having "a heart sincere enough not to want anyone to take me for other than I was" (*ayant le coeur assez bon pour ne vouloir point qu'on me prît pour autre que je n'étais* [48]).[120] This exactly recalls–even to the phrasing—Montaigne's "mortal fear" of being "taken to be other than I am" (*d'estre pris en eschange*).

This concern with how others "take" him leads Descartes to the explanation of why, despite all the good reasons he has just given for not doing so, he finally decided to publish the *Discourse* and its accompanying "essays" in his lifetime. He is concerned with his reputation. He is worried that "many who knew the intention I formerly had of publishing certain writings might imagine that the causes for which I abstained from doing so were more to my disadvantage than they really were" (127). So, where, at the end of part 3, he explains his decision to publish in terms of confirming his existing reputation, in part 6 he explains it as disconfirming his bad one (perhaps as an atheist). He has never, after all, rejected the idea of fame. In the first part of the *Discourse*, he acknowledges that he "did not pretend to scorn all glory like the Cynics" (86); here he states that his official position toward fame is not one of rejection

118. Ibid., 106.

119. Zanger, "I Publish Therefore I Perish."

120. I have given Heffernan's translation (49) here because those that appear in Haldane and Ross ("being at heart honest enough" [100]) and in Cottingham, Stoothoff, and Murdoch ("I was honest enough" [126]) are misleadingly bland.

but one of Stoic or Ignatian "indifference"—which means that he can take it as well as leave it.[121] He has, he says, "always held myself indifferent between the care of being known and not."

Most interestingly, he sees his concern for his reputation—his lack of effort, as he puts it, to remain unknown (*n'ai usé de beaucoup de precautions pour être inconnu*)—as a matter of proper pride.[122] He says that if he had not put forth an accurate—that is, positive—picture of himself into the world, "I would have believed I was wronging myself" (*j'eusse cru me aire tort* [100]).[123] He would also have suffered having the peace of mind that comes with complete self-satisfaction disturbed. He would have had "a kind of disquiet, which would have been contrary to the perfect repose of mind that I seek" (*m'aurait donné quelque espèce d'inquietude, qui eût derechef été contraire au parfait repos d'esprit que je cherche*).[124] As to the nagging matter of experiments, he now acknowledges, again, that there are some that he "cannot perform without the aid of others" (128). But here too there is a matter of pride and of obligation to himself involved. He decides that he cannot bear the idea that he could be

121. On the anti-asceticism of the Ignatian spiritual exercises and the importance to them of this notion of "indifference" toward worldly honors, see the appendix to chapter 4 above.

122. In *The Passions of the Soul*, Descartes's last published work, he defines and discusses proper (that is, justified) self-esteem (see arts. 151–53 in the Haldane and Ross edition of the *Philosophical Works*, 1:401–2). He knows this could be called "magnanimity," but he prefers, following (as in the *Discourse*) "the usage of our language" rather than that of "the schools," to call this virtue "generosity" (*générosité*) instead (art. 161). Descartes sees "generosity" as having the same status that Aristotle gave "magnanimity" (*megalopsychia*), "the key of all other virtues" (art. 161), but Descartes also sees it as compatible with (proper) humility (art. 155). However, the characterization of the humility of the generous is not very convincing (or perhaps even coherent). Pride (*l'orgueil*) is a vice for Descartes, since it is defined as improper self-esteem (art. 157). Article 159 is a strong attack on "vicious humility" ("De l'humilité vicieuse"). On Descartes's substitution of generosity for magnanimity, see Deborah J. Brown, *Descartes and the Passionate Mind* (Cambridge: Cambridge University Press, 2006), 191–195. For the French of *Les passions de l'ame*, I have used the text in Descartes, *Oeuvres philosophiques*, vol. 3, ed. Ferdinand Alquié (Paris: Garnier, 1989).

123. Again, the Haldane and Ross version, "I would have thought it damaging to myself" (127), does not seem to me to convey the force of the phrase. Cottingham, "I would do myself an injustice" (149), is better (and is followed by Heffernan), but still perhaps not strong enough.

124. In article 190 of *The Passions of the Soul*, the self-satisfaction of the virtuous "is called tranquility and peace of mind," and is described by Descartes as "the sweetest of all joys" (*une espèce de joie, laquelle je crois être la plus douce de toutes*). Repentance (art. 191, "Du repentir") is the opposite of this, and is said to be especially characteristic of "weak-spirited people" (*les esprits faibles*).

reproached in the future for not having informed the public "in what way they could have contributed to the accomplishment of my designs" (128). Again, the pronouns are crucial—"*they* could have contributed to *my* designs" (*ils pouraient contribuer à mes desseins*). His ambivalence about autonomy and collaboration remains. Everyone's obligation is to his designs.

In his final general remark about his project and ideas, Descartes again does a complex pirouette, this time on the matter of originality: "[A]s regards the opinions that are truly mine"—as opposed to those that might be fantastically attributed to him—he says, "I do not apologize for them as being new, inasmuch as, if we consider the reasons of them well, I assure myself that they will be found to be so simple and so conformable to common sense, as to appear less extraordinary and less paradoxical than any others which may be held on similar subjects" (129). This is another sentence in which the mixture of pride and humility, focused on the method, is impossible to disentangle; Descartes's opinions are merely "conformable to common sense"—but they are more so "than any others." The *Discourse* ends on an entirely Montaignesque note of rejoicing in freedom from public commitments: "I shall always hold myself to be more indebted to those by whose favor I may enjoy my leisure without hindrance, than I would be to any who may offer me the most honorable position in all the world" (130)—as if kings and princes were lining up to do so!

So what shall we say, finally, of the autobiographical works of Montaigne and Descartes? Neither writer is afflicted with humility. Both, with a good deal of maneuvering and explanation, are quite self-satisfied, and both can be seen to accomplish their goals—Montaigne to justify publication of his idiosyncratic self-portrait, Descartes to justify his self-portrait as ambivalent universal benefactor. It might be said, however, that Descartes's greatest autobiographical work lies not in the sections of the *Discourse* that we have examined but in the whole of the *Meditations*. Where Montaigne in his *Essays* succeeds in presenting both a self and a person, Descartes, in his *Meditations*, succeeds in presenting a first-person speaker who is neither. The fantasy of being born anew as a rational creature is enacted there; autobiography becomes fully impersonal.[125] And so he finesses the issue of pride.

125. Compare Frankfurt, *Demons, Dreamers, and Madmen*, 4.

CHAPTER 6

Milton against Humility

ETHICS AND GRACE

The project or vision of melding classical and Christian values has been a recurrent one in the West, practically since the beginnings of Christianity.[1] Augustine struggled with the issue, and finally came down (in a modified way) on the negative side; Jerome had nightmares about it.[2] Aquinas devoted his life to the project. In the Renaissance, figures like Erasmus and Arminius took up the project, while Machiavelli, for instance, thought the two traditions deeply incompatible.[3] In the nineteenth century, Nietzsche and Kierkegaard also took the negative view, as did Karl Barth in the twentieth century.[4] The negative

---

1. See, for instance (among very many others), Charles Norris Cochrane, *Christianity and Classical Culture: A Study of Thought and Action from Augustus to Augustine* (1944; New York: Oxford University Press, 1957); Jean Leclerq, *The Love of Learning and the Desire for God: A Study of Monastic Culture*, trans. Catharine Misrahi (1961; New York: Fordham University Press, 1977 [original French edition, 1957]); David Knowles, *The Evolution of Medieval Thought* (New York: Random House, 1962).

2. For Augustine, see note 18 below, and the discussion in Jennifer Herdt in *Putting on Virtue: The Legacy of the Splendid Vices* (Chicago: University of Chicago Press, 2008), chap. 2. For Jerome, see E. K. Rand, *Founders of the Middle Ages* (1928; New York, Dover, 1957), chap. 4 (for the nightmares, see 106).

3. For Machiavelli's critique of Christianity as undermining civic values, see his discourses on Livy, Niccolò Machiavelli, *The Discourses*, ed. Bernard Crick, trans. Leslie J. Walker and Brian Richardson (New York: Penguin, 1974), 2:2.

4. For Nietzsche, see, inter alia, *The Genealogy of Morals*, trans. Francis Golffing (New York: Doubleday, 1956); for Kierkegaard, see especially *Fear and Trembling*, trans. Howard V. Hong and Edna H. Hong (Princeton: Princeton University Press, 1983).

view can be held, obviously, from either side of the supposed divide. The argument of this chapter is that while Milton may have thought that he had arrived at some sort of synthesis, the ethical position that runs throughout his work, from beginning to end, is fundamentally and distinctively classical rather than Christian. He consistently resisted the features of Christianity that distinguish its position from that of classical ethics. As we have already seen with regard to Montaigne and Descartes, the key term from classical ethics is the virtue of *megalopsychia—magnanimitas* in Latin, and in English (perhaps) "proper pride" (the English transliteration of the Latin may seem too limited).[5] The key term from the Christian tradition is, of course, "humility." We will follow the course of these terms (and concepts) throughout Milton's corpus.

It is no accident that Nietzsche and Kierkegaard emerged out of a Lutheran context.[6] And this despite the many ways in which the Reformation was a humanistic movement. I have focused on its anti-asceticism and defense of ordinary life and feeling in the world.[7] One might also mention its desire to return *ad fontes* and consequent emphasis on the importance of philology, its insistence on contextual interpretation, its impatience with scholasticism.[8] The careers of figures like Zwingli, Oecolampadius, and Melanchthon testify to these continuities (as does the moment when Luther dubbed himself "Eleutherius").[9] However, on a central ideological issue, on the relationship between the most basic premises of classical ethics—that moral virtue is humanly possible and that reason, properly employed, leads to it—and the process of salvation, the original Reformation, as formulated by Luther and then by Calvin, was fundamentally and implacably at odds with humanism. Despite

5. For the virtue of *megalopsychia*, see *Nicomachean Ethics* (*NE* 1123b–1125a); translated as "high-mindedness" in the Ostwald edition (see chap. 2, n. 28). For Montaigne and Descartes, see the discussion above in chapter 5.

6. See Jaroslav Pelikan, *From Luther to Kierkegaard* (St. Louis: Concordia, 1950).

7. See chapters 1 and 4 above.

8. Helpful on Renaissance and Reformation relations are two essays by William Bouwsma in *A Usable Past* (see chap. 1, nn. 21 and 24): "The Two Faces of Humanism" (19–73) and "Renaissance and Reformation" (225–46).

9. See Charles Garside, Jr., *Zwingli and the Arts* (New Haven: Yale University Press, 1966); E. Gordon Rupp, *Patterns of Reformation* (London: Epworth, 1969), on Oecolampadius; "The German Humanists and the Beginning of the Reformation," in Bernd Moeller, *Imperial Cities and the Reformation*, ed. and trans. H. C. Erik Midelfort and Mark University Edwards, Jr. (Durham: Labyrinth, 1982), 19–37; Jerry H. Bentley, *Humanists and Holy Writ* (Princeton: Princeton University Press, 1983). On Luther as "Eleutherius" (the free man) see Roland H. Bainton, *Here I Stand: A Life of Martin Luther* (New York: New American Library [Mentor], 1950), 97.

their knowledge of and, in many contexts, respect for the classics, Luther and Calvin were committed to asserting the unique, distinctive, and unassimilable nature of biblical, especially New Testament, thought.[10]

Both reformers were fully conscious of this tension. In the period of the indulgence controversy and in the crucial few years thereafter, Erasmus had generally been a friend to the Reformation—to Zwingli he wrote, "I am under the impression that I have maintained almost all that Luther maintains, only without his violence and abstaining from some riddles and paradoxes."[11] Indeed, for a very long period (eight years), he defended Luther despite constant and very high-powered pressure to reject him.[12] When Erasmus finally did come out against Luther in 1525, it was, as Luther said, on "the essential issue," not "trifles" concerning "the papacy, purgatory, indulgences, and such like": the issue of the freedom of the will.[13] It is extremely important to be clear on

10. On Luther and the classics, see E. G. Sihler, "Luther and the Classics," in *Four Hundred Years*, ed. W. H. T. Dau (St. Louis: Concordia, 1917); *Luther and Learning: The Wittenberg University Luther Symposium*, ed. Marilyn J. Harran (Selinsgrove, Pa.: Susquehanna University Press, 1985), esp. articles by Harran and Lewis W. Spitz; Helmar Junghans, *Der junge Luther und die Humanisten* (Gottingen: Vandenhoeck and Ruprecht, 1985); and Carl Springer, "Martin's Martial: Reconsidering Luther's Relationship with the Classics," *International Journal of the Classical Tradition* 14 (2007/2008): 23–50. I am grateful to Professor Springer for bringing his article to my attention, and for conversation on this topic. On Calvin and the classics, see Quirinus Breen, *John Calvin: A Study in French Humanism* (Grand Rapids, Mich.: Eerdmans, 1931); Charles Partee, *Calvin and Classical Philosophy* (Leiden: Brill, 1977); William J. Bouwsma, *John Calvin: A Sixteenth-Century Portrait* (New York: Oxford University Press, 1988), chap. 7; Ford Lewis Battles, *Interpreting Calvin*, ed. Paul Benedetto (Grand Rapids, Mich.: Baker Books, 1996), 47–89; and Paul A. Young, *John Calvin and the Natural World* (Lanham, Md.: University Press of America, 2007), chap. 1.

11. Letter to Zwingli, August 31, 1523, in *The Collected Works of Erasmus*, vol. 10: *Letters 1356 to 1534 (1523 to 1524)*, trans. R. A B. Mynors and Alexander Dalzell (Toronto: University of Toronto Press, 1992), 84.

12. On the pressures that Erasmus was under, see, from the letter cited in the previous note: "I have refused all offers made to me on condition that I would write against [Luther]. The pope, the emperor, kings and princes, and even the most scholarly and dearest of my friends challenge me to do so" (82–83); and see also the previous letter (to Willibald Pirckheimer): "[T]he princes all urge me to attack Luther" (80, and the references there given to other letters).

13. Martin Luther, *The Bondage of the Will*, trans. J. I. Packer and A. R. Johnston (Westwood, N.J.: Revell, 1957), 319. Since there is also a translation of this text in the volume from which I will cite Erasmus's discourse on free will, I will also give page numbers in *Luther and Erasmus: Free Will and Salvation*, ed. E. Gordon Rupp and Philip S. Watson (Philadelphia: Westminster Press, 1969). The Packer and Johnston translation of *Bondage* seems to me more vigorous.

what this issue actually was. It was not the question of determinism. Luther conceded that persons have free will with regard to earthly things ("free will is allowed to man . . . with regard to that which is beneath him").[14] The question at issue was the ethical intelligibility of God and of the relationship between God and man, between divine and human action—the "enigmas and paradoxes" that Erasmus had avoided. Luther understood exactly how his position looked to Erasmus; "doubtless," Luther acknowledged, with regard to predestination,

> it gives the greatest possible offense to common sense or natural reason that God, who is proclaimed as being full of mercy and goodness and so on, should of His own mere will, abandon, harden, and damn men, as though He delighted in the sins and great eternal torments of such poor wretches.

Luther notes (quite correctly, I would say) that "this is why so much toil and trouble has been devoted to clearing the goodness of God and throwing the blame on man's will."[15]

Without some notion of human responsibility—however attenuated—in the process of salvation, the question of grace and the question of ethics split apart.[16] This is exactly what Luther and Calvin intended.[17] Luther mocks those who refuse to believe God to be good "when He speaks and acts above and beyond the definitions of Justinian's Code, or the fifth book of Aristotle's *Ethics*"—the book, that is, concerning justice. Following Augustine, but with what Erasmus would have seen as characteristic hyperbole, Luther insisted that the ancients "were never less upright and more vile than when they shone in their highest

---

For good treatments of Erasmus's attitude(s) toward Luther, see Gordon Rupp, *The Righteousness of God: Luther Studies* (London: Hodder and Stoughton, 1953), chap. 12; Roland Bainton, *Erasmus of Christendom* (New York: Scribner, 1969), chaps. 6–7; and B. A. Gerrish, "*De Libero Arbitrio* (1524): Erasmus on Piety, Theology, and the Lutheran Dogma," in *Essays on the Works of Erasmus*, ed. Richard L. de Molen (New Haven: Yale University Press, 1978), 187–210.

14. *Bondage*, 289; see also 107 (*Luther and Erasmus*, 307, 143).

15. *Bondage*, 217 (*Luther and Erasmus*, 244).

16. For Erasmus's view that the contribution of free choice to salvation is "extremely small," see *Luther and Erasmus*, 89. Throughout *Bondage*, Luther mocks the view that, in this context, any contribution can be seen as "small."

17. On the central matters of Reformation theology, Luther and Calvin were at one. See B. A. Gerrish, "John Calvin on Luther," in *Interpreters of Luther*, ed. Jaroslav Pelikan (Philadelphia: Fortress, 1968), 67–96.

virtues."[18] As examples of this, Luther mentions heroic figures from the Roman republic, including Scipio Africanus, and, among the Greeks, Erasmus's favorite pious pre-Christian, Socrates.[19] This is where the quarrel about God turns into a quarrel about man. The question becomes what and how one thinks about human moral capacities. For Luther, who did not deny that many ancients were able to be constant, make sacrifices, endure pain, serve their countries, and perform other impressive acts, the problem was precisely the (high) motive for which all these actions were done: to attain glory and create self-esteem.

This critique became one of Calvin's favorite topoi. He opens the second book of the *Institutes* by praising "the ancient proverb [that] strongly recommended knowledge of self to man" (*Institutes*, 2.1.1). He sharply distinguishes between normal human self-knowledge and knowledge of the self "according to the standard of divine judgment." In the normal (classical) view, a person "seems to know himself very well when, confident in his understanding and uprightness, he becomes bold and urges himself to the duties of virtue, and, declaring war on vices, endeavors to exert himself with all his ardor toward the excellent and the honorable" (*Institutes*, 2.1.3). According to the standard of the divine judgment, though—in the face, that is, of an ethical and metaphysical absolute (*coram Deo*)—a human being "finds nothing to lift his heart to self-confidence."[20] And the more deeply he looks, the more dejected he becomes, until finally he recognizes "nothing in himself with which to direct his life aright" (*Institutes*, 2.1.3). This "dejection," this giving up completely on the idea of one's moral capacity, is true self-knowledge. There is no danger of man denigrating himself too much (*Institutes*, 2.2.10). Every apparent virtue is tainted with pride (2.2.2; 2.3.4; 3.7.1). The name of the virtue that totally opposes all normal or classical moral schemes is humility. "If we think that we have anything left to ourselves," says Calvin, "I do not call it humility" (*Institutes*, 3.7.6).[21]

18. *Bondage*, 251 (*Luther and Erasmus*, 274); Augustine, *Concerning the City of God against the Pagans*, trans. Henry Bettenson (London: Penguin, 1972), 891 (19:26). For Erasmus's characterization of Luther as *doctor hyperbolicus*, see Gerrish, "*De Libero Arbitrio*," 209n87.

19. For "O sancte Socrate, ora pro nobis," see Desiderius Erasmus, "Convivium Religiosum" in *Opera Omnia* (Hildesheim: Georg Olms, 1961–62), 1:683; also "The Godly Feast," in *The Colloquies of Erasmus*, trans. Craig R. Thompson (Chicago: University of Chicago Press, 1965), 68.

20. On the importance of the phrase and the idea *coram Deo* to Luther, see Rupp, *The Righteousness of God*, esp. chap. 6.

21. In the chapter 5, we saw Montaigne's vacillation between the views in "On Repentance" (though normally his view is the classical one).

As I have already suggested, the conception of classical ethics that Luther and Calvin were attacking was completely accurate. As Alcibiades points out in the *Symposium*, one would have to be a fool to take Socrates's self-disabling professions at face value.[22] There is no conception of humility, of self-disparagement as a virtue (rather than, as in Socrates, a strategy), in classical ethics. The whole idea is foreign to the heroic code, where the ideal is to enact one's excellence, and it is equally foreign to classical philosophy.[23] In the *Nicomachean Ethics*, Aristotle characterizes *megalopsychia* as "the crown, as it were, of the virtues" (*NE* 1124a1). The great-souled man for Aristotle (and I am afraid that this figure is thought of only as male) is someone who "thinks himself worthy of great things *and is really worthy of them*" (*NE* 1123b3; emphasis mine). The correlation of the subjective with the objective is crucial. In Aristotle's picture of great-souledness, as of all the virtues, one can deviate from it in opposite ways (this is the famous doctrine of "the mean").[24] One can think oneself worthy of great things and not be—this is vanity, in which Aristotle has very little interest. On the other hand, which is much more serious, one can think oneself worthy of *less* than one is actually worthy of—that is the vice that truly opposes magnanimity. It is the vice of pusillanimity (*mikropsychia*), of underestimating one's capacities.[25] The worst form of this vice is the case of the self-demeaning person who is in fact worthy of great things. To make great claims for oneself is constitutive of the virtue *as long as the claims are justified*. The key to the virtue is to be justified in one's grand ambitions and self-confidence.[26] And it is part of the virtue to despise those who are less worthy than oneself (*NE* 1124b5).[27] Calvin's description of the ideal figure of classical ethics—"confident in his understanding and uprightness," strenuously exerting himself "toward the excellent and the honorable"—is actually rather tepid in the face of Aristotle's actual characterization of his ethical ideal.

22. Plato, *Symposium* 216a–217b, trans. Walter Hamilton (London: Penguin, 1951), 102–3.

23. See Arthur W. H. Adkins, *Merit and Responsibility: A Study in Greek Values* (1960; University of Chicago Press, 1975).

24. For what this doctrine is (and is not) see J. O. Urmson, "Aristotle's Doctrine of the Mean," in Rorty, *Essays on Aristotle's Ethics*, 157–70 (see chap. 5, n. 67).

25. For Montaigne on *mikropsychia*, see 219 above.

26. In *Putting on Virtue*, chap. 1, Herdt raises the deep question of whether Aristotle's great-souled person acts for the sake of virtue or out of "consciousness of [his] own moral worth" (40–44).

27. This is part of the reason why Descartes substitutes *generosité* for magnanimity in *The Passions of the Soul*. See note 122 in chapter 5 above.

It is obviously difficult to see how one could reconcile magnanimity with humility. Aquinas attempts to do so in the *Summa Theologica*, but ends up basically folding humility into magnanimity. He brilliantly focuses on accuracy of assessment, and sees humility as providing such accuracy to the magnanimous person.[28] He seems to arrive at something like a synthesis in asserting that high ambition is virtuous when it springs from "confidence in divine help," but the discussion gets troublesome again when he takes this seriously and asserts that "without prejudice to humility [persons] may rate the gifts they have received from God *above those apparently granted to others*" (44:99; emphasis mine). Aquinas's attitude toward humility is interestingly and significantly complex. It should not lead a person to be "mindless of his dignity" and it is certainly not the greatest of the virtues. A number of Saint Benedict's "degrees of humility" strike Aquinas as unsatisfactory. Especially troubling are those in which one is "to declare oneself viler than other men," since this involves "a mistaken opinion"—which, following Aristotle perfectly, Aquinas declares "is inconsistent with any virtue" (44:109).[29]

Before turning to Milton, I want to establish one final claim—that the Reformation critique of classical virtue was fully available in the English Renaissance, and especially in English Renaissance poetry. It is possible to read the first book of *The Faerie Queene* in these terms, and I am inclined to do so, but Spenser's theology is notoriously hard to pin down.[30] Milton may well have known (probably knew?) George Herbert's *The Temple*, which includes

28. See St. Thomas Aquinas (question 161, article 1, reply to objection 3), *Summa Theologica*, Latin text and English translation by Thomas Gilby, OSB (New York: Blackfriars and McGraw-Hill, 1972), 44:93; cited hereafter parenthetically in the text.

29. A number of scholars have attempted to defend the coherence or profundity of Aquinas's treatment of magnanimity and humility in the *Summa Theologica*. See, among many others, David A. Horner, "What It Takes to be Great: Aristotle and Aquinas on Magnanimity," *Faith and Philosophy* 15 (1998): 415–44; Mary M. Keys, "Aquinas and the Challenge of Aristotelian Magnanimity," *History of Political Thought* 24 (2003): 37–65. The most thoughtful and historically informed treatment that I have found is R.-A. Gauthier, *Magnanimité: L'idéal de la grandeur dans la philosophie païenne et dans la théologie chrétienne* (Paris: J. Vrin, 1951).

30. For intelligent puzzling over Spenser's theology, see Virgil K. Whitaker, *The Religious Basis of Spenser's Thought* (1950; New York, Gordian Press, 1966); Paul J. Alpers, "Heroism and Human Strength in Book I," in *The Poetry of "The Faerie Queene"* (Princeton: Princeton University Press, 1967), 334–69; Darryl J. Gless, *Interpretation and Theology in Spenser* (New York: Cambridge University Press, 1994); and Carol V. Kaske, *Spenser and Biblical Poetics* (Ithaca: Cornell University Press, 1999).

a number of lyrics that employ the topos of "ironic humanism."[31] "Sinne" (I) pretends to celebrate and manifest "Christian humanism." It thanks God for helping man to virtue through multifarious means—parents, schoolmasters, rules of reason, Bibles, our consciences—but then concludes: "Yet all these fences and this whole aray / One cunning bosome-sinne blowes quite away." The "cunning bosome-sinne" of pride blows Christian humanism "quite away." In the poem entitled "Humilitie," Herbert presents the classical virtues as fundamentally proud and fundamentally competitive.[32] Perhaps the most subtle critique of classical humanism in *The Temple* is the lyric entitled "Unkindnesse," in which Herbert presents himself as simultaneously fulfilling one of Aristotle's highest ethical ideals—that of noble friendship, the focus of books 8 and 9 of the *Nicomachean Ethics*—and completely, even perversely, failing in relation to God.[33] In the way that Herbert uses the contrast between what we might call the virtue framework and what we might call the sin framework, Herbert stands, in many of his major lyrics, as exactly the sort of theologically antihumanist poet that John Milton is not.[34]

31. See Richard Strier, "Ironic Humanism in *The Temple*," in *"Too Rich to Clothe the Sunne"*: *Essays on George Herbert*, ed. Claude J. Summers and Ted-Larry Pebworth (Pittsburgh: University of Pittsburgh Press, 1980), 33–52. "Sinne" (I) and "Humilitie," briefly alluded to in this paragraph, are analyzed in that essay. *The Temple* was widely disseminated in the seventeenth century, across the entire spectrum of competing Christianities. See Robert H. Ray, *The Herbert Allusion Book: Allusions to George Herbert in the Seventeenth Century*, Studies in Philology: Texts and Studies (Chapel Hill: University of North Carolina Press, 1986).

32. On competitiveness as a fundamental feature of classical ethics, along with (or as a version of) pride, see Calvin, *Institutes*, 3.7.4. On the problem of competitiveness in Greek ethics, see Adkins, *Merit and Responsibility*, esp. chaps. 3 and 16.

33. See Strier, *Love Known*, 17–20 (see intro., n. 53).

34. Even Milton's most Herbertian moment, the sonnet on his blindness (sonnet 19), in which (as in many Herbert lyrics) an authoritative voice enters the poem to prevent the speaker from "murmuring," ends on a heroic rather than a self-naughting moment: "They also serve who only stand and wait: (*Complete Poems*, 168 [see intro., n. 59]). To "stand" is a military posture—the blind poet is *en garde*, tensely alert, awaiting a command (see *OED*, "stand," B. 10). Interestingly, the poem of Herbert's that presents a vision of God (his "Kingly" state) and his servants closest to that in Milton's sonnet is Herbert's "To all Angels and Saints," a poem, I have argued, which is uncharacteristic of Herbert (Strier, "'To all Angels and Saints': Herbert's Puritan Poem," 132–45 [see chap. 4, n. 75]). Milton's lack of preoccupation with the power of sin is what leads Stephen Fallon to the claim that Milton is "a theological poet but not a religious one" (*Milton's Peculiar Grace: Self-Representation and Authority* [Ithaca: Cornell University Press, 2007], x, 268). This is surely too strong a claim, but the contrast with Herbert (not made

HUMILITY VERSUS DIGNITY: THE ENGLISH PROSE

In Milton's English prose, "humility" functions primarily as a negative term (out of eleven uses noted in the *Concordance to the English Prose*, six are clearly negative and one is ambiguous).[35] The divorce tracts are crucial here. *Tetrachordon* opens with an attack on the "specious humility" that derives from persons having "a servile sense of their own conscious unworthiness."[36] But to have a sense of "conscious unworthiness" is what humility is normally taken to mean. The opposite of this sort of "specious humility" is not, as one would think, proper humility; the opposite is magnanimity—a nonservile ("manly," Milton and Machiavelli would say) sense of conscious worthiness. The genuine praise of humility in Milton is always in the institutional, not the individual context.[37] The important thing for individual Christians to remember is "the dignity of man" (both as *vir* and *homo*).[38] This is the regulative principle against which all customs, practices, and interpretations are to be judged; "nothing now adayes is more degenerately forgott'n, then the true dignity of man."[39] In the divorce tracts, anything that Milton sees as challenging or undermining "the dignity of man" is condemned. "Affected patience" has exactly the same status as "specious humility."[40] They are among the "abject and servil[e] principles" from which Milton is trying to liberate "the undervalued soul of man."[41]

Lest the divorce tracts be taken as a departure or a special case, it can easily be shown that the appeal to human dignity is central to all of Milton's polemical prose.[42] We can see this in the opening of his first tract. While the stated

---

by Fallon, who compares Milton to Puritan autobiographers) does help make sense of some such claim.

35. See *A Concordance to the English Prose of John Milton*, ed. Laurence Sterne and Harold H. Kollmeier (Binghamton: Medieval and Renaissance Texts and Studies, 1985).

36. *The Complete Prose Works of John Milton*, gen. ed. Don M. Wolfe (New Haven: Yale University Press, 1953–1983), 2:587.

37. See, for instance, the praise of the lowly church in *Complete Prose*, 1:833, 848–49, et passim. I am grateful to Stephen Fallon (personal communication) for helping me clarify this point.

38. *The Doctrine and Discipline of Divorce*, in *Complete Prose*, 2:228 (hereafter *DDD*).

39. *Tetrachordon*, in *Complete Prose*, 2:587.

40. For "affected patience," see *DDD*, in *Complete Prose*, 2:341. I discuss Shakespeare's critique of patience in chapter 1.

41. For "abject and servile principles," see *DDD*, in *Complete Prose*, 2:223; for "the multitude of sorrows," 343; for the "undervalued soul," 249.

42. For a discussion of the hermeneutical continuity of Milton's prose, see the appendix to this chapter.

enemy in *Of Reformation Touching Church-Discipline in England* is formalist ceremonialism, the attack on this soon turns into an extraordinary account of the prominence that ceremonial and traditional religion give to humility. The account of the degeneration of "mysteries" into ceremonies goes (as I reconstruct it) in the following way: through a process something like historical entropy, certain optional procedures in communal worship are declared to be necessary on the pretense of "joyning the body in a formall reverence"; this leads to great attention in worship to the body and the accoutrements thereof; then, through a forgetting of the Gospel, these accoutrements themselves become the focus of conscience, and fear of ritual impurity sets in; this in turn generates exaltation of humility.[43] Looking on outward things with "servile fear," persons

> knew not how to hide their Slavish approach to *Gods* behests[,] by them not understood nor worthily receav'd, but by cloaking their Servile crouching to all *Religious* Presentments, sometimes lawfull, sometimes Idolatrous, under the name of *humility*. (522)

The transformation of humility into a negative term continues. To trace this transformation is Milton's effort in the paragraph that follows the analysis just cited. He presents the (two) sacraments as having been perverted: baptism has become a kind of exorcism; communion "a subject of horror and glouting adoration, pageanted about like a dreadful idol." This latter is especially important because it "some times deceves wel-meaning men, and beguiles them of their reward, by their voluntary humility" (523). This means, I think, that such men fear to receive the sacrament out of a sense of unworthiness in the face of something so "holy." Milton cannot, however, simply let this "voluntary humility" stand as an honest, if unfortunate, mistake. He explains that it is indeed not humility but "fleshly pride," and he completes the transformation of a sense of unworthiness into a form of pride by giving a wonderful Gospel example:

> Such was *Peters* unseasonable Humilitie . . . when *Christ* came to wash his feet; who at an impertinent time would needs straine courtesy with his Master . . . [and] so provok'd by his interruption the meeke *Lord*, that he threat'nd to exclude him from his heavenly Portion, unless he could be content to be lesse arrogant, and stiff neckt in his humility. (524)

---

43. *Of Reformation Touching Church-Discipline in England*, in *Complete Prose*, 1:521.

Milton's account of the perversion of the Eucharist begins to get at the heart of his objections to prelacy and to all ceremonial religion: the deception of well-meaning laypersons through voluntary and improper humility. The "putting of holiness" in ceremonial objects and procedures and in those who are exclusively permitted to perform ceremonies has produced a situation in which "the people of God[,] redeemed and wash'd with *Christs* blood, and dignified with so many glorious titles of Saints, and sons in the Gospel, are now no better reputed than impure ethnicks, and lay dogs" (547). The railed off communion table is one symbol of this improper division of the Christian community.[44] Milton's focus is on the moral and psychological effect of the "priestly" administration of the Eucharist on ordinary "wel-meaning" Christians. They become improperly humble: "And thus the people[,] vilifi'd and rejected" by those who have falsely appropriated the title of "priest," have come to "give over the earnest study of vertue and godlinesse as a thing of greater purity than they need, and the search of divine knowledge as a mystery too high for their capacities, and only for Churchmen to meddle with" (548). For Milton, the dignity of the lay Christian (so-called)—the priesthood of all believers—is at the heart of the attack on prelacy. He is precisely echoing Luther's attack on the way in which the false (so-called) sacrament of ordination established "a seed-bed of unappeasable discord" through which "clergy and laity were to be more widely separated than heaven and earth." It was "the terrible domination of the clergy over the laity" that led Luther to proclaim that "we who have been baptized are all uniformly priests." The aim was to restore "fellowship based on the gospel."[45]

Once we understand this, the rhetoric of Milton's most astonishing antiprelatical tract, *The Reason of Church-Government Urg'd against Prelaty* (1642), becomes intelligible. We should have been expecting the tenor, if not the wit, of the attack on prelacy as a triangle—"the most dividing and schismaticall forme that Geometricians know."[46] We may not have been expecting the defense of sects, but this becomes immediately intelligible when put in terms of

44. Milton's sense of the devaluation of the laity in the Caroline church exactly corresponds to Peter Lake's account of the intended effect of "the Laudian style." See Lake's essay by that title in *The Early Stuart Church, 1603–42*, ed. Kenneth Fincham (New York: Macmillan, 1993), 161–85, esp. 176.

45. *The Babylonian Captivity of the Church*, in *Selections from His Writings*, 345 (see intro., n. 55). Luther sounds like Milton (or, of course, vice versa) not only here but in the previous chapter of *The Babylonian Captivity*, on issues regarding marriage, in which Luther sees a "harshness of man toward men such as God has nowhere demanded" (334).

46. *The Reason of Church-Government Urg'd against Prelaty*, in *Complete Prose*, 1:790.

"the triall of an unfained goodnesse" and—the word is, as we have seen, highly significant—"magnanimity" (795). But we could not have expected a section of autobiography. Here, as in the cases of Montaigne and Descartes, the mystery is why the author would adopt such a mode.

In the Milton passage, as in the final section and elsewhere in the *Discourse on the Method*, one can chart the movement of assertion and anxiety in the prose. The autobiographical passage in Milton's pamphlet is the opening of the second of the two books. When Milton is halfway though this extended medial prologue, just at the point where he is about to turn to genuine auto-biography, he notes, "I shall be foolish in saying more to this purpose" (808). One is inclined (even now) to agree. And yet he proceeds. He is aware of the generic inappropriateness of such self-revelation, and he acknowledges (in a phrase that we have already noted) that he is about to "venture and divulge unusual things of my self." And he does. Halfway though this unusual divul-gence, and having announced, bizarrely in this context, his literary ambitions, he again considers the possibility of stopping—"Time serves not now, and per-haps I might seem too profuse" (812)—yet he goes on to discuss at length his uncertainties about his unwritten future masterworks. There is some powerful impulse at work here, and it cannot be unconnected to the context in which it occurs. I could not answer the question of why Montaigne was consumed by a "hunger to make [him]self known," whereas I spoke of Descartes's sense of "proper pride."[47] This brings us closer to Milton. What is at stake in this sec-tion of *Reason of Church-Government*, and perhaps in the pamphlet as a whole, is Milton's sense of his own dignity.

Milton recognized that the parable of the talents provided an attractive av-enue through which to attempt to unify classical and Christian ethics, but as in Aquinas, the hint of Pharisaism is hard to ignore (recall "without prejudice to humility [persons] may rate the gifts they have received from God above those apparently granted to others").[48] Milton identifies with Tiresias, "bemoaning his lot, that he knew more then other men" [803]). Joan Webber has given a brilliant account of the way in which Milton works to avoid the first-person in this passage ("He that" is the subject), but the moment in which Milton does finally allow himself to emerge in the first-person singular is extremely

47. See 214 and 245–46 above.

48. Already by the late twelfth century, the parable of the talents was regularly used to justify the activity and authority of writers. See Jerry Root, "'*Mustrer*' and the Poetics of Marie de France," *Modern Philology* 108 (2010): 151–76 (esp. note 13).

interesting.[49] He is afraid of being crippled by humility, of being "too inquisitive or suspicious of myself."[50] The great charge that he imagines himself doomed to hear, if he should keep silent, is that he had been "timorous" (804). The final punishment that Milton imagines denounced upon himself, in this future counterfactual mode, is that he would actually become what humility leads one to see oneself as: "[W]hat before was thy sin is now thy duty, to be abject and worthlesse" (805).

As the prologue or "digression" continues, it gets more integrated into its polemical and immediate context. The abolition of prelacy will not only free the pulpits from improper control but provide opportunities, "beside the office of a pulpit," for "free and splendid wit[s]" to "imbreed and cherish in a great people the seeds of vertu" (816). The final sentence of the "digression" explains, with yet further autobiography, why Milton does not himself speak from a pulpit. Refusing to be part of a corrupt institution, he had "thought it better to prefer a blamelesse silence before the sacred office of speaking" (823). The entire effort of this highly wrought prologue can be seen to consist in changing the meaning of "office" here from its sacerdotal to its Ciceronian meaning while still keeping the notion of "the sacred" in place—as in Adriana's appeal to her "office" at the end of *The Comedy of Errors*.[51] This transformation helps us recognize the element in the Presbyterian system that most appealed to Milton: the presence of lay elders (*presbyteroi*) in a governing capacity.[52] In Geneva, the Consistory (or Presbytery), the disciplinary body of the church, was made up of six pastors (that is, ministers) and twelve lay elders.[53] Milton highly prizes this idea:

49. Joan Webber, *The Eloquent "I": Style and Self in Seventeenth-Century Prose* (Madison: University of Wisconsin Press, 1968), 196–97.

50. Recall Descartes's attack on "vicious humility" (*Passions*, art. 159), and its connection to irresolution (art. 170).

51. For *The Comedy of Errors*, see 178–79 above; for a similar reading of this passage in *The Reason of Church-Government*, see Paul Stevens, "Discontinuities in Milton's Early Public Self-Presentation," *Huntington Library Quarterly* 51 (1988): 261–80.

52. On the importance of Milton running the normal English and Scottish Presbyterian analogy between church and state "from the opposite direction"—that is, from state to church rather than vice versa—see Janel Mueller, "Contextualizing Milton's Nascent Republicanism," in *Of Poetry and Politics: New Essays on Milton and his World*, ed. Paul G. Stanwood (Binghamton: Medieval and Renaissance Texts and Studies, 1994), 16.

53. William Monter, *Calvin's Geneva* (New York: Wiley, 1967); Harro Höpfl, *The Christian Polity of John Calvin* (Cambridge: Cambridge University Press, 1982).

[N]othing can be more for the mutuall honour and love of the people to their Pastor, and his to them, then when in select numbers and courses they [the people] are seen partaking and doing reverence to the holy duties of discipline by this serviceable and solemn presence, and receiving honour again from their imployment. (838)

The true schism would be healed; "the terrible domination of the clergy over the laity" would be ended; the people would no longer "be separated in the church by vails and partitions as laicks and unclean, but admitted to wait upon the tabernacle as the rightfull Clergy of Christ" (838). This contemplation of the role of "elders" in the church leads to a moment in *The Reason of Church-Government* that is perhaps even more amazing than the autobiographical excursion: the emergence of Homeric heroism as a model for Christians.

The idea of the presence of "elders" leads Milton to think about shame—"or to call it better, the reverence of our elders, our brethren, and our friends" (840). This "reverence," says Milton, functioned in the classical world as "the greatest incitement to vertuous deeds and the greatest dissuasion from unworthy attempts"—which brings him to Homer.[54] After relating the instance of Hector refusing to retire from battle "lest the Trojan Knights and Dames should think he did ignobly," Milton enthusiastically commends "this generous and Christianly reverence one of another." Homer provides models of people behaving "Christianly," which proper church-government will encourage. After elaborating on this, Milton finally acknowledges that the Homeric poems idealize a rather strong version of a shame culture; he notes that "there is yet a more ingenuous and noble" model available, and that "the feare of infamy" goes only so far as "almost to be vertuous." Yet what is interesting about the more noble ideal is that it is still a shame model, a model of behavior in the eyes of men. Milton does not substitute the Reformation model of evaluating the self *coram Deo*, in the face of God. Instead, he promulgates an internalized version of the shame model, "an esteem, whereby men bear an inward reverence toward their own persons" such that a person does not "fear so much the

---

54. For shame in Homer and in classical Greek thinking, see E. R. Dodds, *The Greeks and the Irrational* (Berkeley: University of California Press, 1951), chap. 2; Adkins, *Merit and Responsibility*, chap. 8; Bernard Williams, *Shame and Necessity* (Berkeley: University of California Press, 1993), chap. 4.

offence and reproach of others, as he dreads and would blush at the reflection of his own severe and modest eye upon himselfe" (841–42).[55]

Milton makes extraordinary claims for this "self-reverence" (the term is Tennyson's).[56] Milton attempts moderation; if "the love of God as a fire sent from Heaven" is "the first principle" of "godly and vertuous actions in men," then "this pious and just honouring of our selves is the second." As the sentence continues, however, this opening concession to fire from above disappears and is supplanted by a liquid source. "Pious and just honouring of our selves" becomes "the radical moisture and fountain head, whence every laudable and worthy enterprize issues forth." Self-reverence becomes the ultimate virtue—"above which there is no higher ascent but to the love of God." And this "ascent" does not involve any change. The love of God "cannot be assunder" from this self-approval (841–42). Presbyterian church-government is praiseworthy because it induces godly and proper heroic pride in the lay Christian.

HUMILITY VERSUS MODESTY: *CHRISTIAN DOCTRINE*

One might argue that the foregrounding of human dignity represents the view of the early and optimistic Milton. In the remainder of this chapter, I will argue that this is not so, that "proper pride" remained a virtue that Milton celebrated throughout his career, and that he never sustainedly adopted the Reformation understanding of humility. The final text I will consider before approaching the poetry is the Latin treatise *On Christian Doctrine*.

Despite the doubts raised by William B. Hunter, I accept the Miltonic authorship of this text and a date of 1655 to 1660 for it.[57] I think, however, that

---

55. For a similar treatment of this passage, with attention to a variety of classical sources, see Scodel, *Excess and the Mean*, 269–75 (see intro. n. 57), although Scodel sees Milton's "commitment to the virtuous, self-esteeming lay person" as having implications that led Milton away from Presbyterianism (271). The emphasis here on acting with regard to one's own image of oneself confirms the cogency of Herdt's question about *megalopsychia* (see note 26 above).

56. In "Oenone," Tennyson's Athena speaks of "[s]elf-reverence, self-knowledge, self-control" as leading to "sovereign power" (lines 142–43). See *Poems of Tennyson*, ed. Jerome Hamilton Buckley (New York: Houghton Mifflin, 1958), 35. Tennyson was a devoted reader of Milton as well as of the classics.

57. See Hunter's articles and the forum discussions they generated in *Studies in English Literature*: "The Provenance of the *Christian Doctrine*," *SEL* 32 (Winter 1992): 129–42, and "Forum," 143–66; "The Provenance of the *Christian Doctrine*: Addenda from the Bishop of Salisbury," *SEL* 33 (Winter 1993): 191–208, and "Forum," *SEL* 34 (Winter 1994): 153–204.

Hunter is correct in calling attention to "the continental context for the treatise," especially the writings of Servetus and Arminius, although I think that
this contextualization works at least as well in support as in denial of Milton's
authorship.[58] The importance of this context, from my point of view, is that it
suggests Milton's continuing distance from normative Reformation doctrine
on the central questions of grace and merit. The ethical structure of *Christian
Doctrine*, as I will try to show, is thoroughly Aristotelian.

That the treatise is a theologically Arminian text, and a very liberal one at
that, has been fully demonstrated.[59] Arminius was a Dutch Protestant theologian who attempted to put Calvinism—that is, predestinarianism—on a rational basis (and thereby profoundly undermined it).[60] The important point
about this "Arminianism," from my point of view, is that it allowed Milton to
accept classical ethics as fully and directly relevant to Christian soteriology.[61]

Hunter collected his papers on this topic in *Visitation Unimplor'd: Milton and the Authorship
of "De Doctrina Christiana"* (Pittsburgh: Duquesne University Press, 1998). The most recent
contribution to this discussion is Gordon Campbell, Thomas N. Corns, John K. Hale, and
Fiona J. Tweedie, *Milton and the Manuscript of "De Doctrina Christiana"* (Oxford: Oxford
University Press, 2007), where the authors affirm Milton's authorship and date the work to the
late 1650s.

58. For the quotation, see Hunter in the forum discussion in *SEL* 34:196.

59. See the introduction to Milton's *De Doctrina Christiana*, ed. Maurice Kelley, trans. John
Carey, in *Complete Prose*, 6:74–86 (page references to *On Christian Doctrine* are to this edition).
In the English context, the term "Arminian" can be confusing, since it is sometimes equated with
Laudianism. Milton was an "Arminian" only in the strictly theological sense; in this other sense,
he is an "anti-Arminian," that is, an anti-Laudian (see Lake, "The Laudian Style," 176). Milton
was unusual in combining anti-Laudianism with anti-Calvinism. On the more normal combina-
tion of both senses of "Arminianism," see Nicholas Tyacke, *Anti-Calvinism: The Rise of English
Arminianism, c. 1590–1640* (Oxford: Clarendon, 1990).

60. See Carl Bangs, *Arminius: A Study in the Dutch Reformation* (Nashville: Abingdon,
1971), and Richard A. Muller, *God, Creation, and Providence in the Thought of Jacobus Arminius*
(Grand Rapids, Mich.: Baker, 1991).

61. For a good discussion of Milton's Arminianism and an apparent exception to it, see Fallon, *Milton's Peculiar Grace*, 182–90. Fallon sees the apparent exception as caused by Milton's
need "to be outstanding in as many ways as possible, or in more ways than are possible at once"
(110). Fallon's book presents a view of Milton generally similar to that presented in this chapter
(of which he used an earlier version), though he sees more anxiety in Milton than I do, and sees
Milton as eventually developing a more "mature" view than that of classical ethics (263; also 232
and 208). Fallon acknowledges the area of convergence in our views (x, 30), but seems to think
that I see Milton's commitment to a classical view of the self as *resulting from* his adoption of Arminianism, whereas in fact I see the chain of causality going the other way around. Fallon argues,
supposedly against me, that "Milton's anti-Calvinist, Arminian soteriology alone is insufficient

The will of man, after the Fall, was not (as Luther and Calvin thought) bound to sin. Sin plays remarkably little role in *Christian Doctrine*. Milton holds that even in the postlapsarian world, "everyone is provided with a sufficient degree of innate reason to be able to resist evil desires *by his own effort*" (186; emphasis mine). This is the basic premise of classical ethics and the absolute center of *On Christian Doctrine*. It explains God's nature: "[H]e considers all worthy of sufficient grace, *and the cause is his justice*" (193; emphasis mine). Salvation and damnation are intelligible in moral terms. Salvation is not by faith alone—"our own effort is always required" (480). The saints are granted perseverance—"so long as they do not prove wanting" (505). The Gospel is "rational" and "manly" (548), not requiring belief in "absurdities" (like the Trinity) or moral unintelligibilities (like Luthero-Calvinist predestination).[62] "Holiness and wisdom" are found "in many of the heathen" (396). Perfect sincerity and good conscience are possible. Good conscience consists of "an intellectual judgment of one's deeds, and an approval of them" which can be directed, Milton startlingly adds, "by either nature or grace"—it apparently makes no difference (*vel naturae vel gratiae judicium mentis*).[63] "By these means," Milton asserts, "we are made absolutely certain of our own sincerity" (*qua sinceritatem nobis inesse certo scimus* [652/40]). One cannot but hear Calvin grinding his teeth.

---

to account for his refusal to acknowledge sinfulness in his self-representations" (31). I am afraid that Professor Fallon and I are in violent agreement here. His early assertion, in "confuting" me, of Milton's "opposition to Arminian teaching in *Areopagitica*" (32n34) is qualified by his own later (and quite proper) puzzlement at the place of Arminius in that text (144).

62. See *Christian Doctrine* on God as one "in the numerical sense in which human reason always understands it" (216), on all other views of the Godhead as "absurd notions which are utterly alien to all human ways of thinking" (222), and on Calvinist predestination as making God completely morally unintelligible (164–66). I have discussed the rationalism of *Christian Doctrine* in "Milton's Fetters, or, Why Eden Is Better than Heaven" (see chap. 3, app. 2, n. 14). For a reminder that Milton did accept a (biblically sanctioned) mystery in his conception of Christianity, see Michael Lieb, *Theological Milton: Deity, Discourse and Heresy in the Miltonic Canon* (Pittsburgh: Duquesne University Press, 2006), 246–47, though Lieb may overstate the importance of this.

63. For the Latin, I rely on *The Works of John Milton*, ed. James Holly Hanford and Waldo Hilary Dunn with the translation of Charles Sumner (New York: Columbia University Press, 1934), 17:40. When quoting the English translation and the Latin together, I will cite first the page number in volume 6 of the *Complete Prose*, followed by the page number in volume 17 of *The Works*.

It must be noted that humility is indeed treated in *Christian Doctrine*, and that the definition given is the Reformation one: "Humility is that whereby we acknowledge our unworthiness in the sight of God" (661; *Humilitas est qua nostram indignitatem coram Deo agnoscimus* [65]). But this treatment is extremely brief (one short paragraph), is unimportant in the argument as a whole, and its structure is distinctly Aristotelian—that is, tripartite rather than binary. Humility is a mean. It is opposed not only to pride (*superbia coram Deo*) but also to "superstitious humility" (*humilitas superstitiosa*). So the negative valence surfaces again, as do Saint Peter's feet (again as a case "where disobedience occurs in the guise of humility" [664/72]). Something like Aquinas's treatment of humility occurs in the course of Milton's discussion of what Carey translates as "the distinctions of public life" (733), and what Sumner more accurately calls the virtues "peculiarly appropriate to a high station" (*virtutes quae in ornamentis vitae versantur* [234–35]). The virtues in question here are *modestia*, which Carey quite misleadingly (if provocatively) translates as "humility" and its corollary—*magnanimitas*.

The discussion of *modestia* is quite remarkable. It begins unexceptionably enough: as Carey translates it (as "humility"), *modestia* "gives a man a modest opinion of himself and prevents him from blowing his own horn" (733). But the definition does not end there. In Carey, it continues, "except when it is really called-for," a slightly stronger but basically accurate rendering of Milton's "unless it is necessary" (*non nisi necessario*). This is pure Aristotle.[64] The question is not whether to praise oneself but when to do so. Milton condemns uncalled-for boasting but, like Aristotle, is very suspicious of undervaluing the self. He warns against "a crafty or hypocritical playing down of one's merit" (734). Allied to *modestia*, Milton asserts, "is the desire for a good reputation," and opposed to it is "a shameless neglect of one's good name" (734–75). Perfectly correlated with *modestia*, as we have said, is *magnanimitas*, which "is shown when in seeking or not seeking riches, advantages, or honors, in avoiding them or accepting them, a man behaves as befits his own dignity" (*pro sua dignitate sibi satis cognita se gerit* [735/245). Behaving as befits one's worth and dignity is what links Milton's conceptions of *modestia* and *magnanimitas*, modesty and high-mindedness. The chapter ends, appropriately with a condemnation of *pusillanimitas*, but the penultimate vice condemned is pride

64. The proof-texts cited are Job 12:3, Judges 5:7 (the Song of Deborah), and Ecclesiastes 12:3. The values of the Hebrew Bible are sometimes more compatible with Greek than with Christian ones. Michael Lieb has stressed this point to me, and I see it as fully instantiated in *Samson Agonistes* (discussed below in this chapter).

(*superbia*), which is given a truly Aristotelian definition. Pride is not a matter of having a high opinion of oneself; it is a matter of doing so "with no or insufficient justification" (*vel indignus vel ultra meritum*).

PROPER PRIDE IN *PARADISE LOST*

But does the ethic of proper pride and the critique of self-abasement find its way into *Paradise Lost?* It might be argued that the presentation of Satan in books 1 and 2 of the poem is the greatest instance of "ironic humanism" in English Renaissance poetry, but the distinction between rejecting the use and rejecting the abuse of various capacities seems to me truly to block that conclusion. The presentation of Satan does not undermine the commitment of *Paradise Lost* to classical ethics. Rather, Milton wishes to present Satan as a preeminent case of a figure who has mistaken opinions about almost everything, and mistaken opinions, as Aquinas, in his most Aristotelian mode, said are "inconsistent with any virtue."[65] The presentation of Satan might, in other words, be part of rather than a rejection of the deep structure of Aristotelian ethics. A more straightforward locus of classical ethics in *Paradise Lost* is the constant assertion of the doctrine of merit. This mainly serves in the poem (as in *On Christian Doctrine*) to guarantee the intelligibility of God's justice, but it also gives the conception of virtue in the poem an Aristotelian flavor. The important question of what constitutes servitude is answered in the characteristically classical way, on purely objective grounds, as serving the unworthy (see 6.174–85). But what I am most interested in establishing is the presence of the doctrine of proper pride or "self-reverence" in the poem.[66]

Adam's desire for "society" is presented in terms of his conscious superiority to all other creatures (8.380–92); and Eve, the answer to this desire, is presented as having both virtue and proper "conscience of her worth" (8.503). Although both Abdiel and the Son manifest proper pride, the fullest exposition of the virtue in *Paradise Lost* is Raphael's commentary, in book 8, on Adam's feelings for Eve. Adam confesses himself susceptible to being powerfully, disturbingly affected by Eve even though he is "in all enjoyments else /

---

65. Whether, in the full context of the poem, Satan is indeed mistaken about almost everything is a different matter. On that, see critics from Shelley on, including Strier, "Milton's Fetters."

66. For a similar argument, with a somewhat different focus, see Scodel, *Excess and Mean*, 269–75.

Superior and," and, in a word from Stoic philosophy to which we shall return, "unmov'd" (8.531–32). Adam speculates that with regard to this unique susceptibility, perhaps "Nature fail'd" in him (8.534), and he notes that "Wisdom in discourse with her [Eve] / Loses discount'nanc't" (8.552–53).

The sufficiency of nature and the regulative power of wisdom are the premises of classical ethics. Raphael's response does not exhort Adam to look beyond nature and natural wisdom for help in the struggle with erotic passion—as, for instance, Saint Augustine did and needed to do.[67] Instead, the message to Adam in *Paradise Lost* is "be not diffident / Of Wisdom" (8.562–63)—an enjambment in which, as in most such cases, the enjambed phrase gives almost the full meaning without the words that continue it. What Adam needs is not divine aid but accuracy in ethical and intellectual judgment.[68] He must avoid the intellectual mistake of "attributing overmuch to things / Less excellent" (8.565–66), and, most of all, he must have proper pride:

> weigh with her thyself;
> Then value: Oft-times nothing profits more
> Than self-esteem, grounded on just and right
> Well-manag'd.
>   (8.570–73)

"Self-esteem, grounded on just and right"—this is the pure Aristotelian ideal (here the enjambment adds nothing, and is almost, in fact misleading; how could "self-esteem, grounded on just and right" not be "Well-manag'd"?). As the placement of this speech near the end of book 8 suggests, and as the Son tells Adam in book 10, proper pride could have prevented the Fall—at least that of Adam, and perhaps Eve's as well. In allowing himself to act out of feeling, Adam forgot his own "real dignity" and objective worth (10.150–56). He failed at self-knowledge in the philosophical, not the Calvinist sense. "Hadst thou known thy self aright" (10.156) means had Adam known his worth, not

---

67. *Confessions*, 8:27–30 (see chap. 2, n. 28).

68. Christopher Tilmouth's attempt to see *Paradise Lost* as somehow combining, if "not quite" synthesizing, an Augustinian (Reformation) and a Thomist (classical) framework seems to me quite unconvincing; it involves seeing Milton's conception of magnanimity as connecting Milton with Herbert. Tilmouth's hesitation about seeing *Paradise Lost* as a "synthesis" expresses his own uneasiness with the role that he wants the poem to play in the chronological narrative to which he is committed (*Passion's Triumph*, 208–9, also 194–95 [see chap. 1, n. 43]).

his worthlessness. Intellectual clarity and proper, unembarrassed self-esteem would have saved both himself and Eve.[69]

Yet the references to book 10 bring up what would seem to be a serious problem for my thesis. Here, surely, in the aftermath of the Fall, Milton must present a distinctively Christian conception of humility. I take it that the dominant critical view is that this conception is signaled in the moments when Adam and Eve say the words, "mee, mee only" (10.832 and 10.936, respectively), and that the conception is most impressively dramatized when Eve at Adam's feet "[f]ell humble" (10.912).[70] Here certainly, humility is presented in a positive light.

I think this view mistaken, and that the values of the poem, even in book 10, remain recognizably classical. Adam's "mee, mee only" is not a cry from the heart. It is part of the central casuistry of the poem, the "great Argument" by which God is absolved from blame for human sin. Adam's words are the result of an elaborate process of ratiocination; the point of them is less Adam's guilt than the exoneration of God. Eve's "plaint" (10.913) is quite different. It is indeed a cry from the heart, and is extremely moving. It is in fact almost as moving as another magnificent "plaint," Adam's words to himself when he falls, a speech that Eve's echoes. Adam had said (or thought—"he inward silence broke"): "How can I live without thee, how forgo / Thy sweet Converse and Love so dearly join'd, / To live again in these wild Woods forlorn?" (9.908–10). Eve asks, "[F]orlorn of thee, / Whither shall I betake me, where subsist?" (10.921–92). "Forlorn"—as Keats said, the very word is like a bell.[71] It appears in passing in book 1 (of hell [1.180]), slightly more resonantly in book 2 (of the fallen angels [2.615]), once in book 4 (almost technically—of unfallen humans from Satan's point of view [4.374]), and once, very powerfully, in the proem to book 7, where the blind Milton evokes what his experience of composition would be like without divine inspiration (7.20). The resonant uses by Adam and then by Eve are the final two instances of the word in the poem. There is no doubt that we are meant to connect them.

69. With regard to the separation scene in book 9, I agree with Joan S. Bennett (*Reviving Liberty: Radical Christian Humanism in Milton's Great Poems* [Cambridge: Harvard University Press, 1989], chap. 4) that Adam ceases argument too soon—or rather, I would say that he is improperly "diffident" of his own wisdom. Scodel (*Excess and Mean*, 279–83) reads the separation scene in detail in this way.

70. For a classical statement of this view in modern criticism, see E. M. W. Tillyard, "The Crisis of *Paradise Lost*," *Studies in Milton* (London: Chatto and Windus, 1951), 8–52. This view has been widely adopted. See, for instance, Joseph H. Summers, *The Muse's Method: An Introduction to "Paradise Lost"* (Cambridge: Harvard University Press, 1962), 183–84.

71. "Ode to a Nightingale," line 71.

But there is more to be said. When Adam decides to answer Eve's plaint, the words he speaks to her may be "peaceful" (946), but they constitute a rebuke. Adam does not praise Eve for her "mee only." Rather, he sharply reprehends it:

> Unwary, and too desirous, as before,
> So now of what thou know'st not, who desir'st
> The punishment all on thyself.
>
> (10.947–49)

Adam points out not the moral grandeur but the absurdity of Eve's desire. He tells her to bear her own guilt first (10.950), and rather unkindly notes that she can hardly expect to bear God's wrath when she endures Adam's displeasure "so ill" (10.952). It is worth recalling that Adam characterized his own "mee only" as a "fond wish" (10.834; compare "Ay me, I fondly dream!" in "Lycidas"). We should, therefore, take it seriously when Adam describes Eve as "too desirous, *as before* . . . of what thou know'st not." "As before"—in other words, when Eve at Adam's feet "[f]ell humble" (10.912), she indeed fell again.[72]

As Adam's rebuke makes clear, book 10 places a very high value on intellectual clarity. What Adam and Eve actually say here *must* matter.[73] At this point in the poem, Adam has begun to exercise the intellectual clarity and leadership that was enjoined on him in book 8, and that he failed at in book 9. When Eve makes her suicide proposal (better to die than to burn), Adam points out that she is presumptuously trying to outsmart God ("to evade / The penalty" [10.1022–23]). The transformative moment is not an emotional but an intellectual one. Adam puts the couple on the right path by an extraordinary hermeneutical maneuver. Surprisingly, he recalls the obscure ("mysterious") prophecy about the woman's seed bruising the serpent's head (10.181). His act of saving faith is a piece of brilliant Miltonic rationalism. Adam notes that if this prophecy is taken literally, it constitutes a pretty minor consolation—"piteous amends," he says (10.1032). Since the literal meaning is so apparently thin, the literal must be discarded. To make this prophecy intelligible, and worthy of its context, Adam makes what he rightly describes as a major

---

72. For a similar reading of this moment, see Jun Harada, "The Mechanism of Human Reconciliation in *Paradise Lost*," *Philological Quarterly* 50 (1971): 547. I owe this reference to Michael Lieb.

73. For Summers's insistence that what Adam and Eve actually say here "does not matter," see *The Muse's Method*, 183; for some shrewd comments on the oddness of this, see Harada, "The Mechanism of Human Reconciliation," 543.

"conjecture" (10.1033)—the serpent stands for "our grand Foe." He then goes on to reinterpret the divine curses as either mild or nonexistent ("what harm" in labor?), and then to invent practical means of survival and improvement (fire-starting mechanisms and fuel). Adam states that he and Eve will experience "humiliation meek," and at the end of the book the narrator tells us—in a very clumsy repetition of Adam's words—that the "humiliation meek" has indeed taken place.[74] Yet it is not dramatically presented. At the beginning of book 11, moreover, Milton reminds us that "thir port" was "[n]ot of mean suitors" (11.8–9)—lest we think that in their contrition they have lost their dignity.[75]

FINAL HUMILITY OR FINAL PRIDE?

I come now to Milton's final published poems, *Paradise Regained* and *Samson Agonistes*. *Samson* might seem to be the work in which Milton comes closest to embracing humility: the blind Samson acknowledges that he (like the blind Milton) has made disastrous marriage choices and (perhaps like the blind Milton) has sinned through divulging divine secrets.[76] But the poem (or "dramatic poem," as Milton calls it) is as thoroughly committed to the classical tradition for its values as it explicitly is for its form (Greek tragedy); it is committed to the values of the heroic tradition, which are presented, quite brilliantly and consistently, as harmonious with those of the biblical tradition.[77]

Samson does, at moments, sound chastened—"[M]y riddling days are past" (line 1064)—and he is certainly filled with misery and self-recrimination. But Greek tragedy is certainly capable of this (witness the Hercules of Sophocles's *Trachiniae* and Euripides's *Herakles*), and Samson's sense of ab-

---

74. Lines 10.1099–1104 repeat lines 10.1088–1092 with only pronouns and tenses changed.

75. Michael Lieb has raised to me the question of whether Adam's "bowing low" to Raphael at 5:360 can be seen as an instance of positive self-humbling. This is an interesting suggestion, but I would note how carefully and nervously Milton prepares for and hedges this gesture. Before getting to it, he emphasizes Adam's self-sufficiency (352–53); differentiates Adam's behavior from that of courtiers (354–57); and insists that Adam's "submiss approach and reverence meek" *does not mean* that Adam was "aw'd" (358–59).

76. This is the line adopted by, among others, Fallon, *Milton's Peculiar Grace*, 250–63.

77. In *The Blaze of Noon: A Reading of "Samson Agonistes"* (New York: Columbia University Press, 1974), Anthony Low sees this continuity (see esp. 175–79), and tries to prevent "the religious meaning of the play" from being seen as too "exclusively Christian" (228). Joseph G. Mayer defends "Samson's pride" in the chapter by that title in *Between Two Pillars: The Hero's Plight in "Samson Agonistes" and "Paradise Regained"* (Lanham, Md.: University Press of America, 2004), 25–39. See his attack on the critics who denigrate this reading (31).

jection is largely social—"The base degree to which I now am fall'n" (414), "at the Mill with slaves," "in slavish habit, ill-fitting weeds" (41, 122); it is a matter of "abject fortune" (169). His self-recrimination is for particular acts of folly and weakness, acts that he had (as Milton always insists) the power not to commit, and that violated both his pact with God and his status as "[t]hat Heroic, that Renown'd, / Irresistible *Samson*" (124–25)—both "Honor and Religion" (412).[78] He feels guilt, but most of all he feels shame. He has been, in an unforgettable word, a "blab" (495); he has been "ignoble / Unmanly, ignominious, infamous" (416–17)—all terms that take their force from (betraying) the heroic tradition. He has behaved, and this is perhaps the ultimate term of shame, "effeminately" (562, and see 410). None of this has to do with feeling ontologically disabled and morally polluted. He defends himself against charges that he feels are unfair (219–233, 1208–15), and the poem celebrates his regaining of "plain Heroic magnitude of mind" (1279). This occurs first when he refuses the command to entertain at Dagon's feast—"Can they think . . . that my mind ever / Will condescend to such absurd commands" (1336–38). Then the process of recovering "magnitude of mind" continues when, through what he experiences as "rousing motions" that turn his thoughts to doing "something extraordinary" (1382–83), he comes to be assured that at the feast he will do nothing unworthy of "[o]ur God, our Law, my Nation," and, last but not least, "myself" (1425).[79]

In the description of Samson resting his arms on the supporting pillars of the Philistine temple, there is a famous, and explicitly marked, ambiguity. Milton writes that Samson stood there "as one who pray'd / Or some great matter in his mind revolv'd" (1637–38).[80] Milton's point might well be that there is

---

78. On the consistency of Samson's assertion of his own free will and responsibility with Milton's commitment to theodicy in *Paradise Lost* and elsewhere, see John Rumrich, "Samson and the Excluded Middle," in *Altering Eyes: New Perspectives on "Samson Agonistes,"* ed. Mark R. Kelley and Joseph Wittreich (Newark: University of Delaware Press, 2002), 307–32.

79. Another connection between the poem and the heroic tradition (and to Achilles in particular) is Samson's inability to conceive of old age as anything but "contemptible" (572). Dalila's vision of a cheerful and coddled old age for Samson (925–97) is utterly rejected. Manoa's imagination of Samson's old age is contradictory. On the one hand, Samson will be housebound, but honored ("sitting in the house, ennobl'd" [1491]), and on the other, his eyesight might be restored, so he could again do something "great" (1499–1501). Lana Cable, *Carnal Rhetoric: Milton's Iconoclasm and the Poetics of Desire* (Durham: Duke University Press, 1995), 177, notes Samson's "dread of further public humiliation."

80. On this moment as "radically indeterminate," see Stanley Fish, "Spectacle and Evidence in *Samson Agonistes,*" *Critical Inquiry* 15 (1989): 587; on the importance of the (non)connective

no difference between the two accounts. The heroic and the religious merge. When the Chorus credits Samson with having experienced an inward illumination, this illumination is represented as having led Samson to rouse "his fiery virtue" (1690–91). The image of the phoenix, so important for Christological readings of the poem, is treated in rationalistic terms as virtue reviving and producing an afterlife of "fame" (1706–7).[81]

Samson's self-immolation, the poem insists, is not willed as such but was an unavoidable consequence of his action as a heroic "deliverer" (1271), a deliverer presented exactly as Machiavelli presented such a figure at the end of *The Prince*: a figure "ordained by God," who, through might, can provide an occasion in which entirely new and liberating forms can be impressed on a body politic that has been reduced to sheer matter if, to return to Milton, the relevant group of people "[f]ind courage to lay hold on this occasion" (1716).[82] The end of the poem celebrates Samson's historical identity in this way, just

---

"or" here and in Milton's poetry generally, see Peter C. Herman, *Destabilizing Milton: "Paradise Lost" and the Poetics of Incertitude* (New York: Palgrave Macmillan, 2005), 173, and chap. 2.

81. For the Christological reading, see Michael Krouse, *Milton's Samson and the Christian Tradition* (Princeton: Princeton University Press, 1949), and Albert R. Cirillo, "Time, Light, and the Phoenix: The Design of *Samson Agonistes*," in *Calm of Mind: Tercentenary Essays on "Paradise Regained" and "Samson Agonistes*," ed. Joseph Anthony Wittreich, Jr. (Cleveland: Case Western Reserve Press, 1971), esp. 228. Merritt Hughes has a lovely page of skepticism about the "phoenix-as-Christ" reading here in his introduction to the poem, *Complete Poems*, 542. William G. Madsen notes that despite the comparison of the phoenix and Christ being "a Christian commonplace," here "the phoenix is not used as a symbol of personal immortality, but as a symbol of the immortality of fame" (*From Shadowy Types to Truth: Studies in Milton's Symbolism* [New Haven: Yale University Press, 1968], 198). But Madsen's commitment to a typological reading forces him to see the poem as needing to be read in terms of the contrast with a more distinctively Christian set of values. In my view, Milton truly sees the final act of Samson as "glorious" (1660) and as needing military and historical, not spiritual completion.

82. See chapter 26 of Mark Musa's bilingual edition of Machiavelli's *The Prince*, 217 (see chap. 3, app. 1, n. 10). Victoria Kahn has urged me to consider that Machiavelli might be using the language of religion here purely ironically and instrumentally, as Machiavelli shows King Ferdinand of Spain successfully doing (in chapter 21), and as he himself perhaps does with regard to Moses in chapter 6 and in the rather heavy-handed language of Exodus here (219). This is possible, and would make Machiavelli highly consistent, but I am not sure that the final chapter of *The Prince* is not an uncharacteristic *cri de coeur*. In any case, Milton might well not have read this chapter (and chapter 6) ironically. For a general treatment of the consideration of "occasions" in *Samson* and in *Paradise Regained*, see David Norbrook, "Republican Occasions in *Paradise Regained* and *Samson Agonistes*," in *"Paradise Regained" in Context: Genre, Politics, Religion*, ed. Albert C. Labriola and David Loewenstein, special issue of *Milton Studies* 42 (2003), 122–48.

as it celebrates Samson's return to heroic status: "*Samson* hath quit himself / Like *Samson*, and heroicly hath finish'd / A life Heroic" (1687–1711). The idea of a figure acting "like himself"—living up to, performing, the ideal version of himself—is a standard feature of the heroic tradition; Ovid wrote of Achilles acting *par sibi*, and Milton is following Shakespeare and many Elizabethan-Jacobean playwrights in adopting this language.[83] Samson enacts his identity, attains "eternal fame" (1717), and provides his nation with what both Milton and Machiavelli call a special sort of *occasione*. But the moment must be seized. As Machiavelli explains, in a sentence that sounds strikingly like Milton, "God does not want to do everything, so as not to take from us our free will and the part of the glory that belongs to us."[84]

Samson Agonistes does, it must be said, include an alternative version of heroism, one much more Christian-sounding. The passage in question is, in fact, the one set of lines in the poem that seem to rely on a distinctively Christian vocabulary or conception. It follows a rousing, almost twenty-line rhapsody on the deliverer in the heroic mold, the queller of tyrants, "with plain Heroic magnitude of mind / And celestial vigor arm'd," who "with winged expedition" executes "[h]is errand on the wicked, who surpris'd / Lose thir defense, distracted and amaz'd" (1268–86). After this, Milton (or the Chorus) draws up short with, "But patience is more oft the exercise / Of saints" (1287–88). "Saints" does suggest Christianity, but the description of these figures, as "each his own Deliverer" is an odd way to speak about salvation, and it turns out that the "deliverance" in question is "over all / That tyranny or fortune can inflict" (1291). It is a mental victory, in this world, and the conception of heroism involved turns out to be Stoic rather than Christian.[85] Moreover, this briefly sketched (five-line) conception of private, individualist mental triumph ("each his own Deliverer") is hardly comparable to being a magnificent force for righteousness like the historical queller of tyrants. The Chorus is clearly trying to resign itself to the idea that Samson, given his disability, might have to settle for this latter, clearly inferior kind of "exercise."[86]

83. See Hereward T. Price, " 'Like Himself,' " *Review of English Studies* 16 (1940): 178–81 (the use in *Samson* is mentioned on 180). Brower, *Hero and Saint*, 121 (see chap. 3, n. 39), points out the Ovidian origin of the phrase (*Metamorphoses* 12:617–19).

84. *The Prince*, 219.

85. See Madsen, *From Shadowy Types*, 188.

86. In *Toward "Samson Agonistes": The Growth of Milton's Mind* (Princeton: Princeton University Press, 1978), Mary Ann Radzinowicz sees the political message of *Samson* as of this sort: "Milton anticipated that other men might learn one way one to free themselves for political ends" (178–79). But I am not sure what licenses her then to privilege Manoa's vision of

But what of *Paradise Regained*? It was published together with *Samson Agonistes* in 1671, although the works are not necessarily a matched pair. The title page suggests only a weak connection between them: "Paradise Regain'd. A Poem." appears in very large letters ("Regain'd" and "Poem" largest), followed, in smaller (but still large) print, by "In IV Books," and then, in small type, "To which is added," and then in italics the size of "In IV Books," *Samson Agonistes*.[87] The layout and typography do not suggest a strong (or any) connection between the poems, and the many critics who see *Samson* as a prefiguration of Christianity, or as showing the superiority of Christianity, need the order of the works to be reversed.[88] Moreover, there is at least a possibility—one that I accept—that *Samson* was composed a good deal earlier than *Paradise Regained*, perhaps early in the Restoration.[89] The two poems are

---

the "Monument" that he will raise for Samson "inflaming" the individual "valiant youth" over Manoa's vision, earlier in his final speech, of Samson having provided the Israelites with a collective "occasion." Moreover, it seems odd to read the "valiant youth" passage as referring to spiritual struggle. "Matchless valor, and adventures high" (1740) does not seem to point in that direction.

87. The title page is reproduced in *Complete Poems*, 470.

88. Stephen Dobranski has no doubt that the poems were meant to be printed together, but, as he says, the "more complicated" and important consideration remains whether Milton conceived of these works as a pair, in the published order, "or whether their combined publication was decided at the printing house" ("Text and Context for *Paradise Regain'd* and *Samson Agonistes*," in Kelley and Wittreich, *Altering Eyes*, 30). Dobranski sees the latter option as quite likely (32–33), but thinks that the lines printed as "Omissa" to *Samson* may have been added by Milton when it was decided to print the two works together (46). Various clever reasons have been advanced for the "reversed" ordering (see Joseph Wittreich, *Interpreting "Samson Agonistes"* [Princeton: Princeton University Press, 1986], chap. 7, and John T. Shawcross, *Paradise Regain'd: "Worthy T'Have Not Remain'd So Long Unsung"* [Pittsburgh: Duquesne University Press, 1988], 107–11), but the fact that cleverness is called for counts against the typological pairing.

89. For the dating of Samson that I accept, see A. S. Woodhouse, "*Samson Agonistes* and Milton's Experience," *Transactions of the Royal Society of Canada*, ser. 3, 43 (1949): 157–75. In "Milton, *Samson Agonistes*, and the Restoration," Blair Worden concurs with Woodhouse; Worden detects in the poem the influence of the trials of the regicides in 1662 (*Culture and Society in the Stuart Restoration: Literature, Drama, History*, ed. Gerald MacLean [Cambridge: Cambridge University Press, 1995], 111–36). An obvious question that confronts those of us who see *Samson* as composed five or more years before *Paradise Regained* is to explain why Milton did not publish *Samson* before 1671. Dobranski makes the intriguing suggestion that the printer might have thought *Paradise Regained* too short to publish by itself, and asked Milton whether he had anything else on hand to add to it. Milton may have seen the publication of *Paradise Regained* as an occasion to put into print a poem with much more incendiary politics, a work that

very different, and the critics who contrast them are indeed on solid ground, though I do not believe that Milton wrote *Samson* with any sense that its view was incomplete, or in need of Christian "correction." On the view of the dating of Milton's works that I accept, *Paradise Regained* is Milton's last major statement. It is there, if anywhere, that Milton finally rejects both the heroic tradition and classical ethics, and adopts the culturally available alternative point of view.

I will argue that he does not do so, that *Paradise Regained* does not sustainedly or even primarily adopt the Reformation critique. It employs, I will argue, a particular version of classical ethics and of the heroic tradition, but the framework remains one in which the central terms are honor, virtue, and merit. It may well add a virtue, that of faith, to the classical set, and this is a significant and potentially unsettling addition—partly substituting (as in *Samson*) waiting for a "motion" for rational deliberation—but the poem may well think of faith as a virtue, as something to which effort and will are relevant.[90] Moreover, most of the "action" of the poem is focused less on the demonstration of faith and more on the demonstration of intellectual and moral clarity. *Paradise Regained* participates much more fully in the Stoic transvaluation of values—the framework in which political and social terms are transformed into psychological and moral ones—than it does in the Christian one, in which love is defined against rather than in terms of justice, and in which abjection and scandal are embraced.[91] *Paradise Regained* sees "the exercise / Of saints" much more positively than *Samson Agonistes* does, but it does not, as we shall see, significantly alter the content of the exercise, the achievement of succeeding

---

he had been keeping from print for this reason. On this (admittedly speculative) account, Milton would have seen *Paradise Regained* as acting as a kind of "beard" for *Samson*.

90. In *Paradise Regained*, 2.247–51, Milton's Jesus distinguishes between a sheer divine gift and a virtue. He says of the forty days that he spent in the desert without food and without appetite "that Fast / To Virtue I impute not," whereas in his situation at the moment of utterance, he does feel hunger, and is, presumably, exercising a virtue. The idea is clearly that a virtue, or any praiseworthy action or state, requires effort.

91. On the Stoics, see, for instance, Malcolm Schofield, *The Stoic Idea of the City* (see chap. 1, n. 19). For the Christian "revaluation of all the values of antiquity," see Nietzsche, *Beyond Good and Evil* (see chap. 3, n. 0), 60 (sec. 46), and Anders Nygren, *Agape and Eros* (see chap. 1, n. 27). For a Catholic insistence on the uniqueness and difference of Christian values, see Mark D. Jordan, *The Invention of Sodomy in Christian Theology* (Chicago: University of Chicago Press, 1997), especially the remarkable "Postlude after St. Ambrose."

in "mental fight." To put my argument in a nutshell, the alternative to classical heroism, for Milton, is another kind of classical heroism.[92]

Milton's choice of subject is always significant. To choose the temptation in the wilderness as the key moment in the life of Jesus allows for a more obviously straightforward continuity with classical ethics than, to take the obvious instance, a focus on the crucifixion might, especially if the latter were to involve any sense of willed abjection and passive physical suffering. Even Socrates, after all, died a noble, tranquil, and cheerful death, a death that involved legal condemnation but not abjection or shame.[93] The only "humiliation" that we see Milton's Jesus undergoing is that of having to listen to Satan's proposals and arguments, and to have to take the (rather minor) trouble to respond to them. Satan is the figure in the poem imagined as "[e]jected, emptied, gaz'd, unpitied, shunn'd" (1.414)—"emptied" is especially rich here (see Phil. 2:7). Satan is the figure to whom shame accrues (see 4.14, 22), whereas, as Satan rightly says, the encounter in the desert gains Jesus "honor" (4.207). The role of Milton's Jesus in the poem is to manifest "amplitude of mind" (2.139). That "his great duel" is not of arms is merely to specify the kind of heroism that he is going to be called upon to manifest, not to question the whole conception of heroic virtue. Milton's Jesus is a figure of immense dignity. He is a figure of temperance in the full Aristotelian sense. The temperate person (*sophron*) is not subject to moral struggle; if he were, he would only manifest the nonvirtue of continence (*NE* 1146a9–15, 1152a1–4). The *sophron* cannot truly be tempted. Thomas N. Corns sees the Jesus of *Paradise Regained* as Milton's most flattering self-portrait.[94]

But taking Milton's poem as representing Jesus, what is most striking in the presentation is what is missing from it. Not only is moral effort missing, but also totally absent is love—as either a topic or a motive. S. B. Liljegren is right in stating that the hero of *Paradise Regained* "does not want to save mankind out of love." Liljegren oversimplifies the matter in describing this figure as merely wanting "to achieve a splendid career," but Liljegren is again right in

---

92. Compare Norbrook, "Republican Occasions," 142.

93. See "*Felix* Socrates" in Gregory Vlastos, *Socrates: Ironist and Moral Philosopher* (Ithaca: Cornell University Press, 1991), 233–35.

94. "It is not that the Son invites the wayfaring Christians to fashion themselves in an *imitatio Christi*; rather, Milton offers a divine figure made in his own image, a daring, almost impudent, *imitatio Miltoni*" (Thomas N. Corns, "'With Unalter'd Brow': Milton and the Son of God," *Milton Studies* 42 [2003]: 108); and see Fallon, *Milton's Peculiar Grace*, 239–50, esp. 242: "The Son offers a model of the kind of perfectibility that Milton smuggled into his own self-representation."

stating that the goal is "the feat of saving a few valuable souls."[95] Milton's Jesus does not want to save *sinners*.[96] As Andrew Milner notes, one of the deepest connections of *Paradise Regained* to Milton's earlier work is his "continued adherence to the notion of a meritocracy."[97] Milton's Jesus is obsessed with the question of worth. He rejects (before even meeting Satan) the idea of militarily liberating Israel in favor of the "more humane, more heavenly" idea of having persuasion "do the work of fear," but this strategy is immediately readjusted to be seen as applying only to "the erring Soul / Not wilfully misdoing" (1.215–25). The rest, "the stubborn," are indeed to be left to the (presumably physical) work of fear (1.226). In responding to Satan's proposal—"Deliverance of thy brethren, those ten Tribes," through an alliance with the Parthians against Rome—Jesus insists that the captive tribes "themselves were they / Who wrought their own captivity" (3.414–15).[98] He notes that God may, at some future time, "bring them back repentant and sincere," but he does not see this as part of his mission. He does not weep for Jerusalem.[99] Similarly, when Satan in book 4 suggests, with regard to Rome, that Jesus may "[a] victor people free from servile yoke," Jesus insists that in the degeneration from virtuous republic to luxurious empire, the Romans have been "[d]eservedly made vassal" (4.134).[100] "What wise and valiant man," Jesus asks, "would seek to free / Those thus degenerate?" (4.144–45).

95. Sten Bodvar Liljegren, *Studies in Milton* (1918; rpt. ed., New York: Haskell House, 1967), xxxviii.

96. For Jesus's project "not to call the righteous, but sinners" (Mark 2:17) as the essence of the Christian "transvaluation" of classical values, see Nygren, *Agape and Eros*, 68. On Milton's reluctance to imagine actual sinners being saved, one of my Press readers brilliantly pointed out "an early instance of this in the opening of *Comus* [*A Mask*] in which the Attendant spirit will only come down to earth to recue the exceedingly virtuous, and will not soil his feathers for the rest."

97. Andrew Milner, *Milton and the English Revolution* (Totowa, N.J.: Barnes and Noble, 1981), 169.

98. Corns, "'With Unalter'd Brow,'" points out the continuity between these lines and Milton's prose of the 1650s with regard to the ethical conditions, on a national scale, for effective and lasting political action in history (116–18).

99. On Jesus's tears as setting him apart from classical ethics, even in Socrates, see chapter 1 above.

100. On the sources for this view of the decline of Rome, especially in Sallust, see Martin Dzelzainis, "Milton's Classical Republicanism," in *Milton and Republicanism*, ed. David Armitage, Armand Himy, and Quentin Skinner (Cambridge: Cambridge University Press, 1995), 3–24, esp. 22–23.

As the above question suggests, Milton's Jesus is as concerned with merit in himself as in those he will and will not save. This returns us to *megalopsychia*. Merritt Hughes plausibly takes "amplitude of mind" at 2.139 as a translation of "magnanimity."[101] We recall the definition of magnanimity in *On Christian Doctrine* as the virtue shown "when in seeking or not seeking riches, advantages, or honors, in avoiding them or accepting them, a man behaves himself as befits his own dignity." The example there cited is the behavior of Christ "when he rejected the empire of the world" (736).[102] In *Paradise Regained*, Milton's Jesus sees his behavior in precisely these terms: "To give a kingdom has been thought / Greater and nobler done, and to lay down / *Far more magnanimous* than to assume" (2.481–83; emphasis mine). Magnanimity is the touchstone. This means that Milton's Jesus will have to deal with the question of honor and glory, since *megalopsychia*, as Aristotle explains, fundamentally involves the question of honor or glory since this virtue concerns management of "the greatest things," and honor is "the greatest of external goods" (*NE* 1123b15–20). The discussion of glory that opens book 3 is one of the richest and most complex passages in *Paradise Regained*; it fully reveals the uneasy mix of Milton's values, and his inability—or unwillingness—to maintain the Reformation perspective.

Satan is at his shrewdest in this discussion. He picks up on Jesus's praise of magnanimity, characterizing glory in heroic and world-renouncing terms, and its possession as the greatest pleasure. Glory is "the reward / That sole excites to high achievements . . . [the] most erected Spirits . . . who *all pleasures else despise*" (3.25–28; emphasis mine). Jesus's response to this is an odd mixture. He first rejects glory as nothing but "fame, / The people's praise," which is worthless because the common people are "a herd confus'd, / A miscellaneous rabble, who extol / Things vulgar, and well weigh'd, scarse worth the praise" (3.47–51). As Liljegren notes, it is "difficult to imagine" the figure who speaks this way of "rabble" as "willing to die for publicans, shoemakers, and tailors."[103]

101. *Complete Poems*, 497. Hughes's "The Christ of *Paradise Regained* and the Renaissance Heroic Tradition," *Studies in Philology* 35 (1938): 254–277, is useful on medieval and Renaissance versions of the heroic tradition, but loses sight of (and downplays) tensions and contradictions within and among traditions. For this tendency, especially among the very learned, see Strier, *Resistant Structures*, chap. 1 (see intro., n. 15).

102. Interestingly, with regard to the matter of asceticism, Milton sees Jesus as also exemplifying proper acceptance of honors. Accepting the ass to ride into Jerusalem is Milton's instance.

103. Liljegren, *Studies in Milton*, xxxviii. There are certainly connections between Milton's Jesus and the radical (Protestant) religious culture of the Interregnum and Restoration, especially the Quakers, but populism is not one of them. There is some unclarity about this (and

Yet this way of speaking is characteristically Miltonic (compare "the worthless approbation of an inconstant, irrational, and Image-doting rabble" at the end of *Eikonoklastes*),[104] and it is squarely within the classical tradition. Aristotle notes that if the great-souled man "is honored by just anyone," he "will entirely disdain it" (*NE* 1124a10). It is simply not true that "Christ's definition of magnanimity as involving more often a repudiation of honors than an acceptance of them has little warrant in the Aristotelian tradition."[105] For Aristotle, to attain true honor and gain the highest self-approbation and the largest share of "what is noble," the great-souled, properly proud person will make great sacrifices and even die for others (*NE* 1169a18–36).

In a discussion of Scipio Africanus as a model (3.100–104), Milton's Jesus provides something like a Reformation critique (Scipio, we recall, was one of Luther's examples). Yet the terms of Jesus' critique are not clear, and the passage is remarkably equivocal.[106] Jesus ends this speech by asserting, "I seek not mine but his / Who sent me, and thereby witness whence I am" (3.106–7). Satan's response to this is perhaps his most brilliant moment—certainly the moment that gets the biggest "rise" out of the Son (the only one to which he "fervently" replies [3.121]). Satan presents Jesus as unlike God in despising glory and also in being classical and elitist. God seeks glory, and does so in a democratic and promiscuous way, "from all men good or bad, / Wise or unwise, no difference, no exception" (3.114–15). Hughes's note on these lines states that Satan "twists" the doctrine of the Westminster Catechism here, but I cannot see where there is any misstatement in the speech. Jesus answers not by denying but by affirming this premise—"And reason." But the next assertion that Milton's Jesus makes would truly render Satan's claim nugatory. Jesus presents the Father as acting "only to show forth his goodness . . . freely" (3.123–25).

This is close to the vision of *agape* (though "show forth" sounds slightly calculating). Yet the vision of undifferentiating and undemanding outpouring is not sustained. The framework immediately shifts back to one of desert and demands—"what could he less expect / Than glory?" (3.126–29). So it turns

---

about suffering in the poem) in David Loewenstein's "The Kingdom Within: Radical Religious Culture and the Politics of *Paradise Regained*," *Literature and History*, ser. 3, 3 (1994): 63–89.

104. See *Complete Prose*, 3:601.

105. Barbara K. Lewalski, *Milton's Brief Epic: The Genre, Meaning, And Art of "Paradise Regained"* (Providence: Brown University Press, 1966), 244.

106. Since the passage is hypothetical ("*if* young African for fame"), it does not affirm what Scipio's motives were, and it keeps qualifying itself ('The deed becomes unprais'd, *the man at least*, / And loses, *though but verbal*, his reward'). Milton seems unwilling to let Scipio's deed become "unprais'd," or even to let his motive be seen as truly base.

out that God, like Scipio, does seek reward, "though but verbal." Yet this focus on the divine nature does then produce one of the clearest assertions in the poem of the perspective from which, as Calvin says, man truly finds "nothing in himself with which to direct his life aright":

> But why should man seek glory? who of his own
> Hath nothing, and to whom nothing belongs
> But condemnation, ignominy, and shame?
>
> (3.134–36)

Yet there is a slight but significant moment of slippage at the end of this speech. After expounding further on human wretchedness and presumption, Jesus adds:

> Yet so much bounty is in God, such grace,
> That who advance his glory, not their own,
> Them he himself to glory will advance.
>
> (3.142–44)

The trouble with this passage is that it has the effect of making God's "bounty" and "grace" motivated. Satan is right; God does seek glory—so much so that he will share some of it with those who acknowledge the priority of his.[107] There seems, in other words, to be something like a deal here, something like the basis for a strategy. This analysis may seem excessively rigorous, but the clearest expounders of the Reformation conception of "grace alone" recognized the subtle as well as the obvious ways in which a position so fundamentally counterintuitive could be undermined. Even the shadow of a bargain would do it. To return to the comparison of Milton with George Herbert, when the speaker of Herbert's "The Holdfast" gets to the point of resolving "to confesse, that nothing is our own," he still has to take the further step of recognizing that even that cannot serve as a basis for action: "But to have nought is ours, not to confesse / That we have nought."[108] Milton does not work to remove the shadow

---

107. Mayer, *Between Two Pillars*, finds these lines completely puzzling after the lines on human sinfulness quoted above ("nothing . . . But condemnation"). Rather than seeing Milton as failing to sustain the (unnatural to him) Calvinist perspective, Mayer reads the lines on God's grace to those "who advance his glory" as applying only to Jesus himself (224). This is not a textually plausible reading, though one can understand Mayer's puzzlement.

108. See Strier, *Love Known*, 66–74, and on bargaining, chap. 4.

of a deal—a deal in which the currency is glory. Nietzsche remarked that "he who despises himself nevertheless esteems himself thereby, as a despiser."[109] As Anders Nygren explains, "one who thinks of humility as a way to fellowship with God, and feels that his own humility gives him an imperishable worth in God's sight, is at bottom anything but humble."[110] Compare "I seek not mine but his / Who sent me, *and thereby witness whence I am*" (emphasis mine).[111]

But surely book 4 of *Paradise Regained* is definitive. The classical philosophers get very short shrift. Jesus's praise of Socrates's self-sacrifice—"For truth's sake suffering death unjust" (3.98)—is apparently forgotten. Socrates's claim to "know" nothing is now taken at face value (4.292–93). The critique stumbles a bit, however, when we hear of the philosophers who "in virtue plac'd felicity" (4.296). They are not criticized for this but for insisting (as Aristotle did) on "virtue join'd with riches and long life" (4.298).[112] Not surprisingly, the longest and most substantive critique is of the Stoics, who did "in virtue plac[e] felicity." Up to this point in the poem, as Milton well knew, Jesus has looked much like a Stoic sage; his achievement has been, through moral and intellectual clarity, to remain "unmov'd" (3.386). The critique of Stoicism should, therefore, make the specifically religious framework of the poem distinct. The charge against the Stoic is pride—"Philosophic pride / By him call'd virtue" (4.300–301). This is the Reformation critique, the presentation of the pagan heroes as, through pride, "never less upright and more vile than when they shone in their highest virtues." The Stoics'

> virtuous man
> Wise, perfect in himself, and all possessing
> Equal to God, oft shames not to prefer,
> As fearing God nor man, contemning all
> Wealth, pleasure, pain or torment, death and life,
> Which when he lists, he leaves.
>
> (4.301–6)

The critique of Stoic pride, however, does not end here. After "when he lists, he leaves," the sentence continues, "or boasts he can." This qualification marks

109. Nietzsche, *Beyond Good and Evil*, 81 (sec. 78); translation emended.

110. Nygren, *Agape and Eros*, 121.

111. Mayer, *Between Two Pillars*, 225, picks up on the oddity of this.

112. See the discussion on whether virtue alone is sufficient for happiness in book 1 of the *Nicomachean Ethics* (1098a19–1101a21).

a major departure from the Reformation position. The trouble with the Stoic sage is that "all his tedious talk is but vain boast" (4.307). The problem, in other words, is not pride but vanity, improper pride—pride as defined in the section on *magnanimitas* in *Christian Doctrine*: "when a man is more puffed up than he ought to be, with no or insufficient justification." This is the Aristotelian rather than the Reformation critique. The problem with "contemning all" on philosophical grounds is not that it is based on or leads to pride but that it cannot (supposedly) be done. The sage is a boaster and a fraud.

Milton returns to the Reformation critique in Jesus's conclusion on the philosophers' ignorance "[o]f how the world began, and how man fell," and on their seeing virtue "in themselves" (4.311–15). But again this perspective is not maintained. Jesus shifts from insisting that the Hebrew scriptures contain essential truths unknown to the classical Greeks to asserting that the scriptures teach what the Greeks teach, only better. This latter perspective emerges when the subject shifts from presentation of religious matters ("Thir Gods ridiculous") to presentation of moral and political ones. The preeminence of the scriptures in teaching the "solid rules of Civil Government" is primarily a matter of style ("majestic unaffected") and method ("in them is plainest taught" [4.361]). And the praise of inspiration as the only reliable source of significant knowledge comes to an abrupt halt "where moral virtue is express'd / By light of Nature" (4.352–53).[113] This is, as Arnold Stein says, "an important second thought"; moral virtue escapes the critique.[114] Moreover, the ambiguity as to whether the critique is of achievement or of shamming continues in the discussion of the Orators and "Statists"—"lovers of their Country, *as may seem*" (4.355; emphasis mine)—and the ambiguity continues, past this dialogue, into the final temptation. The question of human moral capacity remains unsettled.

In puzzling over Jesus's status as "Son of God" in some special sense, Satan asserts that what he has seen so far, though very impressive, has been "th' utmost of mere man, both wise and good, / Not more" (4.535–36). He explains that "Honors, Riches, Kingdoms, Glory / Have been before contemn'd,

113. I do not think that the poem employs the distinction between "knowledge" and "wisdom" on which Lewalski bases her analysis of the Athens temptation in *Milton's Brief Epic*, 290–95. The poem claims to find "all knowledge" in scripture, and it does not designate "wisdom" as specifically religious or scriptural. At the end of book 2, Jesus presents reigning over one's passions as the discipline that characterizes "every wise and virtuous man."

114. Arnold Stein, *Heroic Knowledge: An Interpretation of "Paradise Regained" and "Samson Agonistes"* (Minneapolis: University of Minnesota Press, 1957), 109.

and may again" (537–38). And he is not lying or misrepresenting. Earlier in the poem, Jesus himself had cited republican heroes who could "contemn / Riches though offer'd from the hand of Kings" (2.445–46). So it seems that it is possible for humans to do what Milton presented the Stoics as claiming to do—"contemning all / Wealth, pleasure, pain or torment, death and life" (recall Socrates, "For truth's sake suffering death unjust"). The "utmost of mere man, both wise and good" seems truly worthy. And even when Milton represents a miracle—Jesus simply standing on the spire of the Temple—Milton and many of his readers would have known that to "stand" against temptation, unmoved, was a familiar trope of Stoic heroism. We return to the end of Milton's nineteenth sonnet, where to "stand and wait" is a military posture.[115]

Even in the two epics, then, Milton does not consistently participate in the Reformation attack on the dignity of man as a rational and (potentially) self-governing creature. For Milton, "sufficient grace" may be needed to enable virtue (as Aquinas also believed and, as Milton says, "the philosophers" did not know), but *Christian Doctrine* also makes it clear that God "considers all [persons] worthy of sufficient grace" (193). Moral achievement is genuinely possible and genuinely to be respected. Milton never praises abjection and he does not sustainedly exhort us, with Calvin, to be "consumed with the awareness" of our own ethical poverty. Milton never believed that the person who, "confident in his understanding and uprightness, becomes bold and urges himself to the duties of virtue" is to be scorned and mocked (*Institutes*, 2.1.1). Milton did not ultimately believe that all pride is improper. We must devoutly acknowledge where our gifts come from; and we must "improve" them; and we must thank God that we are not as other—most—men are.

APPENDIX

"Lordly Command?"

As far as I can determine, Milton was never, in any significant matter, a normal anything. When he went to write a masque, he wrote one that attacked festivity, luxury, and spectacle; when he went to write a pastoral elegy in English, he wrote one that condemned most of its own pastoral machinery as "false surmise"; when he wrote an epic based on classical models, he included a sustained mockery of military encounters. So why should we expect Milton to have been a "normal" Presbyterian? My answer, of course, is that he wasn't

115. On the politics of this, see Norbrook, "Republican Occasions," esp. 136–37.

such a thing—and one can easily determine what a "normal" Presbyterian was. But I do not mean to suggest by this that Milton was never "really" a Presbyterian. By the end of his life, he was probably a sect of one, but in 1641 he was truly committed to what Richard Bancroft had mocked as "the pretended holy discipline."[1] As we have seen, however, Milton's reasons for this commitment were quite idiosyncratic and, well, Miltonic; self-esteem was at the center of it. What I want to focus on here is *how* Milton argued for this position. When one understands this—together with the substance of his position—one can see Milton's development with regard to the church as both continuous and coherent.

In making this claim, however, I am running in flat opposition to a mighty force in Milton studies, one by the name of Stanley Eugene Fish. Fish holds that there is a sharp break between the Milton of the antiprelatical tracts—the tracts against church-government by bishops and archbishops—and the Milton of the divorce tracts. The Milton of the antiprelatical tracts, and especially of *The Reason of Church-Government Urg'd against Prelaty*, was, according to Fish, a text man, a writer who justified his position primarily and even solely on appeals to biblical authority, literally understood, while the Milton of the divorce tracts is an antiliteralist committed to "interpretation" and to general principles rather than to texts.[2] This view—although Fish does not, of course, put it this way—makes the Milton of the antiprelatical tracts into what I am calling a "normal" Presbyterian, since the appeal to biblical passages, literally understood, was the normal way of arguing for the Presbyterian position in church-government. One appealed to Paul, especially to the epistles to Timothy and Titus.[3]

1. [Richard Bancroft,] *A survay of the pretended holy discipline; Contayning the beginninges, successe, parts, proceedings, authority, and doctrine of it: with some of the manifold, and materiall repugnances, varieties and uncertaineties, in that behalfe* (London: Printed by John Wolfe, 1593).

2. For the appeal to authority in *The Reason of Church-Government*, see Stanley Fish, "Reason in *The Reason of Church-Government*," in *Self-Consuming Artifacts* (Berkeley: University of California Press, 1972), 265–302 (hereafter cited by page in the text); for the divorce tracts as a new direction in Milton's textual interpretation, see Fish, "Wanting a Supplement: The Question of Interpretation in Milton's Early Prose," in *Politics, Poetics, and Hermeneutics in Milton's Prose*, ed. David Loewenstein and James Grantham Turner (Cambridge: Cambridge University Press, 1990), 41–68.

3. See Calvin, *Institutes*, 4.3.4–9; Thomas Cartwright, *Second Admonition to Parliament*, in *Puritan Manifestoes: A Study of the Origin of the Puritan Revolt*, ed. W. H. Frere and C. E. Douglas, (London: SPCK, 1907), 80–133; and the works of the "Smectymnuans," surveyed in

Fish argues that Milton's major pamphlet on church-government "never progresses beyond its original assertion: church-government by Presbyters and Deacons is commanded of God" (271). A correlate of this, for Fish, is that since *The Reason of Church-Government* entirely works by appealing to inspired biblical authority, it not only doesn't appeal to reason but in fact works to undermine and mock reason, so that reason is identified with prelacy, and the good reader of the tract learns to disregard its discursive structure entirely (275–77). A lovely paradox emerges: there is no reason in *The Reason of Church-Government* (just as there is no progress in *The Pilgrim's Progress*).[4] If this view of the place of reason and of biblical literalism in *The Reason of Church-Government* is correct, then there is indeed a sharp break in Milton's development between this pamphlet (and all the antiprelatical ones) and the divorce tracts, since the latter appeal to reason constantly. But if one doesn't see *The Reason of Church-Government* as working in this paradoxical way, one can see Milton's development (as I have said) as continuous and coherent.

I am afraid that with regard to Fish's view of *The Reason of Church-Government*, I find myself standing with the cynics in *The Tempest*. When Antonio says of Gonzalo's view of the island that Gonzalo "misses not much," Sebastian adds, "No; he doth but mistake the truth totally" (2.1.57–58). I do not think that *The Reason of Church-Government* (1) renounces reason, (2) only appears to progress and argue, or (3) supports its positions primarily through appeals to particular passages in the Bible literally understood. Obviously, I will have to do a good deal of "clubbing quotations" with Fish.[5] But before doing so, I want to give some sense of what a position of the sort that Fish ascribes to Milton actually sounds like. One of the odd things about *Self-Consuming Artifacts* is that Fish never tries to identify contemporary (sixteenth- or seventeenth-century) versions of the positions that he ascribes to his various authors. As I have shown elsewhere, Fish ascribes to George Herbert—explicitly, and at great length—a position that Calvin specifically remarks on and condemns as "Manichean."[6] With regard to *The Reason of Church-Government*, in seeing Milton's fundamental enemy as "the proposition that there is a place for reason

---

the introduction by Don. M. Wolfe to the Yale edition of Milton's *Complete Prose*, 1:76–88 (see chap. 6, n. 36). On the surprising complexity of the Puritan appeal to biblical authority, see John S. Coolidge, *The Pauline Renaissance in England: Puritanism and the Bible* (Oxford: Clarendon, 1970), chap. 1.

4. On *Pilgrim's Progress*, see *Self-Consuming Artifacts*, chap. 4.

5. As in chapter 6, all quotations from The *Reason of Church-Government* (*RCG*), are from volume 1 of the *Complete Prose*. For Milton's dislike of having to "club quotations," see 822.

6. See Strier, *Love Known*, 61–65 (see intro., n. 53).

in the determination of church-government" (277), Fish allies Milton with Reformation antirationalism. There is no doubt that such a thing exists. Luther is the source of it. Luther constantly urged his readers and auditors to "go to the very head of this beast which is called Reason, which is the fountainhead and headspring of all mischiefs"; he argued that part of what it meant for every Christian to be a priest is that "he offereth up and killeth his own reason."[7] This is a tradition that George Herbert actually does fit into.[8] Milton, even in his most Pauline mode, when he attacks "the weak mightiness of mans reasoning" (*RCG*, 827), never sounds like that. Reason plays a nonparadoxical role in *The Reason of Church-Government*.

Let us begin as Fish sensibly does, with the beginning of the tract:

> In the publishing of humane laws, which for the most part aime not beyond the good of civill society, to set them barely forth to the people without reason or Preface, like a physical prescript, or only with threatnings, as it were a lordly command, in the judgement of Plato was thought to be done neither generously or wisely. His advice was, seeing that persuasion certainly is a more winning, and more manlike way to keepe men in obedience then feare, that to such lawes as were of principall moment, there should be us'd as an induction, some well tempered discourse, shewing how good, how gainfull, how happy it must needs be to live according to honesty and justice, which being utter'd with those native colours and graces of speech, as true eloquence the daughter of vertue can best bestow upon her mothers praises, would so incite, and in a manner, charm the multitude into the love of that which is really good as to imbrace it ever after, not of custome and awe, which most men do, but of choice and purpose, with true and constant delight.

Fish finds this opening "conventional" and utterly unsurprising (266). It is always hard to argue with a claim of this sort, since one runs the risk, in doing so, of sounding ignorant or, even worse, naive. But where is the *argument* that this is a "thoroughly conventional" way to open a pamphlet on church- government? It seems to me quite an astonishing way to open such a pamphlet, and to have its only analogues in some passages in the preface and book 1 of Hooker's

---

7. *Commentary on Galatians*, in *Selections from his Writings*, 128, 131 (see intro., n. 48); see also B. A. Gerrish, *Grace and Reason: A Study in the Theology of Luther* (Oxford: Clarendon, 1962).

8. See Strier, *Love Known*, chap. 2.

Laws of Ecclesiastical Polity (1593), an elaborately written work on the other side of the question. Yet even Hooker is less classically oriented than this. To show that the author of this opening actually supports "lordly command[s]" would be something indeed. The framework is that of humanism, especially civic humanism—generosity, persuasion, manliness—and it strongly endorses the coincidence, endorsed by Aristotle in particular, of virtue, happiness, and prosperity.[9]

Fish takes the "well-tempered discourse" invoked here to mean, in the light of the title of the tract, "a formal logical structure, complete with propositions, counter-propositions, the arraying of evidence, and the drawing of conclusions concerning matters in doubt" (266). But, as James Turner points out, it is very odd to read the phrase in this way, since the last third of the passage is all about rhetoric, charm, and—the word with which the sentence (or period) ends—"delight."[10] Much of Fish's case rests on the title of Milton's pamphlet, but it is a striking feature of Fish's chapter on this work that he never cites the pamphlet's full title. Turner points out the importance of the word "urg'd" after "Reason of Church-Government"; it suggests, as Turner rightly says, passion and energy. The final words of the title are "against Prelaty." The pamphlet does not, at any moment (except perhaps in the first half of its title considered in itself) present itself as "a formal logical structure . . . concerning a matter in doubt."[11]

9. For references in the *Nicomachean Ethics*, see chapter 6, note 112, above. On civic humanism, see Baron, *The Crisis of the Early Italian Renaissance* (see intro., n. 4) and *In Search of Florentine Civic Humanism: Essays on the Transition from Medieval to Modern Thought* (Princeton: Princeton University Press, 1988); also Hankins, ed., *Renaissance Civic Humanism* (see intro., n. 4).

10. James Grantham Turner, "The Poetics of Engagement," in *Politics, Poetics, and Hermeneutics*, 263.

11. Thomas Corns also dissents from Fish's reading of *The Reason of Church-Government*, but Corns does so because he sees the pamphlet as less coherent than Fish does, as shifting between the "irreconcilable alternatives" of "Puritan orthodoxy," on the one hand, and the assertion of individual conscience and toleration for heterodoxy on the other (*Uncloistered Virtue: English Political Literature, 1640–1660* [Oxford: Clarendon, 1992], 36). I recognize what Corns sees as the tensions in the pamphlet, but think that his view that the positions involved cannot be held simultaneously and coherently is produced by his awareness of the splits within English Puritanism that develop later in the 1640s. I think that in January of 1642, the positions could all be held coherently within Milton's view at that time of Presbyterianism. Corns alternates between calling Milton's position in the pamphlet "complex" and calling it "confused" (36–37).

Moreover, the initial opposition of "manlike" persuasion to "lordly command" is never, as Fish states, "reversed" (268). Milton shows, following and acknowledging Josephus, that Moses (as the human "author" of the Pentateuch) followed Plato's recommendation and placed Genesis "as a prologue to his laws," so that the Jews "reading therein the universall goodnesse of God to all creatures in the Creation, and his peculiar favour to them ... might be mov'd to obey sincerely by knowing so good a reason of their obedience" (*RCG*, 747). Fish seems to think that obedience always implies constraint, but he has to acknowledge that "reason" does function positively in this sentence. He insists, however, that this is certainly not "a reason in the sense suggested by the title" of the pamphlet. But again, why not? It is not a full-scale argument, but an appeal to general principles and common sense. Why should we not take that to be what Milton has in mind all along? Why not take "reason" in the title as meaning the general principles, the *rationale* of church-government?

The passage that Fish takes to be the clincher for his view that Milton is "mocking" reason is indeed a crucial one, but its point is not to throw us back from reason to authority, but to encourage us to use our reason and our common sense (a faculty that Milton often alludes to, and Fish never). In the final sentence of the preface to the pamphlet, Milton insists on the "clearnesse" of scripture. This looks like the normal Presbyterian position—that church-government is "platformed out" in the New Testament—but this is not what Milton says. He says that the "clearnesse" of scripture is "the cause why in those places of holy writ, wherein is treated of Church-government, the reasons thereof *are not formally, and profestly set downe*" (*RCG*, 750; emphasis mine). This is because "to him that heeds attentively the drift and scope of Christian profession, they [the reasons] easily imply themselves." This is really quite startling. The distinction is not, as Fish says, between "formal reasoning ... and reasons whose force is independent of any chain of inferences" (270)—whatever that means—but between detailed recipes given in proof-texts and general principles. Milton is an odd Presbyterian indeed in giving up proof-texts, but that is what he does here. He is going to urge Presbyterianism against prelaty on the basis of general principles—"the drift and scope of Christian profession." The "clearnesse" of scripture is such that it demands and rewards an attentive reader who grasps large general principles—not through intuition or authority but through reasonableness and common sense. Fish is right that "reason" in the title does not mean abstract rationality; it does mean general

---

These are very different, and the former seems to me to be the more accurate designation, and not to rely on historical foresight or hindsight.

rationale. This kind of "reason" has more to do with reasonableness than with logical form.[12]

Let me try to give some sense, which Fish does not, of how Milton's pamphlet actually proceeds. Fish, adopting a phrase by A. C. Hamilton, sees it as "jumping up and down in one place" (271). Certainly Milton does begin by insisting "that church-government is prescrib'd in the gospell" (*RCG*, 750). But he asserts this on the basis of general rationality—"to say otherwise is unsound." His argument is an appeal to a general principle; it concerns "the importance throughout the whole life of man" of discipline (751)—Christian "discipline" is Milton's name for church-government, as it is Cartwright's. But Milton takes a startlingly optimistic, humanist view of what "discipline" can do, echoing Machiavelli on *virtù* against Fortuna, on the importance of military discipline, and even on human lawgivers ascribing divinity to their products.[13] Milton states that "whatever power or sway in mortall things weaker men have attributed to Fortune, I durst with more confidence . . . ascribe to the vigor, or the slacknesse of discipline." This is such a strong assertion of human capacity that, after "confidence," Milton has to add in parenthesis the words I have elided: "the honor of divine providence ever sav'd." To get to his point about the unlikeliness of God not prescribing, in some sense, ecclesiastical discipline in the Bible, Milton has to stress (as Machiavelli does) how unusual figures like Moses, Lycurgus, and Numa are, and how difficult it is to maintain discipline even in our ordinary domestic lives.[14] In relation to the general conditions of human social and political life, it doesn't make sense that God would leave so important a matter to chance (and therefore "to say otherwise is unsound").

The next chapter claims that to maintain that church-government is not "set down" in the Bible is "untrue." There is, contra Fish (279), a clear distinction between "unsound" on general principles and "untrue" in fact. Milton is

---

12. On the importance in moral philosophy of the distinction between formalization and reasonableness, see "Lifting the Veil," Charles Larmore's review of John Rawls's *Lectures on the History of Moral Philosophy* in the *New Republic* 224 (Feb. 5, 2001): 34.

13. See Machiavelli's *The Prince*, chap. 25, on *virtù* and Fortuna, and chaps. 12–14, on discipline (see chap. 3, app. 1, n. 10); and his *The Art of War*, intro. by Neal Wood, a revised edition of the 1965 Ellis Farnsworth translation [New York: Da Capo, 1990], books 1–3); on the uses of religion, see Machiavelli's *Discourses*, 1:11–15 (see chap. 6, n. 3). On Milton's lifelong engagement with the idea of discipline, I have profited from an unpublished essay by Kenneth Graham, "Milton and the Disciplinary Sphere," which is part of his ongoing project on early modern thinking about "discipline."

14. For Machiavelli on Numa and others, see *The Prince*, chap. 6. On the importance of this chapter, see Pocock, *The Machiavellian Moment*, 167–72 (see chap. 5, n. 99).

not jumping up and down in one place. But what is striking is how little time Milton spends on explicating the details of the church-government set down in scripture, rather than on the general point that it *must* somehow be there: "Did God take such delight in measuring out the pillars, arches, and doores of a materiall Temple" and "should not he rather now by his owne prescribed discipline have cast his line and levell upon the soule of man which is his rationall temple"? (*RCG*, 757–58). The interesting thing here is not the appeal to scripture—which is very general—but the way in which all the terms describing the new dispensation are radically metaphorical. One wouldn't know from a sentence like this that Milton was advocating a particular, concrete institutional system.[15] Even when Milton directs us to one of the proof-texts, there is a much stronger sense of metaphorical and spiritual than institutional focus:

> We may passe over the history of the Acts and other places, turning only to those Epistles of S. Paul to Timothy and Titus, where the spiritual eye may discerne more goodly and gracefully erected then all the magnificence of Temple or Tabernacle, such a heavenly structure of evangelick discipline . . . that it cannot be wonder'd if that elegant and artfull symmetry of the promised new temple in Ezechiel, and all those sumptuous things under the Law were made to signifie the inward beauty and splendor of the Christian Church thus govern'd. (758)

It is very difficult to say what the institutional referent of "evangelick discipline" is here. This "inward beauty" would seem to refer to what Milton, just above this passage, called "the lovely shape of vertues and graces" in the individual Christian. The focus keeps shifting from church-government, and the specifics thereof that are given in Paul's epistles, to the effect of church-government, conceived as instantiating certain general principles, on the spiritual and moral status of the individual Christian under this government.

---

15. This kind of thing is what leads Don Wolfe to assert that *The Reason of Church-Government* is "a weak presentation of Presbyterian claims" (Milton, *Complete Prose*, 1:199). Wolfe assumes that Milton's aim in the pamphlet is "to trace from the Scriptures only the perfect pattern of church government." Instead of disputing this premise, Fish accepts it, but takes the view that Milton must *mean* to be presenting a weak case in those terms. Needless to say, Milton can be seen as presenting a "weak" case for Presbyterianism in the pamphlet only if one assumes that Wolfe is correct about Milton's aim therein. Milton's departures from "normal" Presbyterian ways of arguing have nothing to do with a desire not to present a rational case. In fact, they have to do exactly with such a desire.

The key distinction, for Milton, is not between intuition, inspiration, or authority, on the one hand, and reason on the other, but as the above quotation about "the inward beauty and splendor of the Christian Church" suggests, between inward and outward. This is what allies Milton with Erasmus and the Puritans, and not with Luther and the anti-Puritans. As Roland Bainton puts it, in a brilliant comparison of Luther and Erasmus, for Luther "the great abuse in Catholicism" was "the exaltation of man," whereas for Erasmus, it was "the externalization of religion."[16] The "inward," for Milton (as for Erasmus), means the spiritual and the moral—these are not sharply distinguished—while the outward means the "carnal," the worldly, and the materially or physically oriented. To take "the beauty of holiness" to refer to outward, physical matters is to misunderstand and contradict "the very life of the Gospell" (*RCG*, 765).[17] After sounding for a while (more or less) like an ordinary or normal advocate for Presbyterianism,[18] Milton turns to his major and most characteristic point—that "there is a certain attraction and magnetick force between the religion and the ministeriall form thereof," so that, if, as in prelacy, "the Ministery be grounded in the worldly degrees of autority, honour, temporall jurisdiction, we see it with our eyes it will turne the inward power and purity of the Gospel into outward carnality of the law; evaporating and exhaling the internall worship into empty conformities and gay shewes" (766). "We see it with our eyes" does not refer to something mystical and intuitive here, but rather to something historical; it refers to the Laudian church in England.[19] This is Milton's most basic way of arguing—not through citing texts but through citing principles. And the most important principle of all is the protection and development of the precious internal liquid of "inward power and purity"—the spiritual and

16. Bainton, *Here I Stand*, 199 (see chap. 6, n. 9); also Garside, *Zwingli and the Arts* (see chap. 6, n. 9); and Carlos Eire, *The War against the Idols: The Reformation of Worship from Erasmus to Calvin* (Cambridge: Cambridge University Press, 1986).

17. Fully to grasp Milton's argument here, one would need to understand his use of typology, which he always saw as working disjunctively—to establish the contrast between Old Testament material types and New Testament spiritual realities. For discussions of this, which might be called "spiritualist typology," see William Madsen's *From Shadowy Types to Truth* (see chap. 6, n. 81) and Richard Reinitz's "The Separatist Background of Roger Williams' Argument for Religious Toleration," in *Typology and Early American Literature*, ed. Sacvan Bercovitch (Amherst: University of Massachusetts Press, 1972), 107–38.

18. Kenneth Graham has wisely reminded me that it is important to note that Milton does not *always* sound like a non-normal Presbyterian.

19. On Laud's quite literal understanding of "the beauty of holiness," see Peter Lake's "The Laudian Style," 161–85 (see chap. 6, n. 44).

moral purity of the individual, "whence every laudable and worthy enterprize issues forth" (841). Presbyterianism is superior to prelaty because the form of Presbyterianism conduces to this content.

The connection between Presbyterianism and moral virtue is what allows Milton's classicism and his humanism and his (perhaps still nascent) republicanism to enter into this pamphlet.[20] In arguing against the claim that episcopacy is needed or has been historically useful in preventing schisms in the church, Milton argues that the "apostolic" way of dealing with schism was to call a council—of which every Presbyterian consistory is a model—and to bar from such a gathering "no faithfull Christian . . . to whom knowledge and piety might give entrance" (*RCG*, 789). The apostles rejoiced in such fellowship, and—here Milton warms to his task—"like those heroick patricians of Rome (if we may use such a comparison) hasting to lay downe their dictatorships, they rejoys't to call themselves and to be as fellow Elders among their brethren" (791). The "heroick patricians of Rome" are model presbyters (that is, elders) for Milton. Milton is self-conscious about this—"if we may use such a comparison" is an acknowledgment of the oddity of this association in this context— but he does not back away from the comparison at all. Once we realize that, for Milton, Presbyterianism made room for and encouraged the participation in church-government of "heroick patricians," we can understand further the striking and distinctive features of *The Reason of Church-Government* that we have already discussed: the famous digression on Milton's qualifications and hopes for entering into the public discourse of the nation, and the emergence of Homeric shame as a model for Christian virtue.[21]

In the "digression," Milton is presenting himself as one of those heroic patricians, and he is addressing himself to others, to "the elegant and learned reader" (*RCG*, 807). The pamphlet as a whole makes most sense when it is seen as primarily addressed to educated Puritan burghers and gentry (like Milton himself). As he explains at the end of the pamphlet, Milton is trying to undo the negative and coordinated effects on this group of both living under prelacy and attending the universities—which, he says, teach "sophistry" rather than "generous philosophy," and train their students to "admire a sort

---

20. On the "nascent republicanism" of the early pamphlets, see Mueller, "Contextualizing Milton's Nascent Republicanism," 263–82 (chap. 6, n. 52), and David Norbrook, *Writing the English Republic: Poetry, Rhetoric, and Politics, 1627–1660* (Cambridge: Cambridge University Press, 1998), 109–14.

21. See chapter 6 above.

of formal outside men prelatically addicted" (854).[22] He is presenting himself, despite the odd particularities that he "divulges," as exemplary, as the kind of person—learned, eloquent, courageous, public-spirited—who would flourish under the Presbyterian system.[23] The best features of this system from Milton's point of view are, first, that it resurrects "the wisdom of the Romans" in understanding that the public censor did not need, nor should have, any corporal or punitive power (831–34); and, second, that in providing for this function, "a certain number of grave and faithful brethren"—the presbyters—are called upon to act alongside the ministers (838).

Of the first of these features, the renunciation of physical punishment ("jurisdiction"), Milton assures himself that "every true protestant" will see that "the reason of it" is "coherent with the doctrine of the Gospel"—"besides," he hastens to add, "the evidence of command in Scripture," which he had almost forgotten (834–35). The office of the elder, as we have seen, restores proper pride to the lay Christian, improperly so called—"not now to be separated in the Church by vails and partitions as laicks and unclean, but admitted to wait upon the tabernacle as the rightfull Clergy of Christ, a chosen generation, a royal Priesthood to offer up spiritual sacrifice in that meet place to which God and the Congregation shall call and assign them" (838). Milton appeals to "the equity and just reason" (845) of this vision of human dignity through public participation. He could not be further from merely appealing to authority.

22. For how other opponents of "prelacy" saw its widespread and insidious social effects, see my analysis of the "Root and Branch" petition (1641), "From Diagnosis to Operation," in *The Theatrical City: Culture, Theatre and Politics in London, 1576–1649*, ed. David L. Smith, Richard Strier, and David Bevington (Cambridge: Cambridge University Press, 1995), 225–33.

23. Later on, in *Christian Doctrine*, where Milton proposes a quite different ecclesiology (congregational and baptist), he continues this emphasis, stating that "each believer, *according to his personal talents*, should have a chance to address his fellows" (in *Complete Prose*, 6:608, emphasis mine).

INDEX

Gangi, Mario di, 167n45

Garber, Marjorie, 134n8

Garcia-Villoslada, Ricardo, 190n20

Gardner, Helen, 189n16, 199, 200

Garside, Charles, Jr., 249n9, 291n16

Gataker, Thomas, 15

Gaukroger, Stephen, 235n93

Gauna, Max, 220, 224n65

Gauthier, R.-A., 254n29

Geertz, Clifford, 7, 8n19

George, Charles H., and Katherine George, 188n8

Gerrish, B. A., 251n13, 251n17, 252n18, 286n7

Gilson, Etienne, 234, 235n93, 242n115

Ginzburg, Carlo, 105n21

Gleason, Robert W., SJ, 191n23

Gless, Darryl J., 254n30

Goldberg, Jonathan, 6n14, 23n61, 107n26, 115n40

Goldberg, S. L., 51n69

Golding, Arthur, 50n63

Gouge, William, 15

Gouhier, Henri, 238n100

Gowland, Angus, 18n44

Goyet, Francis, 223n60, 227n73

Grady, Hugh, 107n27

Graham, Kenneth, 289n13, 291n18

Gray's Inn, 42, 185

Greenblatt, Stephen, 7–17, 18, 119n50, 130n7, 131n9, 147n42, 160, 166, 171n59, 182

Greene, Thomas M., 70n35, 71–72n39

Griffin, Miriam, 51n70

Guss, Donald L., 76n50

Hadfield, Andrew, 132n1

Hadot, Pierre, 32n7, 241n107

Hale, John K., 263n57

Hallberg, Robert von, 83n72

Haller, William, and Malleville Haller, 174n71

Halpern, Richard, 12n26

Hamilton, A. C., 289

Hamilton, Donna B., 163n33

Hamilton, Gary, 186n112

Hammond, Antony, 127nn1–2

Hampton, Timothy, 209n7

Handler-Spitz, Rivi, 237n95

Hankins, James, 3n4

Harada, Jun, 269nn72–73

Harran, Marilyn J., 250n10

Harsnett, Samuel, 176n76

Hart, Kevin, 213n19

Hartwig, Joan, 45n51

Hawkins, Michael, 132n1, 144n33

Hawkins, Sherman, 110n35

Heilman, Robert, 109–10

Helmholz, Richard, 178n83

Hennings, Thomas P., 46n53, 165n40, 173n65, 174

Henze, Richard, 163n33

Herbert, George, 20–21, 23, 25, 26, 53–58, 63, 175n75, 189, 199, 200–203, 254–55, 267n68, 280, 285, 286

Herdt, Jennifer, 248n2, 253n26, 262n55

Herman, Peter C., 132n1, 272n80

Hertzler, James R., 186n110

Hill, Christopher, 198n42

Hoffmann, George, 222n61, 226

Holbrook, Peter, 46n53, 98n2, 118n49, 154n4

holiness, differing conceptions of, 21, 23, 38, 39–40, 66, 120, 155, 175, 177–81, 183, 186, 191n21, 228n76, 257–58, 264, 284, 291

Holinshed, Raphael, 132n1, 133, 140n24

Homer, 75, 98–99, 261, 292; *Iliad*, 49n62, 147; *Odyssey*, 147

Hooker, Richard, 132, 286–87

Höpfl, Harro, 260n53

Hopkins, Lisa, 135n10, 145nn37–38, 148n42

Horace, 210, 221

Horner, David A., 254n29

Hubler, Edward, 19n46, 20

Hughes, Merritt, 272n81, 278, 279

Huguenots, 214, 216

Hull, Suzanne W., 116n44

Hulliung, Mark, 2n1

humors (humoralism), 7, 8, 17–21